The Sense of the Past

The Sense of the Past

ESSAYS IN THE HISTORY OF PHILOSOPHY

Bernard Williams

Edited and with an introduction by Myles Burnyeat

PRINCETON UNIVERSITY PRESS

PRINCETON AND OXFORD

Published by Princeton University Press, 41 William Street, Princeton, New Jersey 08540

In the United Kingdom: Princeton University Press, 3 Market Place, Woodstock,

Oxfordshire OX20 1SY

Library of Congress Cataloging-in-Publication Data

Williams, Bernard Arthur Owen.
  The sense of the past : essays in the history of philosophy / Bernard Williams; edited and with an introduction by Myles Burnyeat.
    p. cm.
  "Bernard Williams, complete philosophical publications": p.
  Includes bibliographical references.
  ISBN-13: 978-0-691-12477-3 (alk. paper)
  ISBN-10: 0-691-12477-9 (alk. paper)
    1. Philosophy—History.   I. Burnyeat, Myles.   II. Title.

  B29.W494 2006
  190—dc22   2005047734

British Library Cataloging-in-Publication Data are available

This book has been composed in Sabon

Printed on acid-free paper. ∞

pup.princeton.edu

Printed in the United States of America

10 9 8 7 6 5 4 3 2 1

Contents

Aristotle

Descartes

Hume

Sidgwick

Nietzsche

Preface

Patricia Williams

For a philosopher with an abiding interest in classical civilization, it was, perhaps, fitting that Bernard should die in Rome. The hospital was on the site of an ancient temple to Aesculapius, god of healing, and said by Plato to have been recalled by Socrates in his final words.

He worked on the choice of pieces for this volume while his last book, *Truth and Truthfulness*,* was in press. The majority were to have been on classical philosophy. The essays on Nietzsche have been added to the list at the suggestion of Raymond Geuss, who, with Barry Stroud, advised on the final shape of this volume. I am very grateful for their help. Finding an unpublished essay on Collingwood among Bernard's papers was an added bonus. Sadly, he did not live to write the substantial introductory essay on the history of philosophy he had planned. It was a subject that had engaged him for many years. Adrian Moore, who knew Bernard's thoughts well, has kindly sketched out the likely content as follows:

> In some notes that he left behind, Bernard indicated how he would have used this essay to return to a distinction which he first drew in the preface to his book on Descartes,† and which he draws again in chapter 17 of this collection: the distinction between the history of ideas and the history of philosophy.
>
> The history of ideas is in the first instance history; the history of philosophy, to which both the book on Descartes and this volume belong, is in the first instance philosophy. Bernard did not think that this distinction was a sharp one, but he did think that it was an important one, and he always prized the special contribution to philosophy that he took the history of philosophy to make.
>
> This contribution was not, as philosophers in the analytic tradition used to think, to indicate voices of yore which could be heard as participating in contemporary debates: precisely not. It was to indicate voices of yore which could not be heard as participating in contemporary

---

* *Truth and Truthfulness: An Essay in Genealogy* (Princeton: Princeton University Press, 2002).

† *Descartes: The Project of Pure Enquiry* (Harmondsworth: Penguin, 1978); reprint by Routledge, 2005.

debates, and which thereby called into question whatever assumptions made contemporary debates possible.

In his notes Bernard also wrote that, although it is clear why philosophy needs history (for reasons that he explores in Truth and Truthfulness*), it is less obvious why it needs the history of itself. He surely meant just that: it is less* obvious *why it needs the history of itself. There was no implication that philosophy does not need the history of itself. In these essays he helps to show why it does have this need, and how the need both can and should be met.*

Bernard and I owe a special debt to Myles Burnyeat for the immense amount of time he has devoted to tracking down and checking everything that appears here and, especially, for his introduction. There is no one Bernard admired more in the field of classical philosophy today.

My thanks also to Walter Lippincott, the former Director of Princeton University Press, and the staff in Princeton, whose commitment to Bernard as an author, and to high standards and professional expertise in every aspect of publication are so appreciated at a time when scholarly publishing faces complex financial challenges.

• • •

These papers originally appeared in the places listed below. Permission from the publishers to reprint them is gratefully acknowledged.

1. "The Legacy of Greek Philosophy" in *The Legacy of Greece: A New Appraisal*, ed. M. I. Finley (Oxford: Oxford University Press, 1981), 202–255. By permission of Oxford University Press.
2. "*The Women of Trachis*: Fictions, Pessimism, Ethics" in *The Greeks and Us: Essays in Honor of Arthur W. H. Adkins*, ed. Robert B. Louden and Paul Schollmeier (Chicago: University of Chicago Press, 1996), 43–53. © 1996 by The University of Chicago. All rights reserved.
3. "Understanding Homer: Literature, History and Ideal Anthropology" in *Being Human: Anthropological Universality in Transdisciplinary Perspectives*, ed. Neil Roughly (Berlin: De Gruyter, 2000), 224–232.
4. "Pagan Justice and Christian Love" in *Virtue, Love and Form: Essays in Memory of Gregory Vlastos*, ed. Terence Irwin and Martha Nussbaum, in *Apeiron* 26 (Edmonton, AB: Academic Printing and Publishing, 1993), 195–207. By permission of Academic Printing and Publishing.

5. "Introduction to Plato's *Theaetetus*" in *Plato's Theaetetus*, trans. M. J. Levett, rev. Myles Burnyeat (Indianapolis: Hackett, 1992), vii–xx.

6. "Plato against the Immoralist" in *Platons Politeia*, ed. Otfried Höffe (Berlin: Akademie Verlag, 1997), 55–67.

7. "The Analogy of City and Soul in Plato's *Republic*" in *Exegesis and Argument: Studies in Greek Philosophy Presented to Gregory Vlastos*, ed. E. N. Lee, A.P.D. Mourelatos, and R. M. Rorty (Assen: Van Gorcum, 1973), 196–206.

8. "Plato's Construction of Intrinsic Goodness" in *Perspectives on Greek Philosophy: S. V. Keeling Memorial Lectures in Ancient Philosophy 1991–2002*, ed. R. W. Sharples (London: Ashgate, 2003), 1–18.

9. "Cratylus' Theory of Names and Its Refutation" in *Language and Logos: Studies in Ancient Greek Philosophy presented to G.E.L. Owen*, ed. Malcolm Schofield and Martha Nussbaum (Cambridge: Cambridge University Press, 1982), 83–93.

10. *Plato: The Invention of Philosophy* (London: Phoenix, 1998); also published as a chapter of *The Great Philosophers: From Socrates to Türing*, ed. Ray Monk and Frederic Raphael (London: Weidenfeld and Nicholson, a division of The Orion Publishing Group, 2000), 39–75.

11. "Acting as the Virtuous Person Acts" in *Aristotle and Moral Realism*, ed. Robert Heinaman, Keeling Colloquia 1 (London: UCL, 1995), 13–23.

12. "Aristotle on the Good: A Formal Sketch" in *Philosophical Quarterly* 12 (Oxford: Blackwell's, 1962), 289–296.

13. "Justice as a Virtue" in *Essays on Aristotle's Ethics*, ed. Amélie Oksenberg Rorty (Berkeley and Los Angeles: University of California Press, 1981), 189–199. © 1981 The Regents of the University of California. A less exegetical version appears in Bernard Williams, *Moral Luck: Philosophical Papers 1973–1980* (Cambridge: Cambridge University Press, 1981), 83–93.

14. "Hylomorphism" in *A Festschrift for J. L. Ackrill*, ed. Michael Woods, *Oxford Studies in Ancient Philosophy* 4 (Oxford: Oxford University Press, 1986), 189–199. By permission of Oxford University Press.

15. "Descartes' Use of Scepticism" in *The Skeptical Tradition*, ed. Myles Burnyeat (Berkeley and Los Angeles: University of California Press, 1983), 337–352. © 1983 The Regents of the University of California.

16. "Introductory Essay on Descartes' *Meditations*" in René Descartes, *Meditations on First Philosophy with Selections from*

the Objections and Replies, trans. John Cottingham (Cambridge: Cambridge University Press, 1986), vii–xvii.

17. "Descartes and the Historiography of Philosophy" in *Reason, Will and Sensation: Studies in Descartes' Metaphysics*, ed. John Cottingham (Oxford: Clarendon Press, 1994), 19–27.

18. "Hume on Religion" in *David Hume: A Symposium*, ed. D. F. Pears (London: Macmillan, 1963), 77–88. Reproduced with permission of Palgrave Macmillan.

19. "The Point of View of the Universe: Sidgwick and the Ambitions of Ethics" in *Cambridge Review* 103 (May 1982): 183–191; reprinted in Bernard Williams, *Making Sense of Humanity and Other Philosophical Papers 1982–1993* (Cambridge: Cambridge University Press, 1995), 153–171.

20. "Nietzsche's Minimalist Moral Psychology" in *European Journal of Philosophy* 1 (1993): 4–14; reprinted in *Making Sense of Humanity*, 65–76.

21. "Introduction to *The Gay Science*" in Friedrich Nietzsche, *The Gay Science*, ed. Bernard Williams, trans. Josefine Nauckhoff (Cambridge: Cambridge University Press, 2001), vii–xxii.

23. "Unbearable Suffering." Not previously published in English; German translation in *Zum Glück*, ed. Susan Neiman and Matthias Kroß (Berlin: Akademie Verlag, 2004), 95–102.

25. "Wittgenstein and Idealism" in *Understanding Wittgenstein*, ed. Godfrey Vesey, Royal Institute of Philosophy Lectures, vol. 7, 1972–1973 (London: Macmillan, 1974), 76–95; reprinted in *Moral Luck*, 144–163. Reproduced with permission of Palgrave Macmillan.

Introduction

Myles Burnyeat

These twenty-five essays by Bernard Williams span a period of forty-one years and range from the sixth century BC to the twentieth AD. Together with his book *Descartes: The Project of Pure Enquiry* (1978) and his wonderful booklet *Plato: The Invention of Philosophy* (1998 and reprinted below, chap. 10), they show a depth of commitment to the history of philosophy seldom to be found nowadays in a thinker so prominent on the contemporary philosophical scene. Bernard is a rare example of something that once, before philosophy fell apart into specialisms, was fairly common: a philosopher first and foremost, busy developing new thoughts on modern themes, who yet from time to time writes on a topic in the history of philosophy.

In his abiding commitment to the history of philosophy, Bernard remained true to the Oxford "Greats" tradition in which he was formed. He came up to Oxford in 1947, well before philosophy split into specialisms. His main philosophy tutor at Balliol College (with whom he sparred from the beginning) was R. M. Hare, who, besides his well-known books on moral philosophy, also wrote on Plato. In the "Greats" course of those days Plato and Aristotle were still as compulsory as logic, so it is not surprising that Oxford had long nurtured a tradition of combining independent philosophical thought with historical scholarship. Cook-Wilson, Joachim, Joseph, Mure, Prichard, and Ross had all contributed both to philosophy and to the study of the history of philosophy, with a particular focus on Plato and Aristotle. In scholarly circles several of these names are still influential, even if among philosophers it is only Ross's work in deontological ethics that now has any currency.

But practising the history of philosophy as well as philosophy is not the same as practising the history of philosophy philosophically. One can set out to elucidate the thought of an earlier philosopher without oneself engaging with the issues which that philosopher was interested in. For the most part, up until the Second World War Oxford kept its history of philosophy apart from its philosophy. When Ross, for example, in chapter 7 of his still indispensable book *Aristotle* (1923), gives an account of Aristotle's highly non-deontological ethics, his own very different views inevitably show through (at times, quite assertively), but he does not set up an explicit debate with Aristotle. Contrast Bernard's discussion of Aristotle in "Justice as a Virtue" (chap. 13 below). There is plenty of sympathetic exposition, but also philosophical probing—probing which eventually turns into a critique of Aristotle's attempt to assimilate justice to virtues like courage and temperance. Historical insight into Aristotle's thinking leads to a philosophical lesson about justice and injustice. Yet one would be hard put to it to say which parts of the essay are history, which philosophy. Both are involved throughout, even if sometimes one element predominates, sometimes the other.

The best precedent for this approach to writing the history of philosophy is Gilbert Ryle, who in a number of ways was an important influence on the young Bernard and others of his generation. Ryle took up the Waynflete Professorship of Metaphysical Philosophy immediately after the Second World War, in 1945.[1] But already in *Mind* for 1939, just before the war, he had published the first of several innovative and powerful articles on Plato. "Plato's *Parmenides*" urged that the critique of Plato's Theory of Forms in the first part of that dialogue is valid, and that Plato realized this. Readers were invited to adopt the revolutionary view that the later Plato gave up his most famous theory. (Wittgenstein's repudiation of his *Tractatus* was a powerful exemplum here.) The rest of the *Parmenides* Ryle proposed to treat as "an early essay in the theory of types," in the spirit of Russell.[2]

In retrospect, this paper of Ryle's can be seen as the iconoclastic inaugural manifesto of analytic philosophy's approach to its ancient forebears—the approach that became dominant in Anglophone philosophy departments as they expanded mightily in the post-war years. Ryle was both a friend and an important mentor of G.E.L. Owen, who along with Gregory Vlastos in the United States was one of the institutional leaders who recommended their best pupils for the new posts and helped ancient philosophy to become, not immediately or by their design (quite the contrary!), the specialized profession it now is.

Ryle, of course, would have been dismayed to see ancient philosophy, or any part of the history of philosophy, split off as one specialism alongside others such as epistemology, metaphysics, and ethics. Likewise, when Bernard, writing in a Festschrift for Owen, calls himself "only a part-time student of these subjects,"[3] he is not, I take it, apologizing, but insisting that one need not be a specialist to contribute. And in fact his essay, "Cratylus' Theory of Names and Its Refutation," proved to be one of the more influential essays in that volume. Again,

---

[1] His predecessor was R. G. Collingwood, whom Bernard came to admire greatly.

[2] More about Ryle's invigorating contributions to the study of ancient philosophy can be found in my entry "Gilbert Ryle (1900–1976)," in *Dictionary of British Classicists*, ed. Robert B. Todd (Bristol: Thoemmes Continuum 2004), 3:846–849.

[3] Chap. 9 below, "End-note."

"The Analogy of City and Soul in Plato's *Republic*" (chap. 7), written for the Vlastos Festschrift, has dominated the discussion of its subject ever since. Other papers would have made more of a mark had they not appeared in volumes easy to overlook. (Which makes it all the more valuable to have them reprinted in this collection, planned by Bernard himself.)

Here I think particularly of "The Legacy of Greek Philosophy" (chap. 1), which he wrote when his rooms in King's College Cambridge were next door to Owen's, whose work he acknowledges.[4] He opens with the striking sentence, "The legacy of Greece to Western philosophy is Western philosophy." Bernard had been assigned the impossible task of summing up Greek philosophy in a volume for the general reader designed to cover all aspects of our legacy from ancient Greece. What he actually does in his fifty-plus pages is something much more valuable. Concentrating mainly on Parmenides and Plato, he manages to convey the spirit and excitement of Greek philosophy in a way that grips a modern reader, even one with no previous experience in philosophy. In the process he makes a number of important observations from which specialist scholars can benefit as well. For example, that while the ancient world certainly formulated the view we know as materialism ("Everything that exists is material"), it never entertained the contrary position of idealism ("Nothing ultimately exists except minds and their experiences"). To my knowledge, Bernard was the first person to note this fact (as I believe it to be, though in their different ways both Hegel and Bishop Berkeley thought the opposite). His doing so gave me many happy hours of research and a lengthy paper of my own.[5]

If fifty-plus pages is unusually long for a paper in any area of philosophy,[6] most of the other chapters are unusually short by comparison with the norm in historical studies. The average length of the published articles is just twelve pages. They are also rather sparing with notes (a sane version of Ryle's lifelong policy of total abstention). There are plenty of learned notes in the end pages of *Shame and Necessity* (1993) and *Truth and Truthfulness* (2002), so it is not that Bernard failed to "keep up with the literature." Rather, their uncluttered presentation gives his historical essays the same crisp forcefulness as his contributions to contemporary philosophy. He likes to go straight to a central issue and set about it with

[4] Needless to say, not uncritically. His remarks at p. 18 on "the excursion through what *could* be" reject, correctly in my view, Owen's interpretation of Parmenides frag. 6, 1–2.

[5] "Idealism and Greek Philosophy: What Descartes Saw and Berkeley Missed," *Philosophical Review* 91 (1982): 3–40.

[6] It is the one article listed alongside his books, under the heading "Principal Publications," in his curriculum vitae.

vigour and originality. No fluff. A good example in this book is chapter 8, "Plato's Construction of Intrinsic Goodness," where he starts with the best explanation I have ever read of what exactly Plato's project is when he undertakes in the *Republic* to show that justice is an intrinsic good for the person who has it, and concludes with his own philosophical account of how Plato's project might acceptably be fitted into a less objectivist framework than the *Republic* demands. The result is a profound contribution to the history of philosophy done philosophically.

Only four of the essays predate 1980: in chronological order, they are chapters 11 (1962), 17 (1963), 25 (1972–1973), and 7 (1973).[7] Now in his first teaching job, at New College Oxford from 1954 to 1959, Bernard taught his tutorial students the standard "Greats" fare of Plato's *Republic* and Aristotle's *Ethics*, while his contributions to the University Lecture List included a term-long course on Plato's *Theaetetus* and another in which he would hold a weekly debate with John Lucas on issues in the *Republic*. When he moved to University College London, where the Grote Professor of the day was A. J. Ayer, he regularly gave the departmental course on Plato (i.e., Plato, not just the *Republic*), whom all London philosophy students then, as now, were required to study in both breadth and detail. I shall reminisce later about his Plato course of 1964. He was still lecturing frequently on Plato, and on Aristotle's ethics, in the University of California at Berkeley, his last teaching position. Yet he was slow to commit historical thoughts to print. He had four philosophical articles in print before 1960. But his *Descartes* of 1978 took fourteen years to complete, after being set aside for a number of years.[8] Only the earliest paper in this collection (chap. 12) was sent by him, on his own initiative, to a professional journal. The rest, like his *Descartes*, were commissioned by eager editors who were prepared, if need be (*experto credite*), to delay publication for months or years in the hope of securing his contribution to their volume or series.

All this speaks to a life in which, to begin with, the history of philosophy is an important but subordinate interest. It is only gradually that historical themes become as central to his thinking as they are in *Shame and Necessity* and *Truth and Truthfulness*. Nietzsche was the key influence here, along with Collingwood, which is why it seemed appropriate to include in this collection the three unpublished essays which appear

---

[7] Qualification: his bibliography at the end of *Problems of the Self* (1973) shows two encyclopaedia entries on Descartes, one on rationalism, and a paper on the *Cogito*, none of which he included in his plan for this collection—presumably because they are superseded by his *Descartes*.

[8] *Descartes*, 10, calls this "an absurdly long period." I disagree. Even when you lay a book aside, its future character is maturing as your other work shapes the mind that will eventually return to the task.

below as chapters 22–24. Another factor was Bernard's dismay at the steadily increasing compartmentalization of philosophy. The more professional the separate compartments become, and the more that even those compartments which are quite distant from the sciences (ethics and metaphysics, say, as contrasted with philosophy of language or philosophy of mathematics) acquire something like a research programme, the less reason do philosophers have to take an interest in the history of their subject, or even of their part of the subject. Trapped in the present, they can neither see nor criticize the weak points in prevailing views. They lose one of the traditional functions of philosophy, that of understanding and, if necessary, criticizing the culture they live in.

This, for Bernard, was at least *an* important task, possibly *the most* important task a philosopher can undertake. A task he undertook both theoretically, in *Shame and Necessity* and *Truth and Truthfulness*, and practically as chair of a cogently reforming government Committee on Obscenity and Film Censorship, not to mention his membership of Commissions on gambling and on public schools. As he famously quipped, "I did all the major vices." A joke no other philosopher of his time could match.

It is in chapter 17 of this book, "Descartes and the Historiography of Philosophy," that Bernard gives his most explicit account of how he sees the nature and importance of the history of philosophy. Adapting to the history of philosophy a remark of Nietzsche's about classical philology, he says (p. 259 below),

> I cannot imagine what [its] meaning would be in our own age, if it is not to be untimely—that is, to act against the age, and by doing so to have an effect on that age, and, let us hope, to the benefit of a future age.[9]

He invokes a contrast he drew in the preface to his *Descartes* between the history of philosophy and the history of ideas. By the former he means what I earlier described as the history of philosophy done philosophically; by the latter the exploration of the historical context of a past work, the influences on it and its relation to ideas and issues current at the time. (He ignores altogether the existence of a merely expository type of history which neither contextualizes nor philosophizes.) The great value he sees in the history of philosophy, so understood, is its capacity to revive a sense of *"strangeness or questionability"* (italics mine)

[9] Quoted also in *Shame and Necessity*, 4. The publication date of chap. 16 is 1994. In his last interview, "A Mistrustful Animal: An Interview with Bernard Williams," *The Harvard Review of Philosophy* 12 (2004): 81–92 at 83, he remarks that "This historicist turn has become more prominent in my work in the last ten or fifteen years."

about our contemporary assumptions, both inside and outside philosophy. A fine example is chapter 5 of *Shame and Necessity*, discussing Aristotle's attempt to justify slavery and its bearing on the economic inequalities of our own world. Some of that discussion is put to interesting new use here in "Pagan Justice and Christian Love" (chap. 4), appropriately dedicated to the memory of Gregory Vlastos, who, starting from very different presuppositions, shared Bernard's concern with the present state of society. It is no accident that both wrote, early in their academic career, influential essays on equality, both published in 1962.[10]

• • •

More than half these essays deal, in one way or another, with the ancient world. Like Nietzsche, Bernard began as a classicist and remained a classicist, as well as a philosopher, throughout his life. "The Legacy of Greek Philosophy" (chap. 1) ends with a contrast between the Greek philosophers' sustained pursuit of rational self-sufficiency and the harsher depths of Greek tragedy:

> If there are features of the ethical experience of the Greek world which can not only make sense to us now, but make better sense than many things we find nearer to hand, they are not all to be found in its philosophy. (P. 46 below)

Already we hear the leitmotif of *Shame and Necessity*, published twelve years later, which argues that Homer and Greek tragedy can show us, rather better than ancient or modern moral philosophy can do, what ethical ideas we need in today's world. Since Bernard planned the order of the chapters in this collection, we can assume it is by design that chapter 1 is followed by an essay on Sophocles' *The Women of Trachis*, written for the Arthur W. H. Adkins Festschrift, in which Bernard hails the play's stark presentation of extreme undeserved and uncompensated suffering as "a necessary supplement and a suitable limitation to the tireless

---

[10] Bernard Williams, "The Idea of Equality," in *Philosophy, Politics and Society*, 2nd ser., ed. Peter Laslett and W. G. Runciman (Oxford: Blackwell, 1962), 110–131; reprinted in *Moral Concepts*, ed. Joel Feinberg (London: Oxford University Press, 1969), 153–171, and in *Equality: Selected Readings*, ed. Louis P. Pojman and Robert Westmoreland (New York: Oxford University Press, 1997), 91–104. Gregory Vlastos, "Justice and Equality," in *Social Justice*, ed. Richard B. Brandt (Englewood Cliffs, NJ: Prentice-Hall, 1962), 31–72; parts reprinted in Feinberg, *Moral Concepts*, 141–152, in *Human Rights*, ed. A. I. Melden (Belmont, CA: Wadsworth, 1970), 76–95, and in Pojman and Westmoreland, *Equality*, 120–133; the whole reprinted in Jeremy Waldron, *Theories of Rights* (Oxford: Oxford University Press, 1984), 141–176. More on Vlastos can be found in my memorial, "Gregory Vlastos," *Phronesis* 37 (1992): 137–140.

aim of moral philosophy to make the world safe for well-disposed people" (p. 59). There can be few Festschrift contributions whose content clashes so strongly with the outlook of its dedicatee, who proclaimed in his first and highly influential book *Merit and Responsibility: A Study in Greek Values* that, when it comes to the notions of duty and responsibility, "we are all Kantians now."[11]

Bernard's warning, on the first page of *Shame and Necessity*, that "I am not primarily a classical scholar" may be compared with the phrase "only a part-time student of these subjects," discussed above. Neither is apologetic. The modesty is sincere in both cases, a recognition that to refuse specialization is to risk errors which a specialist would know how to avoid. But Bernard knew that the refusal was, of course, a condition of his being able to write *Shame and Necessity*, which to my mind is of all his books the most profound.

The second and third pages of *Shame and Necessity* express his appreciation for the teaching he received as an undergraduate from Eduard Fraenkel and E. R. Dodds, "two of the most remarkable classical scholars of this century." Now Fraenkel and Dodds were Professors, and Oxford Professors do not give undergraduate tutorials. Bernard is referring to their University classes, open to all members of the University but attended, apparently, only by an enlightened few. It is known that Fraenkel marked him out as a most promising classical scholar. Less well known is Fraenkel's reaction on first encountering Dodds, when he came to read a paper in Oxford. Fraenkel said to the then Regius Professor of Greek, Gilbert Murray, whom Dodds would in due course succeed, that he would like to study under that man for a year.[12] And any classicist will know that the important predecessor of *Shame and Necessity* (1993) is Dodds's groundbreaking *The Greeks and the Irrational* (1951), while both Dodds and Bernard look back to Nietzsche. Both books, moreover, originated as the Sather Classical Lectures at Berkeley, which rank as the most prestigious classical lectures on the planet. For Bernard, the "anxiety of influence" must have been tremendous.

The invitation to give the Sathers came during his long stay at King's College Cambridge, first as Knightbridge Professor of Philosophy (1967–1979), then as Provost (1979–1987). By way of preparation, he read widely in French classical scholarship (Vernant, Vidal-Naquet, and especially Nicole Loraux, plus Foucault), to which King's had always

---

[11] (Oxford: Clarendon Press, 1960), 2. The book began as a doctoral thesis written under the supervision of E. R. Dodds.

[12] This information comes from a letter to the then Prime Minister, Stanley Baldwin, in which Murray recommends that Dodds be appointed his successor. The carbon copy is among Murray's papers in the Bodleian Library (MS. Gilbert Murray 77, fols. 138–140).

been more welcoming than other places in the UK. This added an anthropological dimension to his Sathers which Dodds would have thoroughly approved. With reference to Dodds's work, Bernard writes,

> The Sather Lectures that he gave in 1949–50 yielded one of the most helpful and enduring books in the series, and it is one of the closest in subject matter to the concerns of this study. Since he was also extremely kind to me when I was a student, I should like to feel that my undertaking, even though it is imperfectly related to the kind of scholarship he practised, might count as a homage to him.[13]

• • •

This brings me to the reasons why I am glad to have the opportunity to write this introduction, as my homage to Bernard. Let me go back to University College London in 1964. I was enjoying my first year as a university teacher. The previous year I had been a graduate student under Bernard's supervision. He then left, to become Professor of Philosophy at Bedford College London (the first of his several chairs). I was appointed as his successor to take over one part of his multi-faceted teaching: ancient philosophy. In those days universities (to their credit and benefit) were kinder to young staff than they are now. My sole lecturing responsibility for that first year was one course, on the Pre-Socratics; the rest was tutorials on a variety of subjects with individual students. The Plato course had previously been given by Bernard, and he kindly agreed to return from the other side of Regent's Park to give it once more—to allow me time to work myself into my new job. Naturally, I attended his lectures. They were a revelation. As a graduate of Cambridge, not Oxford, I had never heard Plato discussed with such a blend of philosophy and scholarship. But he kept getting sidetracked; he could not resist a good joke or a digression into some modern theme. The penultimate week of term arrived and we still had not got to late Plato. He suggested that for the final session we should meet for two hours instead of one, so as to give some attention to Plato's later dialogues.

The result was that that last week Bernard spoke non-stop for two hours about Plato's *Theaetetus*. The lecture had everything: acute philosophical analysis of the arguments in the dialogue, the opening up of

---

[13] *Shame and Necessity*, xi. When describing the work of preparing his own Sathers, Dodds wrote, "The labour seemed to me worth while, for in trying to understand the ancient Greek world I was also trying, as I had always done, to understand a little better the world I lived in" (*Missing Persons: An Autobiography* [Oxford: Clarendon Press, 1977], 180–181).

wider philosophical vistas (both ancient and modern), scholarship (a textual crux, a neat point of grammar), literary considerations. Above all, it had a startlingly original, textually convincing, and philosophically wonderful interpretation of the long argument in the first part of the dialogue against the definition of knowledge as perception. I sat spell-bound, saying to myself: this is how I want to do the subject.

From that moment on, the *Theaetetus* became my central interest. A few years later, in 1968, Bernard and I gave a joint seminar on the dialogue at the Institute of Classical Studies in London. (Ryle came twice.) We planned to write a book together—a book that would be the definitive interpretation of the work. Somehow, this never came about. The *Theaetetus* defeats all attempts at a definitive interpretation. But I kept working on the dialogue, and eventually in 1992 (twenty-eight years after that lecture of his) I published *The Theaetetus of Plato*, the long (250-page) introduction to which finally gave to the scholarly world (under the rubric "Reading B") Bernard's interpretation of the argument against the definition of knowledge as perception. He had never got around to publishing it himself.

It is not simply this argument that is owed to Bernard. The entire introduction is inspired by the exact, exacting, but at the same time philosophically generous approach to Plato's text that so gripped me way back in 1964. If I mention that in 1998 a French translation of my introduction by Michel Narcy was published as a book on its own, this is simply to emphasize that the approach I owe to that original lecture—a turning point in my life—has an appeal that transcends the philosophical divide between Anglophone and (so-called) continental philosophy.[14] Two hundred and fifty pages, however, was rather longer than the dozen or so the publisher had asked for ten years earlier. He had envisioned a short, cheap student edition of the *Theaetetus*.[15] Please would I write a very short version of my introduction as well? I said I would find that impossible, and was asked to suggest someone else who could do it. The result was chapter 5 below, carefully placed *before* the essays on the

---

[14] I say "so-called" with an eye to Bernard's scathing remark on the standard contrast between "analytic" and "continental" philosophy in chap. 20, p. 300 below: "This classification always involved a quite bizarre conflation of the methodological and the topographical, as though one classified cars into front-wheel drive and Japanese."

[15] It was Ryle who originally suggested that the Levett translation, which he rightly admired, should be preceded by a short introduction designed to bring out the continuing relevance of Plato's dialogue to present-day philosophical studies. This was when the 1977 reissue was in preparation at the Glasgow University Press. It was hoped that Ryle would write the introduction himself, but he did not live to do so. Nonetheless, when the project landed on my desk in 1979, it came with Ryle's prescription intact: bring out the continuing relevance of the dialogue to present-day philosophical studies. Hence the 250 pages.

Republic, contrary to the generally accepted chronological order which Bernard, with proper caution, endorsed.[16]

My guess is that Bernard chose to place his *Theaetetus* introduction first because it opens with some general remarks about the virtues of the dialogue form: "[I]t is a style of writing that enables Plato to explore philosophical questions in ways more vivid and more intellectually flexible than are available to a treatise" (p. 83). Bernard regarded Plato as the greatest philosopher of all time. His admiration and, I would like to say, love come through on every page of *Plato: The Invention of Philosophy* (chap. 10). For Aristotle, by contrast, whose philosophy has reached us solely in the form of treatises (because his published dialogues, much admired in antiquity, are lost), he professed dislike. Chapters 11–14 show that this dislike did not stop him taking Aristotle seriously and writing well about him. But it is worth noting that vividness and intellectual flexibility are qualities one finds also in Descartes, another of Bernard's favourite philosophers—and in his own writing.

The *Theaetetus* is perhaps the most flexible of all Plato's dialogues, in that it raises and explores many more questions than it answers. Bernard and I share the view that this is because Plato invites his readers, both present and future, to think out answers for themselves to the problems discussed in the dialogue. When it comes to the question "What does it all add up to? What is the final message of the dialogue?" Bernard's introduction and mine offer conflicting answers. Plato would approve.[17]

All Souls College, Oxford

[16] Chap. 10, notes 12 and 14.

[17] I should like to thank Patricia Williams for her help and encouragement during the preparation of this introduction.

GREEK: GENERAL

ONE

The Legacy of Greek Philosophy

THE GREEKS AND THE HISTORY OF PHILOSOPHY

The legacy of Greece to Western philosophy is Western philosophy. Here it is not merely a matter, as in science, of the Greeks having set out on certain paths in which modern developments have left their achievements far behind. Nor is it just a matter, as in the arts, of the Greeks having produced certain forms, and certain works in those forms, which succeeding times would—some more, some very much less—look back to as paradigms of achievement. In philosophy, the Greeks initiated almost all its major fields—metaphysics, logic, the philosophy of language, the theory of knowledge; ethics, political philosophy, and (though to a much more restricted degree) the philosophy of art. Not only did they start these areas of enquiry, but they progressively distinguished what would still be recognized as many of the most basic questions in those areas. In addition, among those who brought about these developments there were two, Plato and Aristotle, who have always, where philosophy has been known and studied in the Western world, been counted as supreme in philosophical genius and breadth of achievement, and whose influence, directly or indirectly, more or less consciously, under widely varying kinds of interpretation, has been a constant presence in the development of the Western philosophical tradition ever since.

Of course philosophy, except at its most scholastic and run down, does not consist of the endless reworking of ancient problems, and the idea that Western philosophy was given almost its entire content by the Greeks is sound only if that content is identified in the most vague and general way—at the level of such questions as 'what is knowledge?' or 'what is time?' or 'does sense-perception tell us about things as they really are?' Philosophical problems are posed not just by earlier philosophy, but by developments in all areas of human life and knowledge; and all aspects of Western history have affected the subject-matter of philosophy—the development of the nation-state as much as the rise and fall of Christianity or the progress of the sciences. Yet even with issues created by such later developments, it is often possible to trace contemporary differences in philosophical view to some general contrast of outlooks which had its first expression in the Greek world.

Granted the size of the Greek achievement in philosophy, and the depth of its influence, it would be quite impossible to attempt anything except a drastically selective account of either. Some very important and influential aspects of Greek philosophy I shall leave out entirely: these include political philosophy (which is the concern of another chapter), and also Greek contributions to the science of logic, which were very important but demand separate, and moderately technical, treatment.[1] Moreover, in the matter of influences, I shall not attempt to say anything about what is certainly the most evident and concentratedly important influence of Greek philosophy on subsequent thought, the influence of Aristotle on the thought of the Middle Ages. Aristotle, who was for Thomas Aquinas 'The Philosopher', for Dante *il maestro di color che sanno*, 'the master of those who know', did much to form, through his various and diverse interpreters, the philosophical, scientific, and cosmological outlook of an entire culture, and the subject of Aristotelianism would inevitably be too much for any essay which wanted to discuss anything else as well. Aristotle's representation in what follows has suffered from his own importance.

After saying something in general about the Greeks and the history of philosophy, and about the special positions of Plato and Aristotle, I shall try to convey some idea of the variety of Greek philosophical interests; but, more particularly, I shall pursue two or three subjects in greater detail than any attempt at a general survey would have allowed, in the belief that no catalogue of persons and doctrines is of much interest in philosophy, and that a feel for what certain thinkers were about can be conveyed only through some enactment of the type of reasons and arguments that weighed with them: of not just what, but how, they thought. In this spirit, if still very sketchily, I shall take up some arguments of Greek philosophers about two groups of questions—on the one hand, about being, appearance, and reality, on the other about knowledge and scepticism. In both, the depth of the Greek achievement is matched by the persistence of similar questions in later philosophy. In another matter, ethical enquiry, I shall lay the emphasis rather more on the contrasts between Greek thought and most modern outlooks, contrasts which seem to me very important to an understanding of our own outlooks and of how problematical they are.

I have said that the Greeks initiated most fields of enquiry in philosophy, and many of its major questions. It may be, by contrast, that there are just two important kinds of speculation in the later history of philosophy which are so radically different in spirit from anything in Greek

---

[1] For an accessible and informative treatment, see William and Martha Kneale, *The Development of Logic* (Oxford, 1962), chs. i–iii.

thought as to escape from this generalization. Greek philosophy was deeply concerned, and particularly at its beginnings, with issues involved in the contrast between *monism* and *pluralism*. It is not always easy to capture what was at issue in these discussions: in some of the earlier Greek disputes, the question seems to be whether there is in reality only one thing or more than one thing, but—as we shall see later—it is not easy to make clear what exactly was believed by someone who believed that there was, literally, only one thing. In later philosophy, and already in some Greek philosophy, questions of monism and pluralism are questions rather of whether the world contains one or more than one fundamental or irreducible *kind* of thing. One sort of monism in this sense which has been known both to the ancient and to the modern world is *materialism*, the view that everything that exists is material, and that other things, in particular mental experiences, are in some sense reducible to this material basis. Besides *dualism*, the outlook that accepts that there are both matter and mind, not reducible to one another, philosophy since the Renaissance has also found room for another kind of monism, *idealism*, the monism of mind, which holds that nothing ultimately exists except minds and their experiences. It is this kind of view, with its numerous variations, descendants, and modifications, which we do not find in the ancient world. Largely speculative though Greek philosophy could be, and interested as it was in many of the same kinds of issues as those which generated idealism, it did not form that particular set of ideas, so important in much modern philosophy, according to which the entire world consists of the contents of mind: as opposed, of course, to the idea of a material world formed and governed by mind, a theistic conception which the Greeks most certainly had.

The other principal element in modern philosophy which is independent of the Greeks is something that first established itself at the beginning of the nineteenth century—that type of philosophical thought (of which Marxism is now the leading example) which places fundamental emphasis on historical categories and on explanation in terms of the historical process. The Greeks had, or rather, gradually developed, a sense of historical time and the place of one's own period in it; and their thought also made use of various structures, more mythological than genuinely tied to any historical time, of the successive ages of mankind, which standardly pictured man as in a state of decline from a golden age (though an opposing view, in terms of progress, is also to be found). Some of the more radical thinkers, moreover, regarded standards of conduct and the value of political arrangements as relative to particular societies, and that conception had an application to societies distant in time. But the Greeks did not evolve any theoretical conception of men's categories of thought being conditioned by the material or social circumstances of their time, nor did they look for systematic explanations of them in terms of history. This type of historical consciousness is indeed not present in all philosophical thought of the present day, but its absence from Greek philosophy is certainly one thing that marks off that philosophy from much modern thought.

It may be that these two, idealism and the historical consciousness, are the only two really substantial respects in which later philosophy is quite removed from Greek philosophy, as opposed to its pursuing what are recognizably the same types of preoccupation as Greek philosophy pursued, but pursuing them, of course, in the context of a vastly changed, extended, and enriched subject-matter compared with that available to the Greeks.

This is not to say that the Greeks possessed our concept of 'philosophy': or, rather, that they possessed any one of the various concepts of philosophy which are used in different philosophical circles in the modern world. Classical Greek applies the word *philosophia* to a wide range of enquiries; wider certainly than the range of enquiries called 'philosophy' now, which are distinguished from scientific, mathematical, and historical enquiries. But we should bear in mind that it is not only Greek practice that differs from modern practice in this way: for centuries 'philosophy' covered a wide range of enquiries, including those into nature, as is witnessed by the old use of the phrase 'natural philosophy' to mean natural science—*The Mathematical Principles of Natural Philosophy* is what Newton, at the end of the seventeenth century, called his great work on the foundations of mechanics. It does not follow, however, that these ages did not have *some* distinction between scientific and what would now be called philosophical enquiries—enquiries which, however they are precisely to be delimited, are concerned with the general presuppositions of knowledge, action, and values, and proceed by way of reflection on our concepts and ideas, not by way of observation and experiment. Earlier ages often did make, in one way or another, distinctions between such enquiries and others—it is merely that until comparatively recently the word 'philosophy' was not reserved to marking them.

It is important to bear this point in mind when dealing with the philosophy of the past, in particular ancient philosophy. It defines, so to speak, two grades of anachronism. The more superficial and fairly harmless grade of anachronism is displayed when we use some contemporary term to identify a class of enquiries which the past writers did themselves separate from other enquiries, though not by quite the same criteria or on the same principles as are suggested by the modern term. An example of this is offered by the branch of philosophy now called 'metaphysics'. This covers a range of very basic philosophical issues, including reality, existence, what it is for things to have qualities, and (in the more abstract and less religious aspects of the matter) God. There is a set of writings devoted to such subjects in the canon of Aristotle's works, and it is called the *Metaphysics*; and it is indeed from that title that the subject got its name. But the work was probably so called only from its position in the edition of Aristotle's works prepared by Andronicus of Rhodes in the first century B.C.—these treatises were *ta meta ta phusika*, the books that came 'after the books on nature'. Aristotle's own name for most of these metaphysical enquiries was 'first philosophy'. Nor is it just the name that was different, but so were the principles of classification, both in the rationale given of them and hence in what is included and excluded. Thus Aristotle has an account of his enquiries into 'being in general' which relates the themes of 'first philosophy' in a distinctively Aristotelian way to the rest of knowledge (roughly, he supposed that it was distinguished by having a subject-matter which was much more general than that of other enquiries); and it excludes some enquiries which might now be included in metaphysics, such as *a priori* reflections on the nature of space and time. These latter Aristotle takes up in the books now called the *Physics*, which were included among the books 'about nature'; the name *Physics* itself being misleading, since what their contents mostly resemble is parts of metaphysics, and also what we would now call the philosophy of science, rather than what we now call *physics*.

These various differences do not stop us identifying Aristotle's enquiries as belonging to various branches of philosophy as we now understand them: this level of anachronism can, with scholarship and a sense of what is philosophically relevant, be handled—as it must be, if we are going to be able to reconstitute from our present point of view something which it would not be too arbitrary to call the history *of philosophy*. But there is a second and deeper level of anachronism which we touch when we deal with writings to which modern conceptions of what is and what is not philosophy scarcely apply at all. With those writers who did not themselves possess some such distinctions, to insist on claiming them for the history of philosophy as opposed to, say, the history of science, constitutes an unhelpful and distorting form of anachronism. So it is with the earliest of Greek 'philosophers', the earlier *Presocratics* (a label which as a matter of fact is used not only for thinkers earlier than Socrates, but for some late-fifth-century contemporaries of his as well).

With regard to the earliest of Greek speculative thinkers, Thales, Anaximander, and Anaximenes, who lived in Miletus on the Greek seaboard of Asia Minor in the first seventy years of the sixth century B.C., it is impossible to give in any straightforward modern terms a classification of the kinds of question they were asking. This is not just because virtually nothing remains of their work (Thales, the oldest, in any case wrote nothing) and we have to rely on disputable reports; even if we had all their writings we could not assign them, in modern terms, to philosophy or to science. They are usually represented as asking questions such as 'what is the world made of?', but it is one achievement of intellectual progress that that question now has no determinate meaning; if a child asks it, we do not give him one or many answers to it, but rather lead him to the point where he sees why it should be replaced with a range of different questions. Of course, there is a sense in which modern particle theory is a descendant of enquiries started by the Milesians, but that descent has so modified the questions that it would be wrong to say that there is one unambiguous question to which we give the answer 'electrons, protons, etc.' and Thales (perhaps) gave the answer 'water'.

We can say something—and we shall touch on this later—about the features of these speculations which make them more like *rational enquiries* than were the religious and mythological cosmologies of the East, which may have influenced them. And this is in fact a more important and interesting question than any about their classification as 'philosophy', something which in the case of these earliest thinkers is largely an empty issue.

CLASSICAL PHILOSOPHY AND THE PHILOSOPHICAL CLASSIC

The involvement of Greek philosophy in the Western philosophical tradition is not measured merely by the fact that ancient philosophy originated so many fields of enquiry which continue to the present day. It emerges also in the fact that in each age philosophers have looked back to ancient philosophy—overwhelmingly, of course, to Plato and Aristotle—in order to give authority to their own work, or to contrast it, or by reinterpretation of the classical philosophers to come to understand them, and themselves, in different ways. The Greek philosophers have been not just the fathers, but the companions, of Western philosophy. Different motives for this concern have predominated in different ages: the aim of legitimating one's own opinions was more prominent in the Middle Ages and the Renaissance (which, contrary to popular belief, did not so much lose the need for intellectual authority, as choose different authorities), while the aim of historical understanding and self-understanding is more important in the present day. But from whatever motive, these relations to the Greek past are a particularly important expression of that involvement in its own history which is characteristic of philosophy and not of the sciences.

It has been a characteristic also of literature, though the nature of the involvement in that case is very different. It has been suggested[2] that our conceptions of Western literature have room for the notions both of a 'relative classic'—a work which endures and has influence and stands at least for a period of time as an exemplar—and of the 'absolute classic', above all the *Aeneid*, which defines for ever the high 'classical' style. Adapting these notions to philosophy, we might say that the classical philosophers Plato and Aristotle are classics in the sense that it has been impossible, at least up to now, for philosophy not to want to make some living sense of these writers and relate its positions to theirs, if only by showing why they have to be rejected: this is a status which they have shared, in the last 200 years, only with Kant. But they might be said also to define a classical style of philosophy—meaning by that a philosophical, not a literary, style. They are both associated with a grand, imperial, synoptic style of philosophy; though beyond that very general description, they have been acknowledged from ancient times to define two different styles, Plato being associated with speculative ambitions for philosophy, seeking to establish that another world of intellectual objects, the Forms, accessible to reason and not to the senses, was ultimately real, while Aristotle renounced these extravagant other-worldly hypotheses in favour of a more down-to-earth, classificatory, and analytical spirit, more respectful of the ordinary opinions of men—but defining a grand style for all that, since the systematic impulse was directed to producing one unified, ordered, and hierarchical world-picture.

Oppositions of the Platonic and the Aristotelian spirits have been a commonplace. In our own century, Yeats wrote, in *Among School Children*:

Plato thought nature but a spume that plays
Upon a ghostly paradigm of things;
Solider Aristotle played the taws
Upon the bottom of a king of kings . . .

Most famously, the received contrast is expressed in Raphael's fresco in the Vatican called *The School of Athens*, which displays the two central figures of Plato and Aristotle, the one with his hand turned towards heaven, the other downwards towards earth. In this connection one must remember the mystical elements which were associated with Platonic thought: not altogether falsely, so far as some of Plato's own writings are concerned, but very heavily selected for and modified by the Neo-Platonist tradition. It is connected with this image of Plato that for a period in the early Middle Ages only the *Timaeus* (in Latin translation)

[2] See Frank Kermode, *The Classic* (London, 1975).

was known, an untypical dialogue in which a theistic cosmogony is advanced.

Looked at more than superficially, the famed contrast is a very complex and ambiguous matter. The spirit of Plato has sometimes been associated with the religious impulse as such; but equally, and in fact more importantly, where the framework of thought is already religious, an expanded Aristotelianism has represented an ordered and stable understanding of the world in relation to God, while Platonism has been taken to represent variously humanism, magic, or individual rational speculation.

The old picture by which the Middle Ages built on Aristotle, but the Renaissance got its inspiration from Plato, has been much qualified by modern scholarship, but it retains enough truth,[3] and more than one important Renaissance thinker agreed with the words of Petrarch, that Plato 'in that group came closest to the goal that may be reached by those whom heaven favours'. Much of this Platonic influence flowed into humane studies and the betterment of the soul, rather than the study of nature; and where the study of nature is pursued in the Renaissance, outside the continuing traditions of Aristotelian science, there is deep uncertainty and disagreement about what kinds of procedure or lore may prove effective in uncoding the messages hidden in phenomena. It is rather later, and with a vision much closer to modern conceptions of mathematical physics, that Galileo expressed what is still a Platonic influence in saying:

> (Natural) philosophy is written in that vast book which stands forever open before our eyes, I mean the universe; but it cannot be read until we have learnt the language and become familiar with the characters in which it is written. It is written in mathematical language, and the letters are triangles, circles, and other geometrical figures, without which means it is humanly impossible to understand a single word. (*Il Saggiatore*, Question 6)

From this point on, the business of decipherment could be more readily detached from notions of an arcane mystery, which were present in the Renaissance, as they were originally in the early Pythagorean sects which influenced Plato; it could become the public task of critical scientific discussion.

Thus in one context Platonism may represent a mystical or cabbalistic interest, against which Aristotelianism stands for a cautious, observa-

---

[3] See P. O. Kristeller, 'Byzantine and Western Platonism in the Fifteenth Century', in *Renaissance Concepts of Man* (New York, 1972), and references. The quotation from Petrarch (*Trionfo della Fama*, 3. 4–6) is taken from this article.

tional approach, concerned to stick to the phenomena; in another, while a Platonic influence encourages rational enquiry into nature, Aristotelianism can be seen (as it was by Descartes, despite his occasional dissimulations) as an obscurantist attachment to mysterious essences and muddled vitalistic analogies. An opposition of the Platonic and Aristotelian spirits is indeed something real, which can be traced through very complex paths in the history of Western thought; but it defines not so much any one contrast, as rather a structure within which a large number of contrasts have in the course of that history found their place.

Various as these contrasts have been, what can be said is that the majority of them have been associated with interpretations of these philosophers' *views* and, in many cases, with what have been believed to be their systems. Under these various interpretations, they have still been seen as authors of large world-views, as classical system-builders. Modern scholarship, encouraged by a philosophical scepticism about system-building, has tended to reduce the extent to which these philosophers are seen as expressing systems. In both cases, their works are now more clearly seen as the product of development over time, with corresponding changes of outlook; while discussions which in the past were taken to be fundamentally expository can be seen to be more provisional, exploratory, and question-raising than was supposed. If this point of view is accepted, does it mean that the importance of Plato and Aristotle, as more than a purely historical recognition, will for the first time be radically reduced? Perhaps not: the power and depth of their particular arguments may come to be what command admiration and interest rather than the breadth and ambition of their systems. Yet it would be superficial to rest too easily on this idea. The interest that these two philosophers have always commanded in the past has been generated not merely by admiration for their undoubted acuity, insight, and imagination, but, very often, by a belief that they had vast and unitary systematic ambitions, of a kind which we now have rather less reason to ascribe to them.

Apart from these issues of how the work of Plato and of Aristotle is to be interpreted, there are in any case other, more general influences likely to affect their traditional standing. Those features of twentieth-century culture which have weakened the hold of the classic, and of the idea that past works can have any authority over the taste of the present, apply in some degree to philosophy. Past geniuses of philosophy, as of the arts, look different under the influence of our idea, deeply felt and largely correct, that twentieth-century experience is drastically unprecedented. Again, in more technical areas of contemporary philosophy, there have been developments from which some of it has attained the research pattern of a science, and in any such area its interest in any of its past, let alone its Greek past, becomes necessarily more external and ultimately anecdotal. For both these reasons, the role of an absolute classic in philosophy, the role which Plato and Aristotle have peculiarly played, is one that quite conceivably may lose its importance. The question here is not whether philosophy might cease to be of interest—there is more than one dispiriting kind of reason why that might prove to be so—but whether, granted philosophy retains its interest, Plato and Aristotle might not do so, and might become finally historical objects, monumental paradigms of ancient styles. It is not impossible, but if it were to happen at all, there is one reason why it is less likely to happen to Plato than to his great companion: the fact that Plato's work includes as a vivid and independent presence the ambiguous figure of Socrates, whose aspect as ironical critic of organized philosophy can be turned also against the Platonic philosophies, which at other points he is presented as expounding.

What We Have

The pre-eminent status of Plato and Aristotle is both the cause and the effect of their work being quite exceptionally well preserved: though in the case of both, and particularly of Aristotle, there was some luck involved. Of Plato's works, we have everything that he is known to have published. Of Aristotle, we do not have his dialogues (for which he was most admired in antiquity), but we do have a large body of treatises which contain material prepared by him or in some cases by close associates or students.

Work later than Aristotle will not in general be touched on here except for some discussion of ancient scepticism; but we should not forget the large influence exercised on Western thought by the later schools, particularly the Stoics and Epicureans, quite apart from those influences on Christianity which are discussed in another chapter. The Presocratics will be of closer concern to us. They are known to us through fragments of their writings, and in many respects the situation is as described in the chapter on Greek science, that we have to rely on summaries and accounts by later writers, who may be remote in time, or stupid, or—as in the case of Aristotle, who was neither—have their own axe to grind. There does remain one very considerable and nearly continuous fragment of Presocratic writing, a substantial amount of the poem of Parmenides (who was born probably *c.* 515 B.C.): we owe this entirely to the Neoplatonist scholar Simplicius, who, in the commentary on Aristotle's *Physics* which he wrote in the sixth century A.D., copied out long extracts from the poem on the ground that Parmenides' book had at that time become very rare. Thanks to Simplicius, we have enough to reconstruct a continuous argument (which we shall turn to in the next section).

By contrast, another challenging figure, Heracleitus, who was almost certainly rather earlier than Parmenides and perhaps born *c.* 540 B.C., is known only from an assemblage of brief disconnected fragments, conflicting and obviously puzzled reports, and a number of unreliable anecdotes illustrating an original, pessimistic, and contemptuous personality. In his case, it is not clear what has been lost, either in terms of works, or, indeed, in possibility of understanding: it seems anyway that he wrote in the form of brief and dense epigrams, and he was famed already in antiquity for his obscurity. Plotinus said of him (*Enneads*, 4. 8), 'He seems to speak in similes, careless of making his meaning clear, perhaps because in his view we ought to seek within ourselves, as he himself had successfully sought.' The idea of searching within oneself was in Heracleitus, as it was in Socrates: 'I searched myself', Heracleitus said (fr. 101).[4] But he was almost certainly not *careless* of making himself clear: rather, his conception of truth was of something that essentially could not be expressed in a direct, discursive way. He probably thought of philosophical speech as he said of 'the king whose oracle is at Delphi: he does not say, and he does not conceal—he gives a sign' (fr. 93). In this, Socrates vitally differed from him.

Heracleitus' views, so far as they can be discovered, centre on the necessity to the cosmos of constant change and 'warfare' between opposing principles, though these are held in some kind of reciprocal relation and balance. They elicited, at some remove, the respect of Lenin, but it was undoubtedly Nietzsche's admiration that came closer to him—and not only because of his greater sympathy for Heracleitus' contempt for the masses. Heracleitus has seldom had followers, but his deliberate ambiguities and startling images (as in fr. 52: 'time is a child at play, playing draughts: the kingdom is a child's') have contributed to the deep resonances which he has occasionally evoked in later philosophy, most recently in Heidegger.

Of the later Presocratics, again no complete work survives; the most numerous fragments are of two contrasted writers. One is Democritus (roughly a contemporary of Socrates, being born *c.* 470 B.C.), who was concerned both with ethical questions and with the explanation of natural phenomena; he is most famous as one of the first theorists of physical atomism. The other is the riddling figure of Empedocles, who came from Acragas in Sicily, and was falsely represented by tradition as having died by throwing himself into Etna. He wrote not later than

---

[4] All references to the Presocratics are to the 6th edition of Diels-Kranz, *Die Fragmente der Vorsokratiker*, in each case to the 'B' section of the material on a given writer.

For an exegesis of these words of Heracleitus, see W.K.C. Guthrie, *A History of Greek Philosophy* (Cambridge, 1962–), i. 417–19.

450 B.C. two poems which later came to be called *On Nature* and *Purifications*. As these titles suggest, naturalistic elements, an interest in physical explanation, coexisted in his thought with a religious strain, and it is still disputed how they were combined, and whether his interest in nature was subordinate to magical concerns rather than the product of curiosity and free enquiry. Curiosity did to some extent motivate the Milesian thinkers, and free enquiry was consciously practised by Democritus and others of similar temper, such as the ingenious thinker Anaxagoras (born *c.* 500 B.C.), who is said to have been prosecuted by the Athenians for holding an impiously naturalistic view of the heavenly bodies.

There is one further group among the predecessors and contemporaries of Socrates, whom we should mention at this point: the so-called 'Sophists', whose interests were neither cosmological nor religious, but more practically orientated, largely towards the training of pupils in techniques for political and forensic success, a training for which they received money. These activities earned them an extremely bad reputation from Plato, whose attitude to them, expressed in all modes from the glittering mockery of the *Protagoras* to the contempt and disgust of the *Gorgias* and *Republic*, has not only left the Sophists in low esteem, but has helped to make the word 'sophist' useless for any historical purpose. This is particularly because Plato tended to conflate four different charges against them: that their teaching had a practical rather than a purely theoretical bent; that they took money; that they produced bad arguments, designed to puzzle and impress rather than to get at the truth; and that they advanced cynical, sceptical, amoral, and generally undesirable opinions.

It is not at all easy to disentangle these elements, nor to establish how far the Sophists, or some of them, had what we would now identify as genuine philosophical interests. They were prone to confuse, as has been well said,[5] the force of reason and the power of the spoken word, two things which Socrates' method of question and answer gave a way of taking apart. Gorgias of Leontini, a celebrated stylistic innovator who influenced one of the greatest geniuses among Greek writers, the historian Thucydides, was a teacher of rhetoric whose excursion into metaphysics, a lost work called *On What Is Not*, may well, to judge from later summaries of it, have been parodistic. But more serious claims can be made for Protagoras of Abdera (born *c.* 490 B.C.), who commanded enough interest and respect from Plato for him to construct in his *Theaetetus* a sensitive elaboration of a relativistic theory of knowledge starting explicitly from a Protagorean basis. It may be true, as a recent writer has said,[6] that 'he dominated the intellectual life of his time with-

---

[5] Edward Hussey, *The Presocratics* (London, 1972), p. 117.
[6] Hussey, p. 116.

out being a truly original thinker', setting rather an intellectual tone, sceptical and irreverent; but it is possible that he articulated more searching and systematic thoughts about knowledge and society than this implies. It would be interesting to know more of his work than we do, both to learn about the radical strain in fifth-century thought, and to form a more detailed idea of developments, which certainly occurred, in the theory of knowledge and the philosophy of language before Plato. It would be interesting, too, as a matter of sheer curiosity, to know how he continued his book *On the Gods*, of which we have only the discouraging first sentence: 'About the gods I cannot know, whether they exist or not, nor what kind of beings they might be; there are many obstacles to knowledge, both the obscurity of the subject and the shortness of man's life.'

The Birth of Metaphysics

Greek philosophy started at the edges of the Greek world: on the offshore islands and the western seaboard of Asia Minor—Ionia—and to the far west, in the Greek colonies of Southern Italy and Sicily. The latter were not in any case independent of Ionian influence. Many received new colonists from Ionia after it was annexed by the Persians in the sixth century, and, in particular, the city of Elea in Southern Italy, famous for the philosophy of Parmenides and his pupil Zeno (thus called the 'Eleatics'), was founded by the citizens of Phocaea, a city in Ionia, who had emigrated in large numbers.

The question has been much and inconclusively discussed, of why systematic cosmological thought, embodying an element of rational criticism, should have arisen in Ionia at this time. The great empires of the East had acquired a good deal of empirical information about measurement, positional astronomy, and such matters, while the Babylonian tradition embodied considerable sophistication in mathematical computation, though with little impulse, it seems, to discover an *a priori* order in the mathematical subject-matter. These various techniques, moreover, coexisted with pictures of the origin and structure of the universe which were straightforwardly mythological. Knowledge of these beliefs, transmitted through the Persian empire, may have played a role in the formation of Ionian cosmology, but, if so, they were essentially modified in a more critical and less mythological direction. The relatively autonomous political life of the small Greek cities perhaps played a part in the growth of critical and reflective thought, as contrasted with those 'Asiatic vague immensities', in Yeats's phrase, of the great empires.

Open speculative enquiry was a necessary condition for the development of Greek philosophy, but it would be a mistake to think that everything which eventually fed into it was equally an example of that openness. The Milesians and Eleatics formed 'schools' only in the sense that these thinkers were connected by ties of intellectual influence and teaching; the Pythagorean school, on the other hand, which was founded in Croton in South Italy towards the end of the sixth century, was more like a religious brotherhood or secret society. The history of this school and its founder is wrapped in obscurity and legend, though we know that Pythagoras himself was another who emigrated from Ionia, having been born and having gained a reputation in Samos. The Pythagorean school played an important, if much disputed, role in the development of mathematics, though it is doubtful to what extent those studies figured in its earlier years. Its life was devoted, more certainly, to an ascetic religious discipline centring on concepts of the purification of the soul and reincarnation: ideas and practices perhaps influenced by shamanistic beliefs which would have reached Greece through the Thracians and Scythians.

Pythagorean ideas were to play an important part in the development of the idea of a rational, immaterial soul, separate from the body, an idea which was much developed by Plato; and which passed from him through Augustine to become the basis of Descartes' dualism—though it lost, in the context of seventeenth-century mechanical science, a basic feature which it shared with all Greek ideas of 'soul', namely the conception that it was the presence of soul which gave living things their life. (Descartes marked the difference when he said something which Pythagoreans, Plato, Aristotle, would all equally have been unable to understand: 'it is not that the body dies because the soul leaves it—the soul leaves it because the body has died.')

Whatever exactly the early Pythagoreans did and believed, they did it in secret, and the concept of being initiated into a mystery applies in their case better than that of making an intervention into an open rational debate. Their existence, contemporary with the later Milesians, reminds us also of something else: that from its beginnings two motives were brought to Western philosophy which have been active alongside one another ever since, the desire for salvation and the desire to find out how things work.

We have already suggested that while the question of how far Milesian thought was philosophical is an unhelpful one, the question of how far its enquiries were rational may be a better one. There are of course various criteria of rationality, but certainly one very important expression of it is to be found in reflection, guided by general principles, on what questions require an answer. There is a very striking example of such thought in a famous argument of Anaximander, who worked in the first half of the sixth century and, according to an ancient writer, was 'the first of the Greeks, to our knowledge, who was bold enough to publish a book on nature'.[7] The argument relates to a question which bothered other Presocratics: what keeps the earth in its place? Others were to appeal to material supports of various kinds: but Anaximander argued that the earth was symmetrically placed in the centre of the universe, and thus needed no support. This argument represents an early application of a purely rational principle, the Principle of Sufficient Reason. If the earth were to move in one direction rather than another, there would have to be a reason for this, in the form of some relevant asymmetry or difference: so, if there is no such asymmetry, the earth will not move in any direction rather than another, i.e. will stay where it is. This impressive argument brings out clearly how the application of rational principle, even if it is to basically primitive cosmological materials, marks out such thought from mythological picture-making.

A different exercise of rationality, however, and a much more purely abstract one is represented by the extraordinary work of Parmenides. Parmenides expressed his philosophy in verse, a choice less eccentric than it would be now, but still a choice (the Milesians wrote in prose). The effort to express abstract and logical considerations in epic hexameters gives an intense but also strained effect, and his style was poorly viewed in antiquity. His aim throughout seems to be to achieve as much clarity as possible, and the syntactical obscurities that remain are the unintended results of the language being drastically bent to his unprecedented subject-matter. His ambiguities are thus of a very different kind from the revelatory puns of Heracleitus. Even the very little we have of Heracleitus (compared with 154 lines of Parmenides) shows that he was the more controlled and sophisticated writer; but Parmenides was attempting something quite different from him or anyone else before,[8] which was to determine the basic nature of reality entirely by argument from premisses self-evident to reflection—just one premiss, in fact, though Parmenides (fr. 5) says that it makes no difference where one starts. Whatever exactly we say about the Milesians, in this undertaking we can certainly recognize the first example of pure metaphysical reasoning: it remains one of the most ambitious.

Parmenides' poem represents a goddess as revealing to him the true way of enquiry. What she gives as the key to the true way is this: 'it is,

---

[7] Themistius *Or.* 26, p. 383, Dindorf.

[8] In this emphasis, as also on some central questions of interpretation, I follow the important article of G.E.L. Owen, 'Eleatic Questions', reprinted in R. E. Allen and D. J. Furley ed., *Studies in Presocratic Philosophy*, vol. ii (London, 1975), pp. 48–81.

and it cannot be that it is not.' We must not try to think 'it is not': for 'you could not know what is not (that is not practicable), nor speak of it (fr. 2). The same thing is there to be thought, and to be (fr. 3). What is there to be spoken of and thought, must be; for it is there to be, but *nothing* is not (fr. 6).'

We will leave for the moment the question of what is meant by 'it' in 'it is' and 'it is not' (in the Greek the verb 'is' stands by itself). Parmenides' first conclusion is that there is no coherent or possible enquiry into what is not, or which uses the thought 'it is not'; this is because 'the same thing is there to be thought, and to be', and what is not, *nothing*, is not available, so to speak, for thought. Parmenides' ultimate backing for this radical claim is hard to recapture with total precision, and is still the subject of controversy. Some believe that the basic argument (as given in fr. 6, 1–2, the last sentence quoted above) is this: with regard to what can be thought and spoken of, it is true (at least) that it *could* be—and this might be conceded even by those of us who suppose that some things which can be thought and spoken of do not, as a matter of fact, exist (unicorns, for instance). But now consider: of *nothing*, it is not true that it could be. So a thing which can be thought and spoken of cannot be identical with nothing. But then it must be something; and so, contrary to what you first thought, *must* actually be.

This is at least a clear fallacy. But in the strange phrase translated as 'is there to be', Parmenides has a more primitive conception than this version captures, a notion of language and thought having a content only because they touch or are in contact with what is—the touching and seeing models of thought and meaning operate more directly on Parmenides' ideas than is quite brought out by the excursion through what *could* be. But however exactly we are to reconstruct Parmenides' rejection of the thought 'it is not', his rejection of it is clear and total, and he proceeds to deduce from that rejection, in order, a series of surprising consequences. What is can have no beginning or end; if it had, then, before or after, it would *not be*, and that is excluded. He adds to this proof of 'its' having no beginning, another based on an elegant use of the Principle of Sufficient Reason: 'what necessity would force it, sooner or later, to come to be, if it started from nothing?' (fr. 8, 9–10).

'It neither was nor will be, since it is altogether now': here Parmenides gives the first expression to an idea of eternity. His conception is not of something outside time altogether, as some later conceptions of eternity have it, something to which no temporal notions apply at all. It is *now*. But, equally, it is not merely indefinitely old—it has no past, and no future. Its time, such as it is, is represented as a perpetual present. 'It' is uniform, unchanging, has no divisions, is the same under any aspect—for to deny any of this would involve thinking that there was some place, or some time, or some respect, with regard to which it *was not*, and this, once more, is excluded.

Above all, there is only one of it. For 'there is and will be nothing besides what is' (fr. 8, 36–7)—anything else would have to be something which *was not*; and 'what is', itself, cannot consist of two distinguishable things or be divided, 'since it all, equally, is; it is not more or less in any way . . . so it is all continuous, for what is sticks close to what is' (fr. 8, 22–5). Once the uniqueness of 'it' is seen to be a conclusion of Parmenides' argument, and not (as some earlier scholars supposed) a premiss, the question of what 'it' is lapses. It is just that thing, whatever it is, that we are thinking and speaking of, when we succeed in thinking and speaking of something—and Parmenides certainly supposes that we can think and speak of *something*, though very evidently it is not what, in our everyday error, we take ourselves to be thinking and speaking of.

The philosophical legacy of this remarkable argument is very extensive and various. The concept of eternal, unchanging, and uncreated being is one which Plato was to use in characterizing his Forms; his debt to Parmenides was explicit and acknowledged, though he had to differ from him, as he gravely concedes in the *Sophist*, by admitting into reality also principles of change. He differed from him already, however, about the world of unchanging being: Plato had held, from the earliest introduction of the Forms, that there were *many* of them, which could be intellectually distinguished. How this could be, however, is something he did not take up until in that same late dialogue, the *Sophist*, he directly faced the challenge of Parmenides' proof and sought to meet it by systematically distinguishing different senses of 'is not'.

That same attempt was also to provide the solution, as Plato hoped, to another problem which directly related to Parmenides' argument, the problem of falsehood. To think, surely, is to think *something*—to think nothing is not to think at all. So what is the 'something' that is thought by one who thinks falsely? Thought or speech which is false cannot be nonsensical: what relation to reality is possessed by speech which has a meaning, but is not true? This problem Plato made a powerfully original attempt to solve, in the course of which he developed a distinction essential to these issues, that between a name and a statement. What is in many ways the same set of questions has recurred in increasingly sophisticated forms to the present day; and Wittgenstein's *Tractatus*, a metaphysical work comparable in both boldness and abstractness to Parmenides', takes its start from a question which implies the converse of Parmenides' principle: 'how can we say what is not?'

Other strains of Parmenidean influence come from his denials of plurality and change. His pupil Zeno invented a series of famous paradoxes which apparently deduce contradictions from the suppositions that there is plurality, or that motion is possible; paradoxes such as that of the Arrow, which (in its shortest form) runs thus: an arrow in flight occupies at each instant a space which is just its own length; but any body which at any time occupies just such a space is, with regard to that time, at rest; so the arrow is at rest at each instant; so it is at rest at every instant, that is to say, it does not move. These paradoxes gave rise to a complex debate which belongs as much to the history of mathematics as to philosophy, from which there emerged eventually the concepts of the continuum and of a limit. But even after mathematical techniques had been established to characterize the phenomena which Zeno thought could not be coherently characterized, there have remained philosophical problems about the application of mathematics to physical space and time in which some of Zeno's arguments have still played a role; while the method which he invented, of generating from a set of assumptions an infinite regress (or progress)—a method which can be used either destructively, or constructively to determine some infinite set of items—has remained an essential resource of analytical thought.

Apart from difficulties for common sense from the Eleatic arguments, there were particular problems for the most advanced form of theoretical pluralism, atomism, which held that the world consisted of atoms moving in empty space—for how was totally empty space to be conceptualized to avoid the Eleatic argument (which impressed others, such as Anaxagoras) that it would have to be *nothing*, and hence could not exist? It seems that the first of the Atomists, Leucippus (born near the beginning of the fifth century) asserted the existence of the void against the Eleatics by saying that void is *not being*, yet *is*—a formulation which seems too much like a contradiction. Aristotle's treatment of this subject in the *Physics* represents a great advance in the conceptualization of empty space, and although he himself does not accept a void, he does not include the Eleatic type of argument among the several bad arguments he uses against it. It is all the more remarkable that Descartes, in the seventeenth century, when he denied a vacuum on the basis of his own physics (which involved a close assimilation of matter and space), was able to use a startlingly Eleatic type of argument: 'If it is asked what would be the case if God removed all the matter from a vessel and let nothing else take the place of what had been removed, then the answer must be, that the sides of the vessel would be contiguous. For if there is nothing between two bodies, they must be next to each other' (*Principles of Philosophy*, ii. 18).

APPEARANCE AND REALITY

Parmenides' poem had a further part, mostly lost, in which the goddess expounded a pluralistic cosmological theory; which, however, she was committed to regarding as nonsense, and probably advanced only as a sophisticated example of the kind of thing she had warned against at the beginning of the poem, the way of ignorant mortals, who 'drift along, deaf and blind, amazed, in confused throngs: they think that to be and not to be are the same, and not the same' (fr. 6, 6–9)—that is to say, they think, confusedly, that it is possible for what *is* here and now, *not to be* at other times and places. There has been much discussion of what relation Parmenides supposed the opinions of men to bear to reality as he explained it. But if that discussion tries to rest anything on what it would be consistent for Parmenides to hold, it must recognize from the beginning the important fact that there is nothing which Parmenides could consistently hold on this subject. For the opinions of men certainly change, and are different from one another: so if everything is (literally) one and (literally) nothing changes, there are no such opinions.

This point applies just as much to the true thought of the instructed philosopher. Some interpreters have claimed that Parmenides believed being and thought to be one, that nothing existed except thought (Parmenides would thus be something like an idealist, in the sense in which it was claimed earlier that no ancient philosopher was an idealist). This view is based partly on highly resistible interpretations of two ambiguous lines (fr. 3; fr. 8, 34), but also on the argument that since Parmenides thought everything was one, and agreed that there was thought, he must have supposed, not being stupid, that thought was the one thing there was. But this type of argument ignores the obliquities of the metaphysical imagination. One might as well argue that since Parmenides thought everything was one, and conceded (since he refers to himself more than once) that *he* existed, he must have supposed that he was the only thing there was. It is clear[9] that Plato regarded himself, more than a century later, as forcing Parmenides to face the question of the existence of thought as part of reality. Let us call Parmenides' one thing 'It'. Then one of Plato's points was that Parmenides agreed that there was at least a name of It; but if there is only one thing, then It must be that name; and since It is a name, then Its name must be the name of a name; so Parmenides' theory comes out as the view that there is only one thing in reality, a name which is the name of a name.

[9] As Owen showed, 'Eleatic Questions', n. 54.

This mildly jocular argument contains in fact both a narrower and a wider point. Since naming is, by both Parmenides and Plato, closely connected with thinking, it raises the question of thought being part of reality, a question which Plato goes on to pursue. But it raises also the general issue of what it is to take a thesis like Parmenides' seriously. Is it, for instance, to take it *literally*? An Eleatic might reply that of course it was never meant to be taken in the literal way in which Plato's argument takes it; but then the question can be pressed, as it was repeatedly pressed against metaphysical arguments by G. E. Moore in the present century, of how it is to be taken. Moore himself was burdened by a prejudice that to take something seriously was to take it literally; we do not have to agree with that, in order justifiably to demand some directions from the speculative metaphysician about how to take him seriously. One guide about how to take him seriously is provided by the direction of his arguments: but in Parmenides' case, this gets us no further on, since his argument either proves nothing at all, or proves just that literal absurdity which Plato objected to.

Parmenides had a theory so simple and radical that, taken literally, it leaves no room even for what he regarded as correct thought. With regard to other, false, ideas, the deluded beliefs of men, and indeed the pluralistic world itself as it seems, he and his followers were disposed to relegate these to the category of 'appearance'.[10] This contrast between appearance and reality can be aligned, as it is by Parmenides (fr. 7), with a contrast between sense-perception and reason: sense-perception is deluded by mere appearance, it is the power of reason that grasps reality. But such a distinction, whatever else may be said about it, does not solve the problem that we have been pressing on Parmenides. For even if men are deluded by the senses, and appearances conceal rather than reveal reality, at least it is true *that there are appearances*, and any full account of what actually exists must include the actual existence of (misleading) appearances. As the English twentieth-century metaphysician F. H. Bradley insisted, appearance must itself be part of reality.

The point was seen, once more, by Plato in that late dialogue the *Sophist* to which we have already referred. But it was a truth which Plato himself had to learn to take as seriously as it needs to be taken. In his middle-period dialogues, above all the *Republic*, he had offered a picture of knowledge and reality which was itself open to this criticism, or at least was deeply ambiguous on the issue. On the one hand, there was the world of Forms, immaterial and unchanging objects of purely intellectual knowledge, which were supposed, in that simple and ambitious theory, to solve a lot of problems at once: to explain, for instance, what

[10] Cf. Parmenides, fr. 8, 37; and also a later monist, Melissus, fr. 8.

mathematical truths are truths about (for evidently they are not about such things as the inaccurate geometrical figures one sees on blackboards), and, at the same time, to be what give general terms a meaning. Over against these, were the objects of sense-perception and everyday belief, the things of the natural world which are mistaken for reality by the 'lovers of sense-experience', who are contrasted with the philosophers, the lovers of truth.

In the *Republic*, the distinction between these worlds is hammered home by a series of dichotomies: in the model of the Divided Line, which separates the realm of Forms from that of matter, and assigns reason to the one, the senses to the other; and in an image which has haunted European thought, which represents the philosopher's education as a journey into the sunlight from a cave, in which ordinary men, prisoners of their prejudices, raptly watch a flickering procession of shadow images. This distinction, and the ordering of value that goes with it, Plato sometimes represents as one between 'being' and 'becoming', where 'becoming', we are told, is constituted by some unsatisfactory and unstable combination of being and not being. Plato was to abandon these formulations, though certainly not his belief in eternal intellectual objects.

Interpreters have not found it easy to capture exactly what Plato meant when, in the *Republic* and other dialogues of his middle period, he claimed 'real being' for the Forms, and denied it to the everyday objects of sense-perception. There is, in fact, more than one level of difficulty. There is the very general philosophical problem, which we have just touched on in the confrontation of Parmenides and Moore, of giving a sense to metaphysical assertions which deny the reality of some large and evident dimension of experience. Problems of that general sort are still with us. But there is also an historical problem, of understanding those particular metaphysical formulations which belong to a time before the development of any systematic logical theory, and which we are particularly likely to misrepresent in the light of later conceptions. Beyond that again, there is a very specific historical problem of understanding Plato, who seems himself to have become dissatisfied with some of these formulations and to have become, in his later work, a critic of his earlier self. If Plato became dissatisfied with these formulations, there is really not much reason to suppose that they ever had some fully determinate sense which we could now recover: it is rather that Plato is one of those who helped to put us into a position from which these formulations may be seen to have no fully determinate sense at all.

His later dissatisfaction with what he had said in the *Republic* lay in some part in technical issues about the idea of *being*: certainly he came to a clearer understanding of that notion, and also to a more patient and analytical conception of the kind of philosophical enquiry that such an understanding demanded. Related developments away from a simple *Republic* image occurred, as we shall see, in Plato's conception of knowledge.

It may be also that, more broadly, he became less governed by images of the rational mind being clogged or imprisoned by the empirical world. Those images themselves, it must be said, always stood in an uneasy relationship to another kind of picture which at the same time he offered of the material world, equally unfavourable to it, but in a contrary direction—that it was evanescent, flimsy, only appearance. The world of matter had to be ultimately powerless but at the same time destructively powerful, two conflicting aspects which stand to one another as the shadows of the Cave stand to the fetters which bind its prisoners. Such tensions express something very real in Plato's outlook (notably, his own deep ambivalence towards political power, and towards art), but their theoretical costs, for so ambitious a theory, are high, and Plato seems to have become aware of them.

The *Republic* theory, however, refuses to go away; it is perhaps Plato's most famous doctrine, and besides its appearances in history and literature as 'the Platonic philosophy', it itself, or at least its terminology, has recurred in many forms. Its tensions themselves help to explain how it keeps a hold on the philosophical imagination; and here one factor to be mentioned—which particularly relates to the associated Platonic doctrine of love, expressed in the *Symposium*—is that there is a constant and vivid contrast, in these middle-period works, between Plato's world-denying theories and his literary presentation of them. The resonance of his images and the imaginative power of his style, the most beautiful ever devised for the expression of abstract thought, implicitly affirm the reality of the world of senses even when the content denies it.

A more general point is that it is only philosophers and historians of philosophy who worry much about what is entailed by a theory such as that of the *Republic* when it is taken strictly. Others—artists, scientists—get what they need out of it, and if Plato's theory is taken broadly enough, much more can be got from it than is strictly in it. That includes the rationalist spirit so important to the seventeenth-century scientific revolution, which we have already referred to in the person of Galileo, the spirit which sought an underlying mathematical structure under the flux of appearances. It is clear how this can be thought to be in the spirit of Plato's *Republic*; it is clear also how it contradicts what is actually said there, since Plato quite explicitly says that there is no hope at all of giving a scientific account of the material world. His message is, and quite clearly, not that physics should be mathematical, but that one should give up physics and pursue mathematics. If philosophers are going to be influential, it is as well that they should be misunderstood.

KNOWLEDGE AND SCEPTICISM

Not all philosophical thought that regards reality as different from appearances need be as drastically dismissive of appearances as Parmenides, or the *Republic* taken strictly. It may rather encourage, like the *Republic* taken loosely, some rationalistic, perhaps scientific method for uncovering the reality from the appearances. One important difference between these attitudes is that the rationalist programme which finds an intellectual order under appearances may also find it to be, to some extent, systematically related to appearances, so that discovery of the hidden order can lead to control of what happens even as it appears: all control of the environment which is grounded in physical theory is of this character.

The fact that the view of the *Republic* was not really of this kind presented a serious difficulty to Plato. He was not, of course, interested in physical technology; but he was concerned with social technology, and the dream of the *Republic* is that philosophers, who have seen the truth about reality, would return to the Cave and, after their intellectual sight had adjusted to the darkness of empirical life, would be able to order things better than those who had never left. But despite some hopeful references to the paradigm that they carry in their memory, he does not provide enough to bridge the disjunction between the two worlds, and, as we shall see rather later, the theory of knowledge which he offers is unable to help in the basic task of political education.

The search for a coherent theory of how scientific knowledge might be possible was a preoccupation of some late-fifth-century thinkers. Anaxagoras had said (fr. 21A) that appearances were 'a glimpse of the hidden', and for this he was praised by Democritus, who evidently struggled with these questions. Democritus took the point that while sense-perception could be misleading, and thought had in some sense to get behind appearances, nevertheless it was only with the help of other perceptions that this could be done: 'colour, sweetness, bitterness, these are matters of convention', he interestingly said (fr. 125), 'and what there is in truth are atoms and the void'; but he represented the senses as replying, 'Poor mind, are you going to overthrow us when you take your beliefs from us? If you throw us, you fall over.'

In trying to resolve the epistemological problems of atomism (and we do not know how far he got), Democritus was facing not only the Eleatics, who thought that they knew something incompatible with his atomism, but also a range of Sophists who thought that they had arguments against anyone's knowing anything at all—or at least, anything of a theoretical, general, or scientific character. The inconclusive speculations of the earlier Presocratics, and in particular the mind-numbing conclusions of Eleatic logic, served to encourage attitudes of scepticism.

A general sense that certainty, at least on any large or speculative issue, is impossible, is itself an early phenomenon. But the Sophists, or some of them, pursued a more aggressive line against philosophical theory of any kind and the use of dialectic to support it; wishing in this to advance their own claims to teach something useful, in the form of rhetoric and the all-important power to persuade in the courts and the political assembly—activities in which, as they agreed with their critics, scrupulous logical demonstration was not at a premium. The arguments used in these attacks on the possibility of knowledge seem now a mixture of almost childish muddles or tricks, and penetrating insights into real difficulties; a few arguments embody both at once, as some of those recorded in Plato's *Euthydemus*, or found in a rather rough and ready compilation of dialectical material called the *Dissoi Logoi* or 'Double Arguments', which is generally taken to date from this period. We do not know how far Protagoras himself developed the positions which Plato ascribes to him, offering a relativized view of truth and knowledge, by which what seems to each man is true *for him*: but we do know that Democritus used against him, and may have invented, a form of argument which was to be very important in the later history of scepticism and the theory of knowledge. This form of argument is called the *peritrope* or 'reversal', and consists in applying a philosopher's criterion of knowledge, truth, or meaningfulness to his own statements—in this case, asking Protagoras whether his own thesis is supposed to be (non-relatively) true.

Some of the material which survives from these early excursions into scepticism seems naïve—naïve, that is, not just by some arbitrary standard of later logical theory, but by the contemporary standards of insight set by Herodotus or Thucydides or, differently, Sophocles—adult persons, compared (it seems) with clever children. The point is not about the individual psychological fact, of the talents or maturity of Sophists compared with those of historians or tragedians; the question is about the social fact, that these arguments were capable of genuinely impressing and bewildering the Sophists' contemporaries. The basic question is, as Nietzsche unforgettably said about Socrates, *how did they get away with it?* Here it is important to remember the gap that always exists between intelligent practice and the theoretical reflective understanding of that practice; and, more particularly, how utterly puzzling the theory of reasoning must have seemed at this point. On the one hand, there existed already startling intellectual achievements in mathematics, and some systematic thought about such subjects as medicine made sense; while, even more evidently, the practice of argument in everyday life could be seen to rest on some assumptions about the connexions between proof and truth—at the very least it was possible to show a person through dialectical refutation that he was contradicting himself and must be wrong somewhere. But at the same time, the Eleatic arguments—which were in fact deep and powerful—led to impossible results; it seemed that one could prove anything. Many other invalid arguments, neither deep nor powerful, could not be decisively shown up because no systematic vocabulary of logical criticism yet existed. The fundamental achievements of Plato and Aristotle in setting logic and the philosophy of language on their feet can conceal from us how random and unstructured reflective logical thought was before the fourth century.

Plato and Aristotle sought foundations for philosophical and (in Aristotle's case at least) scientific enquiry which would resist scepticism. Aristotle's theory of knowledge is complex, and no general account of it will be attempted here. It judiciously combined appeal to some intuitively or self-evidently known principles, with an important role for sense-experience. It also made a very characteristic appeal to the consensus of informed and thoughtful persons: Aristotle champions a programme which applies equally to metaphysics, ethics, and science, of considering and seeking to reconcile the views of the best authorities, and when he says that one's theory should accord with *ta phainomena*, 'the appearances', he includes in that not only data of observation, and what competent speakers would be disposed to say, but also, at least presumptively, existing well-entrenched theoretical opinions. The weight of proof, for Aristotle, is against those who would try to unseat such a consensus. Even granted that the strength of the presumption is not necessarily very strong, so that Aristotle can throw it over with some ease if he thinks he has a strong argument; granted, too, the element of preselection that Aristotle exercises in what is to count as a worthwhile opinion; nevertheless, the fact that he can hope to find any soil in which to ground such a method shows how far things have travelled by his time from the age of the Sophists.

For Aristotle, the advance of knowledge is a collective and on-going enterprise, to which earlier thinkers, unless too exotic, primitive, or capricious, can be seen as contributors. That idea exists powerfully today in the conception of a scientific community, whose practitioners are recruited through an apprenticeship in experimental and observational techniques, and again there is a presumption in favour of expert consensus. But in a world where there were few experimental techniques, the question of who was to be counted as part of the informed consensus was interpreted differently, and there was a strong pull towards intellectual activity coming to be seen (as it scarcely was by Aristotle, but was by many later) as the scholastic undertaking of harmonizing the contents of authoritative books.

This methodological respect for an informed consensus provides a contrast between Aristotle's outlook and Plato's, something which emerges in particularly stark terms with regard to ethics. But there is another set of beliefs about knowledge which they share, and which has been of the greatest importance for the history of philosophy: beliefs which represent knowledge as, in more than one way, quite special, and in particular very different from mere belief or opinion, even true opinion. One idea of this kind is that real knowledge, as opposed to random true belief, should form a system, should be theoretically organized in a way which itself corresponds revealingly to the structure of the subject-matter. This idea relates most directly to an ideal body of *scientific* knowledge, an ideal which Plato (in relation to philosophy and mathematics) did much to form, and Aristotle carried much further. It can be seen, however, also as a condition on what it is for a particular person to know anything. It represents a person's thought as real knowledge only insofar as that thought approximates to the system—the knower is the *savant*, one in whom some part of the ideal body of theoretical knowledge is realized.

This requirement leaves out, needless to say, a good deal of what in everyday acceptance would count as knowledge. This divergence is increased when there is added a further idea, that organized theoretical knowledge can be had only of an unchanging subject-matter, that contingent and particular and changeable matters of fact are no subject for science. Taken together, these ideas yield the conclusion that no person's thought can strictly and properly be said to be knowledge unless it relates to a necessary and unchanging subject-matter. This conclusion—and there are other routes to it besides this—exerted a notable fascination on both Plato and Aristotle, and has since recurred in philosophy more than once.

In Plato's thought, a development on this subject can very clearly be followed. In the *Meno*, a dialogue which marks a boundary between the early and the middle period of his work, his views are in a rich and unstable solution. Faced with a sophistic puzzle about how it is possible to learn anything at all, he introduces for the first time the doctrine of *anamnesis* or 'recollection', which represents the process of learning as the recovery of opinions already in the soul but forgotten. In the dialogue, this process (or, more strictly, its earlier steps) is illustrated by a scene in which Socrates elicits from a slave-boy, by questioning, assent to a geometrical truth of which the boy had no conscious idea before. A great deal could be said about this famous doctrine, and the Pythagorean ideas of pre-existence, reincarnation, and immortality which Plato attached to it, sketchily in the *Meno*, but more extensively in the *Phaedo*. The present point, however, concerns only one feature of it: that as an account of learning, it could not really look appropriate to anything except a necessary or *a priori* subject-matter, such as mathematics. There is indeed something which is striking and demands explanation in the fact that one can elicit from a pupil, by argument, mathematical conclusions which have never occurred to him before; but no amount of Socratic questioning could elicit from anyone a set of particular facts of geography or history which he had not already, in the mundane sense, learned. The reader of the *Meno*, however, finds that Socrates seems to hold also all of the following: that knowledge can be acquired only by such 'recollection'; that there is a distinction between knowledge and mere true belief; and that this last distinction can be applied not only to mathematics, but also to contingent matters—we can distinguish between a man who knows the way to Larissa and a man who merely has true beliefs about it. If we accept the obvious fact that 'recollection' does not apply to such matters (and it is not entirely clear whether the *Meno* accepts that point or not), these claims produce an inconsistency.

However it may be with the *Meno*, there is no such inconsistency in the *Republic*, where Plato makes it clear that for him the distinction between knowledge and belief is a difference of subject-matter: they relate to those two ontological worlds represented by the Divided Line. This neat co-ordination, however, leads to absurd conclusions, compounded by the fact that at this stage Plato has no adequate theory of error. The consequence that there is no empirical knowledge presents a problem, of which we have already seen the outline in discussing the Cave, of how the philosophers' knowledge can play any constructive role in this world at all; for to apply knowledge to this world requires propositions which are about this world, and if no such proposition can ever be more than believed, then it is incurably obscure how the philosopher kings' knowledge can, with regard to the empirical world (which is where, reluctantly, they rule), make them better off than others. Not only can there be no empirical knowledge—equally there can, strictly speaking, be no mathematical or other *a priori* belief, and the situation of apprentice or lucky mathematicians (let alone mistaken ones), which had been discussed in the *Meno*, becomes indescribable. Plato has, indeed, got a place in his classification for something roughly analogous to *a priori* belief, but that, interestingly, concerns not so much individual knowers or believers, as the status of a whole subject, the partially axiomatized mathematics of his day, which he believed to lack foundations.

In his later work Plato went back to the view that knowledge and belief could relate to the same subject-matter, and he may very well have accepted that there was empirical knowledge. The *Republic* represents the high-water mark for him of a theory of knowledge controlled by the categories of subject-matter, by the ideal of a body of *a priori* knowledge, rather than by questions about what has to be true of someone who knows something (as contrasted, for instance, with someone who merely believes that same thing). This emphasis in the *Republic* deeply defeats Plato's own purposes. Plato's anxious question, to which he repeatedly came back, and to which the *Republic* was supposed to give the great answer, was how moral knowledge could be institutionalized and effective in society, as opposed either to the rhetoric of the Sophists, or to the unreasoned and hence vulnerable perceptions of conservative tradition. Knowledge had to be present in society in the form of persons who knew, and who commanded an effective theory of education. Real knowledge, and the ability to impart it—or rather elicit it—went together.

This idea helped in the understanding of the life of Socrates, for it served to join something which Socrates admitted, that he had no knowledge, with something that had to be admitted about him, that his influence did not necessarily make his friends better: it was a fact, which contributed to Socrates' condemnation, that among his associates were such men as the brilliant deserter, Alcibiades, and Critias, prominent among the Thirty Tyrants. Plato's theory of effective moral education was meant to complete the work, and the apology, of Socrates. The *Republic*'s account of knowledge seems at first to yield just such a theory; but in fact it totally fails to do so. It says quite a lot about what it is for a body of propositions to be knowledge, and something about what it is for a person to acquire such knowledge, but it says ultimately nothing about the cognitive difference that that process is supposed to make to a person's handling of matters in the everyday world which, by ontological necessity, lie outside that body of knowledge altogether.

There is another way in which knowledge can seem to make quite special demands. This arises from considering the standards which should govern personal or individual knowledge; whereas the last line of thought was more concerned with the question of what constitutes an impersonal body of scientific theory. More intimate to the concept of knowledge itself, it was equally started in Greek reflection, and has played an even more prominent part in subsequent theory of knowledge. This is the idea that knowledge implies certainty; that an individual cannot be said to know a thing unless he is certain of it, where that implies not only that he feels utterly sure of it, but that—in some sense which it has been a repeated undertaking of philosophy to try to make clear—he could not, granted the evidence he has, be wrong.

This is not, as some modern philosophers have implied, a merely arbitrary condition on knowledge. It is a quite natural suggestion to arise from reflection on knowledge; by more than one route, perhaps, but one could be the following. Obviously, there is a distinction between knowing a thing, and being right about it by luck—even ordinary speech, which is lax about ascriptions of knowledge, distinguishes between knowing and guessing correctly (even where the guesser actually believes his guess). But now consider the condition of a man who believes on ample evidence that a given thing is true, but whose evidence is such that he might still be wrong. Then even if he is not wrong, that seems to be, relative to his state of mind, *ultimately* luck. Here we can take the case of two men, each of whom has, on two different occasions, exactly the same kind and amount of evidential basis for his belief in a certain kind of fact; but, as it happens, one is right and the other is wrong. There is real pressure to say that the one who, luckily, was right, did not really *know*, and a natural English phrase marks this exactly, when it is said of him that *for all he knew* he might have been wrong. By this kind of argument, it can be plausibly claimed that so long as one's evidence falls short in any way of conclusive certainty, one does not, even if one is right, really know.

It is just possible that this powerfully influential line of argument was sketched out near the beginning of Greek philosophy, by the poet Xenophanes of Colophon (born about the middle of the sixth century), who wrote lines which can be translated (fr. 34):

> No man has discerned certain truth, nor will there be any who knows about the gods and all the other things I say: for even if by chance he says what is totally correct, yet he himself does not know it; appearance (*or* opinion) holds over all.

Plato in the *Meno* apparently refers to this as expressing the sceptical view that knowledge is unattainable because you would not know when you had attained it—which is another version of the demand for certainty. But Plato may have been wrong about Xenophanes' meaning; the sense is much disputed, but it is most probable[11] that he speaks only of a distinction, itself very important to Greek thought, between what one has seen for oneself or established at first hand, and what can only be the subject of inference, such as questions about the gods. But besides some good reasons for so taking it, one bad one has been advanced:[12] that on the view of the lines as expressing a general sceptical point, there is no way in which the second sentence could stand as a reason for the first—

[11] The case is argued by H. Fränkel, 'Xenophanes' Empiricism and his Critique of knowledge', in A.P.D. Mourelatos ed., *The Presocratics* (New York, 1974), pp. 118–131; English translation of an article collected in his *Wege und Formen frügriechischen Denkens* (Munich, 1960).

[12] Fränkel, p. 124.

it would rather have to be a consequence. On the contrary, the second sentence might express a subtle and powerful reason for the first—'no-one knows about these things, because if he did know, it would have to be more than luck that he was right, which it cannot be.' The trouble about this as an interpretation of Xenophanes is not that it is too weak an argument, but rather that it is, by a century or so, too sophisticated.

But what Xenophanes probably did not say was eventually said. The requirement of strong certainty having been deduced from the concept of knowledge, a variety of thinkers took the step of claiming that strong certainty, and hence knowledge, were not to be had. Plato attempted to answer such a sceptical conclusion, while sharing the premiss that knowledge demanded strong certainty. But the negative view recurred, and it is interesting that it was, much later, members of the school that Plato founded, the Academy, who made some of the more interesting contributions to the rather episodic intellectual movement which is called Scepticism.

Our knowledge of ancient Scepticism comes in good part from the writings of an undistinguished medical writer of the second century A.D. called Sextus Empiricus. Sextus himself belongs not to the Academic school of scepticism, but to that called 'Pyrrhonian', after Pyrrho of Elis (c. 360–275 B.C.); Pyrrho himself is a shadowy figure, whose views came to Sextus as reported and amplified by his pupil Timon and other writers. Later Pyrrhonism inherited from the Academic Arcesilaus the technique of laying alongside any set of evidences or supposedly convincing argument another with contrary effect, in order to induce total suspension of assent—an attitude which was expressed in a phrase which already had an earlier history in philosophy: *ou mallon* 'no more this than that'. The aim of this technique was practical, to achieve that state of mind which more than one ancient school made its aim, *ataraxia*, quietude of mind or freedom from disturbance.

The Pyrrhonists were careful to withhold assent even from the claim that there was no knowledge; they recognized that, expressed dogmatically, it would be open to the *peritrope* or charge of self-refutation, and this very reflection helped them to get rid of that dogma along with others. The sceptical proposition, they said, was like the purge which 'does not merely eliminate the humours from the body, but expels itself along with them'.[13] Correspondingly, the slogan 'no more . . .' was to be taken, not as a theoretical statement or the right answer to a theoretical question, but as an element in a practice which leads to the same state as having the right answer would lead to, if there were such a thing as having the right answer. *Ataraxia* followed, for the Pyrrhonists, not on answering

[13] Sextus Empiricus, *Outlines of Pyrrhonism*, 1. 206, 2. 188.

fundamental questions, but on being induced to give up asking them. They illustrated the point with a story of the painter Apelles, who, despairing of being able to paint a horse's foam, flung his sponge at the canvas, which produced the effect of a horse's foam.

The later Pyrrhonists criticized the Academic school, of which the outstanding figure was Carneades (c. 213–129 B.C.), for being less prudent in withholding assent, and accused them of dogmatism, for asserting definitely that there was no knowledge. It is clear that Carneades worked very directly on the conception of knowledge as entailing certainty. His target, and the focus of his problems, was set for him by the theory of knowledge advanced by the Stoic school, which had been founded c. 305 B.C. by a gruff eccentric, Zeno of Citium. The theory had been developed in the late third century by a figure important in the history of logic, Chrysippus. (A line of verse said of him that if he had not existed, neither would the Stoic school, and equally elegantly Carneades added, 'if Chrysippus had not existed, neither would I.') The Stoics' theory of knowledge cannot be discussed here, but it is notable for pursuing quite directly the requirements which follow from the argument set out earlier against 'luck': needing, as they believed, some certain criterion of truth, they had recourse to a supposedly self-validating state of mind, one which would eliminate the possibility that what was assented to could be false. They introduced the concept of a 'kataleptic impression'—a form of conviction which was supposedly both subjectively indubitable and objectively unerring. It was this that Carneades attacked, by trying to show that no impression which had the first of these characteristics could be guaranteed to have the second. This was the first enactment of a dispute which was to become central to much modern philosophy, above all through Descartes' appeal, in his notion of a 'clear and distinct perception', to what is, in effect, a kataleptic intellectual impression.

The views of ancient Sceptics are not altogether easy to reconstruct from the accounts, rambling and sometimes inconsistent, offered by second- or third-rate thinkers such as Sextus or Cicero. To some, and varying, degrees they were actually sceptics, denying the possibility of knowledge or indeed of truth, or Pyrrhonianly withholding assent even from these denials. But at the same time there were strains, particularly in Carneades, of what would in modern philosophy rather be called empiricism or positivism, which ascribes certainty only to statements about impressions of sense or subjective appearances, and emphasizes verifiability, the probabilistic character of all empirical inference, and the heuristic uselessness of deduction (J. S. Mill's criticism of syllogistic inference as circular was anticipated by ancient Scepticism). It may be that to Greek thinkers the two strains of scepticism and of radical empiricism seemed more closely associated than they do in modern philosophy, where radical empiricism has sometimes been invoked (as by Berkeley) precisely *against* scepticism. But to Greek thought the distinction between appearance and reality was so basic, and knowledge so associated with reality, that knowledge which was merely *of subjective appearances* perhaps did not count as genuine knowledge at all. This is a large subject,[14] but if this line of argument is correct, it illustrates once more a point made before, that subjective idealism was not a view which occurred to the Greeks.

What is certain is that both the empiricist and the more purely sceptical strains in ancient Scepticism were to be of great importance later. Sextus Empiricus was destined to be one of the most influential of Greek philosophical writers. The translation into Latin and printing of his works (1562, 1569) coincided with an intellectual crisis precipitated by the Reformation about the criterion of religious faith, and it has been shown[15] how sceptical arguments from Sextus became important instruments in subsequent controversies. The weapons of scepticism were used both against, and in defence of, traditional religious faith. One style of defence was expressed by Montaigne, who emphasized the inability of man to reach knowledge, and his pretensions in trying to do so; among the innumerable considerations assembled to support this outlook are the arguments of ancient scepticism. A fideistic, unfanatical attachment to traditional religious belief emerges as the basis of the life of *ataraxia*. As he winningly puts it in his celebrated *Apologie de Raymond Sebond*: 'La peste de l'homme, c'est l'opinion de sçavoir. Voilà pourquoy l'ignorance nous est tant recommandée par nostre religion comme pièce propre à la créance et à l'obeïssance.'

In sharp contrast is the attitude of Descartes, whose use of the armoury of sceptical devices in his Method of Doubt was designed to be pre-emptive, and to enable him to arrive at certainties which, as he put it, 'the most extravagant hypotheses of the sceptics could not overthrow'. Descartes goes through doubt, not to give up philosophy, but to establish it. Finding certainties, as he supposes, first about himself as a rational soul, then about God, then about the structure of the physical world, he attempts a project which is, in effect, to reverse the relation of Carneades to the Stoics: he advances beyond doubt to a new form of kataleptic impression, and it is significant that among his first and basic certainties are those about subjective states of mind which, we have suggested, neither the Stoics nor the Sceptics regarded very highly as truths

[14] For this suggestion and discussion, see Charlotte L. Stough, *Greek Skepticism* (Berkeley and Los Angeles, 1969).

[15] By Richard H. Popkin, in his *History of Scepticism from Erasmus to Spinoza* (Berkeley and Los Angeles, 1979).

about reality. But both Descartes' conception of certainty, and still more some of the propositions which he regarded as certain and which were essential to his system, lacked kataleptic effect on his critics, and Descartes' fundamental achievement, contrary to his hopes, was to help to radicalize doubt, not to eliminate it.

When Montaigne said that Christianity should be taken on faith, because all arguments defeat one another, he almost certainly meant what he said; when Hume and Bayle, in the eighteenth century, spoke in similar terms, they did not. By that time, Pyrrhonian *ataraxia* was to be found not in Christianity, but in as little enthusiasm as possible for any religious issue. In cultivating that, as much against militant atheists as against zealots of the Church, Hume was a genuinely Pyrrhonian thinker, as also in his conservative social views; and besides the standard sceptical material which he used, a basic element in his epistemology, the theory of 'natural belief', can be found crudely prefigured in Sextus.

Hume and the ancient Pyrrhonians had something else in common. For all of them, the rejection of philosophy was the *eventual* rejection of philosophy, and *ataraxia* a state of mind achieved by working at sceptical considerations and then letting natural belief have its sway, so that one ends up living calmly by the customs of one's society (or, rather, by some critical liberalization of them). These thinkers would not have been impressed by the suggestion that it might have been simpler never to have started reflecting at all; or if they express envy for those innocent of reflection, this attitude is formed and expressed at a level of self-consciousness which does not invite the reader to take it simply as it stands. Some, and notably the ancients, believed that people who had never embarked on any reflection did not in general experience *ataraxia*, but were rent by passions and prejudice; but even those who were less sure of that would not have favoured an educational or psychological regime which produced the benefits of a passionless rationality by entirely unphilosophical means. Scepticism remained an *intellectual* posture, and for all these thinkers, the Pyrrhonian outlook was both a minority state and (what is not quite the same thing) an achievement. The Pyrrhonist had, in relation to the rest of society, the role of a sage: a very quiet one.

This is one of several reasons why this posture is no longer possible. There is in modern society no serious role of a sage, as opposed to those of the expert, the commentator, or the entertainer. There is also no serious point of view, or at least none which can be publicly sustained, by which wars, calamities, and social upheaval can be quite so distantly regarded as Scepticism suggested they should be. Again, outlooks shaped by Romanticism and by modern psychological theory demand a deeper view of the emotions than Pyrrhonism had, and a more sceptical view of *ataraxia* itself. These points are well, if negatively illustrated by the thought of Bertrand Russell, whose philosophical stance in the theory of knowledge was, broadly, that of a twentieth-century Humean, but who notably failed to reconcile his social and moral concerns with his theoretical scepticism about ethics, or the strength of his feelings with his understanding of the mind. A book about Russell was called *The Passionate Sceptic*; while there could still be some outlook to which that phrase applied, it is notable, and a significant comment on Russell's own difficulties, that in the terms of ancient or even Humean Pyrrhonism, it is a contradiction in terms.

ETHICAL ENQUIRY

'The discussion is not about any chance question,' Socrates says towards the end of Book I of the *Republic* (352D), 'but about what way one should live.' The discussion was with the sophist Thrasymachus, who had claimed that it was only ever a second-best situation in which a man had reason to act in accordance with the requirements of *dikaiosune*—'justice' as we necessarily translate it, though in the *Republic* it covers a wide ground, and relates to all aspects of being concerned for others' interests as well as one's own. One often does have, according to Thrasymachus, a reason, as things are, for acting in this way, but this is only because one's power is limited—typically, by the greater power of another; one whose power was not so limited would have no such reason, and would be a lunatic if he put others' interests before his own. This view Socrates sets out to refute. Discontented with what he offers against Thrasymachus, and confronted rather later with a more sophisticated version of this kind of thesis, he is represented by Plato as spending the rest of the *Republic* in giving the ultimate answer to it.

Although the speaker is Socrates, and although the question of what exactly in the Platonic Socrates was Socratic is still unanswered,[16] there would be much agreement that the *Republic*'s answer was Platonic, but the problem was Socratic. It was a problem raised by Sophistic scepticism, a form of it more genuinely alarming than scepticism about cosmological speculation or logic, for in this case there existed recognizable and possibly attractive alternatives to the considerations displaced by sceptical criticism.

The nub of the sceptical attack was that there was no inherent reason for anyone to promote or respect anyone else's interests, and that the belief that there was such a reason was the product of various kinds of illu-

---

[16] The state of the question is set out in Guthrie, vol. iii, ch. 12.

sion: in particular, it stemmed from an innocent failure to see that the rules and requirements on people's conduct which were found in different societies obtained only 'by convention', a concept which for the Sophistic critics meant that such rules were social products, about which it could be asked whose interest they served. There were, on the other hand, perfectly good 'natural' motives to self-interested conduct, and this was well illustrated by the behaviour of agents where there was no such framework of convention, notably by the behaviour of one city-state to another—a set of considerations brilliantly and grimly represented in the famous 'Melian dialogue' in Book 5 of Thucydides' *History*.

Part of the problem was set by this kind of use of the concepts of 'nature' (*phusis*) and 'convention' (*nomos*),[17] and the attendant question of what kind of life it was 'naturally' rational to live; together with the suggestion that it was 'naturally' rational to pursue self-interest, the ideally satisfying forms of life being represented, in some of the more uninhibited expositions, in terms of sheer gangsterism. Thrasymachus offers this kind of picture; at this level what is in question is not only an entirely egoistic conception of practical rationality, but also a very simple schedule of egoistic satisfactions, in terms of power, wealth, and sex.[18] This set of considerations just in itself yields the materials of fear and envy, rather than any on-going structure of social relations, and indeed Thrasymachus' view, reduced totally to these elements, turns out to be even descriptively quite inadequate for any account of society.

However, this picture was superimposed on, and derived some appeal from, something different: a picture of a certain kind of social morality, which does offer some impersonal criteria of who is to be admired and respected, but finds them particularly in certain kinds of competitive success and inherited position—an aristocratic or feudal morality. It was from the context of such a social morality that the fifth and fourth centuries inherited the concept of *arete*, 'personal excellence' (the standard translation of this term as 'virtue' is only sometimes appropriate, and can be drastically misleading). This term carried with it certain associations

---

[17] This was not the only use of this celebrated distinction. By some writers, *nomos* was praised for saving us from *phusis*; by others, *phusis* was indeed used in criticism of *nomos*, but in order to extend rather than contract the range of moral ideas, as in a famous fragment of Alcidamas (quoted by the scholiast on Aristotle, *Rhetoric*, 1373b): 'God made all men free: *phusis* never made anyone a slave', and cf. similar opinions referred to by Aristotle, *Politics*, 1253b20.

[18] In the *Gorgias*, a dialogue probably a little earlier than the *Republic*, Plato offered, in the person of Callicles, a more striking, eloquent, and altogether more formidable expression of the egoistic alternative. Socrates' answers to him are less than satisfactory; in part, this is because Callicles is unconvincingly made to accept the idea that egoism must come down to a very crude form of hedonism.

which Plato, and probably Socrates, made strong efforts to detach from it: in particular, the notion of being well thought of and spoken of, cutting a good figure. Here a vital term is *kalos*, 'fine', 'noble', 'splendid', a word more strongly aesthetic than *agathos*, 'good', and an important term of commendation, but bearing with it implications of how one is regarded; as its opposite, *aischros*, 'base' or 'shameful', carries implications of being despised or shunned.

The deeds that made one admired if one was a Homeric hero were typically but not exclusively individual feats of arms, and one's *arete* was displayed in such. One could be shamed and lose repute not only by failing in such feats, but by being mistreated—such things led to the anger of Achilles and the suicide of Ajax. What happened to one mattered for one's esteem as well as what one did, and among things one did, competitive success ranked high: all this, of course, among those who themselves ranked high, for women and members of lower orders had other *aretai* and kinds of repute. In this area, there are two importantly different points, which discussion of this subject has often confused. One is that, for such a morality, shame is a predominant notion, and a leading motive the fear of disgrace, ridicule, and the loss of prestige. A different point is that excellence is displayed in competitive and self-assertive exploits. While socially and psychologically these two things often go together, they are independent of each other: in particular, the occasion of shame and disgrace may be a failure to act in some expected self-sacrificing or co-operative manner. The confusion of these two things is encouraged by measuring Greek attitudes by the standard of a Christian, and more particularly of a Protestant, outlook. That outlook associates morality simultaneously with benevolence, self-denial, and inner-directedness or guilt (shame before God or oneself). It sees the development of moral thought to this point as progress, and it tends to run together a number of different ideas which have been discarded—or at least rendered less reputable—by that progress.

The ideas of *arete*, shame and reputation, were of course much older notions than the self-interest conceptions of the Sophists and the simply reductive social theory that went with those. Insofar as these Sophistic speakers (and, still more, conventional persons influenced by them, such as Meno) appeal to notions of *arete*, and offer for impersonal admiration the ideal of a man of power, they are in fact expressing ethical conceptions which have an aristocratic structure in itself old-fashioned by the end of the fifth century; but these conceptions have been given a new, opportunistic, content, and detached from the base in traditional society which had originally made them part of a working social morality.

This structure of ideas is thus more old-fashioned than another theory presented in the *Republic*, the theory offered by Glaucon and Adeimantus in Book 2. This represents the conventions of justice not as a device of the strong to exploit the weak (which was Thrasymachus' formulation), but as a contractual device of the weak to protect themselves against the strong. This theory, only sketched in the *Republic*, is the prototype of many which view public norms as the solution to a problem which would now be expressed in the language of games-theory. It reaches, in fact, outside the most characteristic terms of Greek ethical theory, concerned as that was with *arete*. In two important respects, it resembles modern Utilitarian and contractual theories. First, the notion of a rule or practice is more fundamental in this theory than notions of character or personal excellence. Second, the desires which are served by the institutions of justice and, generally, the practices of morality are in the first instance self-interested desires: morality is represented as a device for promoting egoistic satisfactions which could in principle occur without it, but which are as a matter of fact unlikely to do so because of everyone's weak position in an amoral state of nature.

This instrumental or contractual view of morality was rejected by Socrates, Plato, and Aristotle. It is in many ways different from the crude Thrasymachean outlook—indeed, in expression it is its opposite. Yet for Plato it shared a basic fault with that outlook: morality was represented by both as an instrument for the satisfaction of non-moral, selfish desires which existed naturally in independence of morality. This was not just a moralizing prejudice on Plato's part, a desire for the moral motivations to appear more dignified. Still less was it the expression of an idea, later insisted on by Kant, that there can be no reason for moral conduct at all, except that it is one's duty—that the very nature of morality requires it to consist in a completely autonomous demand which cannot be rationalized or explained by anything else. The point for Plato was precisely that there had to be a reason for moral conduct, but that no theory of the instrumental kind could provide it. A theory of morality, in his view, had to answer Sophistic scepticism by showing that it was rational for each person to want to be just, whatever his circumstances. The contractual theory failed in this respect: if one were powerful and intelligent and luckily-enough placed, it would cease to be rational for one to conform to the conventional requirements of morality. This is readily admitted by Glaucon and Adeimantus in the dialogue; indeed, they basically agree with the Platonic Socrates in viewing the contractual theory, not as an answer to Sophistic scepticism about morality, but rather as a more sophisticated expression of that scepticism.

The contractual solution was particularly weak because it was unstable relative to a *superior* agent, one more intelligent, resourceful, and persuasive than the average. It was above all for that kind of agent that Plato thought that the sceptical demand had to be met, and the objectives of morality and justice shown to be rational. The life of Alcibiades had been scepticism in action, and the answer had to apply to a man of his superior powers. Here the first feature, too, of the contractual theory had to be rejected, the view that notions of character came second to the notions of a desirable or useful practice. The demand to show to *each* man that justice was rational *for him* meant that the answer had to be grounded first in an account of what sort of person it was rational for him to be. If anything outside the soul (as Socrates and Plato said) or outside the self (as we might put it) is what primarily has moral value—some rule, for instance, or institution—then we are left with a possible contingency, that there could be a man whose deepest needs and the state of whose soul were such that it would not be rational for him to act in accordance with that rule or institution; and so long as that contingency remains possible, the task that Socrates and Plato set themselves will not have been carried out.

It has been said by Kantian critics that Platonic morality is egoistic, in a sense incompatible with the real character of morality. This misses the point. It is formally egoistic, in the sense that it supposes that it has to show that each man has good reason to act morally, and that the good reason has to appeal to him in terms of something about himself, how and what he will be if he is a man of that sort of character. But it is not egoistic in the sense of trying to show that morality serves some set of individual satisfactions which are well defined antecedently to it. The aim was not, given already an account of the self and its satisfactions, to show how morality (luckily) fitted them; it was to give an account of the self into which morality fitted.

For Plato, as also for Aristotle, it was a trivial truth that if it is rational for one to pursue a certain course of life or to be a certain sort of person, then those things must make for a satisfactory state of oneself called *eudaimonia*—a term which can only be translated as 'happiness'. But not everyone now will regard it as a triviality, or even as true, that it is only rational to do what in the end makes for one's own happiness. Moreover, many people who do agree that that is true will not in fact be agreeing with the same thing as Plato and Aristotle meant. These facts are due not only to imperfections of that translation, but also to changes in views of life—changes which themselves have no doubt affected our understanding of the term 'happiness'. A proper charting of the complex relations of these words would involve a whole history of Western ethical thought. What is certain is that *eudaimonia* did not necessarily imply the maximization of pleasure; and when Plato, supposedly having shown in the *Republic* that justice is the proper state of the soul, goes on to argue that the life of the just man is also a large number of times more pleasant than that of the unjust, this is meant to be an entirely additional consideration. It is in this respect much like Kant's assurance that virtue will be rewarded in an after-life, coming as that does after his insistence that it must be regarded as its own reward (a manoeuvre which Schopenhauer disobligingly compared to slipping a tip to a head-waiter who pretends to be above such things). The state of *eudaimonia* should be interpreted as that of living as a man best could, and when one finds some Greek thinkers suggesting that one can attain *eudaimonia* although one is the victim of torture, the linguistic strain that is undoubtedly set up expresses not just a semantic difficulty, but, under that, the substantial difficulty of supposing that being tortured is compatible with living as one best could.

The Platonic aim, then, can be seen as this, to give a picture of the self such that if one properly understands what one is, one will see that a life of justice is not external to the self, but an objective which it must be rational for one to pursue. That is the sense of Socrates' question with which we started, about the way 'one should live': the 'should' is formally that of egoistic rationality, but the task is to reach the right understanding of the ego.

Both Socrates and Plato gave that account in terms of reason and knowledge. Plato saw the fullest expression of these powers in the form of systematic theoretical understanding, something which led to the consequence that the philosopher was the happiest and most fully developed of human beings; it led also to the Utopian political system of the *Republic*. Socrates himself certainly never developed the latter ideas (though the view, popularized by Popper,[19] that Socrates himself was politically a democrat who was betrayed by the authoritarian Plato has no historical basis). The idea, however, that the real self, which is fully expressed in the life of justice, is the self of the discursive intellect, is only a development of Socratic conceptions. It may be that Socrates laid more weight than Plato on 'knowing how to act', and less on knowledge expressed in systematic theory, but certainly the notion that knowledge had to be reflective and rational was already there. An 'interest in definitions', as well as a concern with ethical questions, is what Aristotle plausibly tells us can be ascribed to the historical Socrates, and the interest in definitions with regard to ethical matters certainly took the form of trying to reach a reflective and articulate understanding of the criteria of virtuous action, which would make good practice more rationally lucid and self-critical.

If the essence of virtuous action lay in rational knowledge exercised by the soul, then there could be no separate motives represented by the

[19] In his *Open Society and its Enemies* (London, 1957).

various virtues, as conventionally distinguished: justice, self-control, courage, and the rest. All of them could only be expressions, in different spheres or aspects of conduct, of the same basic rational motivation. When Socrates taught the 'unity of the virtues' under rational prudence or intelligence, he did not mean that there were no ways of distinguishing one virtue from another. He meant rather that they were not basically different motivations: they were the same power of the soul, under different manifestations. Since, further, rationality must be displayed in balancing one kind of demand against another, and an exaggeration of, say, 'courageous' behaviour would not in fact be an expression of real rational understanding of what was required of one, it followed that it would not be an expression of the one underlying power of reason, and hence not of any virtue at all. So the unity of the virtues implied, as might be expected, that one does not properly display any virtue unless one displays all of them.

Virtue is the pursuit of one's interest, construed as a rational agent— the proper interest, as Socrates put it, of the soul, and this was probably already taken by Socrates in a way which implied that the interests of the soul were a separate matter from those of the body, an implication which Plato's drastically dualistic theory of soul and body was to pursue further in the direction of asceticism. Virtous action is a matter of the calculation of what truly matters most to one, and what matters most to one is what matters most for one's soul: these are the demands of the virtuous life, of courage, honour, justice. Hence if one does not act in accordance with those demands, one acts to defeat what matters most to one; no man can consciously act in such a way; so wrong action must involve a failure of knowledge and understanding, and be something which one could not possibly have chosen with open eyes. So all error is involuntary, and 'no-one willingly errs', as Socrates put it: a conclusion still discussed under the name of 'the Socratic paradox'.

The paradox raises in fact two different questions. The first is whether a person can voluntarily do one of two things, while fully and consciously holding that he has stronger reason to do the other. The second question is whether a person must, if clear-headed, admit that he always has stronger reason to do acts of justice, honour, and so forth, rather than acts of mean temporal self-interest. Most would now find it hard to give a simply Socratic answer to the second question, supported as that is by the ascetically dualistic view of the self. One difficulty that such a view inevitably raises, and which Plato himself treats uneasily, is the marked contrast between the spiritual view of one's own interests which is needed by the account of morality's motivations, and the less spiritual view of other people's interests which is needed by its subject-matter.

Socrates thought that the good man cannot be harmed, for the only thing that could touch *him* would be something that could touch, not his body, but the good state of his soul, and that is inviolable. But—apart from other and perhaps deeper weaknesses of that picture—we must ask why, if bodily hurt is no real harm, bodily hurt is what virtue so strongly requires one not to inflict on others?

To the first of those two questions, however, the one in terms purely of conscious action and rationality, some philosophers would still give the Socratic answer. To those of us whose actions seem often very divergently related to what we take to be our reasons, that answer will still seem a remarkable paradox. It should be offered, if at all, not as a demure tautology about action and reason, but rather as conveying an ideal (a highly problematical one) of a state in which action becomes wholly transparent to the agent. That is still, itself, very much a Socratic ideal.

It is surprising how many elements in Socratic-Platonic morality are still to be found in the complex and very interesting ethical theory of Aristotle, different though it is in certain central respects. It is different, most importantly of all, because not all the weight is put on intellectual excellence and pure rationality. Aristotle distinguishes between 'intellectual excellences' and 'excellences of character', and emphasizes the importance to the latter of the correct formation of desire and motivation through training. Without correct upbringing nothing can be done: the hopes for the regenerative powers of philosophy itself which are implicit in the Socratic stance have gone, as has the sense of any combative scepticism against which morality has to be defended. A more settled order is in question. Aristotle, moreover, did not believe in a soul wholly separate from the body, and that denial goes with a rejection of Socratic asceticism, and with more worldly possibilities for *eudaimonia*. The old link of *arete* and public approval, which Plato sought to cut altogether, cautiously reasserts itself in the Aristotelian account, though his theory of the motivation of the virtues is much more sophisticated than anything that had been achieved at an earlier time, or indeed by Plato himself.

Yet, granted these differences, Aristotle still ends by regarding the life of theoretical reason as the highest form of human life, a conclusion which does not follow as directly, or even as coherently, from his premises as it did from Plato's. He preserves also something like the Socratic paradox about action and reason. He even preserves, in effect, the Socratic conclusion about the unity of the virtues, since he thinks that one cannot genuinely have any one excellence of character without the presence of *phronesis*, 'practical reason' (itself one of the intellectual excellences), but if one has *phronesis*, then one must have all excellences of character. This emphasis on the rational integration of character, as also on the integration of a good life over time, its retrospective rational shapeliness, is indeed a central feature of Aristotle's outlook. In the matter of the ultimate unity of virtuous traits of character, certainly this is one issue on which the Greek view seems far from ours: nothing is more commonplace to us than that particular virtues not only coexist with, but carry with them, typical faults. But this is one of the many differences with the Greeks where the contrast itself points to an illuminating area of discussion: what divergences in the understanding of human nature underlie these different conceptions of a rationally desirable life.

It is worth bringing together several features of Greek ethical thought which mark it off in many ways from current concerns and from the moral inheritance of the Christian world. It has, and needs, no God: though references to God or gods occur in these writers, they play no important role. It takes as central and primary questions of character, and of how moral considerations are grounded in human nature: it asks what life it is rational for the individual to live. It makes no use of a blank categorical moral imperative. In fact—though we have used the word 'moral' quite often for the sake of convenience—this system of ideas basically lacks the concept of *morality* altogether, in the sense of a class of reasons or demands which are vitally different from other kinds of reason or demand. The sharp line that Kantianism, in particular, draws between the 'moral' and the 'non-moral' is very partially paralleled by another sharp line, Plato's line between soul and body; but the parallelism is far from total, the distinctions are drawn on quite different principles, and the discussion of the merits and failings of each will be a quite different sort of discussion. Relatedly, there is not a rift between a world of public 'moral rules' and one of private personal ideals: the questions of how one's relations to others are to be regulated, both in the context of society at large and more privately, are not detached from questions about the kind of life it is worth living, and of what is worth having or caring for.

In all these respects the ethical thought of the Greeks was not only different from most modern thought, particularly modern thought influenced by Christianity, but was also in much better shape. There are of course respects in which its outlook could not be recaptured now, and some in which we could not want to recapture it. Some of its thoughts express a certain integration of life which perhaps existed for a short while in the city-state, but which, as Hegel emphasized, would have to be recovered, if at all, only in some totally changed form. Other features of its perceptions, its substantive attitudes to slavery, for instance, and to the role of women, we must hope will never be recovered at all.

At a more theoretical level, it is important that Greek ethical thought rested on an objective teleology of human nature, believing that there were facts about man and his place in the world which determined, in a way discoverable to reason, that he was meant to lead a co-operative and ordered life. Some version of this belief has been held by most ethical outlooks subsequently; we are perhaps more conscious now of having to do without it than anyone has been since some fifth-century Sophists first doubted it. But when all that has been said, it is true that Greek ethical thought, in many of its basic structures and, above all, in its inability to separate questions of how one should relate to others and to society from questions of what life it is worth one's leading and of what one basically wants, represents one of the very few sets of ideas which can help now to put moral thought into honest touch with reality.

In these last remarks I have mentioned 'Greek ethical thought', and that principally refers, of course, to the philosophical ideas of Socrates, Plato, and Aristotle which, very sketchily, I have discussed. But there is a question which I should like to raise in closing, which reaches behind them, and behind some other aspects of Greek philosophy which have been touched on in this chapter.

I have mentioned already Socrates' saying, that the good man cannot be harmed: it expresses an ideal of rational self-sufficiency, of freedom from the damage of contingency. There is an analogy, not merely superficial, between this type of assertion of rationality, and that cognitive demand for the elimination of luck, which appeared in the discussion of knowledge, certainty, and scepticism. The ideal of self-control, always high among Greek aspirations, turned into the aim that, in both cognition and action, what is of highest value, what matters most, should be entirely under the self's control. In later schools, this theme reappeared in various forms: in the Cynic exaggeration of Socratism, that virtue was sufficient for *eudaimonia* and that the good man really could be happy on the rack; in that hope for a state of *ataraxia* which the Sceptics were not alone in cultivating. Aristotle expressly discussed the question of how far *eudaimonia*, the ultimately desirable state, could be subject to risk, and replied that to a small but ineliminable degree it had to be. This represented, however, not so much any large or perilous aspiration, as rather the entirely sensible thought that it is unreasonable to leave out of account the apparatus of social life within which men live and express themselves, and which is subject to fortune. Very notably, a dimension of life which to us is one of the most significant precisely because of its reaching outside the defended self, friendship, is discussed by Aristotle in a way which now seems bizarre in its determination to reconcile the need for friendship with the aim of self-sufficiency.

A deeper sense of exposure to fortune is expressed elsewhere in Greek literature, above all in tragedy. There the repeated references to

the insecurity of happiness get their force from the fact that the characters are displayed as having responsibilities, or pride, or obsessions, or
needs, on a scale which lays them open to disaster in corresponding measure, and that they encounter those disasters in full consciousness. A
sense of such significances, that what is great is fragile and that what is
necessary may be destructive, which is present in the literature of the
fifth century and earlier, has disappeared from the ethics of the philosophers, and perhaps altogether from their minds. Nietzsche found
Socrates to blame for this, with his excessive distrust of what cannot be
discursively explained, his faith in the 'fathomability' of nature, and his
'Alexandrian cheerfulness'.[20] Those remarks belong, in fact, to the first
period of Nietzsche's long and ambivalent relations to the figure of
Socrates, and it was a period in which Nietzsche thought that the 'metaphysical solace' of tragedy could be understood only through a fundamentally aesthetic attitude to life, an attitude which we have even greater
reason to reject than Nietzsche eventually had. But however much he or
we may qualify his account of Greek tragedy and Greek thought, what
he pointed to is truly there: Greek philosophy, in its sustained pursuit of
rational self-sufficiency, does turn its back on kinds of human experience
and human necessity of which Greek literature itself offers the purest, if
not the richest, expression.

If there are features of the ethical experience of the Greek world which
can not only make sense to us now, but make better sense than many
things we find nearer to hand, they are not all to be found in its philosophy. Granted the range, the power, the imagination and inventiveness of
the Greek foundation of Western philosophy, it is yet more striking that
we can take seriously, as we should, Nietzsche's remark: 'Among the
greatest characteristics of the Hellenes is their inability to turn the best
into reflection.'[21]

FURTHER READING

This is a list of some translations of the Greek writers themselves, and a
few books about them; it does not try to include any of the innumerable
works about their later influence.

Details of works marked '(N)' will be found in the notes.

---

[20] *The Birth of Tragedy*, particularly sec. 17. On the question of Nietzsche's attitudes to
Socrates, see Werner J. Dannhauser, *Nietzsche's View of Socrates* (Ithaca N.Y., 1974).

[21] In his lectures on Greek philosophy: *Gesammelte Werke*, Musarion ed. (Munich,
1920–9), ii. 364–9. Quoted by Dannhauser, p. 109.

THE PRESOCRATICS AND SOCRATES

Guthrie, vols. i–iii (N) provides much useful information, but is not very searching in philosophical interpretation. All *translations* of the Presocratics involve vexed questions of interpretation: those offered by G. S. Kirk and J. E. Raven in *The Presocratic Philosophers* (Cambridge, 1957), with commentary, are no exception. Less ambitious is *Ancilla to the Presocratic Philosophers* by Kathleen Freeman (Oxford, 1948).

Hussey (N) is interesting and firmly argued. Allen and Furley (N), and its companion volume Furley and Allen (London, 1970), are useful collections of essays, as is Mourelatos (N). A similar collection on Socrates is edited by G. Vlastos, *The Philosophy of Socrates* (New York, 1971).

PLATO

A *complete translation*, by various hands, is offered in one volume edited by E. Hamilton and H. Cairns (New York, 1961); some of the translations come from the well-known complete translation by Benjamin Jowett (4th edn., revised by D. J. Allan and others, 4 vols., Oxford, 1953).

There are many general accounts of Plato's philosophy, but most suffer from outdated assumptions, and some are very fanciful. *An Examination of Plato's Doctrines* by I. M. Crombie (2 vols., London, 1962, 1963) offers a sober study of the arguments.

A useful series of new commentaries on important dialogues, with translation, is offered by the Clarendon Plato Series (Oxford), general editor M. J. Woods.

A collection of essays parallel to that on Socrates is edited by G. Vlastos (2 vols., New York, 1970).

ARISTOTLE

The standard *translation* is the Oxford Version, in 11 vols., general editor W. D. Ross; extensive selections from this are in *The Basic Works of Aristotle* (New York, 1941). A useful series of commentaries with translation is in the Clarendon Aristotle Series (Oxford), general editor J. L. Ackrill.

General works on Aristotle include: W. D. Ross, *Aristotle* (London, 1923); D. J. Allan, *The Philosophy of Aristotle* (Oxford, 1952); G.E.R. Lloyd, *Aristotle: the Growth and Structure of his Thought* (Cambridge, 1968).

Useful collections of essays include one by J.M.E. Moravcsik (New York, 1967); and *Articles on Aristotle*, ed. J. Barnes, M. Schofield, and R. Sorabji (2 vols. published so far, London, 1975, 1977).

OTHER

On *scepticism*, see Stough (N), and for a more general survey of post-Aristotelian philosophy, A. A. Long, *Hellenistic Philosophy* (London, 1974). The works of *Sextus Empiricus* are translated (facing the Greek text) by R. G. Bury in the Loeb Classical Library (4 vols., London, 1933). An important collection of articles is *Doubt and Dogmatism: Studies in Hellenistic Epistemology*, ed. M. Schofield, M. Burnyeat, and J. Barnes (Oxford, 1980).

The everyday moral ideas which underlie, and differ from, the ethical philosophies of Socrates, Plato, and Aristotle are valuably considered in K. J. Dover, *Greek Popular Morality in the time of Plato and Aristotle* (Oxford, 1974).

Finally, in the context of this chapter it is specially important to mention E. R. Dodds' great book, *The Greeks and the Irrational* (Berkeley and Los Angeles, 1951).

TWO

The Women of Trachis: Fictions, Pessimism, Ethics

> You see the great indifference of the gods
> to these things that have happened,
> who begat us and are called our fathers
> and look on such sufferings.
> What is to come no one can see,
> but what is here now is pitiable for us
> and shameful for them,
> but of all men hardest for him
> on whom this disaster has fallen.
> Maiden, do not stay in this house:
> you have seen death and many agonies,
> fresh and strange,
> and there is nothing here that is not Zeus.
>
> (Sophocles, *Trachiniae* 1266–78)

Philosophy, and in particular moral philosophy, is still deeply attached to giving good news. It is no longer attached (and in the case of Anglo-American philosophy, rarely ever was) to telling redemptive world-historical stories, and its good news no longer takes the forms familiar from such stories. It is not a matter of Leibniz's cosmic cost-benefit analysis, for instance, under which the balance of good over bad is optimal, and—roughly—nothing could have been locally improved without making the whole total worse. Leibniz's story, nevertheless, is worth a moment's attention, before we come back to things that we now can take more seriously.

This statement of Leibniz's view is indeed rough, because Leibniz requires us to accept two ideas which may seem incompatible though in fact they are not, and a proper formulation has to allow for this. The first idea is that we can understand what would count as a local improvement. We must understand this at some level, since Leibniz's theory is offered as a theodicy, that is to say, as a justification offered to people who reasonably see certain local happenings, such as those recounted in *Candide*, as disasters, and ask why those things rather than less disastrous things have to happen.

The second idea is that we cannot really understand what would count as a local improvement. This is because the idea of an improvement gets a grip on us, and in particular prompts a demand for a justification, only if it is understood as possible. We have many mere wishes that go against possibility, to change the past, for instance, or (as a friend of mine once said) to be monogamously married to each of four people at once, but they do not support any serious conception of an improvement and are no focus for a grievance. But on Leibniz's view, there cannot, strictly speaking, be any improvements, since no room for improvement is left by the Law of Sufficient Reason (in its strong form, in which it claims that this is the best of all possible worlds because it combines the maximum of variety with the maximum of simplicity). Nevertheless, it is still true that at a certain, very superficial, level we do understand the idea of a local improvement. For instance, we know that if it were in our power simply to affect the local environment, without consideration for wider regularities, these are the kinds of things we should try to prevent. So the two ideas are not after all incompatible. We think we have a grievance, but when we properly understand the situation, we see that we do not. So, Leibniz told us, there is a theodicy.

Whether this would really be enough for a theodicy raises further questions. For instance, it might be thought a reproach to God that the Law of Sufficient Reason should take the form it does: it suggests a heartless modernist preference on his part for intellectual elegance over a detailed concern for his creatures' interests. If it is then replied that it is fatuous to reproach God for his choice of a creative plan, this seems to be abandoning theodicy rather than contributing to it: that reply could have been given before Leibniz started, as indeed God had already given it to Job.

The context of theodicy of course radically shapes the discussion of what might count as good or bad news. The idea of an *improvement*, in this connection, implies something both better and possible, and the reason why the notion of possibility came into it was that the argument was shaped in order to offer a justification. It was trying to answer a grievance, by showing that the grievance was based on a misunderstanding, an excessively narrow view of things. If we move away from the world in which Leibniz, on God's behalf, dealt with a grievance—a world that now seems immeasurably remote from us—it is less clear how ideas of necessity and possibility shape our reactions to hideous events. If we are not sending complaints, then there seems less reason why our discontents can be lightened by the understanding that what happened was necessary. Perhaps a mere wish, so long as it is not too fantastic, can sustain them. Once the idea of a grievance goes away, with its restriction to the possible—a restriction which itself seems to be grounded in the rather strange idea of being fair to God—then perhaps the room for discontent can expand. We can be relatively discontented even with the necessary.

Alternatively, perhaps the room for discontent should contract. Have we got a focus for discontent at all, when there is no longer anyone to receive and possibly answer a complaint? Discontent makes sense, surely, only if there can be at least some expectation of something better; without that, we are merely unhappy. So should we not say that once we lose the structure of theodicy, the very idea of good news or bad news on a cosmic scale falls away? There is simply the good or bad news that comes to us on the scale of local misfortune, such as is brought about by human action, successful or unsuccessful, helpful or malign. There is no larger question. So philosophical good news, like philosophical bad news, becomes an oxymoron—unless it means the good news, or more often the bad news, about philosophy.

This must be to go too fast. Our "discontents" can surely reach beyond local unhappiness and can be directed to an object which is more than local: directed, for instance, to what we can understand of human history, of human achievements and their costs. This unhappiness perhaps does presuppose the defeated expectation of something better, but not as a focus of complaint: what has failed is not justification but hope. This is illustrated by another redemptive story which has also departed, Hegel's. We can leave aside some of its wider cosmic aspirations: the relevant point here is that the story was meant to provide a focus for the thought that despite the horrors which underlie every human achievement, artistic, ethical or political, the enterprise will have been worthwhile.

As with Leibniz, the thought must be that the horrors were necessary—without that, we simply have another focus for regret. But in Hegel, necessity is supposed to exercise a different kind of leverage on our thoughts. On Leibniz's account, the structure of the necessity is itself part of what makes the totality worthwhile, since it is based on God's choice of the most elegantly complex universe. For Hegel, the necessity need not in itself contribute part of the value, though perhaps it could do so. The complex working of the Geist to turn suffering into historical achievement is not itself the supreme achievement. Moreover, the value of the achievement does not have to transcend a human understanding of that value, as it does with Leibniz. Other considerations laid aside, it is merely that we can reflect "without *this*, *that* could not be, and the value of *that* means that *this*, after all, was worthwhile."

No doubt we do not understand exactly what this reflection might mean. However, we do understand it well enough to recognize at least two different ways of rejecting it. Someone may think that the comparisons involved come out wrong: no achievement could be worth *this*. At the limit, this objection could take the form of thinking that the comparisons were absurd, because there was no sensible way of laying such things alongside one another. The achievement and the suffering are incommensurable, and the supposed justification, which outweighs the one with the other, comes to no more than an affirmation. Even in this form, however, this line of objection is different from that other rejection of such thoughts, which sees the very idea of such a comparison as indecent, a moral outrage. This rejection says rather, in the spirit of Kant, that no *achievement* could be worth this. No good or bad news can be found in history or the actual balance of things at all. That seems to rise above all such questions, and set at least the most important values, moral values, beyond history. However, the Kantian story means more than this formulation reveals. For if no ultimately good or bad news can be found in history, it follows in particular that no ultimately bad news can be found in it, and this of course carries its own kind of good news, a point we shall come back to.

Hegel's own construction had a further feature, that the historical expression of necessity was, in its larger features, total. What had happened was all coherently necessary for the valued aspects of the outcome. We shall want to reject this strongly teleological dimension itself, but it is important that merely in rejecting this, we do not necessarily reject everything that Hegel conveyed. Schopenhauer certainly rejected the triumphalist teleology, but his declaration that life, even if it is incurably a painful and shapeless mess, is redeemed by art, conveyed what he could hardly deny was in some sense good news. At the same time, his view of the world apart from this was likely to give rise only to resignation.[1]

Nietzsche at first accepted Schopenhauer's expression of tragic pessimism, but he later tried to overcome the limitations of that outlook, and I take it that it was as part of this attempt that he was drawn to the model of willing the eternal recurrence. We have to ask: What it is that we need the affirmation of the eternal recurrence to overcome? What bad feeling is it—what discontent, as we put it earlier—that the horribleness of the world is supposed to inspire? This question repeatedly opens up. It opened up in the wake of Leibniz, when we asked what one's discontent is supposed to be if there is no place for a grievance. Similarly, the failure of every possible answer to Hegel's question may leave us with the conviction that there is no such question, and if there is no question, there will be, once again, no possible focus for anything like discontent on a more than local scale. To insist that one must be left with

---

[1] See Nietzsche, "Attempt at a Self-Criticism," added to the 1886 edition of *The Birth of Tragedy*. One of the personal qualities that Nietzsche saluted in Schopenhauer was, notably, his cheerfulness. See "Schopenhauer as Educator," translated by William Arrowsmith in *Unmodern Observations* (New Haven: Yale University Press, 1990), 162.

some focus for one's discontents, even after Leibniz's and Hegel's questions have gone, may seem no better than finding some reason for being unhappy on a large scale—or, perhaps, finding some large scale on which to be unhappy. Something like this indeed seems to have been the situation of Wittgenstein. He insisted that there was no ultimate or metaphysical question about one's discontent with the world, and this left him with a problem of finding a more than personal object for his unhappiness, a problem that he seems to have tried to solve, in part, by directing his unhappiness on to philosophy.

For Nietzsche, there was no metaphysical question raised by the horrors that underlay every human achievement. Yet something was left, something that had to be met, not, certainly, by an answer, but by an affirmation. I take it that what the world's horrors presented him with was the prospect of being crushed by them.

Certainly he did not deny the necessity of the horrors to the achievements. Going beyond Hegel in this as in other respects, he thought that the good not only required the bad but incorporated it: one of the metaphysicians' most basic illusions is their "belief in opposite values."[2] So if there is no honest and affirmative way of acknowledging the horrors, the only way of managing them will be to do what healthy people do all the time, and forget them. But Nietzsche seems to have thought, even if only sometimes, that such a Pyrrhonian reaction would represent weariness and a lack of vitality—a vitality taken, at this point at least, as implying truthfulness. So if there is to be truthfulness about the horrors, and no belief about their being worthwhile under some Leibnizian or Hegelian calculation, there will be only a fully conscious refusal to be crushed, and we shall need a conception, necessarily very schematic, of a life that might adequately express that refusal. The idea of the horrors having been "worth it" is operationalized, as one might quaintly put it, into the thought experiment of being prepared to will everything, with every horror and every hideous triviality, to happen endlessly over again.

It is a good question what this model could possibly achieve. The affirmation is supposed to be immensely costly, an achievement commensurate with the dreadfulness of what it wills. Yet its content, and so, inescapably, the affirmation itself, occurs in the gravity-free space of the imagination. Can the "greatest weight," as Nietzsche calls it,[3] really weigh anything, when it consists in willing an entirely contrary-to-fact recurrence? Can it be more than a Styrofoam rock on a film set of cosmic

[2] Nietzsche's phrase is "der Glaube an die Gegensätze der Werte." See *Beyond Good and Evil*, sec. 2.
[3] Nietzsche's phrase is "das grösste Schwergewicht." See *The Gay Science*, sec. 351.

heroism? The more familiar alternatives to willing the eternal recurrence are better defined in their effects: lying about the horrors, or forgetting about them—where that means *really* forgetting about them, except on the local scale, and getting on with one's life in a suitably unreflective way.

There is no opposition, obviously enough, between unreflective forgetting and working in philosophy. However, there are areas of philosophy which might be supposed to have a special commitment to not forgetting or lying about the horrors, among them moral philosophy. No one with sense asks it to think about them all the time, but, in addressing what it claims to be our most serious concerns, it would do better if it did not make them disappear. Yet this is what in almost all its modern forms moral philosophy effectively does. This is above all because it tries to withdraw our ethical interest from both chance and necessity, except inasmuch as the necessary sets the parameters of effective action. Kantianism and consequentialism, despite their other differences (about free will, for instance), resemble each other, as Iris Murdoch has insisted, in sharing a concern with the practical. The direction of their attention in time is not in all respects the same, consequentialism being more concerned than Kantianism is with what we can now effect, and less interested in what a given agent in the past could have done at the moment of action. Nevertheless, the situation of the rational agent intending to change the world preoccupies them both, and the very plain fact that everything that an agent most cares about typically comes from, and can be ruined by, uncontrollable necessity and chance is no part of their concerns.

When in addition morality itself is disconnected historically and psychologically from the rest of life, as it often is by moral philosophy, and is left as a supposedly self-contained and self-explanatory realm of value, then necessity and chance and the bad news they bring with them are deliberately excluded. This itself, I suggested, counts as an affirmation of good news, and it is more effective as such than any theodicy. This good news, that only the moral really or seriously or ultimately matters, is shown and not said, and one is invited to accept it without even the disturbance of mentioning the matter.

The most important question here, obviously, concerns how we should best think about such things. There are also some questions of how, if at all, moral philosophy within its own limits can conduct itself less evasively. Here I want to take up only a question narrower than either of these, about ways in which the defective consciousness of moral philosophy can be extended by appeal to fiction.

The most familiar appeal in ethics to fiction relies on the idea that fictional worlds can provide thought experiments for ethics. I take it that this is a version of the traditional idea that fiction can yield salutary *exempla* of virtue and vice. The idea has been significantly transmuted from an earlier world of clear statements and plain *exempla* to one in which fictions display ambiguities, moral conflicts that are imperfectly resolvable, multiple ethical interpretations and so forth, and this alteration reveals not merely changes in ethical consciousness but a changed relation of fiction both to ethical life and to moral philosophy. In a world in which there are clear moral statements and plain *exempla*, the relation between the two will tend to be something like that of text to illustration, and the role of the fiction will be that of an efficient aid. Once a certain degree of ambiguity is reached, however, the fiction will come to do things that direct statement cannot do, and working through the fiction will itself represent an extension of ethical thought, and conceivably of ethical experience. How much we can really effect by these means has been a much-discussed question; equally, to present any great fiction just in this light must be to take a limited view of it. However, in this area there is an intelligible and recognized association of fiction and ethical thought, and even of fiction and moral philosophy.

We can ask both what kinds of fiction can significantly help moral philosophy, and what styles of moral philosophy can be helped by fiction. (It could be a test of realism in a style of ethical thinking that it can learn from compelling fictions.) It is not surprising that the fiction that most easily responds to these needs, particularly when ethical thought is directed to traits of character, is (as I shall put it) "dense" fiction, above all the realistic novel, which provides a depth of characterization and social background which gives substance to the moral situation and brings it nearer to everyday experience. It may well be worth considering, for instance, how we would now describe and assess the way in which Mr. Jarndyce, in *Bleak House*, arranges for Esther Summerson's future life without consulting her, and what we can make of the approval of him that Dickens seems to expect from the reader.

The features of dense fictions that lend themselves to these thoughts also have dangers, which recent criticism has helped us to identify. Precisely because the impression of deep characterization and of social reality in such fiction is an artful construct, we can be misled into thinking that our ethical judgments are being extended, that we are gaining moral insight into a situation, when in fact our moral outlook has already done some of the work in constructing that situation. The sense of something hidden and waiting to be interpreted can be an artifact merely of fictional indeterminacy. Equally, the notorious deceptions of narrative closure can impose an ethical significance which would not be available in reality—unless, as often happens, reality itself is interpreted in terms of such deceptions.

Among their other effects, dense fictions can create the impression of necessity, but they do not typically do so in the spirit that will best compensate for the limitations of moral philosophy that have been the concern of this paper. There are, certainly, exceptions: outside the novel, *The Wild Duck* is one. But some of the most sharply delineated reminders of bad news in fiction are presented when necessity comes to the characters in the form of unmanageable chance, and the attempt to deploy this in the context of dense fiction runs the danger of coming too close to the territory that such notions equally supply to comedy and farce. (Some of Hardy illustrates this, including—as it seems to me—the climactic disaster in *Jude the Obscure*.)

There is another kind of fiction, which serves purposes in relation to moral philosophy different from the more familiar ones that are served by dense fictions. I shall call it "stark fiction," and a paradigm of it is offered by the tragedies of Sophocles. It is not merely that its style and structure avoid the anecdotal and the incidental, but that these resources are typically directed in a concentrated way to displaying the operations of chance and necessity. The phrase "a necessary chance," *anangkaia tuchē*, is to be found, twice, in the *Ajax*, and I have said something elsewhere about the ways in which this combination of ideas operates in Sophocles and about ways in which we can use it, although we do not accept all the assumptions of Sophocles' world.[4] We should not suppose, however, that the operations of stark fiction are always the same. One of several disservices that Aristotle rendered to the understanding of Greek tragedy was that of generating the idea that there is some one specific effect that makes tragedy ethically significant. Even among the surviving plays of Sophocles, to say nothing of other writers, each deals with the ethical—and reproves the limitations of our ethical ideas—in a significantly different way.

The play that is perhaps the least familiar among them, *The Women of Trachis*, is particularly relevant to the present discussion because its display of undeserved and uncompensated suffering is so entirely unrelieved. In a sense, it is very simple, compared for instance with the intricacies of the *Oedipus Tyrannus*, which it resembles to the extent of being a play of successive revelations; or compared to the *Philoctetes*, which it resembles in its display of hideous and destructive physical agony, but which deploys complex motives that have no part in this play.

The extreme starkness of the outcome and the simplicity of the effect are, needless to say, achieved by some complex adjustments. The charac-

---

[4] Lines 485, 803. I discuss Sophocles' significance for us (and, more generally, that of tragedy and the epic) in *Shame and Necessity* (Berkeley and Los Angeles: University of California Press, 1993). For the phrase from the *Ajax* see 104, 123–24.

ter of Deianeira has often been seen as peculiarly sweet in a domestic style, a less active and formidable figure than most major Sophoclean women: like Chrysothemis, rather, or Ismene, but, unlike them, the initiator of the action, if a diffident one. She speaks in a way that can make her marriage seem a familiar type of story, as when she says (31 *et seq.*) that they have children now, whom Heracles "sees at times, like a farmer working in an outlying field, who sees it only when he sows and when he reaps." But it would be a mistake to think the aim is a touching naturalism; twenty lines before this, at the very beginning of the play, she had been telling us how she was wooed by a river, which presented itself first as a bull, then as a serpent, and then as a half-human creature from whose beard a waterfall fell. The aim is not naturalism, but an impression, above all, of vulnerability. It is significant, too, that the poison she prepares is, relative to the tradition, underdescribed. The story was that it was made from the centaur's semen, but this element has disappeared from the play. It is tempting to think that this was too sexually assertive an image to suit Deianeira's use of the substance in order to cancel, as she supposes, Heracles' erotic diversion and to regain him as her husband.

It is remarkable, as Nicole Loraux has pointed out,[5] that she kills herself with a sword, a male method of death. This weapon, the same as Ajax used in his suicide, stands in a gendered opposition to the noose, for instance, which Jocasta used. But the effect is certainly not that she is another Ajax, that there has been a transgressive reversal of roles. The image is rather that of passivity, of a brutal thing having been done to her. The nurse's narration of her death does not present us with the act itself: at one moment of that narration, Deianeira is undoing her gown, and the next moment she is dead. It is as though she had been killed rather than killed herself. The message conveyed by the weapon is not that she has killed herself as a male might do, but that she has been killed by males. In just three lines (933–35) we are told that her son had forced her to this act, and that she has without knowing it done the will of Nessus.

Heracles' death, equally, is unsuitable, and the story has again been adjusted, in this case in order to remove any hint of glory from it, to leave it as nothing but unredeemed and hideous suffering. Traditionally, when Heracles died and his body burned, he was deified, and that version is deployed by Sophocles at the end of the *Philoctetes*; but not here, where Heracles' last words only call on his "tough soul to put a steel bit in his mouth and hold back the screams, so that an end can be made of

---

[5] In *Façons tragiques de tuer une femme* (Paris, 1985), translated by Anthony Forster as *Tragic Ways of Killing a Woman* (Cambridge, Mass.: Harvard University Press, 1987).

this unwanted, welcome, task"—welcome only because it will mean the end of the pain.

All the force of the play is directed to leaving in the starkest relief its extreme, undeserved, and uncompensated suffering, and this is what is registered in the famous and strange words with which it ends, quoted at the beginning of this paper. "There is nothing here that is not Zeus" is not a comforting or explanatory remark: it registers only inexplicable necessity, a necessity which may indeed be ascribed to the activities of the gods, but if so, to gods who do not explain themselves or take any notice of the suffering that they bring about. *Agnōmosunē* is what is ascribed to the gods, a negative thing, non-understanding, as contrasted with the *sungnōmosunē* of the line before, the shared understanding that Hyllus finds in his companions. Most remarkable, perhaps, is the idea that what has happened, pitiable for us, is "shameful for them"—and "them" can only be the gods. This doubly underscores the thought that there is no justification. What the gods do will be shameful because there is nothing they could say to excuse it. Moreover, their deeds can be understood as shameful only in the eyes of human beings, and that this can be so, that it even makes sense, shows that they have no authority in their power. They cannot give even the answer that Job received, an answer which offers no justification but which should at least silence the demand for one.

There is, of course, the old question, Aristotle's question, of how pleasure or profit could be got from watching such an enactment, but this is not the question here. It is essential that there is pleasure, and that something is achieved by such a play, and that it does not serve simply as an unwelcome reminder of cosmic awfulness. This is connected with what it achieves as a work of art, and, as Nietzsche already said in *The Birth of Tragedy*, this must lie, in part, in its enabling us to contemplate such things in honesty without being crushed by them. When later he said that we have art so that we do not perish from the truth,[6] he did not mean that we use art in order to escape from the truth: he meant that we have art so that we can both grasp the truth and not perish from it.

It is certainly not that the play's existence as a work of art in some sense *makes up* for the horrors, and to the extent that this is what the early Nietzsche meant by the idea that life is metaphysically redeemed through art, he was wrong, as he indeed came to think. The point of tragedy—or at least of those tragedies that are stark fictions—must lie rather in the fact that it lays its fictional horrors before us in a way that

---

[6] "Wir haben die *Kunst*, damit wir *nicht an der Wahrheit zugrunde gehn*." This is from the *Nachlass* of the 1880's. See *Werke in 3 Bänden*, edited by Karl Schlechte (Munich, 1966), vol. 3, 832.

elicits attitudes we cannot take towards real horrors. With real horrors, we are sometimes practically engaged in them; sometimes, we have some particular reason to be upset by them; most of the time we are necessarily, and (as Nietzsche occasionally brought himself to say) healthily, inattentive to them. What we cannot possibly, or at least decently, adopt towards them is the range of attitudes appropriate to fictional horrors presented in art. Yet such a fiction can carry some understanding of the real horrors. One might say that it reveals their metaphysical structure, their relation, or lack of it, to the universe; except that any such formula follows Aristotle's bad example in trying to give a general account of "the tragic effect," and indeed does worse than Aristotle in hinting, as neither his account nor Nietzsche's does, that some suitably profound philosophical formulation might take the place of the tragedy itself.

It is a mistake to look for one aim even of stark fictions, and the immensely general ideas that I have glanced at here could at best offer a kind of pattern within which the effects of different works might be variously construed. Moreover, most of the things that can be achieved by stark fictions, and through the attitudes appropriate to them, are necessarily obscure. One of their more obvious achievements, however, if not the most basic or important, is to offer a necessary supplement and a suitable limitation to the tireless aim of moral philosophy to make the world safe for well-disposed people.

THREE

Understanding Homer: Literature, History and Ideal Anthropology

I should like to start with some assumptions about anthropology, which I shall state dogmatically and most of which I should like to think are banal. In the peculiar case of homo sapiens, ethological accounts of the species inevitably lead into cultural descriptions of various social groups; this is a version of the old truth that it is the nature of human beings to live under convention (cf. Williams 1995).* Cultures, moreover, display a high degree of secondary elaboration, and while it is true—indeed, blindingly obvious—that significant ranges of human behaviour are to be explained in terms of natural selection, this is for the most part true at a level of fairly general description and in relation to environments which are equally rather broadly identified. For much of human behaviour, cultural description (in the sense in which different societies display different cultures) is going to be an essential element in understanding.

Every society has a past, in the sense that what happened earlier has shaped what is present, and virtually every society has some stories or other to tell about its past. Some societies—in particular, literate ones—have critical views of these stories about their past, views which both provide further evidence for our own enquiries into their past, and are themselves predecessors of those enquiries. In reading those and other written records, and interpreting artefacts or traces of earlier peoples, we have to use some of the same skills as we use in physically encountering peoples who live in a culture unfamiliar to us. In the case of those whom we actually encounter, we have to achieve an understanding of what they say, of what they believe, and of what their aims are, by a process of triangulation that involves all these three elements, and it is a constraint on this process being possible at all that those people's concerns and interests and perceptual powers should be taken not to be too radically different from our own.

However, we need not and should not assume that the processes of interpretation require us to find an equivalent to what they say in terms that we are prepared to use ourselves. It is true that in order to under-

---

* *Making Sense of Humanity and Other Philosophical Papers, 1982–1993* (Cambridge: Cambridge University Press, 1995). —Ed.

stand social transactions and interpret them in this spirit, we need to "get inside" them and to have a sense of what it is to act for the kinds of reasons that these agents have; but this does not imply that these are reasons that we ourselves have. Someone who has the sense of another culture can imagine, improvise, enact and respond appropriately to situations in which he finds himself, and in that sense he has internalised the reasons of people living in that culture; but this does not make them his reasons, any more than the actor's capacity to become an enraged ancient king makes him, even temporarily, into such a king. This is the capacity to take up what I have elsewhere called "the ethnographic stance", and it is a feature of our general understanding of human beings and of the various parts that culture can play in their lives that we should understand that such a stance is possible.[1]

This capacity plays its part also in understanding the past. This is part of the content of the cliché that the past is "another country"—to a certain extent, our approach in historical understanding must share something with our approach to unknown peoples. In some ways historical enquiry is harder. There is, above all, no participant observation: we lack the sight of their doings and the sound of their utterances. On the other hand, we get to the past not just in the ways in which we are figured as getting to exotic peoples, that is to say, by simply arriving in a state of total ignorance. This image of what it is to encounter a previously isolated people, which assimilates it to the entirely schematic situation of "radical translation" that has so interested philosophers, is itself in almost all cases a drastic exaggeration,[2] but it does make a difference that we are linked to the historical past by a self-conscious set of traditions. We reach the past by a route each step of which, in the favourable case, stands in explanatory relations to the steps before and after it. For these and other reasons, the case of historical cultural understanding is different enough from the situation of the social anthropologist as participant observer for it to be foolish to regard the past simply as another country. Nevertheless, there is enough in common in the ideas of interpretation, coming to see how things went in another cultural situation, for us to signal the connection by calling certain kinds of historical understanding "ideal anthropology". It is anthropology, because it shares these forms

---

[1] The general idea of interpretation I am using is of course familiar from the work of Donald Davidson. For the "ethnographic stance" and the possibility of understanding without identification, see Williams 1986. ["Reply to Simon Blackburn," *Philosophical Books* 27 (1986).—Ed.]

[2] It no doubt also carries heavily ideological presuppositions about the relations between "scientific" investigators and "primitive" peoples. The purely philosophical concentration on radical translation need not in itself carry such presuppositions: it is a device for isolating what is taken for granted in interpreting anyone.

of understanding, and it is ideal, not because it is perfect, but because it does not have the kinds of evidence which are central to the paradigm examples of social anthropology in action.

Some of our evidence from the past consists of physical objects, artefacts and other similar traces. Some of it consists of documents. Some of it, as we have already seen, may consist of documents in which a past society sought to record its own history. Some of it, which is the present concern, consists of what we may call works of literature. We do not have to assume that the society we are studying had a notion of "literature" or applied it to these documents. If they did not, then manifestly we have to take extreme care in using any such notion. However, in the case of a self-conscious society with a developed critical stance, there may be enough in the local practice to back up our seeing these writings as works of literature, or something like that. Literature can provide evidence for ideal anthropology; as we might also say, the interpretation of literature can be part of the interpretation that is the business of ideal anthropology.

There are familiar and enormous problems in this process. For instance, in the case of the ancient Greeks, which is the example that will be my concern here, there is a well known problem with regard to using the surviving tragedies as evidence about the society in which they were written. Greek tragedy tended to adopt a "high", archaising, manner, which means that as direct evidence of the ethical or other concepts of its audience, it has to be taken with extreme caution. This is the reason why Sir Kenneth Dover, in writing about popular conceptions of Greek morality, relied more on comedy (because it had to make people laugh) and legal speeches (because they had to persuade a jury) than on tragedy or epic (Dover 1974, 1–45).* However, it is still true that tragedies had to be intelligible to their audience. Indeed, they were produced in competition to impress and engage that audience, perhaps to overwhelm them, and that should be able to tell us something about the relations between the ethical conceptual structures of Greek tragedy and the outlook of such an audience.

In the case of Homeric epic, however, there is a still more radical displacement involved. It is not merely that the Homeric poems are expressed in formulaic language which no-one ever spoke. In addition, the people in classical Athens who read and discussed these poems when they had been written down knew that they belonged to an earlier time, that they had in some way or another been transmitted from an earlier society. The actual history of the poems is, of course, a very complex and

---

* K. J. Dover, *Greek Popular Morality in the Time of Plato and Aristotle* (Oxford: Blackwell, 1974).

still unresolved question, and I am not competent to discuss it, any more than I can discuss their relations to the archaeology of archaic Greece. However, if we assume, uncontroversially, that they stem from an oral tradition, we have to suppose an earlier non-literate audience to whom these poems, or parts of them, were recited; and to this audience, too, they already spoke of an earlier time.

This means that anyone who is engaged in interpreting the concepts used in these poems, or, as we may say rather vaguely, the "outlook" of the poems (though we should not assume that the outlook of the poems is always the same, in particular between the *Iliad* and the *Odyssey*) has a complex task. Indeed, there is more than one possible task. We may be concerned with the world or worlds represented in the poems, for instance with the kinds of concerns, motives or beliefs that Achilles or Odysseus is represented as having. Or we may be interested in the outlook of the poems' original audience, something which for more than one reason is very difficult to recover: one thing that we should not assume is that this is just the same as the outlook of the poems, any more than we can believe that their artefacts or their social organization were the same as those represented in the poems—as I have already said, the poems spoke even to their first audience about a past time. Yet again, we may be most interested in the outlook of the poems' readers in classical Athens, and in what the poems meant to them.

The first of these undertakings is importantly not independent of the third. We can hope to recover something we could call the outlook of the poems only by reconstructing what they meant to some audience, and that audience must be the first recipients of the poems about whom we know anything very much. In the light of what we know, we can try to "lay off" for the elements in the poems which that audience would have found different from their own life, as opposed to those that they found familiar. It may seem that there is an impossibly circular task here, of constructing the audience from the poems, and reading the poems in the light of what they might mean to such an audience. But this is to neglect the fact that about this audience there is a lot of extra evidence, and it also overlooks the vital point that, with regard both to this extra evidence and to the Homeric poems themselves, this is very far from a situation of radical translation, even in the fairly attenuated sense of this in which it applies to our encounters with previously unknown people. These poems are linked to us by an enormously complex and powerful tradition, in which the business of reading and understanding them has been transmitted from one historical period to another. People certainly disagree on the question of how far we understand "the world of Homer". But, unless they are being exceedingly cautious or provocative, they are usually prepared to admit that there is such a thing as understanding Homeric

Greek, something which informed Greek scholars mostly do rather well, and beginners do badly. We can, to a considerable degree of agreement, translate the poems into English. The firm conviction that we can do this is supported by the historical traditions that link us to the ancient world, by the fact that informed readers today are not arriving at these texts by historical parachute, but have learned ancient Greek from someone who learned ancient Greek from someone who. . . . This does not, of course, guarantee "correctness", or remove huge interpretative and historical problems, but it does provide the absolutely essential foundation of conducting the operations of ideal anthropology on these works at a level at which they can produce results and make some sense. A jokey classical scholar of my acquaintance, in parody of the methods of deconstruction, cheerily suggested that the word "album" in a poem of Horace might be taken to mean a book in which you stick photographs; it is quite instructive to consider how many reasons, of how many kinds, there are why this is not a good idea.

In my book *Shame and Necessity* (Williams 1993)* I tried to reach an understanding of certain ideas in the Homeric poems, in particular ethical ideas such as agency, responsibility, shame, and constraint. In the case of some of these ideas, I argued that they were more like ideas that we ourselves possess than many commentators have supposed. It is important that it was not implicit in the method of enquiry that this should be the result, or at least to this extent. I in fact concentrated on those ideas about which I was convinced that they bear a rather close relation to our own, in particular because I was concerned with using those ideas to help us understand ourselves, but there are of course many other conceptions employed by the ancient Greeks (some of which I discussed) which are much more alien to us, and I did not in any way wish to deny it. While all this is true, there are some ideas which we share with the ancient Greeks, and in particular with the audience of the Homeric poems, which are so basic to the understanding and construction of human action that one would need very powerful evidence (to put it mildly) to make one believe the claims made by some previous scholars that these concepts were lacking in the Greek world.

The claims made by Bruno Snell, for instance, that "Homeric people" (a concept which he used in an unclear way to provide a bridge between Homer's characters and Homer's readers or listeners) lacked any idea of a unitary agent capable of making decisions, or even of an agent who had a unitary body—such a suggestion runs up against a very strong presumption that unless one ascribes some such notions to the people represented in these poems and to the people who heard or read them, one

* Hereafter Williams 1993.—Ed.

would not be able to make sense of the poems at all. It is not offered as a dogmatic universal claim. As with other kinds of natural history, it is exceedingly rash to anticipate the marvels that one may encounter in the way of cultural development: or, to put the point in a rather more sophisticated way, while there must be common materials that we ourselves and those under study share, one must be aware that they may present themselves in quite unexpected forms and combinations. However, with regard to notions which are as central to our understanding of human activities as the idea of a decision, or that of a human being's purposively moving his or her limbs, one should try a number of other explanations before one concludes that they are absent from the world that one is trying to interpret.

In the case of Snell and those who thought like him, there are at least four reasons why he arrived at these mistaken conclusions. One is simply a failure to read the text carefully enough and to think consequently about it. For instance, with regard to motivational elements such as *thumos*, which on Snell's view were regarded in the Homeric world as virtually autonomous sources of action, the text itself makes clear that a bodily agent is needed if an action is to spring from such a principle: the primary idea is not that *thumos* does things, but that an agent does things in or with his *thumos*. Second, there is a failure to allow for the "literary" distance between the epic style and its audience. "We should be cautious about moving . . . from poetry to culture" as James Redfield has well said (Redfield 1975, 22),* and some of the inferences about the supposed psychology of Homeric characters, in particular of Homeric heroes, are based on an artefact of style, a refusal of the anecdotal which lends a certain dignity and inevitability to the narrative. One example of this is the development of Achilles' willingness to reach an agreement with Agamemnon; another, perhaps, is the postponement of Penelope's recognition of her husband (cf. Williams 1993, 46–48). In such cases, it is naive, not merely to read off an implied psychology from the structure of the narrative, but even to suppose that there is anything that could be read off simply from the narrative and taken to be an implied psychology.

Another mistake has been to impose on the Homeric poems, or indeed any other work of ancient literature, the misguided conclusions of modern philosophies. In particular, in the case of agency and the psychology of action, it is a crudely Cartesian philosophy that is to blame. This is particularly so with regard to the absence from Homer or other Greek writers of a (supposed) concept of the will. This is an area in which there

---

* James Redfield, *Nature and Culture in the Iliad* (Chicago: University of Chicago Press, 1975). —Ed.

is a peculiarly sensitive relation between similarity and difference, between materials that have to be taken for granted in making sense of the text at all, and materials which are the subject of specific cultural elaborations, as the notion of the will quite certainly is in our own history. Some of that local history is involved with the Cartesian philosophy, which has both influenced people's conceptions of what action might be, and is itself the product of previous constructions, some of them (such as those of Augustine) of considerable ideological power. If one tries to interpret conceptions used in the ancient world by reference to these ideas, one will misinterpret them. The misinterpretation, in this kind of case, consists in more than anachronism. It is part of the argument against the Cartesian misinterpretation of Homer that it forces us to neglect or deny phenomena which are basic to our making sense of human action at all, and hence basic to our making sense of human action as it is described in the Homeric poems. But to the extent that these phenomena are basic to making sense of action at all, then they are basic to making sense of action in our own cultural context as well, and the Cartesian misinterpretation is not simply an historical misunderstanding, but a philosophical mistake, a misunderstanding of ourselves.

Another error that can be cured by reflection on the principles of ideal anthropology is that embodied in Snell's so-called "lexical principle", which is to the effect that the Greeks had a particular idea only if they had a word that expressed it. One particularly strong version of this is that if the Greeks had a certain idea, then they had to have a word which expressed this idea and nothing else, and in these terms it has been argued that the Homeric poems contain no idea of practical deliberation. This cannot survive the very obvious reflection that equally in modern English there is no expression that means practical deliberation and nothing else, except the expression "practical deliberation" itself, which is first of all virtually a term of philosophical art, and secondly not an expression likely to turn up in a poem. But even if it is more liberally construed, the principle is naive, because it elides the distinctions between the relatively untheorised language of everyday transactions, and the more theoretical kind of vocabulary that will be needed if we are going to compare the categories used by one society with those used by another.

Yet another problem with the lexical principle is the question of what direction we should look in for the expression in question. It has been remarked, for instance, that in the Homeric poems there is no word that means "intention", or "intentional" as an attribute of actions. This may well be true. However, there is an adjective, *hekon*, which almost always means "intentionally", and indeed, though it is an adjective, effectively functions as an adverb. It is a very striking fact that in the *Iliad* and the

Odyssey it occurs only in the nominative singular, a phenomenon which ties it very firmly to the sense of "intentionally"; its negative counterpart, *aekon*, by contrast, occurs also in other cases, and this is appropriate to its sense, which is more often "unwillingly". Such straightforward philological facts as these are a basic part of the evidence on which ideal anthropology must depend in studying a society from which we possess written texts.[3] Of course, it is only in the light of certain philosophical presuppositions, which help to form the assumptions of such a method, that the evidence can be identified as evidence, as telling us something relevant about the conceptual structures that belonged to a past society.

Several of the points in this discussion have related in one way or another to issues of what may be expected to be universal in our understanding of human societies, and what is culturally variable. I have already said that we should be cautious in dogmatically asserting that some given elements must be universal: in assuming, as one might put it, that philosophical reflection on the methodology of an ideal anthropology can yield a body of synthetic necessary truths. Much of the history of philosophy, particularly in the last two centuries, is littered with the rubble of constructions that have aimed to achieve such results. I said earlier that we are well advised to preserve our willingness to be surprised by the natural history of human conventions. However, even if we do not offer any rich body of what are claimed to be substantive universal necessities, there is, in the area of action and its ethical surroundings, a set of very basic ideas which, at the least, lay an extremely heavy burden of proof on anyone who claims to find a society in which these conceptions were not operative.

Until that proof or argument arrives, as it notably failed to do in the case of the Homeric Greeks, we may claim that everywhere:

1. There are actions—people do things, and are recognised by others as doing things.
2. Actions are understood to lead to outcomes, some of which are intended and some not.
3. Sometimes the outcomes are bad, to be regretted by the agent or by someone else or both.
4. When there is an outcome regretted by someone else, there can be a demand for a response.

There is another item which might be added to these, though it is perhaps less utterly banal than the others:

---

[3] As has already been explained, the relations of the written texts to "Homeric society" are more complex than this formulation implies.

5. People are sometimes in unusual or untypical states which affect their actions and their intentions.

This last idea relates particularly to the interest that members of a society have over time in their fellow agents, and in the extent to which they can be expected to behave in a steady or an unreliable manner.[4] It may be that in most places there is some interest in such a consideration, though certainly the ways in which it is understood, and also the factors that may be understood as affecting an agent's actions or intentions at a given time, will be very different in different societies.

These are the materials of something like an idea of responsibility, and it is reasonable, until we meet firm evidence to the contrary, to expect that they will be found in every society. However, what is quite certain is that there is no one idea of responsibility to be found in every society, but rather a range of notions that vary between them. These notions interpret the materials in different ways, and give them very different emphases in relation to one another. This is the kind of account that I tried to give, in outline form, in *Shame and Necessity* (cf. Williams 1993, 50–74), considering the Greek and specifically the Homeric case, about which it has often been asserted that ideas of responsibility in anything like our sense were missing. The present point is that, if anything like this account is correct, it represents a clear, but also an untypically simple, example of the relations between the universal and the local. Certain materials or elements are universal; what is local and various are the ways in which the materials are arranged, emphasised and interpreted. It is perhaps unlikely that in general the universal can be identified and deployed in such a simple way: indeed, it may well be that such an account is too simple for this case itself.

However, if, as I have suggested, anthropology must involve itself in an interpretational task; and if the study of past societies must, in part, consist of a kind of anthropology without participation, which I have called "ideal anthropology", which applies, though with special features, to those societies from which we possess written, and in particular "literary" remains: then certainly we have to reflect very keenly on how strong the assumptions of the interpretational activity must be, and how far they do yield universal elements. It remains a pressing task for the philosophy of anthropology and, as a special case, for the philosophy of history.

[4] For some speculations in this area cf. Williams 1990, 1–10. [Reference cannot be identified. —Ed.]

SOCRATES AND PLATO

FOUR

Pagan Justice and Christian Love

In his article 'Socrates' Contribution to the Greek Sense of Justice',[1] Gregory Vlastos claimed that in classical Greek thought and practice the norms of justice were 'discriminately applied' to two classes of people: one's enemies and one's social inferiors—in particular, among the latter, slaves. He argued that Socrates, while he had nothing to say about the second of these restrictions, took an important step forward with respect to the first, and originated the idea that one's treatment of other people should be guided not by the matter of their being friends or enemies, but by moral considerations. Socrates accepted that this policy could put one, in material terms, at a disadvantage in relation to people who did not share it, in particular people whom the traditional view would regard as one's enemies, and since he thought that one certainly had no reason to pursue a policy that was not in some basic sense to one's advantage, he had to think that a virtuous life was sufficient for one's ultimate advantage—the position that he argues, for instance, in the *Gorgias*.

All this was part of Vlastos's aim, sustained over a long period, of showing that Socrates did much to originate a higher view of norms applying to social and personal conduct, one that transcended the perceptions of his contemporaries and led in the direction of an ideal of a life shaped basically by moral considerations. Those considerations laid a lot of weight on an idea of equal concern for others, and on values that put considerations of personal need and moral merit in place of determinations made by rank and power. They were thus historically, and in Vlastos's case personally, associated with some (typically Protestant) interpretations of Christianity. He was scrupulous in not taking what might be called a 'Fourth Eclogue' view of Socrates or of any other pagan thinker. But he did associate Socrates with a number of moral advances that he saw as eventually forming part of a Christian moral outlook.

In these remarks, I should like to touch on three aspects of the large and deep issues that are raised by this picture of our ethical history.

---

[1] *Archaiognosia* 1,2 (1980).

What did the traditional view, rejected by the Socratic outlook,[2] think about justice towards friends and enemies? What did the Socratic outlook want to put in the place of that view? How far could it go on the path it had chosen without running into a problem familiar to Christianity and unknown to earlier paganism, that the value of an individual human being, by becoming morally infinite, runs the risk of becoming effectively zero?

1   PAGAN JUSTICE

When Vlastos said that the norms of justice were discriminately applied to enemies and to slaves, as contrasted with other people, he meant that the traditional Greek practice allowed one to behave unjustly towards those groups. This itself could mean either of two things: that the Greeks allowed behavior towards these groups that indeed was unjust and would be seen by us to be so; or that they allowed behavior towards those people that the Greeks themselves saw as unjust. Vlastos of course meant the first of these things, but he meant the second as well. This might seem a surprising claim, and it is natural to reply that Greek practice would be better described in the following terms: behavior that would be unjust in other circumstances can be regarded as just if it is directed towards slaves or towards one's enemies. If the Greeks' thought is expressed in these terms, the Socratic outlook can still be taken to have introduced a reform, but the reform has to be differently described, as altering the criteria of justice rather than taking the criteria of justice and widening their application. In the case of friends and enemies, I think that this is, roughly, what we should say. However, this is not the case with slaves, and although slavery is not the main subject of this paper, it will be helpful to say something about it first.[3]

With regard to slaves, something like Vlastos's formulation does indeed apply. Between masters and slaves there was no justice, and bad treatment of a person's slave was a wrong against that person, not against the slave. This followed from what it was to be a slave. If any question arose about the just or unjust treatment of slaves, it was not a question within the institution of slavery but a question about it: whether

---

[2] In using the expression 'Socratic outlook', I am laying aside the questions, discussed by Vlastos, of the extent to which Socrates himself originated these changes. For possible antecedents see Albrecht Dihle, *Die Goldene Regel* (Göttingen 1962), pp. 45–8, and Mary Whitlock Blundell, *Helping Friends and Harming Enemies* (Cambridge 1989), p. 56, to whom I owe the Dihle reference.

[3] I have developed the argument that follows at greater length in *Shame and Necessity* (California U.P. 1993), ch. 5.

it could be a just arrangement that permitted one human being to be possessed by another, with the result that their relations were not regulated by justice. This question was occasionally raised, but not very often. There are one or two surviving remarks about the injustice of slavery, based on the idea that it was a matter of pure chance, the result of arbitrary force, who gets enslaved,[4] and it is an objection of this kind that Aristotle tried to answer in the famous discussion in Book I of the *Politics*. Aristotle saw very clearly what he had to show. He thought both that slavery was (roughly) necessary to the life of the polis, and that the polis was naturally the best organization of human life. From this it already follows in a sense that it is natural that there should be slaves. What Aristotle had to show, however, if the claims of nature were to silence complaints of injustice, was something more, that for some particular people, it was natural that they should be slaves rather than somebody else. His attempt to deliver this conclusion appears to have been hardly better received in the ancient world than it has been by modern critics, and it is obvious why this should be so. If Aristotle were right, and if slavery were properly conducted, then the slaves themselves would have nothing to complain of. But the ancient Greeks quite rightly thought that the condition of slavery was one that any human being had reason to complain of. From Homer on, being captured into slavery was a paradigm of human disaster, a brutal form of bad luck. In the classical period, free people were constantly reminded of the contingencies of slavery, if not by the capture of slaves, which at least happened elsewhere, then by manumission, which happened in front of them.

The standard Greek attitude to slavery was not that it was a just institution; nor, again, that it was an unjust institution, a view which would have encouraged the thought that it should be replaced by something else, and they had nothing with which to replace it. Their view rather was that the institution was necessary, and that for those subjected to it it was bad luck. In that sense, it lay outside the considerations of justice.

For us it does not lie outside those considerations, and is a paradigm of injustice. However, this does not mean that those same traditional materials, economic or cultural necessity and bad luck, make no contribution to our thinking about social life. We use them all the time. It may be that we have the aspiration that no social or economic relation should

---

[4] What is perhaps the best known of these comments is still regularly ascribed to the comic writer Philemon, of the 4th century BC, but this is a mistake: for details, see *Shame and Necessity*, pp. 202–3, note 19. The author and date of the famous verses are unknown.

lie outside considerations of justice. To the extent that we have that aspiration, we try either (with the Left) to replace necessity and luck with justice, or (with the Right) to show that the results of necessity and luck can be just. Neither project is such a success as to enable us to say that in these matters we have decisively gone beyond the ethical condition of the ancients.

In the case of slavery, then, we can say that both the institution itself and what went on inside it lay, for the most part, outside considerations of justice. With friends and enemies, on the other hand, it was different: it was rather that the categories of 'friend' and 'enemy' structured what was just and unjust. Not to help a friend or return benefits received was a clear case of injustice, while returning violence with similar violence (or with more) was not only comprehensible but could be demanded.

In his article, Vlastos tends to express the traditional view in terms of 'returning wrong for wrong', and in this he follows the passage of Plato [*Crito* 49 B 8 seq] in which Socrates expresses his rejection of such a view. But it is hardly surprising that this is not how the traditional view standardly described itself.⁵ The only direct statement I have been able to find that explicitly links injustice with a favorable view of the 'friends and enemies' principle is by Gorgias [*Pal.* 18, DK 82 B 11a]: 'So was it a matter of wanting to help one's friends or harm one's enemies? For in these interests someone would do injustice. But my own case was altogether the opposite . . .' Even this does not legitimate the injustice, and in any case the speaker mentions the matter only to walk away from it.⁶ The famous passage from the *Choephoroi* [306 seq], which Vlastos mentions, about the age-old maxim *drasanti pathein* says twice that the repayment of killing with killing is a matter of *dikê* or *dikaion*.* On this matter, as opposed to slavery, the traditional view is not appropriately expressed in terms of the limitations of justice, but rather in terms of what was thought to be just.

Of course, the actions that the principle could legitimate might be exactly the sort of actions that in other circumstances would be unjust: that is part of its point. Pindar (a little out of character perhaps) says [*Pyth.* 2.83 seq] 'as an enemy against an enemy I shall creep up like a

---

⁵ The verb *antadikein* is a Platonic coinage, first occurring in the *Crito*.

⁶ A passage cited by Vlastos from Euripides [*Ion* 1046 seq] says that it is a fine thing for those in good fortune to honor *eusebeia* [piety, reverence—Ed.], but no law stands in the way of those who want to treat their enemies badly. *Eusebeia* always refers to a specifically religious type of requirement; it is not clear how the remark (made by an aged paidagogos) relates to justice.

* *Dikê* and *dikaion* mean "justice"; *drasanti pathein* means "The doer should suffer what he has done." These phrases, along with *trigerôn muthos* ("the age-old maxim") p. 80 below, come from Aeschylus, *Choephoroi* (*Libation-Bearers*) 306–14. —Ed.

wolf, padding one way and another in crooked paths'. Herodotus [8.105–6] tells an appalling story about a man who had been castrated, and who contrived 'the greatest repayment to someone by whom he had been wronged that we have ever heard of.' Thucydides [2.67.4] tells how the Athenians killed without a hearing and threw into a pit some Lacedaimonian envoys and others, 'thinking it justified or right' (*dikaiountes*) to do the same thing as the Lacedaimonians had done to some Athenians and their allies at the beginning of the war. There are, of course, many other such examples.[7]

2 SOCRATIC REFORM

If, in this traditional way, A does some horrible thing to B because B is his enemy, there are at least three different sorts of objection that may be made. (i) Not A: if anyone is to do that to B, it should not be A. (ii) Not B: these are not circumstances in which B should have any such thing done to him. (iii) Not that thing: no-one should do that thing to anybody. Of course, the situation may be such as to invite more than one of these comments, possibly all of them, at once. (i) and (ii) represent different aspects of a demand that the return for harms should be depersonalized. (i) may demand that personal vengeance should be replaced by a public, impersonal agency. This change has two desirable results. One is that what happens to B is not an expression of A's rage, prejudice, and possibly error, and so may bear a more reliable relation to what B has done, if anything. The other benefit is that an impersonal agency is less likely to provoke a further round of violence from the person whom it has (as we may now put it) punished: its action may, if we are lucky, finish the matter. This speaks to (ii), as the concerns of the *Oresteia* make very clear: the mere fact that I am in the third or fourth generation of a family with a history of violence need no longer operate to involve me in it. The same applies, very obviously, to vendettas between families or other groups. Another advantage of the public authority may be its regulation of (iii). What A does to B in the primitive situation may be, as much as any other feature of the transaction, determined

---

[7] Thucydides also, interestingly, gets Cleon to say in the Mytilinean debate [3.40.3] 'pity is justly returned to people who are similar [*tous homoious*] but not to those who do not show pity in return, and who necessarily are in the position of being enemies'. Classen well argues on the strength of the last clause that *homoious* should mean 'in a similar situation' rather than 'like-minded'. But the previous clause does suggest 'like-minded', and, when one recalls that the necessity in question was applied by the Athenians themselves, the slippage between the two senses provides a compact rhetorical demonstration of the move from the justice associated with the traditional rule to that invoked in the Melian dialogue.

by rage; even apart from issues of justice, it may easily be hideous enough
to make it certain that this will not be the end of the affair.

The effect of pressing these kinds of objection, and in particular of establishing a public authority, is to leave the category of an enemy with
less ethical significance. For one thing, when the vendetta and similar relationships are rejected, B will not be A's enemy just because he falls into
a certain class, e.g. by belonging to a certain family; if he is A's enemy at
all, it will be because of what he himself has done. This thought is precisely expressed by Demosthenes [23.56]: 'there is no class [*genos*] of
friends and enemies, but each of them is brought into being by what is
done.' Further, even if B is A's enemy, and is so by these improved criteria, there are many things that A cannot do to B, because he cannot,
within the approved procedures of society, do them to anyone: these include the forms of violence that have become the monopoly of the public
authority. In respect of what with us would be criminal proceedings, the
only enemies will be public enemies. With private proceedings, the processes of the law will to some extent have drawn the teeth of enmity. By
the 4th century, it was an Athenian commonplace that compensation
sought in litigation was legalized revenge.[8]

Such ideas are very familiar, for instance in relation to a Lockean justification of the state. As this point suggests, they are also familiarly related to matters of justice. To reduce in these ways and to this extent the
ethical significance of enmity serves the purposes of civil peace, co-
operation and personal security, but it more specifically serves the ends
of justice, because it brings it about that if anything disadvantageous
happens to B in the name of justice, then the nature and severity of what
happens to him bears a non-arbitrary and publicly intelligible relation to
what B can reasonably be supposed to have actually done. This makes it
very clear that laying aside in these ways the 'friends and enemies' rule
does not imply that one has given up the principle of *drasanti pathein*,
the idea that one who has done wrong should suffer. On the contrary,
what the elimination of private vengeance brings about *in the order of
justice* is best explained by saying that it makes it more certain that one
who has done wrong will be brought in an orderly and reliable way to
suffer in an appropriate degree. Of course, someone might have grounds
for giving up both the 'friends and enemies' rule and the principle of
drasanti pathein. We should ask what those grounds might be, and what
they might have to do with justice. We must also ask whether Socrates
was such a person.

The argument in the *Crito* goes: one should not be unjust to anyone,
so one should not be unjust to anyone in return for injustice. One should

---

[8] Lys. 1.4, 7.20, al.; Dem. 21.28, 22.3, al.; Whitlock Blundell, p. 54.

not do anything bad to others, even when they have done something bad to oneself, since doing bad and doing injustice are the same. So one should not do injustice in return, or do anything bad to others, whatever they have done to oneself. Socrates says that this is and will be an unpopular doctrine. As we saw earlier, he is happy to say that the popular view is that one can do injustice in return for injustice, but this inaccurate and question-begging formula does not focus his disagreement with the popular view. Indeed, it is not yet clear what exactly his disagreement is with the popular view, because it is unclear what it is to do something bad (*kakôs poiein*) to someone else. If this simply means that we should never do anything to another that involves our acting badly, we are left where we were: the traditional view will simply say that being horrible to one's enemies does not involve acting badly. What Socrates means, rather, is that we should not do anything to others that is bad for them. This is equivalent to saying that we must not harm them. This is what Socrates believed, and Xenophon, in his encomium on Socrates at the end of the *Memorabilia* [4.8.11], says of him that he was a just man, so as never to harm anyone in any way.

If suffering were a sure sign that one was being harmed, then this would dispose of *drasanti pathein*. But it is not, as becomes clear in Book I of the *Republic*. There, Polemarchus expresses the traditional doctrine by saying that it is justice to harm bad people and one's enemies, and he is refuted by Socrates on the ground that harming something must mean making it worse with regard to its special excellence, so that harming a person must consist in making him a worse person, which is something that justice could never require of us. It is this sense, equally, that gives rise to the Socratic doctrine, deployed in the *Gorgias* in heroic defiance of the prejudices of common sense, that the good man cannot be harmed.

If justice imposes sufferings, and those sufferings can serve one's interests in being a good person, then *drasanti pathein* may, to that extent, remain in place. Can its purely retributive aspects remain in place? In one sense, perhaps yes, since what is in the interests of a person's virtue includes being *treated justly*: if the just treatment of a malefactor consists in appropriate punishment, then punishment should be applied merely because it is just, and that constitutes a form of retributivism. On the other hand, the Socratic view will go beyond retributivism when that is understood in the most primitive sense, that all we need mention in explaining what a wrong-doer deserves is a balancing of his act and our response: on the Socratic view, we must refer also to the wrong-doer's interests.

Socrates's attack in the *Crito* on 'doing injustice in return' directs itself only obliquely to what the traditional view meant, and not at all to what it said. In deploying his new, ethicised, conception of harm, implicitly in the *Crito* and explicitly in the *Gorgias* and *Republic*, Socrates addresses himself directly to what the traditional view said, but—it now turns out—not at all to what it meant. When the old view instructed one to harm one's enemy, it did not mean that one should make him worse: it meant that one should make him suffer. Socrates instructs us not to harm anyone. But that turns out to mean that one should not make him worse: what has that got to do with not making him suffer? The most that Socrates seems to have done is to instruct those who accepted the old view to think about something they perhaps thought too little about, their own and others' interests as virtuous or potentially virtuous people, but he does not seem to have said anything to discourage them from making other people suffer.

Moreover, it is far from clear that he could or indeed needed to say anything of that kind. Socrates takes it to be a consequence of his new doctrine that the just person may well be at a disadvantage in worldly terms by not, for instance, taking pre-emptive action against the unscrupulous. He does not deny (as some pacifists do) the cynical predictions of Polus and the rest about what may happen to the just person; he merely rejects the relevance of those predictions, on the ground that worldly disaster cannot threaten one's real interests. The good man cannot be harmed. But if that is so, then it is even less clear what is wrong with the old vengeance, or indeed with any form of cruelty or exploitation. If I cannot really harm anyone's interests by attacking their bodies or their possessions, what is wrong with doing so? It looks as though the most that we can say against the old view is that those who seek vengeance are going to be disappointed, because they hope to be more radically horrible to their enemies than, as it turns out, they can be.

Socrates will presumably say that, if we think in these terms, we shall be looking in the wrong direction. What is wrong with exploitation and cruelty lies not in what those things do to the sufferers, but in what they do to the perpetrators. But this does not solve the problem, because if we do not have an adequate account of what is bad about the activities in relation to the victim, we have little idea why they are bad for the perpetrator. At best, the complaint would seem to be of a kind of triviality, as though the cruel were wasting their time with superficial things.[9]

---

[9] These questions are related to a more general point, that it is a mistake to think that ethical conceptions typical of the archaic age were more narcissistic than those associated with Platonic or, again, modern morality. I discuss this in *Shame and Necessity*, ch. 4 and Endnote 1.

3 INFINITE VALUE

Rather than thinking in political terms, of regulating and normalizing the responses demanded by the old rules and creating an impersonal power to control them, the Socratic approach tries to transcend those responses altogether, by appealing to a different order of value and a different understanding of people's deepest interests. In this, it resembles Christianity, and the difficulties that we have just glimpsed have indeed been shared by some kinds of Christianity, for instance of a Gnostic character, which placed the significance of human life so radically beyond its worldly operations as to leave it quite mysterious why what happens in the worldly dimension should matter at all. Christianity labored hard, notably in the person of Augustine, to give an answer to that question, and it was helped to do so by a doctrine of history, an account of why God should have an interest in a finite world. Even given those resources, it remained a constant source of tension in Christianity, whether it was the aim of its special truth to transform the secular world, or merely to redeem it.[10]

Socratism generated a similar problem, with fewer resources to deal with it. Vlastos was surely right in holding that Socrates did not want to accept the most extreme conclusions about the worthlessness of worldly things, that he did not agree with Antisthenes and the Cynics in thinking that all non-moral goods were indifferent. Socrates thought it better to be healthy rather than sick, in the company of friends rather than friendless, free of bodily pain rather than in agony. So how is it that the good man cannot be harmed? If we say, as Vlastos does in the article from which I started,[11] that for Socrates virtue had infinite value, and non-moral goods only finite value, we are still left with the question of what attitudes adequately acknowledge those respective values. How can we avoid the conclusion that a subtraction of non-moral goods is either no loss at all, because it is a subtraction from an infinite sum, or else a loss that we have reason to fear, because it is a subtraction from a finite sum

---

[10] Vlastos himself, in the period when he was publicly identified with Christianity, believed passionately that it should transform it. In his book *Christian Faith and Democracy* (New York 1939) he tells how a friend of his, 'a decent pagan, asked: "Why are you a Christian?" I replied: "Because I believe in love." ' Vlastos explains how uneasy he felt with this reply in the face of social inequality, the 'impassable barrier' between rich and poor. No one had made it. 'But it is there. And as long as we let it stand, faith in love will lack the substance of action, and no one can profess it without a measure of hypocrisy.' [pp. 40, 42.]

[11] He takes a different view in his book *Socrates*, based on a distinction between the conditional and the unconditional.

that we reasonably care about? We are also still left with the problem we have already encountered, about the content of the virtues that have infinite value—a content that is directed almost entirely to protecting other people's possession of finite goods.

Socrates surely did think that non-moral goods had some value, and that their loss constituted some loss. The sense in which the good man cannot be harmed has to be that he cannot ultimately be harmed. But Thrasymachus, Callicles, and their less theoretical associates can press Socrates painfully on what *ultimately* means. In the long run, as Maynard Keynes used to remind people, we are all dead. Unless, of course, we are not: and it is hard to resist the conclusion that this aspect of Socratic doctrine can make sense only if it is completed, as it was by Plato and by Christianity, with a belief that this is not the only or the most important life we lead.[12] Under those auspices, the negotiations between finite and infinite can take on another aspect, one that leaves behind the bleak truth underlying the old rules, that these are the only life and the only friends that we shall ever have.

We have seen two ways of going beyond the old rule. One is the political way, of regulating enmity and replacing its exchanges by impersonal authority. This is a way that all societies, to various degrees and with varying success, try to take. Another way, which Socrates proposed, was to transcend enmity and its relations altogether, and I have suggested that at the level at which Socrates seemingly wanted to pursue it, this path leads intelligibly only to metaphysics and religion, a transcendence of finite life altogether. But it may be thought that there is a third, and strictly ethical, way of going beyond the old rule. This agrees with the old dispensation that there is only one life, but enjoins, as a beneficial way of living it, that one should never hate anyone, and should encourage in oneself only positive sentiments. Paganism itself found resources for limiting the indulgences of hatred or the enjoyment of others' suffering,[13] and more generally for controlling the destructive and obsessional emotions of hatred and the desire to hurt. Such projects of ethical education and of self-management are still very much with us, and there is good reason why they should be. But should they try to exclude *drasanti pathein* entirely?

Here we need a distinction. The *trigerôn muthos** of the *Choephoroi* said that blow for blow was *demanded* (it was this demand that was

---

[12] On Socrates facing death, see Vlastos, *Socrates*, pp. 233–5; *Shame and Necessity*, pp. 184–5, note 60.

[13] Already in the *Odyssey* Eurycleia is told not to gloat [22.411]. Similar ideas at Lys. 2.8, Ar. *Nub.* 549 seq, Democr. DK 68 B 293, Herod. 4.205; and Diogenes Laertius ascribes to Pittacus and to Solon [1.76, 1.54] sayings to the effect that forgiveness is better than revenge: Whitlock Blundell, p. 56.

* Cf. footnote p. 74 above. —Ed.

controlled and redirected by public institutions). But there is a different thought, that disagreeable or unhelpful conduct towards a particular person is not indeed demanded of me, and if I act against him I shall not be acting in the role of an agency of justice, but nevertheless it may be allowed in view of what he has done, to me or to my friends. That last possibility brings in an important consideration. Socrates and others seeking to overcome the old rule have been agreeably less disposed to get rid of its first clause than its second; they have little objection to one's being nice to one's friends, unless it involves the corruption of some process demanded by justice. But by the transitivities of friendship and enmity, which can work such chaos when friendship provides the basic protection system[14] and which still operate to some extent even when it does not do so, my support for my friends may well involve my being less than friendly to those who have behaved badly towards them.

But need this involve harming those people—harming them even in the less spectacular ways that are still available when many ways of harming them have been fortunately taken away by the law? We have to ask, once again, what counts as harm. 'Being less than friendly' requires some expression, and certainly it is not enough of an expression of it that one should be, simply, less friendly. Being less friendly to someone than I am to my friends is, in itself, simply treating him like everyone else; it is certainly not adequate to register the special fact that I and my friends have *got something against him*.

The problems raised by this are real, but not in themselves philosophical. A problem of principle does arise, however, if we want there to be a *universal* sentiment that can be called, as Christians have called it, love. If love, or anything that could collect such a name, is what we should feel for everyone, then there is no way in which one can fall below that level of concern without failing in a required virtue, even when it is a matter of what one should feel towards those who have behaved badly towards oneself or one's particular friends. There are only two ways out from that position. One is that one should have no particular friends, including oneself. The other is that towards people who have behaved badly in relation to oneself or one's friends one should feel and act in ways that are less than (particularly) friendly, but that one should do so specifically in the interests of charity: *to do those people a good turn*. This state of mind has a familiar psychology and, we can now perhaps see, an interesting history. It takes the archaic idea that expressions of enmity are legitimated in the name of justice, and the Socratic idea that

<hr />

[14] Whitlock Blundell, discussing this [p. 48], points out that it led to extended networks, particularly in conjunction with the further friendship relation of *xenia*: she mentions the example of Axylos [*Il*. 6. 14–16] who had many friends, 'because he lived by the road.'

in applying justice to someone I must be benefiting him, and combines the two in a way that achieves, with an awesome dialectical horribleness, the worst of two worlds.

The conclusion must be neither Socratic nor Christian. The old rule has to be tamed and directed, both politically and psychologically, rather than metaphysically transcended or transmuted into universal *agapê*.

FIVE

Introduction to Plato's *Theaetetus*

Like all of Plato's dialogues, the *Theaetetus* presents a conversation that did not actually take place. The dialogue form is not meant to give an historical record; it is a style of writing that enables Plato to explore philosophical questions in ways more vivid and more intellectually flexible than are available to a treatise. Above all, the dialogue form enables Plato not to speak in his own person. The leading figure in the dialogues, except for some of the last that he wrote, is Plato's teacher Socrates. The ideas which Socrates expresses in the dialogues, or helps to construct in conversation with the other characters, are not necessarily ideas that were known to the historical Socrates, and in many of the dialogues, including the *Theaetetus*, the materials of the discussion are quite certainly Plato's.

Questions are raised not only by Socrates' presence, but also by Plato's absence. We should not assume that there is a straightforward route from any given dialogue to Plato's beliefs. We are used to the idea that philosophers have theories or even systems, which they lay before us in articles or monographs. Reading Plato's dialogues, we may easily think that they are just a literary device for putting across opinions which he might, if he wished, have expressed more directly. There are a few dialogues of which that is a fair description; in some the form of dialogue is almost abandoned. But the very fact that in some cases Plato is clearly talking to us through the dialogue should make us question the assumption that he is always doing so.

Hardly anyone now thinks that all Plato's dialogues, or all except the earliest, express the *same* theory, roughly that of the *Republic*. Most people accept that Plato developed, questioned, and even perhaps changed his theories. But we still need to guard against the idea that every time Plato wrote a dialogue he was acting as curator of his own system, keeping it in place or monitoring its developments. Plato certainly had some systematic beliefs, and still more some guiding metaphysical and ethical concerns, which are variously and powerfully expressed in his work. He has always been regarded as one of the greatest Western philosophers, by some people as the greatest of them all. Notwithstanding the achievements of his remarkable predecessors whose writings are lost to us (several are mentioned in this dialogue), he virtually invented the subject, philosophy. He was the first to express many distinctively philosophical questions and concerns; in the *Theaetetus*, he explores in an intense and closely argued way ideas which have shaped the ways in which people have subsequently discussed what knowledge might be, and whether we can have any. But as well as explicit philosophical content, Plato lays before us in his dialogues various attitudes which also belong to philosophy, such as curiosity, puzzlement, and intellectual surprise. His characters may be excited, bored, confused, or impressed; they take up, in such moods, all sorts of analogies, metaphors, stories, and models (for instance, of the human mind); they learn something from them, and often then throw them away. The dialogues, very often, embody these processes of inquiry—they do not merely present, in coded form, its results. If we are going to get the most from reading one of Plato's dialogues, we have to keep in close touch with its tone, sustaining a sense of what is a joke, what is merely provisional, what is being tried out or tried on.

The *Theaetetus* is a dialogue to which this advice particularly applies. Socrates reiterates a theme familiar from Plato's earliest dialogues, that he himself knows nothing, and that he is merely there to discuss and criticize other people's ideas, and to help them formulate them; it is here that, in a famous image, he compares his role to that of a midwife (150). On its central question, 'what is knowledge?', the dialogue's results are negative, but it is not supposed that we have learned nothing in disposing of the various answers which are proposed in the course of the argument. Moreover, the various answers themselves, as we shall see, are not merely suggestions randomly elicited by the question. They speak to various important preconceptions, and they help to identify theoretical problems which will have to be faced in any later discussion of knowledge.

Many scholars have assumed that there is definite doctrine to be gathered from between the lines of the dialogue. Partly, this is because it is agreed that the dialogue was written after the *Phaedo*, the *Symposium*, and the *Republic*, with their ambitious metaphysical speculations about a changeless order of 'Forms' separate from the world of ordinary material happening, and it is felt that the *Theaetetus* must have something to say about those matters since it concerns knowledge (which in the *Republic* is confined to the Forms), and indeed seems to express in the Digression (172–177) some of the same attitudes to philosophy, contrasted with the world of practical affairs, as are to be found in these dialogues. Indeed, there is a reading of the first and longest Part of the dialogue, discussing the idea that knowledge is perception, which represents the argument of that Part as relying on the kind of view of the material world that is to be found in the *Republic*.[1]

Whether we accept that reading or not, we should not assume that because there are theoretical commitments in the offing and Plato here refers to various philosophical theories, the dialogue is all the time trying to get some doctrine across to us, as opposed to making us think about the issues. Moreover, as Myles Burnyeat has said:

> . . . readers of the *Theaetetus* are required to contribute more and more as the dialogue proceeds. As I see it, your task in Part I is to *find* the meaning in the text and follow the argument to a satisfactory conclusion. In Part II you are challenged to *respond* to the meaning in the text by overcoming the problems and paradoxes that it leaves unresolved. In Part III the task is nothing less than to *create* from the text a meaning which will solve the problem of knowledge.

The three Parts of the dialogue discuss, at very different lengths, three different suggestions for what knowledge is: that it is perception, that it is true judgement, and that it is true judgement together with 'an account'. Before the first of these ideas is taken up and submitted to a long examination, Socrates helps to set up the inquiry with a demand for a general account of the notion in question: It is no good giving, as Theaetetus first does, a list of kinds of knowledge, because that will not tell us what *makes* those things kinds of knowledge. When Socrates makes this demand, as he does in several other Platonic dialogues, it is often objected by modern critics that, for many of our notions, there is no reason to suppose that we can give a definition which captures their various applications. In trying to understand the ways in which many different things can be called a 'game', for instance, or a 'machine', or 'honest', or 'natural', it is unlikely that we shall get far by looking for the kind of neat formula that pairs 'vixen' with 'female fox'. Why should we

---

[1] In his introduction to Miss Levett's translation, Burnyeat calls this Reading A, as opposed to another, Reading B, which understands the use of the "flux" material in this section as part of a long *reductio ad absurdum*, not something that Plato himself believes about the material world. Burnyeat, very carefully laying out the alternatives, leaves the decision between them (or yet another) to the reader. Anyone who wants to arrive at a serious conclusion about the meaning of the dialogue should work his or her way through Burnyeat's invaluable discussion of the arguments, both here and throughout the dialogue. The present, very much shorter, Introduction is indebted at several points to his, while both have their origins in past discussions which he and I have had about the dialogue.

The quotation in the following paragraph is from the Preface to his Introduction, pp. xii–xiii. See Myles Burnyeat, *The Theaetetus of Plato*, with text translated by M. J. Levett, revised by Myles Burnyeat (Hackett: Indianapolis & Cambridge, 1990).

expect there to be one for knowledge? The general point is well taken. But, equally, there is good reason to wonder whether Socrates, at least in this dialogue, is really looking for such a formula. The first suggestion offered by Theaetetus and taken up for discussion is that knowledge is perception, and this is certainly not a definitional formula. For one thing, Socrates makes it quite clear later on (165d) that it is not to be tested by merely considering whether 'perceive' and related terms can be substituted for 'know': It will not count against the proposal, for instance, that one can be said to see or hear dimly or faintly, but not to know something dimly or faintly. Moreover, it is immediately obvious that an identification of knowledge with perception will not fit the examples of knowledge that came up when Theaetetus was assembling a list. Those were all cases of a skill or a kind of expertise, and they are not kinds of perception. Indeed, the relations of expertise to knowledge as perception will turn out, rather later in Part I, to be altogether problematic.

The list is rejected for a more general reason, that it will not give any insight into the nature of knowledge. The idea that knowledge is perception is worth considering as possibly giving insight (though not if it is treated simply as a definition). Socrates examines the idea by working it up into a theory. First he says (151e) that Theaetetus' suggestion is what used to be maintained by Protagoras, a famous teacher who was a contemporary of Socrates and who appears in one of Plato's most brilliant dialogues, which bears his name. Protagoras claimed that 'man is the measure of all things', a saying which is here taken to mean that each man is the measure of the things that are *for him*: in the sense that if, for instance, one person finds the wind cold and another finds it warm, the right thing to say is that the wind is cold for the one and is warm for the other. If we say this, relativizing the statement made by each person to his or her own perception, neither person can be wrong. There is no room for error, since no claim is being made beyond what later philosophy was to call the 'immediate experience' of each person. Indeed, it is wrong to imply that there is any such thing as the state of the wind *in itself*. Protagoras' thought is that the wind is cold for one person and warm for another, and that is all there is to it. We may say in ordinary speech that the wind is 'really' warm, but that is at best a statistical judgement, to the effect that it is warm for more people than not. (There is an important question, to which we shall come back, whether Protagoras, sticking to his preferred forms of speech, can in fact make those statistical claims.)

From this, it is an easy step—one needs to ask, when reading the dialogue, how easy a step it is—to saying that everything which really happens can be reported simply by statements of immediate experience: Everything that is, in any sense, is for some individual. Individuals themselves, moreover, exist only as participants in these perceptual encounters. Understood in this way, Protagoras' doctrine turns out to be a version of the theory associated with Heracleitus (a philosopher who flourished around 500 B.C., whose work survives only in obscure but often deeply impressive fragments), that 'everything is in flux': nothing *is* anything without qualification. So Socrates is able to say (160d) that three theories come to the same thing: the view of Heracleitus and others, 'that all things flow like streams; of Protagoras, wisest of men, that man is the measure of all things; and of Theaetetus that, things being so, knowledge proves to be perception.' The central problem about the meaning of Part I of the *Theaetetus* is to decide the sense in which these three things do 'come to the same thing'.

In the course of reaching this conclusion, Socrates questions the basis on which people conventionally suppose that some of their experiences better tell them how things 'really' are than others do: the experiences they have when they are well, for instance, as opposed to those they have when they are sick, or waking experiences rather than those had in dreams. Indeed, most radically, he asks how one can tell whether one is awake or dreaming, and with this question he helped to start a sceptical tradition of questioning which, above all through the influence of Descartes, has continued into modern philosophy.

Developing the Heracleitean aspect of the view, Socrates brings in a theory about 'slow' and 'quick' motions. A modern critic will want to know whether this is a physical theory—a sort of scientific hypothesis— or, alternatively, a metaphysical model, a vivid way of representing the implications of sticking to Protagorean certainties. This question did not present itself to Plato in quite that form, and it is probably better to leave it to be settled in the light of other interpretative answers one needs to give. Above all, one needs to decide whether Plato brings in the Heracleitean material as something that he himself believes about the material world, or whether it is elicited simply as a consequence of the Protagorean view, itself constructed as offering the only sense in which perception could be knowledge—because immediate perception is the only kind of perception that, like knowledge, has a content which, necessarily, is true. (Plato gives several opportunities to ask whether knowledge and immediate perception do have some such feature in common.) If one takes the second line, the argument that leads to the rejection of the Heracleitean view constitutes a long *reductio ad absurdum* of Theaetetus' suggestion. It is not even plausible (this argument will go) that knowledge is perception, unless immediate perception is meant, to which Protagoras' maxim applies, but if one sticks to what is determined by that maxim, one has a Heracleitean world, and if the world is Heracleitean, no language or thought is possible (181–83).

It may be asked why, on this line, Protagoras has to lead to Heracleitus. Even if the only *knowledge* lies in the indubitable data of immediate perception—'hot for me now'—might we not be able to think of enduring things, such as material objects and people, as the objects merely of belief? There is more than one way of approaching that question, but Plato's outlook on it is probably shaped by an important assumption, one that has been shared in one form or another by many subsequent philosophers: that knowledge must be self-sufficient, and cannot need anything weaker than itself. If Protagoras' statements offer all the knowledge there is, they cannot presuppose an understanding of the world which rests in mere belief. If Protagorean statements constitute all the knowledge there is, then we must be able to understand the idea that what those statements present as a world is all the world there is.

Before he reaches his eventual refutation of the Heracleitean element, Socrates engages in some complicated maneuvres against the Protagorean element by itself. After rejecting some charges against Protagoras as purely *ad hominem*, he isolates the powerful objection that Protagoras' theory cannot account for its own claim to be true; indeed, if others think the theory false, they cannot be wrong in thinking this. (This is one of the first uses of a pattern of argument that has often been used since, by which a philosopher's theory is applied to itself.) It has been objected that in this argument Socrates falls back on an unrelativized sense of 'true' which Protagoras' theory has eliminated, but that objection raises some deeper questions. Protagoras' formulae did not rely on deploying a relativized sense of *true*. What were relativized were the perceptual terms, such as 'hot'. '*It is hot* is true for me' got its content by meaning 'It is hot for me'. In the light of this, Socrates' objection has force, because it is quite unclear what Protagoras might be doing in asserting things such as a philosophical theory, which cannot be expressed in such terms. He has, for instance, no way of claiming that someone who comes to accept his theory will be replacing false views with true ones.

At this point in the dialogue, it is indeed suggested that Protagoras might dispense with this claim altogether, and say instead that he can help people to replace states of mind that are less nice (for them) with states of mind that will be nicer (for them). But in reply to this, in one of Plato's most brilliant insights, Socrates points out that any claim to be able to do such a thing involves predictions, and a prediction about future Protagorean certainties cannot itself be a Protagorean certainty: no-one possesses a 'a criterion within himself' (178c) of what *will* be, even of what will be for himself. (There has been earlier, at 166b, a suggestion that Protagoras might have more success with statements about the past, reducing memories to present impressions.) In the case of the future (and the same applies, we may add, to those 'statistical' questions of *how many* people are having certain kinds of experience) nothing can eliminate the fact that two people can have conflicting beliefs, and there is nothing such as immediate experience to guarantee that one rather than the other is right. In these cases, unlike that of immediate experience, the parties are symmetrically related to the subject matter of the judgement—for neither of them is it peculiarly 'his'. It is precisely in such cases that there is room for expertise, and because of this, as Socrates makes clear, the objection against Protagoras, that he destroys his own claims to be wiser than others, is not merely personal rhetoric. Rather, by removing any realm for expertise, he removes one of the most important applications of the notion of knowledge. It begins to look as though, when at the beginning we turned away from kinds of expertise to immediate perceptual experience and its subjective certainties, we may have turned in the wrong direction.

Before we leave the first Part of the dialogue, another argument is offered against the claim that knowledge is perception, independently of the long discussion that ran through Protagoras and Heracleitus. This argument, which again has had an immensely important influence on later philosophy, rests on the idea that each sense can grasp items only of a certain kind, as sight relates to colors, hearing to sounds, and so forth. But knowledge requires concepts that are not tied in this way to any of the senses, concepts such as sameness, difference, and being. By which of the senses could we gather that a sound is something different from a color? Yet this is certainly something we know, and indeed everything we know involves concepts of this nonsensory kind. So knowledge is not perception, and this, at any rate, is something we have come to understand, as Socrates says. There are other things, as well, that we can come to understand in thinking through the long and wonderfully subtle route that has led to this conclusion.

The dialogue now takes a new turn, and Theaetetus offers a different suggestion: that knowledge is true judgement. This suggestion is also refuted, at the end of Part II (200–201), with a very swift argument which is a paradigm of the arguments still used to make this point. Someone may have a true belief about a certain matter, but it may be sheer luck that his belief is true—acquiring it as he did, he might just as well have acquired a false one. If this is so, his true belief does not count as knowledge. This is Plato's argument, and it is conclusive, even though it is not entirely clear from the example what contrast Plato has in mind between sound and unsound sources of belief. His scene is a law court, in which a lawyer or orator persuades the jury of something which may indeed be true, but where the conditions prevent their coming to a sound judgement on the matter. Does Plato want to emphasize the distinction between firsthand experience, such as an eye-witness might have, and mere secondhand testimony? Or rather the distinction between a thorough argument and a hasty, superficial one? The distinction does not make much difference to the use of the example for this particular purpose. It would make a difference if Plato were to try to develop an account of knowledge by building directly on such examples, as many modern theorists do, but as we shall see, he does not try to do so.

The jury example, which refutes the suggestion that knowledge is true belief, takes only a page at the very end of Part II. Almost all of the Part is devoted to a preliminary question, whether there can be such a thing as false judgement. Two lines of argument are introduced to suggest that false judgement may be impossible. One of them (188–89) is to the effect that false judgement must involve 'thinking what is not', which is hard to distinguish from thinking nothing, which, in turn, must be equivalent to not thinking at all. This kind of argument is not pursued in the *Theaetetus*, but is discussed at length in its successor dialogue, the *Sophist*; so, too, are the views of Parmenides and others already mentioned (180–81, 183–84), who held that everything is, in some sense, one, and that there can be no change or difference in the world. The *Sophist* displays, among other things, Plato's insight that these two issues, of falsehood and of change, are closely related to one another, and that both demand a close examination of ideas of 'being'.

The *Theaetetus* itself pursues only the other of the two problems about false judgement which it mentions, one that centers on the idea of taking, or mistaking, one thing for another. The argument is that this must be impossible. One cannot make a mistake about something one does not know (how could one even think of it?), and from this it follows that one cannot mistake two things one does not know for each other, nor something one does not know for something one knows. But, further, one cannot mistake for each other two things one knows, since this would be enough to show that one did not know them: If someone could say to himself, and believe it, 'Theaetetus is Theodorus', then he would literally not know what he was talking about. But of everything it is true that either one knows it or one does not know it, so these are all the conceivable combinations; so nothing can be mistaken for anything else. The upshot of the argument, in effect, is that it is a necessary condition of mistaking two items for one another that one should know them both, but this is also a sufficient condition of knowing them apart—that is to say, of not mistaking them.

Faced with this puzzle, Socrates introduces a possibility which helps the discussion to make a little progress. The assumptions of the argument are not quite true, because one may mistake something one perceives for something one knows, and the thing or person one perceives may be either known or unknown to one. Thus I may take someone I see in the distance for Theaetetus, who is known to me, and the person I see may in fact be someone else I know, such as Theodorus, or it may be a stranger. In such a case, I can make a mistake. Socrates works out all (or almost all) the possibilities that this new idea permits, illustrating it with a model of the mind as a wax block which takes and preserves images of items one has previously perceived. (The wax block is here a model just of memory, and not, as it became in later philosophy, of perception.) When I later perceive something, I may fit that perception to an image on my Block, and in this process there lies the possibility of mistake.

However, this model cannot be enough. We can make mistakes about things that are not perceived at all. Thus someone who asks what seven and five add up to may, if he is bad at arithmetic, think that the answer is eleven rather than twelve, and this mistake cannot be explained in terms of the Block. So a second model is introduced, of an aviary or birdcage. As one acquires knowledge of the numbers, one comes to possess, as it were, birds of knowledge which enter the cage of the mind. Seeking the answer to a given question, one tries to grasp the right bird, and one may grasp the wrong one, as the person does who thinks that eleven, rather than twelve, is what seven and five add up to.

With the Aviary, Plato introduces a distinction which is very important to the theory of knowledge, between dispositional knowledge and knowledge in action, represented by the model in terms of merely possessing a bird in the cage as opposed to holding it in one's hand. This distinction (which was later expressed by Aristotle in terms of having knowledge and using it) is useful, but it does not solve the present problem. If there is a puzzle of how one can take one thing one knows for another thing one knows, it arises just as much with the birds in the model—the Aviary has simply replaced one mistake with another. It is no help, either, to add to the Aviary, as Theaetetus rather desperately suggests, 'pieces of ignorance': That raises the same problem again, and some others as well.

Scholars have wondered how the Block and the Aviary are to be reconciled with things that Plato says elsewhere about knowledge, perception, and our grasp of arithmetic. These worries are pointless. The models are designed to deal with a specific question, and we should concentrate on the aspects of them that are relevant to that question. Thus 'having in one's aviary the bird that is the knowledge of eleven' merely represents the capacity to think of the number eleven, and we need not bother here with such matters as the metaphysical status of numbers. We are left with enough questions, even when we leave aside the irrelevant ones, and each of the models has given rise to much discussion. With the Aviary, for instance, are birds corresponding to seven and to five involved in the mistake that Socrates describes? Is there a separate bird labelled 'the sum of seven and five'? The best answer to these questions seems to be that only birds corresponding to eleven and to twelve are mentioned, and Plato leaves us with the unsolved problem of how one of them can be mistaken for the other, as it seems it must be if 'eleven' is thought to answer the question 'What are seven and five?'.

A question that needs to be considered is whether Plato intends to leave us with any positive result from the Wax Block. Does it make a contribution to understanding mistakes that involve perception, and fail only to the extent that it cannot explain others? Or does its failure to explain others mean that it gives too shallow a view even of the mistakes involving perception? Here we must bear in mind that our expectations of a theory to deal with these matters are different from Plato's. Modern philosophy thinks of these as semantic problems, concerned with the correct understanding of thoughts such as 'The sum of seven and five is eleven' or 'The man I can see over there is Theaetetus'; we are concerned with the ways in which reference to a given item may be secured by different expressions. If we expect a semantic theory, we shall probably think that the Block gives us no more help than the Aviary. Plato indeed says that we should consider thought processes in terms of speech that the soul conducts with itself, a fruitful line of inquiry which he takes further in the *Sophist*. But the distinctions deployed in the Block and the Aviary—unlike some of those made in the *Sophist*—do not belong to semantic theory, and there is no direct relation between semantic conceptions and processes mentioned in the models: There is no suggestion, for instance, that when I think 'The man I can see is Theaetetus', what I *mean* is 'My present perception of a man fits my memory of Theaetetus'. Rather, the idea is that the process of having the thought involves my fitting the perception to my memory. Plato tries to proceed by distinguishing perceptual and nonperceptual ways of grasping, or getting at, an item—a distinction which, disastrously, has no analogue when we get to the Aviary.

How exactly the distinction between 'ways of grasping' is supposed to help with the problems, and how exactly it relates to what would now be discussed as semantic problems of reference, are questions that deserve careful consideration. We need to ask, too, why Plato is so concerned here with questions of mistaken identity. A simple answer is that this is the puzzle he has chosen to discuss here, a puzzle expressed in terms of taking one thing for another; later, in the *Sophist*, he will turn to descriptive falsehood, such as that involved in saying that Theaetetus is flying when he is in fact sitting. But Plato's concentration in the *Theaetetus* on identity mistakes does not come only from the puzzle he happens to have set himself. It relates, rather, to a radical discovery which Plato had made, and which resonates through the later part of the *Theaetetus* and in the *Sophist*: that *knowledge is necessary for error*.

In his earlier work, Plato had tended to assimilate error to ignorance. Ignorance, not knowing about something, can be seen as simply the negation of knowledge. In the case of expertise or a skill, ignorance is, basically, a void, the lack of the appropriate knowledge; equally, with ignorance of particular items, not to know of something is to have no thought about it. The *Republic*, in particular, in its dealings with knowledge, is overwhelmingly concerned with two topics, the kinds of skill that distinguish the rulers from the other classes in the city, and the distinctive subject matters to which various states of mind, and various studies, such as philosophy and mathematics, are addressed. Neither of these concerns is well designed to bring out distinctions between ignorance and error. The *Theaetetus* and the *Sophist*, on the other hand, address the fundamental point that error is not only different from mere ignorance, but, in a certain way, excludes it. I can make a mistake about something only if I know it, or know something about it, or know enough about it for my false belief to be a belief *about that thing*. These requirements could only seem very puzzling, until Plato took the first steps towards making them clear. Those steps required him to ask what it was that one needed to know in order to be in a position to make a mistake, and this naturally led first to problems about misidentification.

This concentration carries over into Part III, where the proposal is taken up that knowledge may be true belief together with a *logos*—an 'account', as we may best translate this very versatile word. Part III is the most compressed, and in some ways the most problematical, part of the dialogue, and the first problem which has to be faced is that it never discusses what, as we may be inclined to think, it should be discussing. The proposal in terms of an 'account' immediately follows the example of the jury, which straightforwardly refutes, as we saw earlier, the conception of knowledge as merely true judgement. Knowledge and true judgement cannot be the same thing, says Socrates (201c). 'That's just what I once heard a man say,' Theaetetus replies, 'he said that true judgement with an account is knowledge.' After this, we would expect the dialogue to pursue the kind of 'account' that could have turned the jurors' true belief into knowledge—their being able to offer a more reliable basis of such a belief, perhaps, such as that available to an eye-witness, or their being able to rehearse the details in a consistent way and to give good explanations in the face of objections (such considerations had indeed put in an appearance in a much earlier dialogue, the *Meno*). But nothing of this sort follows: The 'man's' proposal is elaborated in terms of a 'dream' recounted by Socrates, of a very abstract theory which seeks to construct knowable complexes from unknowable elements. The jury example serves as a transition to a discussion which does not pursue such examples, but rather reverts to a more basic level and seeks a better understanding of what it is to know a certain thing, to have a grasp of it. This contributes in itself to finding out what knowledge is, but it also has a broader theoretical relation to the puzzling conclusion which has emerged, that error presupposes knowledge.

The Dream has been much discussed, and scholars are not entirely agreed on the extent to which it refers to the theories of any specific thinker, as well as differing about its exact interpretation. More generally, critics have been puzzled by the extremely unspecific nature of the model: We are told nothing about the kinds of elements or wholes involved. However, the lesson to be drawn from the discussion is perhaps so general that it does not matter what the unspecified elements might be. The lesson is that there is going to be a systematic difficulty with any proposal to the effect that knowledge of a certain item should be explained in terms of an analysis into *unknowable* elements (202e). Exploiting some claims—seemingly very dubious—about the relations between notions such as 'whole', 'sum', and 'totality', Socrates is able to argue that either the complex is a knowable whole which must have knowable parts, or, alternatively, if the supposed parts or elements really are unknowable, then they cannot be *parts* of a complex at all. These arguments may seem specious, but once more we must bear in mind what they are supposed to do. Relations of part and whole puzzled Plato, as they did other Greek thinkers, but here he is undoubtedly clear that there is a difference between the complex or 'syllable', S-followed-by-O, and the mere pair of items, S and O. He is also aware that you can spell the syllable SO, but you cannot spell the letter S. His point, rather, is that spelling cannot be an adequate analogy to knowing: However exactly wholes are constructed of parts, knowable wholes cannot be constructed of unknowable parts. We must remember all the time the challenging requirement which has now emerged, that one must know a thing if one is to have a true or false belief about it. It follows from this that each of a set of letters (or any other such elements) will have to be known, if one is to believe of it that, together with the others, it forms a given complex; but, according to the Dream's account, this is exactly what someone will have to believe of each element, if he is to know the complex.

After rejecting the theory of the Dream, Socrates turns back to consider, more generally, what 'an account' might be. He lays aside the sense in which it means 'an expression of thought', for the obvious reason that true belief itself can receive such an expression—this cannot be what turns belief into knowledge. Two further candidates each raise, in turn, a very general difficulty of principle. One goes back to the sort of idea offered in the Dream, that an 'account' of a whole is to be given by listing its parts, and raises another problem, independent of the special point (about the parts being themselves unknowable) which has already been made against the Dream. If someone gives a correct enumeration of parts, we can always raise the question whether he knew that this was a correct enumeration of them, or whether (for instance) he got it right by luck. So we shall have to say that knowing a thing, or what a thing is, involves having a correct conception of it and *knowing* its composition in terms of its parts; and this gets us no further with an account of knowledge. If, last of all, it is proposed that the 'account' of a particular thing which will give us knowledge of it is to be found in a grasp of its distinguishing characteristics, of what marks it off from other things, we run into a difficulty very directly related to those raised by the Block and the Aviary: unless one grasps a thing's distinguishing characteristics, so that one can tell it from other things, one cannot even think of it, and so cannot get as far as having any conception of it at all, even one that falls short of knowledge.

The arguments of Part III make no secret of the fact that they leave much to be discussed. But the third Part is like the second, which more explicitly spells out its difficulties, and also like the first, which extensively deploys a complex argument, to the extent that they all belie the formally negative conclusion of the dialogue. We do not know at the end of it what knowledge is, but we understand better than we did at the beginning what might be involved in knowing what knowledge is. Thanks to a discussion which, even by Plato's standards, is exceptionally rich, inventive, and profound, we have been alerted to basic and very general problems not only in understanding knowledge, but in grasping what true or false belief might be, and what it is to think about a particular thing, whether correctly or incorrectly.

Plato says in the *Republic* that the dialectician, the person who pursues philosophy, is one who 'sees things together'. The *Theaetetus*, though it is one of the most analytical of Plato's dialogues and also, superficially, one of the more discontinuous in its argument, has a remarkable power to help to do just that.

BRIEF BIBLIOGRAPHY

The major commentaries on the *Theaetetus* are all in English. The revised version of M. J. Levett's translation included in this volume was first published, together with a more extensive introduction, in Myles Burnyeat, *The Theaetetus of Plato* (Indianapolis: 1990).

A commentary on the Greek text will be found in
Lewis Campbell, *The Theaetetus of Plato*, with a revised text and English notes, 2nd edition (Oxford: 1883).

The following are commentaries on other English translations, which the reader may find it useful to compare with Miss Levett's.
Francis Macdonald Cornford, *Plato's Theory of Knowledge*. The *Theaetetus* and the *Sophist* of Plato translated with a commentary (London: 1935).
John McDowell, *Plato: Theaetetus*. Translated with notes (Oxford: 1973).

A study of the dialogue without translation is
David Bostock, *Plato's Theaetetus* (Oxford: 1988).

More general books on Plato that contain substantial discussions of the *Theaetetus* include
W. G. Runciman, *Plato's Later Epistemology* (Cambridge: 1962).
Kenneth M. Sayre, *Plato's Analytic Method* (Chicago & London: 1969).
Nicholas P. White, *Plato on Knowledge and Reality* (Indianapolis: 1976).

There are many articles that throw light on particular aspects of the dialogues. The reader who wants to take the discussion further should consult the helpful list given by Myles Burnyeat in *The Theaetetus of Plato*, pages 243–48.

SIX

Plato against the Immoralist

Plato continually confronted ethical sceptics of various kinds; in their most radical form they may perhaps be called, if rather anachronistically, "immoralists". Such characters typically offer a theoretical position in favour of thinking that self-interested and exploitative strategies are rational and that an attachment to ethical values such as justice is not, except perhaps for some instrumental or second-best reason.

In Athens at the end of the 5th century BC, in the time of Plato's youth, there was a current of thought to the effect that the values of the older generation had not been transmitted to its children, who had lost confidence in their fathers', and perhaps any, ethical code. It is a familiar theme in Aristophanes, and it is explicit, in relation to that time, in more than one Platonic dialogue, notably in the observation central to the argument of the *Meno*, that worthy men such as Thucydides son of Melesias had sons who turned out badly (*Men.* 92 seq.). Similar ideas, in relation to public morality, came from the reflection that whatever the aspirations of Periclean democracy at home, it kept the empire together by ruthless and unprincipled means.[1]

Whatever the historical sources of his concern, it is true that Plato considers such theories with a seriousness and urgency which have few parallels in the history of philosophy besides Machiavelli and Nietzsche. The seriousness with which Plato regards the immoralists comes out, revealingly, in the fact that he is prepared to regard a remarkably wide range of positions as immoralist. Correspondingly, he makes very exacting demands on any account of ethics that can hope to answer those positions. In reacting to the challenge of the immoralists, he is not satisfied with an account of ethics which merely meets, more or less, our everyday demands on the ethical life, and provides some motive for people, under normal conditions, to live that life. That is what Glaucon and

---

[1] The display of this idea in the Melian Dialogue (Thuc. 5, 84–111) has to be read in parallel with the account of Athens in the Funeral Speech (2, 35–46): neither need undermine the other. Plato, of course, believed that democracy was essentially unprincipled, in all its operations. One might read the startlingly vicious attack on Pericles (the most admired democrat) in the *Gorgias* (515 d ff.), as implying that the distinction offered by Thucydides cannot be sustained. (Notably, the charge against Pericles is that like other democrats he flattered the crowd, something explicitly denied by Thucydides, 2, 64.8.)

Adeimantus offer in Book II of the *Republic*, and Plato finds it as unsatisfactory as Thrasymachus' manifestly immoralist view. It is important
to ask exactly why he does so. In particular, it is important to answer
this question if we are to understand what Plato is seeking when he
moves the search for justice from the individual to the city.

Thrasymachus had said in Book I that justice was "the advantage of
the stronger" (338c). This was not offered as a *logos* or definition of justice: if it were, it would lead to the conclusion that since the stronger certainly pursues his own advantage, he must pursue justice, which Thrasymachus of course denies. Closer to what he principally wants to say is
his later statement (343c) that justice is an *allotrion agathon*, something
that always does somebody else some good. Thrasymachus' own account operates at the very primitive level of dividing agents (whether
they be individual people or cities) into two types, the strong and the
weak, and identifying justice simply as a device used by the strong to exploit the weak. This immediately raises the question of what makes one
agent stronger than another. In particular, what makes a collective agent,
such as a city or a group of bandits, strong? Indeed, what makes it a collective agent at all? The answer, as Socrates points out at 351 ff., must
be, to a significant degree, the practice of justice between the individuals
who form the collective agent. So Thrasymachus' primitive model must
be wrong.

This implies, further, that we cannot go on saying simply that justice
"always does someone else some good". Thrasymachus himself, when
he said this, did not mean that the only benefits secured by any just act
were benefits to someone other than the agent. He did not deny that
when the weaker party acts in accordance with justice, he secures a benefit for himself; he claimed that when this is so, it is only because of
power possessed by someone else who is stronger and who also gains a
benefit. Justice is always in someone else's interest, because when an
agent has an interest in doing some just act, it is always (leaving aside
errors, which are discussed at 339 seq.) because it is in someone else's
interest that this itself should be so.

However, not even this much will be true, once we accept that justice
helps to make collective agents strong. In place of Thrasymachus' view,
that justice is a device used by the strong to exploit the weak, we have the
idea put forward by Glaucon in Book II, that it is a device of the (individually) weak to make themselves (collectively) strong—to make themselves
stronger, in fact, than those who, before this association, were individually strong. On this account, Thrasymachus' first formulation, that justice
is the interest of the stronger, might be replaced with an equally crude slogan to the effect that it is the interest of the weaker. When the association
of the (previously) weak is formed, and the collective agent comes into

being, justice does each of the participants some good in a way that does not depend on its doing some other, exploiting, party some good.

Expressed in these terms, Thrasymachus' and Glaucon's accounts seem to be opposed to one another. It is not simply that they can easily be formulated in terms that are contrary to one another: the opposition may seem to us to extend to their ethical value. The Thrasymachean account, to the extent that it can be made coherent at all, is fiercely reductive and "unmasks" justice as an exploitative device. Glaucon's theory, on the other hand, is the ancestor of honourable contractualist accounts which show why justice is the basis of collective endeavours and the division of labour, and why it is of great value to human beings.

Granted these differences, it is significant that every party to the discussion in the *Republic* treats Glaucon's position (and its elaboration by Adeimantus) as essentially a somewhat refined version of Thrasymachus'. "I shall renew Thrasymachus' argument", Glaucon says (358b–c); and Adeimantus, who, like his brother, does not accept this outlook himself but wants to hear it refuted by Socrates, says that he has put as strongly as he can the view of Thrasymachus and others who agree with him (367b). The reason for this is, at one level, obvious. There is an opinion about justice that Thrasymachus on the one hand, and Glaucon and Adeimantus on the other, certainly share, despite their other differences: that the life of justice[2] is in some sense *a second best*. This is the issue that is picked out at the beginning of Book II, when the distinction is made between things that are valued in themselves, things that are valued for their consequences, and things that are valued for both (357–358).[3] What Socrates is encouraged to show, contrary to the common opinion which has been expressed in different ways by Thrasymachus and by Glaucon, is that justice falls into the first class. It is obvious that this is the issue, but there is another question to which the answer is rather less obvious: Why should the discussion take this form? Why are the standards for the value of justice raised so high? This is the question I shall take up in the rest of this paper.

The first point to emphasise is how radically individualistic the issue is taken to be. Glaucon's account might be said to show that we have an interest in pursuing justice, and if we assume that "we" is taken collectively, this is straightforwardly true. Indeed, as we have already seen,

---

[2] Granted the wide range of the term *dikaiosynê* in the *Republic*, the issue under discussion can be taken to be the value of the ethical life as a whole. "Justice" is the only appropriate translation of the term, and I shall stay with it, but the broad scope of the issue must be kept in mind.

[3] "Consequences" translates more than one expression: *ta apobainonta* 357b6; *hosa gignetai ap'autôn* d1, 358b6. There are also, of course, various references to specific consequences of justice, or rather of the reputation for it.

granted the collective "we", justice does not even come out as a second best—without justice there will be no collective "we". But the collective "we" has a tendency to unravel, and in the discussion with the immoralist, we are not allowed to assume it. The question whether *we* have reason to pursue justice is taken, by Socrates as it is by the immoralist, to refer to each of us. The question each of us must ask is: "What reason do I have to be just?"; "What does justice do for me?". This is the force of Socrates' earlier remark (352d): our discussion is not about a trivial matter, but about how one should live.[4]

The question, then, is about the best life for the individual, and already at 347e Socrates has said that he regards it as an issue "bigger" than Thrasymachus' first formulations, whether he was right in thinking that the life of the unjust person was better (*kreittô; ameinon* 358c) than that of the just. A closely related idea is that no-one would choose to be just if he had an alternative ("no-one is willingly just", 360c). The force of this is supposedly given to us by the thought-experiment which Glaucon presents. It is helpful, I suggest, to see Glaucon as presenting two different thought-experiments. The first is that of the ring of invisibility (359d–360)[5]; the second (360e–361d), that of the contrast between two men, one of whom has all the social rewards of justice without being really just, while the other has genuine justice and none of its conventional rewards.

Glaucon claims (on behalf of Thrasymachus and his associates) that someone armed with Gyges' ring would act unjustly, as (effectively) an exploitative and self-seeking bandit. An immediate objection to this is that, with regard to many people, it is not very plausible. Even if justice is in some abstract sense a second-best, a contractually acceptable midpoint (359a) between the best option (unpunished self-seeking) and the worst (being the victim of others' injustice), it is likely, if an ethical system is to work at all, that the motivations of justice will be sufficiently internalized not to evaporate instantaneously if the agent discovers invisibility. Moreover, it is not clear in any case how much such a thought-experiment tells one about justice in real life. What is the precise relation between the two questions: "How would you live if you could become

---

[4] . . . *chrê zên*: for the force of *chrê*, cf. B. Williams, *Shame and Necessity*, Berkeley 1993, 184 n 57, and materials cited there. By the time of Plato, the term bears a certain contrast with *dei*, which introduces rather a notion of (relatively) external necessity. So in the *Republic*, the idea that the just life is a life one "should" (*chrê*) live is contrasted with the idea that one "has to", is "forced to", live it: cf. 358c, people pursue justice as necessary, not as good.

[5] Often called, as I shall call it, "Gyges' ring", though the reference is explicitly to an ancestor of Gyges.

invisible at will?" and "What is the value of justice to you as things actually are?" To try to answer the second of these questions by answering the first, as Glaucon suggests by introducing Gyges' ring, is to compare reality with fantasy, and that hardly seems a helpful way to address the question of whether and why one wants the life of justice. It is rather like assessing one's actual sexual happiness by comparing one's sexual life with pornography.

The second thought-experiment is at least nearer to reality. It is not entirely clear, in fact, what the situation is supposed to be with one of the figures in the contrast, the misunderstood or mistreated man of justice,[6] but the general idea is clear enough, and the contrasted figure, the unjust man who enjoys a reputation of justice, is certainly familiar. One is invited to consider which of these figures one would prefer to be, and to consider this in the light of what one currently thinks about the value of justice. This gives a sharper sense than is given by the story of Gyges' ring to the question "Do you pursue justice for its own sake or for the sake of the rewards and the reputation that conventionally go with it?"

The question gains in force when we take into account Adeimantus' contribution. The general effect of that contribution is to reinforce Glaucon's insistence that we should "take away reputation" (367b), and we may wonder why, at the start of his remarks, Adeimantus says that the argument has not been adequately expressed by Glaucon, and that "what most needed saying has not been said" (362d). His point is that as Glaucon has put it, it is the enemies of justice such as Thrasymachus who emphasise the idea that people pursue justice for the sake of the conventional rewards. On the contrary, Adeimantus says, the real problem is that the friends of justice, people who are trying to encourage the young to be just, themselves emphasise those rewards, and so sell justice short; and he cites passages from the poets to this effect (prefiguring some of the objections that will be brought against them later in the dialogue).

All this, then, gives some sense to the idea of pursuing, and praising, justice "for its own sake". But now we must ask why Plato thinks it so important that we should value justice in this way. What is the point of insisting that one does not value justice properly unless one values it, in

---

[6] It is not clear, in particular, whether the genuinely just man "appears" unjust because he has an unconventional notion of justice, so that the world judges unfavourably the character he really has; or, rather, the world factually misunderstands what his character is. The latter makes a neater parallel with the contrasting case, but the former presents a more relevant challenge, and is also of course closer to the case of Socrates. I have discussed the passage (and considered the ideal of ethical autonomy which it expresses) in: *Shame and Necessity*, 98 seq. with n 46; and see n 47 for the point that the reference to Aeschylus does not help.

this sense, for its own sake? A modern reader may easily be misled at this point, and take the answer to this question to be more familiar than it is. He or she may take Plato to be thinking of a pure, self-sufficient moral motivation, in terms of which the agent does good or right actions simply because that is what they are, and for no other reason. (The starkest version of such an idea is to be found in Kant, but it takes more forms, and is more generally familiar, than its strictly Kantian expression.) This implies that if one reflects on the value of a moral life, one will insist simply on its moral value: this is what counts as "intrinsic" value, as being concerned with justice and other moral values for their own sake, and it is contrasted with measuring those values against anything else at all, such as one's own welfare. But this, certainly, is not Plato's concern. The argument with the immoralist can be formulated only because there is one, univocal, kind of question in practical reason, "How should I live?", "What is the best life?", "How shall I do best?", to which Thrasymachus and his friends give the wrong answer, and Socrates, on behalf of justice, will give the right answer. It is not that the pursuit of justice "for its own sake" has a quite special, moral, value which vindicates itself and cannot in principle be measured by any other sorts of consideration. The question of its value, rather, is the question of what makes a life worth living, a question to which other "non-moral" goods might in principle, as the immoralist suggests, provide the answer.

Another way of putting the point is that the idea of "pursuing justice for its own sake" occurs in Socrates' answer to the question, not in the question itself. The question is not "What is the value of justice pursued for its own sake, as opposed to the sake of its consequences?"—a question to which the answer is, virtually by definition, "moral value". The question is: "What is the value of justice?", and Socrates' answer is: "It has no value (really), unless it has value when it is pursued for its own sake." So the question remains: Why does Plato's Socrates think this? Why does he raise the standards for the vindication of justice so high? Why must it pass the test of being desirable "for its own sake", in isolation from all social rewards and encouragements?

The answer to this question has an ethical aspect and a political aspect, and in virtue of the analogy between the individual and the city, which plays such an important part in the *Republic*, they are closely tied to each other. Before we come to the political aspect and to the analogy, however, it will be helpful in understanding the ethical aspect if we look outside the *Republic*, to the *Gorgias*.[7] This dialogue presents conversations that Socrates has with three speakers, Gorgias, Polus, and Callicles,

---

[7] It is generally supposed that the *Gorgias* is earlier than Books II to X (at least) of the *Republic*, but nothing turns on this for the present discussion.

who take in succession increasingly radical positions. The discussions are structured by the use that is made of three distinct value-oppositions, all of them important to Greek ethical life. One is the contrast between *dikaion* and *adikon*, the just and the unjust: this relates, as in the *Republic*, to values that concern fair dealing with others, respect for their persons and their property, and generally a prohibition on exploiting them.

The terms of the second distinction, *kalon* and *aischron*, are harder to translate, and the contrast between them harder to summarize. They can have a purely aesthetic sense, but in their connection with action and character, they relate centrally to dimensions of honour and shame. This is often in Greek thought understood in an external and conventional sense, so that it is a matter of one's reputation, how one is seen or spoken of, but the values can be more deeply internalized, and the distinction becomes one between things that agents can be proud of, and think well of themselves for having done or been, as opposed to things for which they despise themselves, feel ashamed or embarrassed or contemptible.[8]

The contrast, lastly, between *agathon* and *kakon*, good and bad, is often, in the course of the discussion, interpreted in terms of self-interest: one seeks the *agathon* in seeking what is best for oneself. The basic idea, however, is something rather more general and abstract, the idea of what an agent has good reason to pursue or not. These are the terms which are, throughout these conversations, unquestionably tied to the conclusions of practical reason, and it makes no sense, in this discussion, to say that an agent knows that something is (on balance) *kakon*, and that he has decided that this is what (on balance) he has reason to pursue.

Gorgias, the first speaker, accepts the conventional idea that all these values go together, so that what is *dikaion* is also *kalon* and *agathon*: we have reason to pursue the just and should think well of ourselves and others for doing so. It is in these terms that he defends his practice of rhetoric. Polus enters the discussion to offer a more radical position, which separates *dikaion* and *agathon*: we should stop thinking that the *dikaion* is what we have reason to do. However, he takes a less radical line with the dimension of *kalon* and *aischron*, and is manoeuvred by Socrates into claiming both that to behave unjustly is *aischron*, and that what is *aischron* is *kakon*—that is to say, that we have reason to avoid it.[9] This is inconsistent with his attempt to hold that injustice is not *kakon*.

---

[8] For the role of shame in Greek (and, indeed, our own) ethical experience, see: *Shame and Necessity*, in particular chapter IV and endnote 1.

[9] Gorg. 474c seq. *Kakon* and *aischron* mostly appear in this discussion in their comparative forms.

Polus' mistake is to sustain at once a conventional link between *dikaion* and *kalon* (just behaviour is admired, injustice is something to be ashamed of), and a natural link between *kalon* and *agathon* (we have reason to do what will make us admired, no reason to do what will make us ashamed of ourselves). The last speaker, Callicles, sees Polus' mistake, and takes the further step of denying the conventional link between *dikaion* and *kalon*. In doing this, he wants to keep the link between *kalon* and *agathon*: the rational person will want to be admired and envied, to think well of himself, and not to be an object of contempt, but he will bring this about, Callicles urges, through power and the exploitation of others, having no concern for considerations of justice.[10]

Callicles is the most brilliantly represented and intimidating of Plato's immoralists, and it will be disappointing for the friends of the ethical life if Socrates fails to refute him. He is, supposedly, refuted, but it is very easy to feel that Plato, in constructing the discussion, has deliberately dealt Callicles a hand of losing cards. Although there are several complexities in the argument, Callicles effectively ends up (from about Gorg. 491 onwards) defending a crudely gluttonous form of hedonistic activity, which very few are likely to envy. But this was not supposed to be the idea. The immoralist was supposed to be a rather grand, powerful, stylish figure—the aesthetic echoes of *kalos* are relevant here—whom others, if they were honest, could admire and envy; but he has ended up, in Socrates' refutation, as a low addict or at best a heartlessly boring *bon viveur*, whom anyone with any taste would despise. It is easy to think that Socrates wins the argument only by changing the subject.

However, there is more to the strategy than this suggests. Callicles (491b) wants to say that the successful unjust man will be *kalos*, and admirable in recognizable ways: he will, for instance, be intelligent and brave. But the direction of Socrates' argument, which brings it close to the concerns of the *Republic*, is to suggest that Callicles has no right to suppose that, on the assumptions he and his unjust man are left with, there could be a basis either for admiring virtues such as intelligence and courage, or for thinking that the unjust man could actually sustain them. How does the immoralist explain the values of courage and intelligence? He may do so in terms of political power: but quite early in their discussion (488–489), Socrates shows that there is a conflict between such a political conception and Callicles' ideal of an individual person who is

---

[10] My very bare summary follows what I take to be the points in the dialogue that are most significant for the present question. Needless to say, other important patterns can be extracted from what is a very rich set of arguments (which also raise some specially acute questions about Plato's use of fallacy).

"better", since political power is a collective enterprise, in which the individuals are not going to be in his sense "better", above all in a democracy.[11] The alternative is that the immoralist explains the value of these human qualities simply in terms of the satisfaction of desire—that is to say, as Plato puts it, in terms of pleasure. But that is not convincing, since someone can think of himself as *kalos* only if he can admire himself, and that implies grounds on which others can admire him, which implies more generally that one person can admire another.[12] The criterion which consists merely in the individual's desires being satisfied provides no basis for admiration at all. The immoralist is left only with hedonism.

Socrates in the *Gorgias* argues that any basis of admiration implies *taxis* and *kosmos* (503d seq.), order and discipline, and these, applied to the soul, constitute justice. This implies, in effect, the Socratic idea of the unity of the virtues, and the immoralist may well say that this is to go too fast. Even if Callicles was not very good at showing it, perhaps the immoralist can have his own disciplines, not including justice.

Now we are precisely at the point that we had reached in the *Republic*. We are asking what is *agathon*, what makes a life worth living. The immoralist would like this to include some things that are not merely pleasant, but worthy of admiration: he wants there to be, as we might say, a basis for value. He would hope that these might include courage and intelligence, say, but not justice. Socrates wants to say, first, that if we think solely in terms of desire-satisfaction, there will be no basis for value, nothing to admire at all, and, moreover, life will not be worth living, since it will be a mess. Some discipline is necessary for there to be any stability, and that requires there to be a product of thought, something that can be better or worse, which indeed implies that there are some characters to be admired, others to be despised (the dimension of the *kalon*). So far the *Gorgias*, and the same point is of course repeatedly made in the *Republic*. But Socrates in the *Republic* will offer further arguments to bind justice more closely into these thoughts, and he addresses them to two different parties. To the immoralists he says: You need some structure and discipline if life is not to be a mess, and (as this itself implies) there is something to be admired, some basis of value. I shall show you that the structure and discipline which you must accept if you are to admire and value anything (say, courage and intelligence) are

[11] In connection with the later discussion of Pericles, Socrates is in effect presenting Callicles with a dilemma for the aristocratic or oligarchic immoralist: the Athenian empire, which was run in ways he should admire, was run by a democracy. Cf. n 2, above.

[12] It is a Calliclean idea, obvious in his opening speech about nature and convention (482e seq.), that the respectable secretly admire the ruthless, unless they have been intimidated into not doing so. This is very close to the inspiration of the Gyges' ring story.

such that you must also admire and value justice; and "admire and value" means, admire and value for its own sake. To the friends of justice, Glaucon and Adeimantus, he adds: I am not going merely to show the immoralists that they cannot do without justice; I am going to show them that they cannot do without valuing it for its own sake, which is what you wanted in the first place.

There is a political aspect, as I said earlier, to the same argument. The "analogy" between the individual and the city which is introduced at *Rep.* 368d is officially put forward to help us understand justice in the individual: it is as though the same message were written in larger letters. (In fact, the whole development of the *Republic* shows that the matter of justice in the city is pursued, not only to help with the original question, but for its own sake.) The basis of the supposed analogy is in fact dubious, and I have argued elsewhere[13] that Plato moves between two different principles which pull in different directions: that the account of a given character in a city and in an individual is the same, and that a city has a certain character if all, most, or a leading section of its citizens have that character. Plato's political conclusions, I suggested, exploit this ambiguity. In particular, he implies both that in the just city all the citizens are just (which is what one might hope), and also that citizens of the lower classes are no more just than the lower sections of the soul are rational, which is why they need to be dominated by the Guardians.

However this may be, it is certainly true that the lower classes in the city, like the lower sections of the soul, cannot look after themselves: they have no inherent principles of order and discipline. The order and discipline that they need come from elsewhere: in the political case, from the Guardians. This means that the Guardians must be ethically self-sufficient, and this means that they must be able to see that justice is worth pursuing for its own sake. If justice were, as Glaucon explains, valuable only as a second-best, there would be no motive for the Guardians to be just, since they are not in anyone else's power. The constitution of Plato's city essentially depends on justice being good in itself, or for its own sake.

Plato could not use this conclusion, of course, to *demonstrate* that justice was good in itself. Those who accept Glaucon's account will reasonably not trust Plato's constitution. For them, a just city will reject ethical aristocracy and will consist of imperfect citizens keeping an eye on each other. This is why the ethical and the political parts of Plato's enterprise

---

[13] "The Analogy of City and Soul in Plato's Republic", in: Lee, Mourelatos and Rorty (eds.), *Exegesis and Argument: Studies in Greek Philosophy presented to Gregory Ulastos*, Assen 1973 [= chap. 7 below—Ed.].

help each other. The ethical argument we have already followed suggests that people's lives will be incoherent if they are the sort of people who (the political analogy suggests) form the lower two classes of the city, and if, in addition, they try to be ethically self-sufficient. Democracy, in particular, is the project of such people trying to be ethically self-sufficient as a collective, and that is a doomed venture which ends in tyranny, just as the immoralist (Plato claims), though he would like to be a free spirit who admires and is admired by some other free spirits, can in the end be nothing but a sordid slave of desire.

We need not accept Plato's outlook, and not many people do. But one needs to go on a long ethical journey to find what exactly it is that one rejects, and it will be important, for each person, to decide what this will be. Certainly, the claim that justice has to be valued in itself, or for its own sake, is not a mere moralistic assumption of Plato's, and he has not simply set himself a gratuitously difficult task of demonstrating it. It is deeply rooted in the whole enterprise. One important question we are left with now, reading the *Republic* in a very different, and differently democratic, time, is not so much whether we agree with Socrates or with Glaucon, but how far they might both be right. What is it to admire and practice justice "for its own sake"? Perhaps the lesson of Glaucon's argument is just this, that precisely because we need justice as an instrument we need to admire it for its own sake; and that what we need to do is to learn how to do this, while not forgetting why we are doing so.

SEVEN

The Analogy of City and Soul in Plato's *Republic*

In making the first construction of the city, there is an assumption that it should be able to tell us something about δικαιοσύνη* in the individual: we look to the larger inscription to help us read the smaller one, 368D. But, as Plato indeed implies, the larger inscription will help with the smaller only if they present the same message. What is Plato's reason for expecting the same message? Basically, it is that δίκαιος applies to both cities and men, and that it signifies one characteristic: "So the just man will not differ at all from the just city, so far as the character of justice is concerned, but will be like it" (καὶ δίκαιος ἄρα ἀνὴρ δικαίας πόλεως κατ' αὐτὸ τὸ τῆς δικαιοσύνης εἶδος οὐδὲν διοίσει, ἀλλ' ὅμοιος ἔσται 435B). That there should be some kind of analogy between cities and men in respect of their being δίκαιος would seem to be a presupposition of asking the question "what is δικαιοσύνη?" and expecting one answer to it.

Indeed at 434E Plato says that when we transfer what we have said about the city back to the man, we may find that it does not work out; but the moral will be that we should go back and try again and "perhaps by looking at the two side by side and rubbing them together, we may make justice blaze out, like fire from two sticks. . . ." Plato clearly has a fair confidence that this technique will work: his confidence is in what I shall call the *analogy of meaning*.

At 435E, however, he takes what is in fact a different tack. Proceeding there to the division of the soul, he seems at first sight to be backing up the "analogy of meaning." "Are we not absolutely compelled to admit that there are in each one of us the same kinds and characteristics as there are in the city? For how else could they have got there? It would be ridiculous to imagine that among peoples who bear the reputation for being spirited . . . the spirited character in their states does not come from the individual citizens, etc." This looks as though it means that we call a city, people, etc. "spirited" because most or all of its individual persons can be called "spirited"—and for certain terms, this style of account is very reasonable.

---

* A glossary of untranslated Greek words can be found at the end of this essay. —Ed.

But for such terms (the three examples that Plato gives at 435E correspond, it is worth noting, to the three elements of his analogy), so far from having something that backs up the previous principle of finding a common characteristic in virtue of which both cities and men are called so-and-so, we have something that defeats it. For if we say that "F" is applied to the city just because it is applied to the men, we have already explained how the term can be applied to both cities and men, and to go on from there to look for a similar explanation of how "F" applies to men is at least pointless, since the phenomenon which set off the search for the analogy in the first place, viz. the fact that "F" applies to both cities and men, has already been explained. If, moreover, the rule for applying "F" to cities is taken as itself the common λόγος that we were looking for, then we have not just pointlessness but absurdity, since the common λόγος will have to be something like "x is F if and only if x has constituent parts which are F," which leads to a regress. Thus the argument at 435E, so far from backing up the "analogy of meaning," defeats it.

Plato in any case does not seem to think that every term which can be applied to both cities and men obeys the rule of 435E. Thus at 419A ff. (the beginning of Book IV), answering Adeimantus' objection that the guardians get a thin time of it, Socrates says that a city's being sublimely happy does not depend on all, most, the leading part, or perhaps any, of its citizens being sublimely happy, just as a statue's being beautiful does not depend on its parts being severally beautiful. This contradicts the principle of 435E, and certainly contains a truth. Leaving the importantly, and indeed deeply, contentious case of "happy," we can certainly agree that a large crowd of sailors is not necessarily a crowd of large sailors, while an angry crowd of sailors, on the other hand, is a crowd of angry sailors. So what Plato has here are two classes of term: one class ("angry," "spirited," etc.) obeys the rule of 435E, which we may call *the whole-part rule*; while the other class ("large," "well-arranged," etc.) does not.

However, Plato does not proceed along the lines of this distinction. Rather, for an indeterminately large class of terms, possibly including δικαιοσύνη, he wants to say both:

(a) A city is F if and only if its men are F;

and

(b) The explanation of a city's being F is the same as that of a man's being F (the same εἶδος of F-ness applies to both).

The combination of these, as we have already seen, could lead to a regress, but Plato avoids this by holding (a) only for the city-man relation, and not for the relation of the man to any further elements—that is to say, he does not take (a) as itself identifying the λόγος of F-ness. Thus "F" does not occur again in the explanation of what it is for a man to be F: at that stage, it is reduced to something else. Thus the explanation of a man's being δίκαιος, and the λόγος of δικαιοσύνη in general, are alike given us by the formula.

(c) Each of the elements (λογιστικόν, θυμοειδές, and ἐπιθυμητικόν) does its job,

which of course implies

(d) λογιστικόν rules.

Applying (a) to the particular case of δικαιοσύνη, we get

(e) A city is δίκαιος if and only if its men are;

while at the same time, for a city as for a man, we have the requirement that its being δίκαιος consists in (c)'s being true. But what does (c) mean of a city? For like cities, the elements of cities consist of men: and how are the characters of these elements to be explained? Here it seems the whole-part rule must certainly apply—it was, we remember, with reference to these characteristics that Plato introduced us to it. We shall have

(f) An element of the city is logistic, thymoeidic, or epithymetic if and only if its men are.

But the δικαιοσύνη of a city, as of anything else, consists in (c)'s being true. So in order to be δίκαιος a city must have a logistic, a thymoeidic, and an epithymetic element in it. Since it must have an epithymetic element, it must, by (f), have epithymetic men: in fact, it is clear from Plato's account that it must have a majority of such men, since the lowest class is the largest. So a δίκαιος city must have a majority of epithymetic men. But an epithymetic man—surely—is not a δίκαιος man; if he is not, then the city must have a majority of men who are not δίκαιοι, which contradicts (e).

This contradiction is, I believe, powerfully at work under the surface of the *Republic*. Remaining still at a very formal and schematic level, we get another view of it by asking what follows if we accept (e) and also take the analogy between city and soul as seriously as Plato at some points wants us to. Since the men are δίκαιοι, of each man (d) will be true, and λογιστικόν (no doubt in some rather restricted way) will be at work in each member even of the lowest and epithymetic class. Some minimal exercise of λογιστικόν would seem to be involved in bringing it about that each man sticks to his own business, which is the most important manifestation of social δικαιοσύνη: though it is very notable that Plato repeatedly uses formulations abstract and impersonal enough to prevent such questions pressing to the front. (A very striking example of this is at the point where δικαιοσύνη is first, after the hunt through the other cardinal virtues, pinned down. At 433C–D we have a reference to the beneficent effects of the φρόνησις of the guardians, but by contrast with this, "that which is in" [τοῦτο . . . ἐνόν] even slaves, artisans, women, etc., and which makes the city good, is represented not as a characteristic of theirs, but merely as a *fact*, that each minds his business [ὅτι τὸ αὑτοῦ ἕκαστος εἷς ὢν ἔπραττε καὶ οὐκ ἐπολυπραγμόνει, 433D4–5]. Clearly, this fact cannot be "in" these people—the question is, what has to be in these people to bring about this fact.)

But now if the epithymetic class has in this way to exercise some λογιστικόν, and this helps it to stick to its tasks, recognise the rulers and so forth, and if we read this result back through the analogy to the individual soul, we shall reach the absurd result that the ἐπιθυμητικόν in a just soul harkens to λογιστικόν in that soul through itself having an extra little λογιστικόν of its own. Recoiling from this absurdity, we recognize that in the individual soul, the ἐπιθυμητικόν cannot really harken; rather, through training, the desires are weakened and kept in their place by λογιστικόν, if not through the agency, at least with the co-operation, of θυμοειδές. If with this fact in our hand we come back once more across the bridge of the analogy to the city, we shall find not a δίκαιος and logistically co-operative working class, but rather a totally logistic ruling class holding down with the help of a totally thymoeidic military class, a weakened and repressed epithymetic class; a less attractive picture. The use of the analogy, it begins to seem, is to help Plato to have it both ways.

Does Plato intend us to accept the proposition (e), that the citizens of the δίκαιος city are themselves δίκαιοι? The question is not altogether easy. The passage 433–4, from which I have already quoted the most notable evasion, manages to create the impression that the answer must be "yes" without, so far as I can see, ever actually saying so. An important contributory difficulty here is the point which has been often remarked, that the earlier account of σωφροσύνη has left δικαιοσύνη with not enough work to do, so that it looks like merely another way of describing the same facts. In the case of σωφροσύνη, he comes out and says that it is a virtue of all citizens (431E–432A); but the route to this conclusion has several formulations which make even this seem shaky (431B–D, particularly: "the desires in the many and vulgar are mastered by the desires and the wisdom in the few and superior"). The tension is always the same. The use of the analogy is supposed in the upshot to justify the supreme rule of a logistic element in the city, where this element is identified as a class of persons; and it justifies it by reference to the evident

superiority of a soul in which the logistic element controls the wayward
and chaotic desires. But this will work only if the persons being ruled
bear a sufficient resemblance to wayward and chaotic desires—for instance, by being persons themselves controlled by wayward and chaotic
desires. And if they are enough like that, the outcome of Plato's arrangements will be less appealing than first appears.

Suppose, then, we give up the proposition that all or most people in
the δίκαιος city are δίκαιοι; thus we give up the whole-part rule for
δικαιοσύνη. We might, at the same time, put in its place something
rather weaker than the whole-part rule, which we might call *the predominant section rule*:

(g) A city is F if and only if the leading, most influential, or predominant citizens are F.

The effect of using (g) with δικαιοσύνη is of course to cancel any implication that the citizenry at large are δίκαιοι—it merely gives us something
that we knew already, that the guardians are δίκαιοι. But the importance
of (g) is in no way confined to the case of δικαιοσύνη—it is a rule which
Plato appeals to often, and particularly in his discussions of the degenerate forms of city in Book VIII. It is in the light of the *predominant section*
idea that we should read the reiteration of the whole-part idea which introduces those discussions at 544D. If we look at some of the things that
Plato says about the degenerate cities, this will lead us back again to the
just city, and to the ineliminable tension in Plato's use of his analogy.

With the degenerate cities, it is clear in general that not all the citizens
are of the same character as the city, and there are references to citizens
of a different character. The tyrannical city is, not surprisingly, that in
which there is most emphasis on the existence of citizens different in
character from the tyrant: 577C "the whole, so to speak, and the best element is dishonourably and wretchedly enslaved"; cf. 567A, 568A "the
best people hate and flee the tyrant." In other kinds of city, there may
be a minority of citizens of a character inferior to that of the city as a
whole: there may be a few men of tyrannical character in cities where the
majority is law-abiding (575A); if few, they have little influence, but if
there are many, and many others who follow their lead, then they produce a tyrant (575C). We can notice here that even in a tyranny there is
a requirement that a substantial and influential section of the citizens
should share the character of the city. Again, at 564D we are told that
the "drones" are already present in an oligarchy, but in a democracy
they become the leading element (τὸ προεστὸς αὐτῆς).

The democracy, however, presents a special difficulty. Plato says that
the distinguishing mark of a democracy is that it is the state in which one
finds men of every sort (παντοδαποί, 557C), and like a garment of many

colours it is decorated with every sort of character (πᾶσιν ἤθεσιν, ibid.).
Having said this, it would be impossible for Plato to say that all the citizens were "democratic" men as described at 561D *al.*—always shifting, without expertise in anything, prepared to indulge any ἐπιθυμία, etc. Nor should it be easy for him to say that the majority are such men. Yet this is precisely what he has to say. The "predominant section" rule says that the character of the state is derived from that of the ruling citizens. In the cases where the rulers are few, this will not necessarily imply much about the character of other citizens, for the few may hold their power by force, threats, etc. (as in the case of the tyrannical state, already considered: and cf. 551B, the origin of the oligarchy). Plato says that a democracy will also come into being by threat of force, 557A—but this is merely vis-à-vis the ruling oligarchs. A democracy is a state in which the many rule, and if it gets its character from that of its rulers, then the majority must have a "democratic" character. This, on the face of it, sorts none too well with the claim that the democratic state will particularly tend to contain all sorts of character—the "democratic" character seems in fact to be a special sort of character. Moving between the social and the individual level once more, Plato seems disposed to confound two very different things: a state in which there are various characters among the people, and a state in which most of the people have a various character, that is to say, a very shifting and unsteady character.

These people, moreover, are the same people that constitute the lowest class in the δίκαιος city; so we are led back once more to the question we have already encountered, of how, consistently with Plato's analogy and his political aims, we are to picture their quiescent state when λογιστικόν (in the form of other persons) rules. It may be said that in the difficulties we have found about this, we have merely been pressing the analogy in the wrong place. The essential analogy here might be claimed to be this: just as there is a difference between a man who is controlled by λογιστικόν and a man who is controlled by ἐπιθυμία, so there is such a difference between states, and to try to infer the condition of the epithymetic class when it is ruled from its condition when it is not ruled is like trying to infer the condition of a man's ἐπιθυμίαι when *they* are ruled from their condition when they are not. What we are concerned with (it may be said) is the healthy condition of man or city, and relative to that the difference between a good and a bad state of affairs can be adequately—and analogously—explained for each.

Such attempts to ease out the difficulties only serve to draw attention to them. For, first, certain things *can* be said about the ἐπιθυμίαι when they are "ruled." For instance, there is the notable difference between a man who has his ἐπιθυμίαι under control, so that he does not act on them except where appropriate, but for whom they are nevertheless very active, so that control is the outcome of struggle and inner vigilance; and a man whose λογιστικόν has achieved inner peace. That inner peace, again, might be of more than one kind: some ἐπιθυμίαι might be mildly and harmoniously active, or there may have been some more drastically ascetic achievement—*solitudinem faciunt, pacem appellant** could apply to inner peace as well. But these differences, read back into the political case, precisely revive the earlier problems. Inner peace is what Plato must want, but that in the political case requires the allegiance of the epithymetic element, and we are back to the question of how we are to picture that being secured. Again, a difference between the barely self-controlled man and the man of inner peace is that the first has some ἐπιθυμίαι which the latter does not have—if a man has inner peace, then some ἐπιθυμίαι he will have eliminated or never had. But does the difference between the good city and democracy then lie partly in the emergence in the latter of extra and more violent epithymetic persons? If so, then Plato has to explain why the working class even in the good city has to be thought of as though they were already potentially such persons. If not, we are faced with the original problem once more, of what it was in those potentially violent persons that kept them in their place in the good city.

Let us suppose that it is the inner peace model that Plato has in mind, and that it is achieved through the exercise of λογιστικόν, on a modest scale, by the individuals in the working class. (They might have been said to possess some measure of ὀρθὴ δόξα, if that were not inconsistent with the eccentric theory of knowledge which the *Republic* presents). If their individual λογιστικόν helps in keeping the workers in their place, then (as we saw earlier) the analogy is no longer in full working order, since that feature cannot be read back into the soul without absurdity. But let us waive that point, and ask what has to be presupposed to keep even the remnants of the analogy going for Plato's purposes. It is not enough that in its economic function, the role of the lowest class should bear some analogy to the role of the ἐπιθυμίαι in individual life. For if we stick merely to the nature of certain roles or functions, no argument will have been produced against the view of Plato's democratic enemy, that those roles or functions can be combined with the business of ruling. Criticism of Plato often concentrates on his opinion that ruling is a matter of expertise; but he needs more than that opinion to reach his results in the *Republic*, and has to combine with it a set of views about what characteristics and talents generally co-exist at the level of individual psychology. In that area, he has to believe not only that λογιστικόν comes in two sizes (as we might say, regular size and king size), but also

---

* Tacitus, *Agricola* 30: "They make a desolation and call it peace." —Ed.

that the talents and temperament that make good soldiers go with thymoeidic motivations, and the talents and temperament that make good workers go with epithymetic motivations.

Of these, the former looks plausible enough—indeed, soldierly temperament and thymoeidic motivation are perhaps necessarily connected (that is a question we shall come back to). Again, logistic supremacy and fitness to be a guardian are of course for Plato necessarily connected. But how about epithymetic motivation and fitness to be a δημιουργός? Not even Plato at his loftiest can have believed that what actually qualified somebody to be a cobbler was the strength of his ἐπιθυμίαι. The most he can have thought is that the sort of man who made a good cobbler was one who had powerful ἐπιθυμίαι; and this is also the least he can think, if he is to keep any of the analogy going and justify the subordinate position of cobblers by reference to their epithymetic disposition. So what we have to believe, it seems, is that cobblers are characteristically men of powerful passions—of more powerful passions, indeed, than soldiers—who nevertheless have enough rational power to recognize the superiority of philosopher kings when there are philosopher kings, but become unmanageably volatile when there are no philosopher kings.

There have been those who thought that the working classes were naturally of powerful and disorderly desires, and had to be kept in their place. There have been those who thought that they were good-hearted and loyal fellows of no great gifts who could recognize their natural superiors and, unless stirred up, keep themselves in their place. There can have been few who have thought both; Plato in the *Republic* comes close to being such a one, even though we can recognize that his heart, and his fears, lie with the first story. His analogy helps him to combine both stories, in particular by encouraging us to believe in an outcome appropriate to the second story from arrangements motivated by the first.

What about θυμοειδές and the military class? Here there is a slightly different kind of tension in the structure. At no point, we must remember, does the structure present a simple contrast of the psychological and the political, for on both sides of that divide we have two sorts of thing: elements, and a whole which is affected by those elements. On the political side we have classes, and a state which is affected by which class is predominant among them (hence the "predominant section rule" we have already looked at); the theory is supposed to yield both an analysis and a typology of states. On the psychological side, we have "parts of the soul," and persons in which one "part" or another is dominant; this yields, first, a classification of motives within the individual, and, second, a typology of character. The difficulties we have just been considering, about the epithymetic class, are generated across the political-psychological boundary, in the relations that Plato finds between, on the one hand, the working class and a state dominated by that class, and on the other hand, epithymetic motivation and a character dominated by such motivation. In the case of the θυμοειδές, the most interesting difficulty (it seems to me) breaks out earlier, in the relations between the type of motivation that is represented by this "part of the soul," and the type of character that is produced by its predominance. Once the type of character is established, the political consequences follow, granted Plato's general outlook, fairly easily. Indeed, it is just the appropriateness of those consequences that seems to dictate the connection of ideas on the psychological side; whatever may be the case elsewhere in the *Republic*, here the political end of the analogy is dictating certain features of the psychological end.

I shall not attempt here any general discussion of the divisions of the soul, which, particularly with regard to the distinction between λογιστικόν and ἐπιθυμητικόν, is a large subject of great independent interest;[1] I shall make only some remarks about θυμοειδές. When it first appears, it already has a rather ambivalent role. On the one hand, it seems to be something like *anger*, and we are told, in distinguishing it from λογιστικόν, that it is manifested by children (441A) and animals (441B), and we are reminded of the Homeric figure who reproached his own anger. However, right from the beginning it takes on the colour of something more morally ambitious (as we might put it) than mere anger or rage; the case of Leontius and other examples (439E–440E) take it rather in the direction of noble indignation, and we are told (440E) that rather than class it with ἐπιθυμητικόν, we should rather say that "in the strife [στάσει, a significantly political word] of the soul it takes arms on the side of λογιστικόν." If θυμοειδές merely represented anger this would indeed be a surprising psychological claim.

The claim is indeed weakened a little at 441A, when it is said that θυμοειδές acts as ἐπίκουρος to λογιστικόν "if it has not been corrupted [διαφθαρῇ: it can scarcely mean "destroyed"] by bad upbringing." But the concession is not adequate. For so long as there is any conflict at all—and if there is not, the question does not arise—it clearly is possible for anger to break out, not merely against λογιστικόν, but on the side of ἐπιθυμητικόν against λογιστικόν. What is more interesting than that psychological platitude is the fact that Plato reveals elsewhere that he is perfectly well aware of it, and indeed in a passage where he is defending exactly the same doctrine as in the *Republic*. In the image of the chariot and the two horses in the *Phaedrus*, when the black (epithymetic) horse bolts, the white (thymoeidic) horse helps the (logistic) charioteer to bring

[1] For a very brief suggestion on this matter, see my "Ethical Consistency," in *Problems of the Self* (Cambridge, 1973), p. 169.

it to a halt; and when the black horse is finally stopped, it turns on its companion and "abuses it *in anger*" (μόγις ἐξαναπνεύσας ἐλοιδόρησεν ὀργῇ, 254C). Mere anger, Plato's dramatic realism reveals, can always side with the devil. The thymoeidic element in the soul is from its inception more than mere anger, or indeed any other such motive which there might be good reason on purely psychological grounds to distinguish from ἐπιθυμίαι (a drive to self-destructive risk-taking, for instance).

It is to be understood, rather, by working backwards from the character which is determined by its dominance, a character which is in turn to be understood in terms of a form of life: the military or competitive form of life which it was a standard thought to contrast with the life of contemplation on the one hand and the life of gain on the other (cf. Aristotle *EN* I.5.1095b17, with, in particular. *Rep.* 581C), a contrast embodied in the Pythagorean saying about the three sorts of people that come to the Games (Iamblichus *De Vit. Pythag.* 58). In this contrast of types of character there is also a political or social thought, of course, and that is why, as I suggested earlier, Plato has great ease in adjusting psychology and politics in the case of θυμοειδές: as the passage in question makes explicit (440E–441A, 440D), politics is there at its introduction. Ἐπιθυμητικόν has an independent psychological foundation, and Plato makes a lot of it and of its psychological relations to λογιστικόν in the individual, as a type of motivation. With that, I have argued, there are grave obstacles to Plato's reading back into the city what he needs for his political conclusions, obstacles to some extent concealed by his use of the tripartite analogy.

GLOSSARY OF UNTRANSLATED GREEK WORDS

δίκαιος, δίκαιοι: just
δικαιοσύνη: justice
εἶδος: character
ἐπιθυμία, ἐπιθυμίαι: appetite, appetites
ἐπιθυμητικόν: appetitive (epithymetic) part
ἐπίκουρος: auxiliary
δημιουργός: craftsman
θυμοειδές: spirited (thymoeidic) part
λογιστικόν: reasoning (logistic) part
λόγος: account
ὀρθὴ δόξα: correct belief
σωφροσύνη: temperance
φρόνησις: wisdom

EIGHT

Plato's Construction of Intrinsic Goodness

I

Thrasymachus says in Book I of the *Republic* that justice is 'the advantage of the stronger' (338C). This is not offered as a λόγος or definition of justice: if it were, it would lead to the conclusion that since the stronger certainly pursues his own advantage, he must pursue justice, which Thrasymachus of course denies. Closer to what he principally wants to say is his later statement (343C) that justice is an ἀλλότριον ἀγαθόν, something that always does somebody else some good. Thrasymachus' own account operates at the very primitive level of dividing agents (whether they be individual people or cities) into two types, the strong and the weak, and identifying justice simply as a device used by the strong to exploit the weak. This immediately raises the question of what makes one agent stronger than another. In particular, what makes a collective agent, such as a city or a group of bandits, strong? Indeed, what makes it a collective agent at all? The answer, as Socrates points out at 351 seq, must be, to a significant degree, the practice of justice between the individuals who form the collective agent. So Thrasymachus' primitive model must be wrong.

This implies, further, that we cannot go on saying simply that justice 'always does someone else some good.' Thrasymachus himself, when he said this, did not mean that the benefits secured by any just act were uniquely benefits to someone other than the agent. He did not deny that when the weaker party acts in accordance with justice, he secures a benefit for himself; he claimed that when this is so, it is only because of power possessed by someone else who is stronger and who also gains a benefit. Justice is always in someone else's interest, because when an agent has an interest in doing some just act, it is always (leaving aside errors, which are discussed at 339ff.) because it is in someone else's interest that this itself should be so.

Some passages in this paper are reprinted or adapted, by permission of the publishers which we gratefully acknowledge, from B. Williams, 'Plato against the Immoralist', in O. Höffe, ed., *Platons Politeia*, Berlin: Akademie Verlag, 1997, 55–67, and B. Williams, *Plato: The Invention of Philosophy*, London: Phoenix, 1998 [respectively chap. 6 above and chap. 10 below—Ed.].

However, not even this much will be true, once we accept that justice helps to make collective agents strong. In place of Thrasymachus' view, that justice is a device used by the strong to exploit the weak, we have the idea put forward by Glaucon in Book II, that it is a device of the (individually) weak to make themselves (collectively) strong—to make themselves stronger, in fact, than those who, before this association, were individually strong. On this account, Thrasymachus' first formulation, that justice is the interest of the stronger, might be replaced with an equally crude slogan to the effect that it is the interest of the weaker. When the association of the (previously) weak is formed, and the collective agent comes into being, justice does each of the participants some good in a way that does not depend on its doing some other, exploiting, party some good.

Expressed in these terms, Thrasymachus' and Glaucon's accounts seem to be opposed to one another. It is not simply that they can easily be formulated in terms that are contrary to one another: to us, the opposition may seem to extend to their ethical value. The Thrasymachean account, to the extent that it can be made coherent at all, is fiercely reductive and 'unmasks' justice as an exploitative device. Glaucon's theory, on the other hand, is the ancestor of honourable contractualist accounts which show why justice is the basis of collective endeavours and the division of labour, and why it is of great value to human beings.

Granted these differences, it is significant that every party to the discussion in the *Republic* treats Glaucon's position (and its elaboration by Adeimantus) as essentially a somewhat refined version of Thrasymachus'. 'I shall renew Thrasymachus' argument,' Glaucon says (358B–C); and Adeimantus, who, like his brother, does not accept this outlook himself but wants to hear it refuted by Socrates, says that he has put as strongly as he can the view of Thrasymachus and others who agree with him (367B). The reason for this is, at one level, obvious. There is an opinion about justice that Thrasymachus on the one hand, and Glaucon and Adeimantus on the other, certainly share, despite their other differences: that the life of justice[1] is in some sense *a second best*. This is the issue that is picked out at the beginning of Book II, when the distinction is made between things that are valued in themselves, things that are valued for their consequences, and things that are valued for both (357–8).[2]

---

[1] Granted the wide range of the term δικαιοσύνη in the *Republic*, the issue under discussion can be taken to be the general value of ethical constraints on one's relations to other people. 'Justice' is the only appropriate translation of the term, and I shall stay with it, but the broad scope of the issue must be kept in mind.

[2] 'Consequences' translates more than one expression: τὰ ἀποβαίνοντα 357B6; ὅσα γίγνεται ἀπ' αὐτῶν D1, 358B6. There are also, of course, various references to specific consequences of justice, or rather of the reputation for it.

What Socrates is encouraged to show, contrary to the common opinion which has been expressed in different ways by Thrasymachus and by Glaucon, is that justice falls into the third class. It is obvious that this is the issue, but there is another question to which the answer is rather less obvious: why should the discussion take this form? Why are the standards for the value of justice raised so high?

The first point to emphasize is how radically individualistic, at this stage of the discussion, the issue is taken to be. Glaucon's account might be said to show that we have an interest in pursuing justice, and if we assume that 'we' is taken collectively, this is straightforwardly true. Indeed, as we have already seen, granted the collective 'we', justice does not even come out as a second best—without justice there will be no collective 'we'. But the collective 'we' has a tendency to unravel, and in the discussion with Thrasymachus we are not allowed to assume it. The question whether *we* have reason to pursue justice is taken, by Socrates as it is by Thrasymachus, to refer to each of us. The question each of us must ask is 'what reason do I have to be just?', 'what does justice do for me?'. This is the force of Socrates' earlier remark (352D): our discussion is not about a trivial matter, but about how one should live.[3]

The question, then, is about the best life for the individual, and already at 347E Socrates has said that he regards it as an issue 'bigger' than Thrasymachus' first formulations, whether he was right in thinking that the life of the unjust person was better[4] than that of the just. A closely related idea is that no-one would choose to be just if he had an alternative ('no-one is willingly just,' 360C). The force of this is supposedly given to us by the two thought-experiments that Glaucon presents, the ring of invisibility (359D–360) and that in which we are invited to think about two men, one of whom has all the social rewards of justice without being really just, while the other has genuine justice and none of its conventional rewards (360E–361D).

There are difficulties with each of the thought-experiments: the second, because it is not clear what exactly we are invited to suppose,[5] and the

[3] χρὴ ζῆν: for the force of χρὴ, cf. B. Williams, *Shame and Necessity*, Berkeley: California University Press, 1993, 184 n.57, and materials cited there. By the time of Plato, the term bears a certain contrast with δεῖ, which introduces rather a notion of (relatively) external necessity. So in the *Republic*, the idea that the just life is a life one 'should' (χρὴ) live is contrasted with the idea that one 'has to', is 'forced to', live it: cf. 358C, people pursue justice as necessary, not as good.

[4] κρείττω; ἀμείνων 358C.

[5] It is not clear, in particular, whether the genuinely just man 'appears' unjust because he has an unconventional notion of justice, so that the world judges unfavourably the character he really has; or because the world factually misunderstands what his character is. I have discussed the passage in *Shame and Necessity*, 98f. with n.46; and see n.47 for the point that the reference to Aeschylus does not help.

first, because it is unclear what it could tell us about real life. But they are intended, in any case, to sharpen the question 'do you value justice for its own sake or for the sake of the rewards and the reputation that conventionally go with it?' The question gains in force when we take into account Adeimantus' contribution. The general effect of that contribution is to reinforce Glaucon's insistence that we should 'take away reputation' (367B), and we may wonder why he says that the argument has not been adequately expressed by Glaucon, and that 'what most needed saying has not been said' (362D). His point is that as Glaucon has put it, it is the enemies of justice such as Thrasymachus who emphasize the idea that people pursue justice for the sake of the conventional rewards. On the contrary, Adeimantus says, the real problem is that the friends of justice, people who are trying to encourage the young to be just, themselves emphasize those rewards, and so sell justice short; and he cites passages from the poets to this effect (prefiguring some of the objections that will be brought against them later in the dialogue).

II

All this, then, gives some sense to the idea of pursuing, and praising, justice 'for its own sake'. But now we must ask why Plato thinks it so important that we should value justice in this way. What is the point of insisting that one does not value justice properly unless one values it, in this sense, for its own sake? A modern reader may easily be misled at this point, and take the answer to this question to be more familiar than it is. He or she may take Plato to be thinking of a pure, self-sufficient moral motivation, in terms of which the agent does good or right actions simply because that is what they are, and for no other reason. On this conception, if one reflects on the value of a moral life, one will insist simply on its moral value: this is what it is to be concerned with justice and other moral values for their own sake, and it is contrasted with relating those values to anything else at all, such as one's own happiness. But this, certainly, is not Plato's concern. His argument can be formulated only because there is one, univocal, kind of question in practical reason, 'how should I live?', 'what is the best life?', 'how shall I do best?', to which Thrasymachus and his friends give the wrong answer, and Socrates, on behalf of justice, will give the right answer. It is not that the pursuit of justice 'for its own sake' has a quite special, moral, value which vindicates itself. The question of its value, rather, is the question of what makes a life worth living, a question to which other 'non-moral' goods might in principle, as the others suggest, provide the answer.

Another way of putting the point is that the idea of 'pursuing justice for its own sake' occurs in Socrates' answer to the question, not in the question itself. The question is not 'What is the value of justice pursued for its own sake, as opposed to the sake of its consequences?' The question is: 'What is the value of justice?', and Socrates' answer is: 'It has no value (really), unless it has value when it is pursued for its own sake.' So the question remains: why does Plato's Socrates think this? Why does he raise the standards for the vindication of justice so high?

The question has been put in terms of someone's desiring or valuing or pursuing justice for its own sake. This might equally be expressed in terms of justice being valued or pursued as an end, or as a final good. This, so far, does not give us a sense for justice *being* a final good, as distinct from some agent's pursuing it as a final good, but the discussion between Socrates and the Thrasymachean party already suggests a direction in which one might get to that notion: what was to be the Aristotelian way, to the effect that justice is a final good if a rational, reflective, or wise person would pursue it as a final good. We shall need to keep this idea in mind.

However, my title uses a different phrase, 'intrinsic goodness', and we must not assume that this is the same idea. Christine Korsgaard has pointed out[6] that the standard contrast to 'final' is 'instrumental', while the contrast to 'intrinsic' is 'extrinsic', and you need a theory to show that these two distinctions come to the same thing. Korsgaard makes several important points, but I do not want simply to accept her account as the basis of my discussion. She writes:

> To say that something is intrinsically good is not by definition to say that it is valued for its own sake: it is to say that it has its goodness in itself. It refers to the location or source of the value rather than the way we value the thing.

Extrinsic goodness, on the other hand, is value that something gets from some other source.

One consideration that Korsgaard uses in separating the intrinsic/extrinsic distinction from the final/instrumental distinction does not seem to me to have the effect that her account requires. There are, as she says, various ways in which the goodness of one thing can be dependent on the goodness of another without the first being a means to the second. But many of these possibilities apply to practical reason itself. As

[6] 'Two Distinctions in Goodness', *Phil. Rev.* 92 (1983); reprinted in *Creating the Kingdom of Ends*, Cambridge: Cambridge University Press, 1996. The quotation, and the one that follows, occur in the reprint at p. 250.

David Wiggins and others have pointed out in discussing Aristotle, one may value going to the concert as a way of, not as a causal condition of, having a good evening. This kind of example is among those that Korsgaard uses to distinguish extrinsic from instrumental value. But these examples need not lead us to a notion which, in contrast to the final/instrumental distinction, refers to 'the source of the value rather than the way we value the thing'. It need lead us only to the conclusion that even within the scope of practical reason, or again, 'the way we value' something, the contrast to 'final' should be something broader than 'instrumental'; there are various ways of pursuing something 'derivatively', as we might say, as opposed to pursuing it as an end or final good, and one species of this is pursuing it as a means or instrument.

There is a second question about Korsgaard's account of these distinctions which is very relevant to the present discussion. As Korsgaard formulates her central point:

> One [distinction is that] between things valued for their own sakes and things valued for the sake of something else—between ends and means, or final and instrumental goods. The other is the distinction between things which have their value in themselves and things which derive their value from some other source: intrinsically good things versus extrinsically good things.

But we do not need Aristotle to remind us that a rational or wise person can pursue or value a certain thing both for its own sake and for the sake of something else. We have already seen that what Socrates wants to show, and will claim in the end to have shown, is that justice should be valued both for itself and for its consequences—that it is both a final and an instrumental good. Let us take 'a good' to be some type or general object of pursuit or valuation, such as justice, or honour, or pleasure. (This is the sense in which two rival politicians each of whom is pursuing honour are both pursuing the same good.) If one and the same good can be both final and instrumental, then *that* distinction is not one between different classes of goods; it is a distinction between kinds of goodness or ways in which things may be found good, and not, as Korsgaard puts it, a distinction between different things. But the intrinsic/extrinsic distinction, as she explains it, *must* be a distinction between things: if something 'has its value in itself'—whatever exactly that means—it presumably cannot also 'derive its value from some other source'. This shows that we are not merely taking apart two distinctions that operate in the same field.

I do not propose to pursue the idea of intrinsic goodness, as distinct from final goodness or goodness as an end, directly. My aim is to work round, in Plato's thought, to a certain idea of intrinsic goodness and to see what function it performs there. At the end of the paper I shall suggest that we need, for our purposes, an idea of intrinsic goodness which is rather different from the one that we shall have ascribed to Plato; rather paradoxically, it is Plato's own argument that will have helped to make this clear.

For the immediate discussion of Plato, at any rate, there are three ideas which I should like us to keep in mind from Korsgaard's formulations and the discussion of them. The first is Korsgaard's own point that we cannot assume that a notion of intrinsic goodness must be the same as that of final goodness or goodness as an end. The second idea, which we may take from Korsgaard's language of 'sources', is that the notions of intrinsic and extrinsic goodness have something to do with the ways in which the goodness of various things is explained; and, closely connected with this, that the notion of something intrinsically good is that of a thing whose goodness is in some sense self-explanatory. Third, there is an obscurity about what it is that these distinctions serve to distinguish: in particular, whether they distinguish good things, or ways in which good things are conceived or valued.

III

Now I should like to start again, from a different point in Plato's work—Diotima's speech in the *Symposium*.

The symposiasts have been talking about what ἔρως is, what it is to be a lover. We know that the lover has desires. We know that the lover and his desires have some relation to τὸ καλόν or καλά, beauty or beautiful things; in particular, beautiful young men. Now we learn more precisely what these desires are, and what their relation is to the beautiful. It is certainly not—as opposed to what some earlier speeches said—that the desire itself is beautiful. Nor is the desire a desire for the beautiful, at least in any sense that is at all transparent: (206E2–5) 'love is not love of the beautiful, as you think.—What is it, then?—Of reproduction and birth in the beautiful.' This desire itself turns out to be an expression, or form, of a desire to be immortal.[7]

Now this provides a schema, to put it in rather formal terms, which can be filled out differently for different types of ἔρως. A man's ἔρως for a woman defines birth, τόκος, literally; ἐν, 'in association with', is sexual; and the immortality in question is genetic. But a man may bring

---

[7] The dialogue may suggest that this itself is an expression of the desire that the good should be with one for ever, 206A. I shall not take this up here.

forth or generate not babies but ideas or poems, and live for ever (or at least for longer) through those. The beauty in question may now be that of a particular youth, or something more general—as we might say, youthful beauty; again, that may be beauty of soul rather than of body. There is nothing in all this to imply that the various refinements, as perhaps we may call them, necessarily keep step with one another. Socrates has been disposed to generate ideas and good thoughts but in association with youths who had beautiful bodies; though he may have got at least some of the way towards being 'a lover of all beautiful bodies' (210B), rather than being obsessed with one person. Conversely, Alcibiades, we learn later, is drawn to Socrates' beautiful soul (215–217), but he has little idea of what an appropriate τόκος would be.[8]

Then Diotima gives her account of the end of the progress, to the 'final and highest mysteries of love' (210A), which she doubts that Socrates can achieve. Here, in a famous passage, the lover is said to turn to the great sea of beauty, and will come to see something 'wonderfully beautiful in its nature', which

> always is and neither comes to be nor passes away, neither waxes nor wanes; it is not beautiful in one way and ugly in another, nor beautiful at one time and not at another, nor beautiful in relation to one thing and ugly in relation to another, nor beautiful in one place and ugly in another, as it would be if it were beautiful to some people and ugly to others;

and it is not embodied in any face or body, or idea, or knowledge, or, indeed, in anything. This culminating, ultimately fulfilling, encounter still fits the original schema. This would indeed be a worthwhile life for a man (212A); he would bring forth, not images of virtue, but true virtue, and his relation to τὸ καλόν, which is now the item that has just been described, would be that of seeing it and being with it, words reminiscent of the language originally applied to sexual relations with a beautiful person.

There are several things which, it is important to see, this account does not imply. It has been thought to imply that no-one ever really loves a particular person, but only the beauty in that person, a beauty of which that person is at best a poor exemplar. On the contrary, the account gives a sense to loving a particular person, in the form of a range of different contents laid down by the schema, and it denies that love is for beauty itself. Moreover, there is no suggestion that the particulars,

---

[8] This helps to answer the question which dogs Plato's account of Socrates, why being loved by Socrates did not transform Alcibiades: it is loving Socrates that should have done that, and he did not know how to do it.

these bodies or souls, were only seemingly or illusorily beautiful. They are indeed not unconditionally, or unqualifiedly, or perhaps we can say (as opposed to 'relatively') absolutely, beautiful, which is what the item of the final vision is. Indeed, retrospectively from the point of view of the vision, human bodies and colours and other such things are said to be merely 'mortal nonsense', but that is a comparative judgement of value, and it does not imply that it was simply a mistake to have thought that those things were beautiful, or even that one was mistaken to have pursued them. We may say that it is like a growth in aesthetic taste, from kitschy music, say, to more interesting music. It does not altogether deny the point or the object of the earlier taste, and indeed the earlier taste is a condition of the process, which is a progress rather than the mere detection of error or the elimination of a misunderstanding.

Diotima says that the earlier pursuits were 'for the sake of' (ἕνεκα) the final secrets, 210A, and she also says of one who comes to the vision that he is coming to the τέλος* of the erotic, which may imply a similar idea, though it need not. But, emphatically and several times, she says that this is so only for one who is going about the erotic in the right way.[9] This does not mean that unless the ultimate state is reached, the earlier states are pointless. It means that from the later perspective we can see a point to them which they do not reveal at all to some people, and reveal only imperfectly even to those who are going about them in the right way. For those who do go about them in the right way, that imperfection is expressed in an obscure unsatisfactoriness or incompleteness in those relationships, which can be traced to their failure to express adequately the desire to have the good for ever.[10]

Diotima at some points makes it seem that once one has got going in the right way the ascent or refinement is almost inevitable: (210B) 'if one is to pursue beauty of form, it would be great foolishness not to recognize that the beauty in all bodies is one and the same.' Yet she also describes the ascent as involving tasks (E6). All this refers to the higher levels of the progress, above the point which she is doubtful that Socrates himself will be able to pass. Now Socrates is not liable to great foolishness, and what is to come later, the speech of Alcibiades, will show that he is not incapable of ethical tasks which may be involved. I take it that we are being told that Socrates was not in a position really

---

* Goal—Ed.

[9] 210A2; A4; E3; 211B5.

[10] How far, and in what ways, such a feeling may come, in an uninterpreted form, even to those who are not going about the erotic in the right way, is a question to which the earlier speeches suggest answers.

to 'pursue beauty of form', and that the discovery of the sea of beauty, the final vision, involves intellectual tasks that were formulated by Plato himself.

The object of the final vision is absolutely or unconditionally beautiful. If we associate the idea of the intrinsic with a notion of explanation, we may also say that this object is intrinsically beautiful; although Plato does not make much of it in the *Symposium*, he certainly thought that this object would explain, in some sense, why anything, including itself, was beautiful. The object is also, I suppose, a good thing: to reach it was the τέλος of a progress inspired by the desire to have the good for ever. However, just in virtue of the account (or, rather, the apology for an account) which we have suggested for 'intrinsic', we must not suppose that because this object is intrinsically beautiful, and it is good, it is intrinsically good. If it were intrinsically good, its goodness would not be explained by anything else. But we know, not from the *Symposium* but from the *Republic*, that its goodness is explained by something else, the Form of the Good, which explains the goodness of everything including itself (as the sun enables everything including itself to be seen, 508B). On the provisional account of intrinsic goodness, the Form of the Good is, for Plato, the only intrinsically good thing.

There are significant differences of tone between the *Symposium* and the *Republic*. The *Symposium* more emphasizes the pathos of the finite, the attractiveness of the contingently and transitorily beautiful which nevertheless carries with it a yearning for something the beauty of which will not be transitory, something to which some people may be able to ascend. The ascent of course has parallels in the *Republic*, but many of that dialogue's most powerful images are those of descent, which convey the regret of the return to the cave, of leaving the unconditioned for the conditioned. Relatedly, the *Republic* makes more of the idea that the contrast between the conditioned and the unconditioned is a contrast between appearance and reality, and its images of the contingent, particularly in relation to the Cave and in the discussions of art, are of illusion, deceit and dreams (476C); even though, when Socrates in Book V (479A) explains why the 'lovers of sights' are in a state of belief (δόξα), the 'appearances' he cites are in fact matters of comparison or relativity.[11]

Yet the end of the educational story that the *Republic* tells, the vision it offers, is strikingly similar to that of the *Symposium*. The Guardians are drawn to the intellectual world by love: they love study which tells them about being (485B), and the Form of the Good is the 'greatest

---

[11] A6 τῶν πολλῶν καλῶν μῶν τι ἔστιν ὃ οὐκ αἰσχρὸν φανήσεται; means '... will not appear as ugly', not '... will not appear to be ugly.'

study' (505A2). 'And so we shall say that they will admire and love (ἀσπάζεσθαί τε καὶ φιλεῖν) the things of which there is knowledge' (479 *fin*), and notably at 490B we are told that

> the genuine lover of learning . . . would go on and would not be discouraged and would not cease from ἔρως* until he seized with the appropriate part of his soul each thing that by its nature is, and drawing near to what really is and being united with it (μιγείς), he would bring forth reason and truth, he would know and would live in truth, and would be nourished and so would cease from his painful labour. . . .[12]

The intrinsically beautiful in the *Symposium* was not something that it would make sense to want: what one wanted was to generate the right kind of offspring (virtue, in fact) in its presence, which means in its cognitive presence. In exactly the same way, the Form of the Good, that which is, and alone is, intrinsically good in an explanatory sense, is not anything that one wants: what one wants is to generate reason and truth in its presence—that is to say, in its cognitive presence and by its intellectual light.

IV

Aristotle famously said (*EN* 1096b33–5) that if there were a separate and absolute Good, 'it is obvious that it could not be achieved or possessed by man; but it is to something of that sort that our inquiry is directed.' If Aristotle means by this (he may not) that Plato unfortunately overlooked this feature of the Form of the Good, that it is not achievable in action, he has missed the point: it would be a category mistake to suppose that it could be any such thing. If he means (equally, he may not) that Plato introduced the Form of the Good, a supposedly self-explanatory intrinsically good thing, in place of a final good, which is what Aristotle himself was looking for, then he is also mistaken. Plato has more than one final good, and the most significant is the life of the intellect—living, as he put it, in the presence of Forms—and this involves living in the light of the Form of the Good. So there is a final good, one among others, which is related to the intrinsic self-explanatory good, but it is not the same as that good, and it would not make sense to suppose that it was.

For reasons that Aristotle gave, and which Plato began to explore in his later work, there are grave problems in even understanding the

---

* Desire, love—Ed.
[12] For ᾧ προσήκει ψυχῆς, cf. *Symp.* 212A1, ᾧ δεῖ.

notion of something that is absolutely good or beautiful in the sense of the *Symposium* and the *Republic*. The problems do not come simply from the idea that the goodness or beauty of such a thing must be self-explanatory. A major problem is that the thing is meant to explain the goodness or beauty of everything else which is good or beautiful; hence that it cannot be any specific sort of good or beautiful thing; hence that there is nothing else about it which explains its goodness or beauty; and hence, seemingly, that it is good or beautiful and nothing else at all. This is surely unintelligible.

Some of the notorious problems, then, come from the idea that there is just one intrinsically good item which is both self-explanatory and other-explanatory. Yet some of the recalcitrance of the Form of the Good, the difficulty in saying anything about it, would surely arise also with a larger class of self-explanatory intrinsic goods, forming a class of objects whose goodness was to be explained in advance of any human valuation. Such items (unlike the Form of the Good) will have other properties, and the sense in which their goodness will be self-explanatory is, presumably, that it will be explained by those properties. But then what is the nature of the a priori guarantee (as it will have to be) that such an explanation cannot refer to something else: for instance, that it might not be *improved* by referring to something else? Might it not be improved, for instance, by relating these properties to things that we value? Moreover, what is the a priori guarantee that some of those same properties could not causally depend on some other intrinsically good thing, as they cannot, if intrinsic goods and extrinsic goods are to form two disjunct classes? I shall not try to explore these questions here, but I find it hard to believe that the problems posed by Plato's Form of the Good are entirely due to its special role as a unique and explanatorily very ambitious intrinsic good.

The main point I want to emphasize, however, is not how hard it is for Plato to specify the Form of the Good, but how much he manages to say without specifying it. The criticism of Plato in Aristotelian style, to the effect that his account of the good is too intellectualist and inadequate to the claims of practical reason, is likely to distract us from a rather obvious feature of the *Republic*, that a lot of what it actually tells us about the Form of the Good consists of considerations that relate it to practical reason. It tells us almost nothing about the intellectual content of encountering the Form of the Good; it leaves us uncertain how much Socrates himself knows about it, and certain that he cannot at this point explain whatever he does know about it (506E, 517B, 532–3). Yet Socrates is supposed, by the end of the dialogue, to have met fully the challenge set in Book II; so it must be possible to understand why justice is a final good without understanding adequately, or barely at all, what the one and only intrinsic good is, or what is involved in its theoretical contemplation. We can understand Socrates' answer because we can gather from his account at least the following: that the wise or rational person needs to regard justice as a final good, and that he can make sense of it as a final good. We can take away some more as well, about the role of the Form of the Good in this, and I shall come back to that, but the central point is that we can take away these two conclusions.

The first conclusion, that the rational person needs to regard justice as a final good, has both an individual and a political form. In its individual form it is implicit in the description of the divisions of the soul in Book IV, and in the associated account of the various virtues. A less schematic expression of it occurs in the studies of degeneration in Books VIII and IX, but it may be less easy to see, partly because those studies, for obvious reasons, tend to mix psychological and political considerations, and partly because the story of degeneration is shaped by comparisons with a completed state of justice which by this stage is taken for granted, and so the story may not help us to see what exactly the individual's need for justice is. To get a slightly different view of Plato's account of this, it may be helpful to look outside the *Republic* again, to a dialogue which has many of the same preoccupations, the *Gorgias*.

V

This dialogue presents conversations that Socrates has with three speakers, i.e., Gorgias, Polus, and Callicles, who take in succession increasingly radical positions. The discussions are structured by the use that is made of three distinct value oppositions. One is the contrast between δίκαιον and ἄδικον, the just and the unjust: this relates, as in the *Republic*, to values that concern fair dealing with others, respect for their persons and their property, and generally a prohibition on exploiting them. The terms of the second distinction, καλόν and αἰσχρόν, are understood here not in their directly aesthetic sense as in the *Symposium*, but in their connection with action and character, where they relate to honour and shame. I take it, as I have argued elsewhere, that this is not merely a matter of one's reputation; the distinction is one between things that agents can be proud of, and think well of themselves for having done or been, as opposed to things for which they despise themselves, feel ashamed or embarrassed or contemptible.[13]

---

[13] For the role of shame in Greek (and, indeed, our own) ethical experience, see *Shame and Necessity*, above n.3, in particular chapter IV and Endnote 1.

The last contrast, between ἀγαθόν and κακόν, good and bad, is often, in the *Gorgias* as elsewhere, interpreted in terms of self-interest: one seeks the ἀγαθόν in seeking what is best for oneself. The basic idea, however, is something more general and abstract, the idea of what an agent has good reason to pursue or not. These are the terms which are, throughout these conversations, unquestionably tied to the conclusions of practical reason, and it makes no sense in this context to say that an agent knows that something is (on balance) κακόν, and that he has decided that this is what (on balance) he has reason to pursue.

Gorgias, the first speaker, accepts the conventional idea that all these values go together, so that what is δίκαιον is also καλόν and ἀγαθόν: we have reason to pursue the just and should think well of ourselves and others for doing so. It is in these terms that he defends his practice of rhetoric. Polus enters the discussion to offer a more radical position, which separates δίκαιον and ἀγαθόν: we should stop thinking that the δίκαιον is what we have reason to do. However, he treats the dimension of καλόν and αἰσχρόν in a less radical way, and is manoeuvred by Socrates into claiming both that to behave unjustly is αἰσχρόν, and that what is αἰσχρόν is κακόν—that is to say, that we have reason to avoid it.[14] This is inconsistent with his attempt to hold that injustice is not κακόν.

Polus' mistake is to sustain at once a conventional link between δίκαιον and καλόν (just behaviour is admired, injustice is something to be ashamed of), and a natural link between καλόν and ἀγαθόν (we have reason to do what will make us admired, no reason to do what will make us ashamed of ourselves). The last speaker, Callicles, sees Polus' mistake, and, takes the further step of denying the conventional link between δίκαιον and καλόν. In doing this, he wants to keep the link between καλόν and ἀγαθόν: the rational person will want to be admired and envied, to think well of himself, and not to be an object of contempt, but he will bring this about, Callicles urges, through power and the exploitation of others, having no concern for considerations of justice.[15]

Callicles is a more powerfully eloquent, and in some ways more sophisticated, version of Thrasymachus. He is supposedly refuted, but it is easy to feel that Plato has deliberately dealt him a hand of losing cards. Although there are several complexities in the argument, Callicles

---

[14] *Gorg.* 474C seq. κακόν and αἰσχρόν mostly appear in this discussion in their comparative forms.

[15] My very bare summary follows what I take to be the points in the dialogue that are most significant for the present question. Needless to say, other important patterns can be extracted from what is a very rich set of arguments.

effectively ends up (from about *Gorg.* 491 onwards) defending a crudely gluttonous form of hedonistic activity, which not many are likely to envy. But this was not supposed to be the idea. The successfully unjust man was supposed to be a rather grand, powerful, stylish figure (the aesthetic echoes of καλός are relevant here) whom others, if they were honest, could admire and envy; but he has ended up, in Socrates' refutation, as a low addict or at best a heartlessly boring *bon viveur*, whom anyone with any taste would despise. It is easy to think that Socrates wins the argument only by changing the subject.

However, there is more to the strategy than this suggests. Callicles (491B) wants to say that the successful unjust man will be καλός, and admirable in recognizable ways: he will, for instance, be intelligent and brave. But the direction of Socrates' argument, which brings it close to the concerns of the *Republic*, is to suggest that Callicles has no right to suppose that, on the assumptions he and his unjust man are left with, there could be a basis either for admiring virtues such as intelligence and courage, or for thinking that the unjust man could actually sustain them. How does Callicles explain the values of courage and intelligence? He may do so in terms of political power: but quite early in their discussion (488–489), Socrates shows that there is a conflict between such a political conception and Callicles' ideal of an individual person who is 'better', since political power is a collective enterprise, in which the individuals are not going to be in his sense 'better', above all in a democracy.[16] The alternative is that he explains the value of these human qualities simply in terms of the satisfaction of desire—that is to say, as Plato puts it, in terms of pleasure. But that is not convincing, since someone can think of himself as καλός only if he can admire himself, and that implies grounds on which others can admire him, which implies more generally that one person can admire another.[17] A criterion that consists merely in the individual's desires being satisfied provides no basis for admiration at all. All that is left is hedonism.

Socrates in the *Gorgias* argues that any basis of admiration implies τάξις and κόσμος (503D seq), order and discipline, and that these, applied to the soul, constitute justice. The argument for this, which in the *Gorgias* could politely be called schematic, is strengthened in the *Republic*, with its account of the parts of the soul and their functions. At the same time, the *Republic*'s account is more complex, since it allows types

---

[16] In connection with the later discussion of Pericles, Socrates is in effect presenting Callicles with a dilemma for the aristocratic or oligarchic amoralist: the Athenian empire, which was run in ways he should admire, was run by a democracy.

[17] It is a Calliclean idea, obvious in his opening speech about nature and convention (482E seq), that the respectable secretly admire the ruthless, unless they have been intimidated into not doing so. This is very close to the inspiration of the Gyges' ring story in the *Republic*.

of individual between the perfectly just person and the democratic or, worse, tyrannical person to whom Callicles' ideal, according to the *Gorgias*, must inevitably be reduced. But of course the *Republic* claims to show that the intermediate types are not as they would wish to be if they understood their natures better; and even they must, to some extent, regard justice as a final good.

Moreover, we need there to be people who regard justice as a final good if there is to be any stability for anyone. This is the political aspect of the argument. The 'analogy' between the individual and the city which is introduced at *Rep.* 368D is officially put forward to help us understand justice in the individual: it is as though the same message were written in larger letters. In fact, the way in which the *Republic* proceeds means that justice in the city and in the individual cannot be separated from one another, and the answers that the dialogue eventually gives to Thrasymachus and to the questions of Glaucon and Adeimantus are essentially political.

Whatever exactly the state of the lower classes in the city is meant to be,[18] it is certainly true that they are like the lower sections of the soul in this respect, that they cannot look after themselves: they have no inherent principles of order and discipline. The order and discipline that they need come from elsewhere, from the Guardians. This means that the Guardians must be ethically self-sufficient, and this means that they must be able to see that justice is worth pursuing for its own sake. If justice were, as Glaucon argued, valuable only as a second-best, there would be no motive for the Guardians to be just, since they are not in anyone else's power. The constitution of Plato's city essentially depends on its rulers seeing justice as good in itself, or for its own sake, and if it is to be more than a virtuous tyranny, the lower classes will have to have some kind of belief to the same effect.

Plato could not use this conclusion, of course, to *demonstrate* that justice was good in itself. Those who accept Glaucon's account will reasonably not trust Plato's constitution. For them, a just city will reject ethical aristocracy and will consist of imperfect citizens keeping an eye on each other. This is why the ethical and the political parts of Plato's enterprise help each other. The ethical argument we have already followed suggests that people's lives will be incoherent if they are the sort of people who (the political analogy suggests) form the lower two classes of the city, and if, in addition, they try to be ethically self-sufficient. Democracy,

---

[18] I have discussed a difficulty about this, implicit in the supposed analogy, in 'The Analogy of City and Soul in Plato's *Republic*', in E. N. Lee, A.P.D. Mourelatos and A. O. Rorty eds., *Exegesis and Argument: Studies in Greek Philosophy presented to Gregory Vlastos*, Assen: van Gorcum, 1973, 196–206 [= chap. 7 above—Ed.].

in particular, is the project of such people trying to be ethically self-sufficient as a collective, and that is a doomed venture which ends in tyranny, just as Callicles, though he would like to be a free spirit who admires and is admired by some other free spirits, can in the end be nothing but a sordid slave of desire.

The city needs just people as rulers, but, equally, just people need the city. This is to some degree concealed by the downward movement of the *Republic*, which emphasizes the sacrifice of the Guardians in becoming rulers. But the question of that sacrifice can come up only in a context in which the able young have received an education which enables them to be Guardians, that is to say, the education offered in a just city. Guardians will not emerge, and young people will not become fully just, unless the institutions replicate themselves (which is what, the tale of decline tells us, will eventually fail to happen); and it is precisely the strongest spirits that will be corrupted without those institutions (492). So not only does the city need people who will see justice as a final end; such people, and young people who would like to become such people but do not yet fully understand what is involved, need the just city, or some approximation to it which can also bring it about that there will be such people.

So we can reply to the challenge of Book II. The rational person needs to regard justice as a final good. Moreover, he, and we, can make sense of regarding it as a final good, because that is exactly what the various arguments of the *Republic* have enabled us to do. These were the two conclusions that I said we would be able to take away from Socrates' argument. If we accept them, then, I suggest, we have been shown that justice is a final good.

VI

The Form of the Good, the item that we identified as being, on Plato's account, the one and only intrinsic good, has played a role in this account, but it is significant what a very small role it is. We are told that if we were to grasp it and work down again from it, we would understand the point of all the virtues, as well as of everything else. But as I have already said, the really significant thing is that Socrates has been able to meet the challenge of Book II, and get us to understand his answer, without any of us getting a glimpse of the Form of the Good. There is indeed an element which is essential to the answer even as we, or Glaucon and Adeimantus, understand it, an element in which the Form of the Good is mentioned. This is the motivation of the Guardians, which makes them reluctant, and hence uniquely reliable, rulers: they are driven by the love of truth, which, Plato tells us, expels other wants (485), with the result that they want no rewards, and so will not squabble or conspire as other rulers do (520 seq). The search for truth, Plato seems to think, is the only genuinely selfless motive; at the same time, it is connected with the truth-seeker's own self, since it is only as a mind seeking truth that one can fully satisfy the desire for immortality. The Form of the Good is the ultimate object of this search for truth. But once again, it is significant how little difference it would make to the argument if it were not. For the Guardians to have what, on Plato's account of things, is this essential motive, they need to have in mind a certain final good, the aim of understanding; perhaps, given his ideas of immortality, this must be, more specifically, the aim of understanding eternal reality. It makes no difference to this whether or not this reality has as its highest element the one and only intrinsic good.

It is just because the Form of the Good, which for Plato is the uniquely intrinsic good, is so retiring and inexplicable, that Plato's account of justice as a good, and, more generally, of what should concern one who is living the best possible life, has so little to do with it. He can answer the basic challenge of the *Republic*, to show that justice is a final good, and answer it in a way which he can reasonably suppose we shall understand, without his doing much more than to salute the intrinsic good. This is paradoxical, and the paradox suggests some lessons for the way in which we should think about these notions. They are no more than suggestions, but I think that both the failures and the successes of Plato's enterprise should encourage us to take them seriously.

First, we should abandon the idea that the distinction between intrinsic and extrinsic goodness determines two classes of things. I have already suggested that this idea contributed to the opaque and unhelpful character of absolute beauty and the Form of the Good. If we accept that one and the same thing can be both intrinsically and extrinsically good, then we can, to this extent, bring the intrinsic/extrinsic distinction into line with the final/instrumental distinction.

The next suggestion is that we should take a further step in the same direction, and treat final goods as a species of intrinsic goods. I argued earlier, in criticism of Christine Korsgaard, that the contrasting term to 'final' need not be merely 'instrumental', but something more general: I proposed the label 'derivative'. This, in itself, was intended to be a fairly uncontentious proposal. It is more contentious to suggest, as I am now suggesting, that the final/instrumental distinction altogether should be understood as an application of a more fundamental distinction between intrinsic and—using the term now more broadly than before—derivative goodness. The reason why this proposal is more contentious relates to a point about final goodness which we have accepted throughout the discussion: that the basic notion in this connection is that of someone's wanting or pursuing something as an end or final good, and that the notion of something's *being* a final good is to be explained in terms of this, for instance as what a wise or rational person would pursue as an end.

On the present proposal, intrinsic goodness will be treated in a similar way. The notion of something's being an intrinsic good will be explained in terms of a more basic notion of someone's valuing something as an intrinsic good.[19] It is important that this does not imply that all valuing is reducible to practical attitudes: 'valuing' does not entail 'wanting' or 'pursuing' or 'trying to bring about' (or a disjunction of them). This is particularly significant for us who, unlike Plato, regard a range of things in the world as having intrinsic goodness, although they are not ends or final goods: works of art, for instance, or natural beauty. Valuing such things cannot be reduced to practical attitudes. It can of course, in various connexions, be expressed in practical attitudes, and it would be an empty thing if it could not be expressed in such attitudes, even if there are some circumstances in which it can be expressed in no more than wishing. What exactly valuing involves in various circumstances, including what practical attitudes it may involve, is a significant question, and we should expect the answers to it to be fairly open-ended. This is indeed part of the point of the very abstract notion of 'valuing'.

There should be answers to this question, of what is involved in valuing a certain thing as an intrinsic good. There should be an answer, too, to the further significant question, of why we should value it in this way. This leads to the place of explanation among these notions. It is common to all accounts, presumably, that the extrinsic or derivative is explained in terms of the intrinsic. The interesting questions concern the explanation of the intrinsic. Up to now we have assumed, as Plato assumed when he was concerned with the Form of the Good, that intrinsic goodness should be self-explanatory. This idea turned out to be unfruitful. However, when we considered Plato's account of the final good of justice, we found that (relative to his own assumptions) he was able to explain it in terms of our needing to treat justice as a final good, and our being able to make sense of our doing so.

My last suggestion is that we should extend this schema to intrinsic goodness in general. We give up the unrewarding idea of intrinsic goodness being self-explanatory. We say that something is intrinsically good if we need to value it as intrinsically good, and we can make sense of our doing so.[20] The formula 'we can make sense of our doing so' is intended

---

[19] This means, of course, that we cannot explain 'we value X as an intrinsic good' as 'we value X because we believe that it is an intrinsic good'.

[20] I do not think that 'need to' is too strong, granted that an account is being given of 'X is an intrinsic good'. The account leaves room for people to treat something as an intrinsic good (for instance, as an end) without their having to claim that it is an intrinsic good *überhaupt*.

to secure a place in this discussion for something that is almost always a good idea in philosophy, explanation without reduction.

We may take the case of trust, or, more generally, honest relations between people.[21] This is widely regarded as a good thing, and there is quite a lot to be said about why it is a good thing. The value of trust and trustworthiness is not self-explanatory, and to claim that it was would be to leave it unexplained, an object of blank intuition. Yet the goodness of these things is not merely derivative, either. We do regard it as intrinsic. Moreover, we have to regard these things as intrinsically good if they are even to be derivatively good, since many of their good effects, and indeed their existence, depend on their being valued as intrinsic goods. So what is needed for us to be able to make sense of them as intrinsic goods? We have to be able to think reflectively about trust and trustworthiness as fitting into a structure of human qualities and social relations, in a way that relates them to other things that we value, and which does not reduce them to a device for maximizing utility or for getting out of the Prisoners' Dilemma. If they appeared to reflective understanding as simply such a device, the idea that they were intrinsically good would unravel, and we could not make sense of them as intrinsic goods. If we can make sense of these things as intrinsic goods, we are not *pretending* that they are intrinsic goods. That would be something else: it would be to pretend that we needed them, or to pretend that we could make sense of them as intrinsic goods, and neither of these things need be so. If we can make sense of trustworthiness in such terms, then we shall have *constructed* an intrinsic good.

Plato's Form of the Good is a peculiar and very extreme example of what an intrinsic good has to be if it is regarded as a kind of thing that presents itself as self-explanatorily good, prior to any considerations of how we might value it. We have seen how little it contributes to Plato's enterprise. On the other hand, we have seen how much Plato achieves, in his own terms, by asking the questions 'do we need to value justice as a final good?' and 'can we make sense of our doing so?' If we use 'intrinsic' in the new and broader way, Plato will be asking these questions about justice as intrinsically good, and in answering them, he will have constructed an intrinsic good.

---

[21] I discuss in detail this example of constructing an intrinsic good in *Truth and Truthfulness*, Princeton: Princeton University Press, 2002.

NINE

Cratylus' Theory of Names and Its Refutation

At the very beginning of Plato's *Cratylus* Hermogenes explains Cratylus' view by saying that it supposes there to be a certain natural correctness (*orthotēs*) of names; that this correctness is the same for all linguistic groups; and (very strongly) that it has nothing to do with what name anyone actually applies to anything—so that, he is quoted as saying to Hermogenes, 'your name would not be Hermogenes, even if everyone called you that' 383b). This last point implies something which explicitly emerges later, that, for Cratylus, the question whether some word 'N' is the *correct* name of a given item is the same as the question whether 'N' is that item's name at all.

The assumption that the answers to those questions must be the same is not shared by everyone in the dialogue. It is shared by Hermogenes, for reasons which are (roughly) the opposite of Cratylus'. It is not shared by Socrates, whose final position requires us to distinguish the questions; or rather, to put it more precisely, it requires us to make a distinction which can be handily put by us in terms of a possible divergence between *the name of X* and *the correct name of X*, and is often so put in the dialogue, but which can also be expressed, as we shall see later, in terms of two kinds of correctness.

In trying to give some account of Cratylus' theory of names, I shall particularly emphasise that distinction and Cratylus' denial of it. Some of what I include in that theory is not advanced by Cratylus in the dialogue, but by Socrates in the course of his attempt, with Hermogenes, to elaborate a notion of 'the correctness of names' (see 391b for the start of their enquiry); but Cratylus fully adopts their theory (428c), and, whatever other status these conceptions may have, they are (at least in outline) consequences of the general views which are refuted in the argument against Cratylus at the end of the dialogue. Whether Plato displays any independent attachment to them is a question I shall touch on at the end.

According to Cratylus, then, if 'N' is not the name of a given item, it makes no difference if people call it 'N'—or, perhaps, try to call it so: the embarrassment at this point will grow into an objection. Equally, if it is the name of that item, it makes no difference if people do not so call it. The name-relation is purely binary, relating a word and an item. Names can, of course, be of different kinds, and while the first examples are proper names of people, this is not the basic case, and the theory applies to general terms; indeed, it applies to proper names because it applies to general terms. Exactly what kind of item is named by a general term is a question on which the dialogue gives us no help, and it need not concern the present discussion.

What could such a binary relation be? The first level of discussion which contributes to answering the question gives us the principle that if 'N' is the name of a given item, and 'N' can be resolved etymologically into other names, then the combination of those names must be appropriate to the item. But this, clearly, only raises another question; we eventually have to invoke a theory of elements, and these achieve their relation to what is named through imitation (*mimēsis*) (422 seq.), the basic idea, sketchily enough conveyed, being that the action of producing a certain vocal sound resembles some process in the domain of what is to be named. This theory, elaborated in detail through the labours of the etymological section, and presented with an immense degree of irony by Socrates to Cratylus, is agreed by him to represent his view (428c).

We originally saw that Cratylus holds

(1) If 'N' is the name at all of an item, it is the correct name of that item.

We have now learned

(2) If 'N' is the name of an item, 'N' bears a certain complex relation to that item.

Let us call that relation *the φ-relation*. The relation is to be explained in terms of the procedures for resolving names into other names, and, ultimately

(3) the φ-relation is grounded in the idea of an element of a name being a *mimēma* (430a9) of a process or natural feature.

There is a difficulty lurking in this which Plato seems to mark without pursuing. (3) requires that there should be elements of names which are related to reality through *mimēsis*, but it does not require that they should themselves be names: indeed they are not, and an elementary name—the simplest thing which is itself a name—is, relative to these elements, itself a complex.[1] While the theory permits this, there seems no reason why it should actually require it. Socrates is obviously right in saying at 422b that the correctness of those names that are elementary

---

[1] The point is discussed by Norman Kretzmann: 'Plato on the Correctness of Names', *American Philosophical Quarterly*, 8 (1971), 126–38.

will have to be tested 'by some other method'—i.e. not by etymological resolution; but it does not follow that they must be resolved into something other than names. They might be names whose correctness is to be tested by a method which does not involve resolving them at all.

It is unclear why the theory should not yield this outcome. There is indeed the point that the ultimate simples are sounds, which, except for the vowels, cannot be uttered by themselves: the nearest we can come to isolating them in speech is to add further and arbitrary elements to make them pronounceable. This point is of course made at 393e, merely in order to illustrate, early in the argument with Hermogenes, the general idea that the addition or subtraction of some elements need not destroy the effect of a name. But the status of the elements surely raises a question about the theory of the φ-relation. Why is it that the ultimate elements, when made with a little assistance into isolable names, turn out to be the names of those sounds (or letters), and not names of the natural features to which they are linked by *mimēsis*? The problem for Cratylus should not just be that the word for hardness can be either *sklērotēs* or *sklērotēr* (434c), but that it is not *rh(ō)* itself.

When Cratylus enters the dialogue at 428, he asserts claim (1) of his position in the strongest possible terms, resisting at the same time Socrates' suggestion that 'legislators' (*nomothetai*), regarded as originally imposing names, might be expected to have done their work better or worse. 'So are all names correctly applied (*orthōs keitai*)?', Socrates asks, and Cratylus answers, 'Inasmuch as they are names' (429b10–11). In reply, Socrates makes explicit the distinction denied by (1), in the form of distinguishing between the view that the name 'Hermogenes' does not apply (*keisthai*) to the third person present, and the view that it does apply, but 'not rightly'; and Cratylus says that it does not apply to him at all, but is rather the name of someone who has the appropriate nature, i.e. to whom that name bears the φ-relation.

Socrates' essential step in refuting these claims is to show that they leave Cratylus with nothing coherent to say when one introduces the dimension of what speakers actually do with names, a dimension necessarily left out by any view which finds the whole account of naming in the φ-relation, since that relation is simply a relation between words and things. Socrates' first example (429e) ingeniously introduces the act of addressing someone (*proseipein*) with the wrong name. The example is of one who, in foreign parts, greets Cratylus and says 'Welcome, Athenian visitor, Hermogenes, son of Smikrion!'[2] The question is, does he not

---

[2] Hermogenes' father's name was Hipponikos: 384a8, 406b8. It has been conjectured that Cratylus really was son of Smikrion: cf. Diels–Kranz, *Die Fragmente der Vorsakratiker* (6th edition), 11 65.1 and note.

even *address* Cratylus, but rather Hermogenes? Or no-one? When Cratylus replies that such a person would seem to him *phthenxasthai allōs*, 'to speak'—one could take it to mean—'to no purpose', his answer leaves Socrates still with the room to ask (rather oddly) whether what he spoke was true or false; but this elicits the explanation that he would be making a noise, like someone banging a pot, and this retrospectively offers the possibility of a different reading for *allōs*: he would *merely* be producing speech.[3]

This conclusion can be related quite simply to Cratylus' position. It is important that Cratylus does not have to say (what would be simply false) that the speaker addresses Hermogenes rather than Cratylus. He can reasonably say that there is a speech-act, which may be called 'addressing someone by name', such that there are two separate necessary conditions of its being true that X addresses Y by name:

(i) X addresses (speaks to, directs words to, etc.) Y;
(ii) In the course of (i), X uses a name which is a name of Y.

It will follow that in the situation which Socrates puts to Cratylus, the speaker does not address anyone by name: not Cratylus, because of condition (ii), and not Hermogenes, because of condition (i). If the purpose of his speaking was to address someone by name, then indeed he spoke *allōs*—even if Cratylus' final gloss on that failure is a little exaggerated.

However, that does not get Cratylus very far, and once the speech-act aspect of the question is raised at all, Socrates is in a position to show that even to understand Cratylus' theory requires one to understand possibilities which Cratylus denies. He shows this, first, with regard to mistakes, and, ultimately, with regard to convention.

Cratylus denied that, in the imagined situation, the speaker addressed anyone by name, since he did not satisfy both the conditions of doing that with respect to any one person. But he cannot deny that the speaker satisfied condition (i) with respect to the man in front of him: he certainly, for instance, spoke to him. Moreover, he used a particular name in relation to him; and Cratylus must know all that, or he could not diagnose the situation as he does. So Cratylus must accept that the speaker performed *some* speech-act in relation to the man in front of him, and indeed he must know what it is for X *to call* Y 'N'. But if so, then he

---

[3] This sense of ἄλλως, for instance in Sophocles *Ph.* 947, 'a mere image', is admittedly well attested only where ἄλλως occurs with a substantive (see Jebb, *ad loc.*). But the reading suggested, besides tying up with Cratylus' later remark, has the advantage that it gives him a reply which relates to, and undercuts, *all* the alternatives that Socrates presents in his question. φθέγξασθαι is of course a standard term not only for human sounds, but for animal cries (cf. Arist. *HA* 535a30) and for noises from inanimate things—for instance, a pot when struck, *Tht.* 179d. (I am grateful to the editors for comments on this matter.)

must know what it is for X to call Y 'N' although 'N' is not Y's name, and he is in a position to recognise mistake. Moreover, he must know what it is for almost everyone usually to call Y 'N', and he is in a position to recognise convention.

The argument about mistake is developed in terms of the allocation (*dianomē*) of names. One can identify Y and a particular name independently of one another, and one can bring that name to Y's attention (431a1–2, cf. 430e6–7, very forceful expressions of perceptual confrontation), just as one can bring to his attention a certain picture; and one can claim that what is displayed is his name or picture. Whatever relation constitutes a particular name's being his name—if, for instance, as Cratylus believes, it is much the same relation as constitutes a picture's being his picture—that claim may be false. Even when it is, there has certainly been an allocation; hence there are mistaken allocations of names.

It is important to see what a *dianomē* is. It is an activity which can be performed on either names or pictures in relation to their objects, and, according to Socrates' introduction of it (430d), has the properties that, in the case of a picture, if the picture is allocated to a person of which it is the picture, then the *dianomē* is correct (*orthē*), while in the case of a name, if it is allocated to the person of which it is the name, then the *dianomē* is both correct and true. This suggests that the *dianomē* does not simply involve the claim 'this is your picture (name)', for in any sense in which that is true or false, as well as right or wrong, with names, it is equally so with pictures. We should rather expect that *dianomē* is an activity which, when done with a name, yields a *logos*, something that can be true, and when done with a picture, does not. We can imagine wordless *dianomē* of a picture—handing it to the subject, for instance; and we can imagine a partly worded one, in the form of someone's saying, for instance, 'You are . . . ' and presenting a picture. The analogy to this in the case of names would be saying 'You are . . . ' and presenting a name. But 'presenting a name' is itself a linguistic activity (cf. 387c6 'naming is part of speaking'), and saying 'You are . . . ', followed by presenting 'N', comes to saying 'You are N', which, unlike its picture analogue, can be true as well as correct.[4] Of course, there is also a kind of statement that is available in both cases; that statement which Socrates gives, and which in the name case takes the form 'this is your name'.

Nothing here, any more than elsewhere, restricts the discussion to proper names. Indeed, in the picture case it seems that the pictures can be taken as ascribing the general properties of male and female (431a3–4). The model therefore has some potential to destroy those

[4] Cf. the formulation at 429c6 of the question to which the discussion of *dianomē* helps to give an answer: 'Is someone not mistaken who says *that he is Hermogenes?*'

general arguments against the possibility of falsehood, naturally associated with Cratylus' position, which put in an appearance at 429d; and that is recognised, in a rather sketchy way, at 431b. Those arguments rest, in one way or another, on the idea that an expression 'E' cannot misfit reality, since it must be allocated either to nothing, or to whatever it is that it fits. But this critic must have some conception of what counts as 'fitting', as I have called it, and of what it is that a given 'E' would fit. But then he has an understanding of some (at least) statements of the form ' "E" fits *that*', an understanding which allows also for the possibility of such a statement's being false; and that possibility is the same as that of 'E' misfitting reality.

This has the same structure as the *dianomē* argument in the *Cratylus*. Of course, the potential for destroying the argument against falsehood cannot be fully realised until a *general* way is found of locating independently the item which 'E' fits or misfits, and this is not achieved until the *Sophist*, if then. The point that the *Cratylus* does not achieve this has been made by John McDowell,[5] who points out that 'the function of indicating what is being talked about is not credited to a constituent in the account' but has to be discharged by an act of confrontation. (A similar limitation, it may be said, can be found in the account given by the *Theaetetus*, insofar as that is even partly successful, of false identity statements.) The *Cratylus*, however, disclaims any attempt to give a general answer (429d7–8), and what it does say perhaps has a greater potential for being generalised than the criticism allows. McDowell also objects that the *Cratylus*' contribution is not merely limited but misguided, on the ground that it tries to assimilate falsehood to partial accuracy, as though an expression could be discovered to misfit reality only if its general shape were right but other features wrong. But this is to connect the discussion of *dianomē* too closely to what follows. That discussion lasts to 431c3, and indeed relates, though not in very general terms, to the puzzles of falsehood; from 431c4, Socrates takes off on a further discussion (*au*, c4), designed to deal with the φ-relation itself.

This discussion reverts to issues of name-*giving*, and the activities of a *nomothetēs*. Plato might be thought to invite confusion by moving so easily between name-giving and the use of established words, since the possibilities of mistake are evidently so different in the two. But—as Plato clearly sees—they are different only if certain assumptions are made, assumptions which are denied by Cratylus. According to Cratylus, there is no act which a *nomothetēs* or anyone else can perform to *make* 'N' the name of Y—'N' either bears the required φ-relation to Y or it does not. Hence what is called 'name-giving' will be merely a trivial variant on

[5] *Plato Theaetetus* (Oxford 1973), 236.

describing. The distinction between name-giving and using an established name will collapse also at the other end of the spectrum, with that radical Humpty-Dumpty view which Hermogenes offers early on (384d1–2, 385a) as one version of what he opposes to Cratylus. As Cratylus assimilates name-giving to describing, so this assimilates describing to name-giving. The view, opposed to both of these, that what is Y's name depends on 'agreement and custom',[6] precisely leaves room for the distinction, since there is an important difference between following a practice and trying to initiate one.

In his attack on the φ-relation itself, Socrates first shows that there is a conflict between Cratylus' faith in *mimēsis* (his thesis (3)) and the all-or-nothing view that he takes of the name-relation, since *mimēsis* depends on resemblance, and resemblance is a matter of degree. The very notion of one thing's being an *eikōn*, a representation, of another, involves this point; for the only *absolute* notion of resemblance that could be used is that of indistinguishability, but an item indistinguishable from Cratylus would not be a representation of Cratylus, but 'another Cratylus'. The very idea of a representation of X, such as Cratylus takes a name to be, already implies at least a selection among the properties of X. The following argument, including the examples at 434–5, works from this point to show that we can recognise that 'N' is the name of Y independently of the exactness of its representation, and this, like the argument about *dianomē*, undermines thesis (1). But it goes further, for the same considerations show that one can recognise 'N' as the name of Y independently of resemblance altogether. (3) is wrong, and, as Hermogenes said (414c2), getting resemblance to do this job is a sticky business,[7] and we have to fall back on agreement. It is merely custom and agreement that makes a given name the name of a given item, and this excludes not merely this particular candidate for the φ-relation but any kind of φ-relation as constituting the name-relation itself.

The conclusion may be put in terms of the conditions for something's being a name; and that could leave it open whether there was some further question about the correctness of the names which, as things are, we use. Alternatively, the conclusion may itself be expressed in terms of correctness, as it is at 435c. In those terms, the conclusion will be that agreement and custom govern everyday correctness—they will be the determinants of whether someone has correctly used a name which we

---

[6] συνθήκη καὶ ἔθος, the standard phrase in the dialogue: cf. ἔθει τῶν ἐθισάντων, 384d8. As Robinson pointed out, it is only in that passage and in conjunction with that phrase that νόμῳ in this dialogue expresses the contrast to φύσις: see 'The Theory of Names in Plato's Cratylus', in *Essays in Greek Philosophy* (Oxford 1969), 112.

[7] 435c4–5: see the end-note for this translation.

have in our language. In that case, the further question that might possibly arise would be about the correctness of our language. We may then distinguish two ways in which questions about correctness may be raised. There are certainly questions of internal correctness, to be settled by reference to our linguistic practices. There may or may not be a question of external correctness, a question about the correctness of our linguistic practices.

Socrates agrees with Hermogenes that custom and agreement are the sole determinants of internal correctness. Hermogenes, however, thinks that there is no further question of external correctness, while Socrates thinks that there is: there are requirements on what a language has to be, which follow from what it has to do. This is the point of the tool analogies at 387 seq. But this, as Kretzmann[8] has made very clear, has nothing to do with any idea of the material properties of words resembling the world, as was claimed in the theory of the φ-relation. The resources of the language can be better or worse adapted to the requirements of dialectic, and that will make it better or worse in an external sense, but it will be so only in virtue of its structural properties and the semantic relations of its terms to each other, and not in virtue of their shape or sound or any such feature.

Socrates, then, differs from both Hermogenes and Cratylus in thinking that there are two questions, of internal and external correctness; or, in the alternative formulation, that there is one question about what the name for a given item is, and another about whether the practices that undoubtedly assign it that name are correct. Hermogenes thinks that there is only one question, settled by the appeal to our practices. Cratylus thinks that there is one question, to be settled by the basically external device of the φ-relation; but Socrates' own answer to the external question will be on totally different lines from that.

Socrates' conclusions are not formally inconsistent with claiming that names do as a matter of fact possess some mimetic features; nor do they strictly exclude the aim of remodelling the language so that names acquire such features. Many have thought that Plato does show some real attachment to the mimetic principle. But, so far as the actual language is concerned, the treatment of the etymological enterprise as a whole, and particularly the mimetic aspect, is loaded with irony and warnings (cf. 426b1, the reference to the expert; 428d, Socrates' doubts; and many other passages); while it is a notable fact that Socrates is prepared to rerun the entire diagnosis of the language on lines opposite to the Heraclitean principles which he and Hermogenes have used. He indeed says

[8] Op. cit., especially 135.

at 435c2–3 'it pleases me that names should be as far as possible like things', a formulation neutral between explanation of the actual language and aspiration for a better one; but it is permissible to take this as referring to what Socrates indeed claimed long before, that the structure of language should represent the structure of things.

Certainly that is all we should expect Plato to find important. Here one must bear in mind not just the conclusions already discussed, but the powerfully demystifying arguments towards the end of the dialogue about what might be learned from language. Cratylan *mimēsis* is not what makes our names function as names, and, if they display such features at all, the question arises of how they came to do so. They will, at best, be a flickering record of observations made by the *nomothetēs* (as one might say, by human experience). As a recipe for linguistic improvement, again, the mimetic principle has nothing to offer. The functions of language, and the purposes for which it might be improved, are to teach, learn, inform, divide up reality. The knowledge required for that can appear in language only if someone possesses it already; and while there might be point in making that knowledge appear structurally, and thus improving language dialectically, there can be no such point to altering it in the direction of Cratylan *mimēsis*.

Even if it is not formally inconsistent with them, an attachment to Cratylan *mimēsis* is in fact banished by the conclusions of the *Cratylus*. This brilliant, tough-minded and still underestimated dialogue does not only show that the idea of language's having mimetic powers could not explain what language is; it leaves the belief in such powers looking like what it is, a belief in magic.

END-NOTE

The phrase at 435c4–5, γλίσχρα ἡ ὁλκή αὕτη τῆς ὁμοιότητος, has received various translations. LSJ incautiously offers 'clinging' for γλίσχρα and 'attractive force' for ὁλκή. Jowett[4] treats both this, and Hermogenes' use of γλίσχρως at 414c2, which is explicitly mentioned here, in terms of 'hunger', and *Rep.* 488a2, ὡς γλίσχρως εἰκάζω is usually taken on the same lines: 'how greedy I am of similes'. Others have taken γλίσχρα to mean 'shabby', but this sense (e.g. d.23.208) clearly comes from the notion of tight-fistedness or being sticky with one's money, which does not fit; in any case, it hardly goes well with the comment that the appeal to agreement is something φορτικόν. Neither line pays enough attention to 414c, where the adverb has to be attached to verbs which express the addition or subtraction of letters by the etymological interpreter, while Socrates' reply cites, in the usual ironical tone, conditions that supposedly make these elaborate manoeuvres necessary. This would fit an interpretation of 435 which gives the γλίσχρα ὁλκή as, straightforwardly, 'a sticky haul', like getting a ship to move over a gummy slip-way: one has to work hard to try to keep the resemblance theory moving.*

---

* Anyone who knows Gwil Owen and is interested in ancient philosophy will have learned from him. I myself, though only a part-time student of these subjects, have had the good fortune of being able to learn from him for more than thirty years.

However, I hope, as other contributors must hope, that this book will be read by many people who will never have known Gwil at all. That reflection often tempts contemporaries to reminisce, in the hope of preserving the essence of their friend and teacher for the future. With regard to Gwil as teacher, that temptation need not be indulged. His writings, in their compression, intense power of argument, and brilliantly resourceful learning, convey better than any selection of anecdote what his influence has been.

TEN

Plato: The Invention of Philosophy

Plato invented the subject of philosophy as we know it. He lived from 427 to 347 BC,[1] and he is the first philosopher whose works have come down to us complete. He is also the first to have written on the full range of philosophical questions: knowledge, perception, politics, ethics, art; language and its relations to the world; death, immortality and the nature of the mind; necessity, change and the underlying order of things. A. N. Whitehead said that the European philosophical tradition consisted of 'a series of footnotes to Plato'[2], and his remark makes a point. Of course, the content of the questions has changed in all sorts of ways, with the development of the sciences and radical transformations in society and culture. It is important, too, that we, unlike Plato, have a strong sense of the importance of history in understanding human life, but this sense has come about quite recently, and is absent not only from Plato but from most other philosophers before the nineteenth century, who tended, like him and under his influence, to think of the most important truths as timeless.[3]

Western philosophy not only started with Plato, but has spent most of its life in his company. There was a period in the Middle Ages when almost all his works were unknown, but before that, and after the rediscovery of his texts (Petrarch in the fourteenth century had a manuscript of Plato), he has been read and has been a point of reference. Some thinkers, in various different styles, have thought of themselves as 'Platonists'; most others have not, and many reject every one of his distinctive positions, but they are all indirectly under his influence. We are all under the influence of thinkers we do not read, but in Plato's case, people also turn back continually to his work itself. He is in any case a great writer, who can command extraordinary ingenuity, charm, and power, but beyond that, his genius as a philosophical writer is expressed in a special way. Many philosophers write treatises, analysing the problem, arguing with other positions, and setting out their own solutions. Plato did not: he wrote dialogues. With the exception of some *Letters*, which are doubtfully genuine,[4] all Plato's works are in this form. Because they are dialogues, there is always something more and different to be drawn from them, not just in the way that this is true of all great works of philosophy, but because Plato specially intends it to be so. The dialogue form is not, for the most part, just an artful way of his telling one something. It is an entry and an invitation to thought.

Plato never appears in the dialogues himself.[5] In most of them, a major part is taken by the striking figure of Socrates, Plato's teacher. They are by far our most important source for what Socrates was like.[6] Socrates is the inspiration of the dialogues in more than one way. He himself wrote nothing, and indeed claimed to know nothing, devoting himself, it seems, to engaging people in conversations in which he questioned their most basic beliefs and showed that they had no basis for them. This method is described in several of Plato's dialogues, and many of them display it in action. But Socrates' legacy was not just a matter of method. His life, and more particularly his death, left Plato with some of his deepest concerns. Socrates was tried by the Athenian courts in 399 BC and executed, on charges, among other things, of 'corrupting the youth', and this disaster starkly raised a range of questions: what the evil was in a political order that could do this; how it was that Socrates' presence had not made his fellow citizens (including some of his associates) better people; and how much it mattered—whether in the end it mattered at all—that Socrates' life was lost, granted that his character was uncorrupted. All these were to be central themes of Plato's philosophy, a philosophy expressed through the dialogue form which was itself a tribute in writing to Socrates' style of life and talk.*

In some of the dialogues, particularly some that can be dated to late in Plato's life, the conversational form withers away, and they do function almost as treatises. In a few, characters other than Socrates do not express much more than puzzlement, agreement, or admiration. But for the most part, the dialogue form is an active presence, and this affects in more than one way our relations to Plato's ideas. In some dialogues, no one offers a definite conclusion, and we find that we have been presented with a question, a refutation, or a puzzle. This particularly applies to those which we can take to have been written in Plato's earlier years, but it is also true, to a considerable extent, of a notably powerful later dialogue, the *Theaetetus*.[7] Even when an authoritative figure in a dialogue, usually Socrates, seems to leave us with a conclusion or theory to be taken away from it, we should not necessarily suppose that this is what Plato is telling us to believe.[8]

Not everything asserted in a dialogue, even by Socrates, has been asserted by Plato: Socrates asserting may be Plato suggesting. Because Plato is an immensely serious philosopher, who indeed set philosophy on the path of claiming to address our deepest concerns by means of argu-

* As a help in identifying the various dialogues mentioned in this book, there is a list of them, with brief descriptions, at p. 180.

ment, orderly enquiry, and intellectual imagination, and because we project on to him images of seriousness which are drawn from other philosophy[9] and from later experience, we may well underestimate the extent to which he could combine intensity, pessimism, and even a certain religious solemnity, with an ironical gaiety and an incapacity to take all his own ideas equally seriously. It is a weakness of scholars who study philosophers to think that philosophers are just like scholars, and it is particularly a mistake in the case of Plato. Plato gathered about him a group of people who pursued philosophical discussion, teaching and enquiries into mathematics and astronomy. This gave rise, eventually, to a new kind of institution, a place for what we would now call 'research'. From the public space on the edge of Athens in which Plato carried on his discussions, it was called the Academy[10], and in this way Plato gave the word 'academic' to the world, but it is an irony that he should have done so. We should not be trapped into thinking of him as a professor.

This point bears on a passage which itself raises a question of how far we should trust his written works. Towards the end of the *Phaedrus*[11], there is this conversation:

SOCRATES: Well, then, someone who thinks that he can set down an art in writing, and equally someone who accepts something from writing as though it were going to be clear and reliable, must be very simple-minded ... how can they possibly think that words which have been written down can do more than serve as a reminder to those who already know what the writing is about?

PHAEDRUS: Quite right.

SOCRATES: You know, Phaedrus, writing shares a strange feature with painting. The offspring of painting stand there as if they were alive, but if anyone asks them anything, they are solemnly silent. The same is true of written words. You'd think they were speaking as if they had some understanding, but if you question anything that has been said because you want to learn more, it gives just the same message over and over. Once it has been written down, every discourse rolls about everywhere, reaching just as much those with understanding as those who have no business with it, and it does not know to whom it should speak and to whom not. And when it is faulted and attacked unfairly, it always needs its father's support; alone, it cannot defend itself or come to its own support.

PHAEDRUS: You are quite right about that too.

SOCRATES: Now tell me, can we discern another kind of discourse, a legitimate brother of this one? Can we say how it comes about, and how much better and more capable it naturally is?

PHAEDRUS: Which one is that? How do you say it comes about?

SOCRATES: It is a discourse that is written down, with knowledge, in the soul of the listener; it can defend itself, and it knows to whom it should speak, and with whom it should remain silent.

PHAEDRUS: You mean the living, breathing discourse of the man who knows, of which the written one can fairly be called an image.

SOCRATES: Exactly—and tell me this. Would a farmer who was sensible and cared about his seeds and wanted them to yield fruit plant them in all seriousness in the gardens of Adonis in the middle of summer and enjoy watching them become fine plants in a week? Or would he do this as an amusement and in honour of the holiday, if he did it at all? Wouldn't he use his knowledge of farming to plant the seeds he cared for when it was appropriate, and be satisfied if they bore fruit eight months later?

PHAEDRUS: That's how he would handle those he was serious about, Socrates, quite differently from the others, as you say.

SOCRATES: Now what about the man who knows what is just, noble and good? Shall we say that he is less sensible with his seeds than the farmer is with his?

PHAEDRUS: Certainly not.

SOCRATES: Therefore he wouldn't be serious if he wrote them in ink, sowing them, through a pen, with words that are unable to speak in their own defence and unable to teach the truth properly.

PHAEDRUS: He surely wouldn't.

SOCRATES: No—he is likely to sow gardens of writing just for fun, and to write, when he writes, to store up reminders for himself when he arrives at old age and forgetfulness, and for other people who follow in his footsteps, and he will like to see them sweetly blooming; and while others take up other amusements, refreshing themselves with drinking parties and such things, he is likely to enjoy himself, rather, like this.

PHAEDRUS: Socrates, you are contrasting a vulgar amusement with a very fine one—with the amusement of a man who can while away his time telling stories of justice and the other things you mentioned.

SOCRATES: That's just how it is, Phaedrus. But there is a much finer concern about these things—that of someone who uses the art of dialectic, and takes a suitable soul and plants and sows discourse accompanied with knowledge: discourse which is capable of helping itself and the sower, which is not barren but produces a seed from which other discourse grows in other lives, and in turn can go on to make the seed immortal, making the man who has it as happy as any man can be.

Phaedrus, 275c–277a

By 'the art of dialectic' here Socrates means argument in speech, teaching through conversation. There has been discussion of why Plato, after this, should have gone on writing. But even if we take Socrates' remarks (a little stolidly, perhaps) entirely at their face value, they do not mean that Plato should not write—they give him a reason to write, and that reason is obviously only one among similar reasons we might imagine. This passage does not mean the end of philosophical writing. But it does express an important idea about the limitations of philosophical writing, an idea which, I shall suggest, is important in relation to the spirit in which Plato wrote his works and the spirit in which we should read them.

PLATO'S DEVELOPMENT

A complication in trying to extract Plato's philosophy from the dialogues is that they do not all present the same philosophy, and his views and interests, not surprisingly, changed over time. It is thus very important to establish, if we can, the order in which the dialogues were written. There are various sorts of evidence that can be brought to bear on this. There are occasionally references to historical events. Some dialogues refer explicitly or by implication to others. There is a technique called 'stylometry', which treats certain features of Plato's style statistically to establish gradual changes in them over time. In addition, there is the content of the various dialogues, in terms of which we can try to make sense of Plato's philosophical development. Here there is an obvious danger that we shall fall into a circle, dating the dialogues in terms of their ideas, and working out the development of the ideas from the order of the dialogues. However, with the help of all these methods together, scholars have arrived at a fair measure of agreement.[12]

The earliest is a group of short dialogues often called 'Socratic' because the role played by Socrates does not go beyond what, it is generally thought, can reasonably be ascribed to the historical Socrates himself. There is then a pair of dialogues, the *Gorgias* and the *Meno*, which, as we shall see, seem to mark a transition from the concerns of the Socratic dialogues to those of Plato's Middle Period, in which, as everyone now agrees, he goes beyond the interests of the historical Socrates, and develops very distinctive ideas of his own. The Middle Period contains what may be the most famous of his dialogues, the *Phaedo*, the *Symposium*, and the *Republic*.[13] These dialogues have particularly helped to form the traditional picture of 'the Platonic philosophy', which contrasts with the everyday physical world of appearance a realm of intellectual, eternal objects, which are the objects of real knowledge and can be directly attained, in some sense, by the immortal soul. These objects are called 'Forms', and we shall be concerned later with questions of what Plato thought they could explain, and how far he had a consistent theory of them.

These famous dialogues of the Middle Period were not by any means Plato's last word, and among the hardest questions in Platonic scholarship is to decide exactly which dialogues are later than the Middle Period, and to form a picture of how much, and in what ways, Plato may have changed his mind and his approach as he got older. The late dialogues include the *Theaetetus, Sophist, Statesman, Philebus* and *Laws*.[14] The last (from which Socrates has finally disappeared) is probably the least read of Plato's major dialogues: it is a long discussion, in twelve books, of political and social arrangements, in a more realistic but also much darker tone than that of the *Republic*.

There are two dialogues that, together, give rise to problems of dating in a particularly acute form. On stylometric grounds, the *Timaeus* seems to be a late dialogue. However, it gives an elaborate account of the creation of things by a 'demiurge' who imposes form on matter (there is no question in Plato of a divine creation of the world from nothing, as in the Christian tradition), and it refers to the Forms in terms very similar to those used in Middle Period works such as, above all, the *Republic*. On the other hand, the *Parmenides*, which cannot be distinguished stylistically from Middle Period dialogues, contains a number of extremely serious criticisms of those ways of talking about Forms, criticisms which many, including Aristotle, have regarded as fatal. They occur in the first part of the dialogue, where a very young Socrates is represented conversing with the old and sage figure of Parmenides, who in fact wrote a bold metaphysical poem claiming the unity of everything and the impossibility of change, and who was held in great respect by Plato.[15] (It is just possible, in terms of dates, that Socrates should have met Parmenides, very unlikely that he did so, and quite certain that they could not have had such a conversation.) Socrates advances an account of Forms to which Parmenides (virtually quoting from the *Phaedo*), makes a series of objections which Socrates cannot answer. Parmenides says that he needs training in 'dialectic' (which was, significantly, Plato's favourite term for more than one method in philosophy which, at various times, he found most promising). He suggests that Socrates listen to a demonstration on a theme taken from Parmenides' companion and pupil, Zeno,[16] and is prevailed upon to mount the demonstration himself. The second part of the dialogue consists of a very elaborate set of entirely abstract arguments, the content, and indeed the whole point, of which are still not agreed.

On one picture of Plato's development, he started with the modest methods of enquiry that he acquired from Socrates. He then developed a 'theory of Forms', with the very ambitious doctrines, particularly about immortality, that are associated with it in the *Republic*, the *Phaedo*, and the *Symposium*. He then became convinced that there were deep difficulties with the theory, difficulties which are expressed in the *Parmenides*. Then, in later works, notably the *Theaetetus, Sophist*, and

Statesman, which are without doubt more technical, he pursued in much more severely analytical detail problems that had been latent in the grand theories of the Middle Period.

I think that there is some truth in this schema[17] and some of what I say about Plato's outlook will be in this spirit, but we should not be tied to any simple version of it. In particular, we should not ask whether or when Plato gave up 'the Theory of Forms', because, as we shall see, there is no Theory of Forms. In any case, it is artificial[18] to discuss these matters as though Plato wrote his dialogues in an order, in the sense that he always finished one before starting another. He may have had more than one unfinished at once; still more, the ideas that appeared in various dialogues were at work in his head at the same time.

Above all, it is a mistake to suppose that Plato spends his time in the various dialogues adding to or subtracting from his system. Each dialogue is about whatever it is about, and Plato pursues what seems interesting and fruitful in that connection. We often cannot know, in fact, exactly what made a consideration seem to him interesting and fruitful at a given point. Plato was recognizably, I think, one of those creative thinkers and artists—it is not true of all, including some of the greatest—who are an immensely rich source of thoughts and images, too many, perhaps, for them all to have their place and use. We may think of him as driven forward by his ideas, curious at any given point to see what will happen if some striking conjunction of them is given its head. We should not think of him as constantly keeping his accounts, anxious of how his system will look in the history of philosophy.

The Socratic Dialogues

In the early dialogues Socrates typically appears discussing with one or more characters a question about the nature of the virtues, and refutes some claim to knowledge which they have made, while offering his habitual disclaimer to the effect that he himself knows nothing. To this extent, the dialogues are 'aporetic', that is to say, negative in their outcome, but there is often some significant suggestion in the offing. In the *Laches*, a characteristic example, Socrates is asked by two distinguished citizens, Nicias and Laches, whether young men should be trained to fight in armour; he draws them into a discussion about the nature of courage. Their common-sensical suggestions are refuted, and no conclusion is reached. By the end, however, Socrates has implicitly advanced a distinctive view, by associating the virtue of courage with knowledge, as he does elsewhere with other virtues. Moreover, the dramatic frame of the dialogue introduces a theme which was to be of constant concern to Plato, and which is brought to focus later in the *Meno*: how is it that worthy people in an earlier generation, who basically, if unreflectively, lived by decent values, were unable, as Plato believed, to pass them on to their children?[19]

One of the dialogues that is assigned to the early group on grounds of its style and, in general terms, its content, is the *Protagoras*, but it is a strikingly special case. Socrates tells how he was woken early in the morning by an enthusiastic friend wanting him to come to a house where they could see the great teacher, Protagoras, who is visiting Athens. Protagoras is a 'sophist', someone who takes fees for teaching, in particular for teaching young people how to be successful and happy. Plato repeatedly attacks such people, and it is to him, principally, that they owe their bad reputation, but he clearly had a genuine respect for Protagoras. He comes out very well from this dialogue, and later, in the *Theaetetus*, though he does not appear himself, Plato discusses as his invention a sophisticated theory based on his well-known saying, 'man is the measure of all things.'

Admitted to the house, Socrates and his friend find Protagoras surrounded by admirers, and there is also a notable group of other sophists, sketched by Plato with a lightly malicious touch. Socrates raises the question whether virtue can be taught. Protagoras gives a long and brilliant speech in which he tells a story about the natural defencelessness of human beings and their survival through their intelligence and inventiveness, and he lays out what may be seen as a theory of knowledge for democracy:[20] virtue can be taught, but, unlike the arts, where there is a division of labour and conspicuous experts, in the matter of virtue citizens teach their children and each other.

Plato gives Protagoras a compelling and thoughtful expression of such an outlook, though it is exactly what he himself rejected. He himself came to believe that there were distinctive kinds of knowledge that must underlie virtue, and the project of the *Republic* is to design a social order which will indeed be authoritarian, because it will use political power to express the authority of knowledge. There is no place in this for democracy. Plato typically compares a democratic city to a ship navigated by majority vote of the passengers, and in the *Republic* it is represented in hostile and embittered terms, as, in the *Gorgias*, the greatest of Athenian democratic leaders, Pericles[21], is brutally attacked as a demagogue. Here, however, Protagoras is allowed to offer a different and more benign conception. It is an example of something that is one of Plato's strengths, even if his polemics sometimes conceal it—that he can understand, not just the force of contrary arguments, but the power of an opposing vision.

In the course of the exchanges that follow, Socrates demands, as he often does in the presence of sophists and teachers of rhetoric, that there should be a real conversation, proceeding by question and answer, and that there should be no long speeches. The idea (which no doubt came from the historical Socrates himself) is that only through question and answer is it possible to construct and follow a logical argument, which will actually prove or disprove a definite conclusion: speeches allow irrelevance, bad logic, and misleading emotional appeals. Quite often, characters in the dialogues complain about Socrates' method. Even if they do not put it in quite these terms, they might be said to see the question and answer form as itself a rhetorical contrivance, one that helps Socrates to force his opponents down a favoured train of thought, often a chain of misleading analogies, instead of giving them a chance to stand back and ask what other kinds of consideration might bear on the issue. The criticism certainly occurs to many of Plato's readers.

When Socrates' procedure invites that criticism, one must in any case ask, as I suggested earlier, whether Plato necessarily expects the reader to accept his argument or to question it. But there is a further point, that we should not assume that 'the force of argument' is an entirely fixed and determinate notion. It is not so anyway, and it is less so in Plato, for the special reason that he more or less invented the idea.[22] What one sees in his dialogues is a process, of his seeking in many different ways to distinguish sound argument from the mere power of persuasive speech, as it might be heard in an Athenian law court, for instance. Ancient Greeks, and particularly, perhaps, the notoriously litigious and political Athenians, were very impressed by the power of speech. It is significant that the common Greek word *logos* had semantic roots in both speech and reason; it can mean 'word', 'utterance', 'story', 'account', 'explanation', 'reason', and 'ratio', among other things. One of Plato's major and ongoing undertakings was to construct models of what it is for an utterance not just to tell a story but to give a reason.

In the *Protagoras*, after his protests against speeches, Socrates makes a long one himself, which is an engaging parody of another sophistic method, that of advancing a view by commenting on a poem, a method which he shows, in effect, can be used to prove anything you like.[23] He then turns to refuting Protagoras's position, but this, too, takes a strange turn, since he claims as the basis of his argument that the only good is pleasure, something that Plato himself quite certainly did not believe. At the end of this brilliantly inventive dialogue, the two protagonists, Socrates and Protagoras, find themselves in a puzzling situation, with great respect for each other, and much work still to be done:

—I have only one more question to ask you. Do you still believe, as you did at first, that some men are extremely ignorant and yet still very courageous?
—I think you just want to win the argument, Socrates, and that is

why you are forcing me to answer. So I will gratify you and say that on the basis of what we have agreed upon, it seems to me to be impossible.

—I have no other reason for asking these things than my desire to answer these questions about virtue, especially what virtue is in itself. For I know that if we could get clear on that, then we would be able to settle the question about which we both have had much to say: I, that virtue cannot be taught, you, that it can. It seems to me that the recent outcome of our argument has turned on us like a person making fun of us, and that if it had a voice it would say 'Socrates and Protagoras, how strange you are, both of you. Socrates, you said earlier that virtue cannot be taught, but now you are insisting on the opposite, trying to show that everything is knowledge—justice, temperance, courage—in which case virtue would appear to be eminently teachable. On the other hand, if virtue is something other than knowledge, as Protagoras has been trying to say, then clearly it would not be teachable. But if it turns out to be wholly knowledge, as you are now insisting, Socrates, it would be very surprising indeed if virtue could not be taught. Protagoras maintained at first that it could be taught, but now he thinks the opposite, urging that hardly any of the virtues turn out to be knowledge. On that view, it hardly could be true that it was teachable.'

Now, Protagoras, seeing that everything is upside down and in a terrible confusion, I am most eager to clear it all up, and I would like us, having come this far, to continue until we come through to what virtue is in itself, and then to enquire once more whether it can or cannot be taught . . . If you are willing, as I said at the beginning, I would be pleased to investigate these things along with you.

—Socrates, I commend your enthusiasm and your ability to find your way through an argument. I really don't think I am a bad man, and certainly I am the last man to be envious. Indeed, I have told many people that I admire you more than anyone I have met, certainly more than anyone in your generation. And I say that I would not be surprised if you came to be very well regarded for wisdom. We shall examine these matters later, whenever you wish. But now the time has come to turn to other things.

Protagoras, 360d–361e

VIRTUE IS NOT YET KNOWLEDGE

The question whether virtue can be taught is taken up in the *Meno*, and again it leads to another: how can one answer this question if one does not already know what virtue is? To ask what a particular virtue is, is a standard Socratic move, as he asked about courage in the *Laches*, but now Plato explains rather more fully than he had earlier what the answer to any such question might be like. It cannot consist of a list of examples—that will not show what the examples have in common. It cannot merely be a characteristic that necessarily goes with the item in question: we cannot say, for instance, that shape is 'the only thing that always accompanies colour'[24]—that is true, perhaps, but it does not explain what shape is. This discussion of method gives us some ideas that were implicit in Socratic questioning, but were not all clearly recognized. One is that the account we are looking for (in this case, of virtue) must be explanatory—it must not simply capture an adequate definition of the word, but must give us insight into what virtue is. This in turn raises the possibility that the account may have to be part of a larger theory.

A further idea is that the account will not leave everything where it was. It may revise the ideas that people typically have of the virtues. Indeed, it may well require them to change their lives. That, certainly, was part of Socrates' project, even if it was not clear how it could be so. The distinctively Platonic idea, which begins to grow in the *Meno*, is that it is theory that, in one way or another, must change one's life.

But now Meno finds an obstacle to the search for what virtue is:

MENO: How will you look for something, Socrates, when you do not know at all what it is? What sort of thing will you set as the target of your search, among the things you do not know? If you did meet with it, how would you know that this was the thing that you did not know?

SOCRATES: I understand what you want to say, Meno. Do you realize that this is a debater's argument you are bringing up: that a man cannot search either for what he knows or for what he does not know? He cannot search for what he knows—since he knows it, there is no need for a search; nor for what he does not know, since he does not know what to look for.

MENO: Does that argument not seem sound to you, Socrates?

SOCRATES: Not to me.

MENO: Can you tell me why?

SOCRATES: I can.

And he goes on to say something which in terms of the earlier dialogues is extraordinary:

SOCRATES: I have heard from men and women who are wise about divine things . . .

MENO: What do they say?

SOCRATES: Something, I thought, both true and beautiful.

MENO: What is it, and who are they?

SOCRATES: Those who say it are among the priests and priestesses whose care it is to be able to give an account of their practices. Pindar too says it, and many other poets, those who are divine. What they say is this; see whether you think they speak the truth. They say that the human soul is immortal; at times it comes to an end, which they call dying, at times it is reborn, but it is never destroyed. So one must live as holy a life as possible:

> Persephone will receive the debt of ancient wrong;
> In the ninth year she will give back their souls to the sun above.
> And from these there will grow noble kings, and men great in
>   strength and skill,
> And for the rest of time they shall be called sacred heroes.[25]

As the soul is immortal and has been born often and has seen everything here and in the underworld, there is nothing that it has not learned; so it is not surprising that it can recollect the things it knew before, about virtue and about other things. As the whole of nature is akin, and the soul has learned everything, nothing prevents a man, after he has recalled just one thing—the process that people call learning—discovering everything else for himself, if he is brave and does not tire of the search; for searching and learning are simply recollection.

Meno 80d–81d

These are stories, Socrates admits, not demonstrations, but perhaps there can be a demonstration. He summons a slave boy, and, in a famous scene, gets him, merely by questioning him, to see the solution to a geometrical problem which he had never even heard of at the beginning of their conversation. How can this be possible? Socrates' suggestion is that the demonstration reminded the boy of the answer; he knew it already, but until now had forgotten it. Since he knew it already, he must have learned it already; but he did not learn it in this life, so he learned it in an earlier life. The soul is immortal.

It is not much of an argument. There is in any case an objection, that even if we have been shown by this episode that the boy's soul existed earlier, there is nothing here to show that it will exist later—pre-existence is less than immortality. Plato fills in the missing piece by pure sleight of hand.[26] But there is a deeper and more interesting problem. It is often objected to in this scene that Socrates leads the boy in the demonstration. This misses the point. If the question had been one in history or geography, the boy could not, in any comparable way, have come to see the answer: in such subjects, if one does not know, one does not know. It is essential that the exercise is in mathematics and involves what is called *a priori* knowledge, knowledge which is independent of experience. Plato offers here the first theory of such knowledge.

The demonstration may well show something about how we become conscious of *a priori* knowledge. Indeed, many philosophers have agreed with Plato to this extent, that such knowledge is in some sense innate. Very few, however, have agreed that this has anything to do with an earlier existence. For why should we say that there was some more direct way in which the boy must have originally learned it? Learning in the way that the boy has just learned, the way displayed in the demonstration, is how we learn mathematics: how could there be some more direct, original, way of doing so? Plato thinks, or will come to think, that there is an answer to this question, that the naked soul once saw mathematical objects directly by the eye of the intellect. But how could such a process possibly be a way of coming to know mathematics? It is a strange, and typically metaphysical, reversal; Plato praises reason over sense perception, the intellectual over the material, but, trying to give an account of *a priori* knowledge, he straight off interprets it as an intellectual version of sense perception.

Socrates says that the boy does not yet properly know this mathematical truth (in this life), because he has no secure hold on it, will no doubt forget it, and, most importantly, cannot explain it. At the moment it is a mere belief, which will become knowledge only if it is 'tied down by a chain of reasoning'. Later on in the *Meno*, he illustrates this important distinction between knowledge and true belief by a different sort of example. He contrasts a man who knows the way to Larissa,[27] because he has been there, with one who simply happens to have got it right. Put like this, the distinction is not confined to any particular subject matter: if you have a true belief, and you have the reasons, the backing, or the experience appropriate to that kind of belief, then you have knowledge. This does not suggest, as the experiment with the geometry problem might perhaps suggest, that only *a priori* knowledge is really knowledge. Still less does it suggest—indeed, it contradicts the suggestion—that knowledge might have one subject matter and belief another. As we shall see, Plato does come to some such position in the *Republic*, but that is to move a long way, and in a rather perverse direction, from what is first offered in the *Meno*.

Socrates uses the *Meno*'s distinction between knowledge and true belief to answer the familiar question: how can decent men have failed to teach their sons to have their own virtues? He and Meno, even though they do not know what virtue is, have agreed to conduct their argument on an assumption: if virtue is knowledge, then it must be teachable. Certainly virtue has not been taught. The sophists claim to do so, but if they have any effect at all, it is to make their pupils worse people. More significantly, worthy men, who care above all that their sons should share their virtues, have failed to bring this about. So, it seems, virtue is not teachable, and therefore, on the assumption which they have accepted, it is not knowledge. That is, in a way, correct, but given the *Meno*'s distinction, it does not mean that virtue could not become knowledge. What we learn from the worthy men's experience is only that *their* virtue was not knowledge. It was not nothing, however: they did have virtue, but it took the form of true belief. That worked all right for them in practice, just as a true belief about the road to Larissa will get you there, and will enable you to lead others there if they are actually with you. It does not enable you to teach another to get there by himself. But if we could find the right chains of reasoning to tie these beliefs down, so they do not run away, then they might become knowledge, and then they could be taught. Philosophy will provide those chains of reasoning, and this is how it will change our lives.

That Plato should present Socrates as making this point has a special pathos about it, for the most striking instance of someone who failed to teach his virtue was Socrates himself. Socrates had a pupil and a lover,[28] Alcibiades, who was very talented and, it seems, very beautiful. His life was a disaster: vain and petulant, he betrayed Athens and others as well, and died a ruined man. The case of Alcibiades was a reproach to Socrates as a teacher, and Plato's recurrent and developing concern with the issues discussed in the *Meno* is a response to that reproach, an ongoing apology. In the *Symposium* Plato confronts squarely the relations between Socrates and Alcibiades, and one of the less obvious features of that wonderful dialogue is the ethical assurance with which he does so. In his own contribution to the series of speeches, Socrates had already said that the goddess Diotima had told him[29] that he himself would not reach the highest level of intellectual love, which in outline she describes to him, love in the presence of the Form of beauty; this signals the metaphysical deficit, so to speak, which Plato diagnosed in Socrates' experience. Alcibiades, drunk, bursts into the party after the speeches (his part has to be something separate, dramatic, not a contribution under the rules of the occasion). He gives a vivid account of Socrates, and of their strange relations. It is an encomium, and we are to take it as true; it reveals some understanding; but at the same time it shows that, whatever might possibly be learned from Socrates, Alcibiades, inside an invincible vanity, could not learn it.

THE ETHICAL CHALLENGE

It was not merely that decent people did not manage to pass on their values, because they did not grasp and could not explain reasons for leading a decent life. There were also people who argued that there was no reason to lead a decent life, and that the best idea would be a life of ruthless self-interest. How many people argued this as a philosophic position we do not know, but certainly there was a social attitude, to the effect that the conventional values of justice—to behave fairly and co-operatively, keep one's word, consider others' interests—were a racket, which was encouraged by people who were intelligent and powerful and did not need to live like this themselves.

There are two characters in the dialogues who express this view. One, the more colourful and formidable, is Callicles in the *Gorgias*. Callicles' first speech offers a powerfully expressed challenge both to the life of justice and to the activity of philosophy, as contrasted with a political life in which one can exercise power. Besides the reference to Socrates' trial and execution, perhaps one can hear, too, what Plato knew might be said of himself if he had got it wrong about applying his talents to philosophy:

> We mould the best and the most powerful among us, taking them while they're still young, like lion cubs, and with charms and incantations we subdue them into slavery, telling them that one is supposed to get no more than his fair share, and that this is what is fair and just. But I believe that if there were to be a man whose nature was up to it, one who had shaken off, torn apart, and escaped all this, who had trampled under foot our documents, our trickery and charms, and all those laws that are against nature—he, the slave, would rise up and be revealed as our master, and then the justice of nature would shine out . . .
>
> Philosophy is no doubt a charming thing, Socrates, if someone is exposed to it in moderation at the appropriate time of life. But if one spends more time on it than he should, it is the undoing of mankind. For even if someone has great natural advantages, if he engages in philosophy far beyond the appropriate time of life, he will inevitably turn out to be inexperienced in all those things in which a man has to be experienced if he is to be admirable and good and well thought of. Such people have no experience of the laws of their city or of the kind of speech one must use to deal with people on matters of business, public or private; they have no experience in human pleasures and appetites; no experience, in short, of human character altogether. So when they venture into some private or political activity, they become a laughing stock . . .
>
> So when I see an older man still engaging in philosophy and not giving it up, I think such a man by this time needs a flogging. As I was just saying, such a man, even with natural advantages, will end up becoming unmanly and avoiding the middle of the city and its meeting places—where, as the poet said, men become really distinguished—

and will slink away for the rest of his life, whispering with three or four boys in a corner, never coming out with anything free-spirited, important, or worth anyone's attention . . .

As it is, if someone got hold of you or of anyone else like you and took you off to prison on the charge that you're doing something unjust when you're not, be assured that you wouldn't be able to do yourself any good. You would get dizzy, your mouth would hang open, and you would not know what to say. You would come up for trial and face some no-good wretch of an accuser and be put to death, if death is what he wanted as your sentence. How can this be a wise thing, Socrates, 'the craft which took a well-favoured man and made him worse', not able to protect himself or to rescue himself or anyone else from the gravest dangers, to be robbed by his enemies, and to live a life without honour in the city? To put it rather crudely, you could give such a man a smack on the jaw and get away with it. Listen to me, friend, and stop this refuting. 'Practise the sweet music of an active life and do it where you'll get a reputation for being intelligent. Leave these subtleties to others'—whether we call them merely silly, or outright nonsense—'which will cause you to live in empty houses', and do not envy those who go in for these fiddling refutations, but those who have a life, and fame, and many other good things as well.

Gorgias, 483e–486d (with omissions)

Socrates has already had two conversations before Callicles appears, and they are carefully structured to show how radical Callicles' outlook is. The first speaker is Gorgias, a famous orator and teacher of rhetoric, who gives a defence of his profession. Plato believes that this profession is dangerous and its claims to any expertise hollow, and in this notably angry dialogue he goes on to denounce the rhetorician as a technician of mere appearances, like someone who serves the sick with rich and unhealthy pastries or paints the face of the dying. But Gorgias himself is treated with some respect. He indeed gives a respectable defence: he thinks that his skills serve the cause of justice, that the life of justice is worth living, and that to be a just person is *kalon*—a significant ethical term for the Greeks, which means that it is worthy of admiration, and that a person would properly be well regarded and would have self-respect for living such a life.

He is succeeded in the conversation (as, Plato believes, also in social reality) by a younger and more belligerent figure, who is called Polus. He thinks that the life of justice is not reasonable; given an alternative, it is not worth pursuing. Under Socrates' questioning,[30] however, he makes the mistake of admitting both that justice is *kalon*, worth admiring, and also (reasonably) that something worth admiring is worth pursuing. Having said that justice is not worth pursuing, he is faced, Socrates shows him, with a contradiction. Granted that he thinks that we have reason to do what will make us admired, and no reason to do what will make us feel foolish or ashamed of ourselves—that is to say, he still attaches value to the *kalon*—he should not go on saying that just behaviour is to be admired and injustice is something to be ashamed of. This is what Callicles, stormily breaking into the conversation, points out. It is a purely conventional idea, he insists, which must be given up if we are going to have a realistic view of what is worth doing. Callicles himself does still subscribe to the value of the *kalon*, but he does not apply it to justice. He thinks that a reasonable person will want to be admired and envied, to think well of himself, and not to be an object of contempt, but the way to bring this about is through power and the exploitation of others, having no concern for justice. Implicit in this, indeed very near the surface of it, is the idea that people do secretly admire the successful exploiter and despise the virtuously exploited, whatever they say about the value of justice.

Socrates does refute Callicles, but only by forcing him into a position which, critics have thought, he has no reason to accept. He ends up[31] defending a crudely gluttonous form of hedonism, which not many people are likely to envy. But this, surely, was not supposed to be the idea. The successfully unjust man was supposed to be a rather grand and powerful figure, whom others, if they were honest, would admire and envy, but he has ended up in Socrates' refutation as a squalid addict whom anyone with any taste would despise. It is easy to think that Socrates wins the argument only because Plato has changed the subject. But Plato does not suppose that he has changed the subject. His point is that without some idea of values that apply to people generally, there will be no basis for any kind of admiration, and if Callicles wants still to think of himself in terms of the *kalon*, he will have to hold on to something more than bare egoism, which by itself offers nothing for admiration and really does lead only to an unstructured and unrewarding hedonism. Plato himself, of course, believes something that goes beyond this, that only a life of justice can offer the structure and order that are needed to make any life worth living.

This is what the *Republic* is meant to show: 'It is not a trivial question we are discussing,' Socrates says towards the end of the first book of that dialogue: 'what we are talking about is how one should live.'[32] He says it to Thrasymachus, Plato's other (and rhetorically less impressive) representative of the enemies of justice. Thrasymachus has been defending the idea that if a person has a reason to act justly, it will always be because it does somebody else some good.[33] It is not very hard for Socrates to refute this in the version that Thrasymachus offers; attached as he is to the rather flashy formula 'justice is the interest of the stronger', Thrasymachus has not noticed that the 'stronger' typically take the form of a group, a collective agent (such as the people in the Athenian democracy), and that they can be a collective agent only because they individually follow rules of justice.

This leads naturally to the idea that justice is not so much a device of the strong to exploit the weak, as a device of the weak to make themselves strong. This idea is spelled out in Book II by two further speakers, Glaucon and Adeimantus, who say that they do not want to believe it themselves, but that they need to have it refuted by Socrates. It is bound to seem to us ethically a lot more attractive than Thrasymachus's proposition: it is the origin, in fact, of the social contract theories that have played an important part in later political philosophy. It is interesting, then, that Glaucon and Adeimantus, as much as Socrates himself, regard this position as only a more effective variant of Thrasymachus's.[34] The reason for this is that on this account justice still comes out as a second best. Just as much as in Thrasymachus's cruder account, it is an instrument or device for satisfying one's desires. An adequate defence of justice, Plato thought, must show that it is rational for each person to want to be just, whatever his circumstances, and the suggestion of Glaucon and Adeimantus fails this test: if someone were powerful and intelligent and well enough placed, he would reasonably have no interest in justice. What Socrates must show is that justice is prized not simply for its effects, but for its own sake.

But why is this the demand? Why is the standard for a defence of justice raised so high? The answer fully emerges only after one has followed the whole long discussion of the *Republic*. That discussion takes the form of considering justice both in an individual and in a city, and Plato constructs a complex analogy between the two. He discusses in great detail what the institutions of a just city must be. He pursues this, as indeed Socrates makes clear, for its own sake, but the main features of the analogy are needed to answer the question about the value of justice 'in itself', and indeed to show why that has to be the question in the first place. A just person is one in whom reason rules, as opposed to the other two 'parts' of the soul that Plato distinguishes,[35] a 'spirited', combative and competitive, part, and a part that consists of hedonistic desires. Just people, who will have this balance and stability in their soul, need to be brought up in a just city, one that is governed by its own rational element; that is to say, by a class of people who are themselves like this. Those people certainly need to see justice as a good in itself; there is nothing to make them pursue it except their own understanding of justice and of the good. They will be able to do this, since their education will give them a philosophical understanding of the good, and of why justice represents the proper development of the rational soul. So, Plato hoped, the *Republic* would have answered the question about the transmission of virtue from one generation to another: it could be brought about only in a just city, and a just city must be one in which the authority of reason is represented politically, by the unquestioned authority of a class of Guardians who—and Socrates recognizes that it will be seen as a very surprising solution—have been educated in philosophy.

In one sense, the foundation of a just city is supposed to be the final, the only, answer to the question of how to keep justice alive. But even in the *Republic* Plato does not suppose that it could in practice be a final answer, for no earthly institution can last uncorrupted, and even if we imagine the city coming about, it will ultimately degenerate, in a process which Plato lays out in Books VIII and IX. There is a parallel story about the effects of the ethical degeneration among individual people, and together they give an opportunity, not only for an evaluation of different kinds of society, but for a good deal of social and psychological observation.

OUT OF THE CAVE

Books V to VII of the *Republic* are devoted for the most part to the education of the Guardians, and they also express some of Plato's highest metaphysical ambitions. This is because the further reaches of what the Guardians learn extend to a reality which in some sense lies beyond everyday experience, and it is only an encounter with this reality that secures the firm hold on the good that underlies the stability of their own characters and their just governance of the city. (It is worth mentioning that Plato says that women should not, as such, be excluded from the highest and most abstract studies, an idea that sets him apart from most of his contemporaries and, as often, from the more conventional Aristotle.[36])

Plato pictures the progress of the soul under education in terms of an ascent from what, in a vivid and very famous image, he represents as the ordinary condition of human beings:

> —Next, compare our nature, and the effect of its having or not having education, to this experience. Picture human beings living in an underground dwelling like a cave, with a long entrance open to the light, as wide as the cave. They are there from childhood, with chains on their legs and their necks so that they stay where they are and can only see in front of them, unable to turn their heads because of the fetters. Light comes from a fire which is burning higher up and some way behind them; and also higher up, between the fire and the prisoners,

there is a road along which a low wall is built, like the screen in front of puppeteers above which they show their puppets.

—I can picture it.

—Now imagine that there are men along this wall, carrying all sorts of implements which reach above the wall, and figures of men and animals in stone and wood and every material, and some of the men who are doing this speak, presumably, and others remain silent.

—It is a strange image you are describing, and strange prisoners.

—They are like us: for do you think that they would see anything of themselves or each other except the shadows that were cast by the fire on the wall in front of them?

—How could they, if they are forced to keep their heads motionless for all their lives?

—And what about the objects that are being carried along the wall? Wouldn't it be the same?

—Of course.

—And if they could talk to each other, don't you think they would suppose that the names they used applied to the things passing before them?

—Certainly.

—And if the prison had an echo from the wall facing them? Wouldn't they suppose that it was the shadow going by that was speaking, whenever one of those carrying the objects spoke?

—Of course.

—Altogether then, they would believe that the truth was nothing other than the shadows of those objects.

—They would indeed.

—But now consider what it would be like for them to be released from their bonds and cured of their illusions, if such a thing could happen to them. When one of them was freed and forced suddenly to stand up and turn his head and walk and look up towards the light, doing all these things he would be in pain, and because he was dazzled he would not be able to see the things of which he had earlier seen the shadows. What do you think he would reply if someone said to him that what he had seen earlier was empty illusion, but that now he is rather closer to reality, and turned to things that are more real, and sees more correctly? Don't you think he would be at a loss and would think that the things he saw earlier were truer than the things he was now being shown?

—Much truer.

—And if he were forced to look at the light itself, wouldn't his eyes hurt, and wouldn't he turn away and run back to the things he was able to see, and think that they were really clearer than the things that he had been shown?

—Yes.

—And if someone dragged him by force up the rough steep path, and did not let him go until he had been dragged out into the light of the sun, wouldn't he be in pain and complain at being dragged like this, and when he got to the light, with the sun filling his eyes, wouldn't he be unable to see a single one of the things now said to be true?

—He would, at least at first.

—He would need practice, if he were going to see the things above. First he would most easily see shadows, and then the images of men and other things reflected in water, and then those things themselves; and the things in the heavens and the heavens themselves he would see more easily at night, looking at the light of the moon and the stars, than he could see the sun and its light by day.

—Certainly.

—Finally he would be able to look at the sun itself, not reflected in water or in anything else, but as it is in itself and in its own place: to look at it and see what kind of thing it is.

Republic, 514a–516b

This image brings together two different ideas of what is wrong with the empirical world and with the skills, such as rhetoric, that live off it and its politics of illusion: that it is all empty appearance, and that nevertheless it involves coercive forces (symbolized by the chains) from which people need to be freed. The everyday world, with its sensations, desires, and inducements, is at once flimsy and powerful. In this it resembles what later times would understand as magic: the world that Prospero brings into being in *The Tempest* is merely the baseless fabric of a vision, and yet he can claim

> graves at my command
> Have wak'd their sleepers, op'd, and let 'em forth
> By my so potent Art.[37]

It is just this profound ambivalence, about its power and its emptiness, that inspires Plato's attack on painting, poetry, and the other arts, an attack which is expressed at various points in the *Republic* but most concentratedly in Book X.

When the future Guardians go up from the cave into the open air, they may eventually even be able to look directly at the sun. The sun, in Plato's story, stands for the Good, and the analogy is a complex one. As the sun makes living things grow, so the existence of everything is explained by the Good; as the sun enables everything to be seen, including itself, so the Good enables everything, including itself, to be known.

What this means is that explanation and understanding must reveal why it is 'for the best' that things should be so rather than otherwise.[38] Plato's conception of 'the best' must be understood in a very abstract way: he is concerned with such matters as the mathematical beauty and simplicity of the ultimate relations between things, an interest which he seems to have derived (together, probably, with his belief in immortality) from the mystical and mathematical tradition of the Pythagoreans, which he encountered on his visits to Greek communities in Italy, first in about 387 BC.

When Plato talks of things being 'for the best', we should not think of him as like Dr Pangloss in Voltaire's *Candide*, who claims that this is the best of all possible worlds and that if we knew enough we would see that everything, however disastrous, is ultimately for the best in humanly recognizable terms such as happiness and welfare. That outlook is a shallow version of Christianity, a religion which is committed (at least after Augustine) to believing that human history and everyday human experience do matter in the ultimate scale of things. Plato, in the *Republic* and, notably, in the *Phaedo* (but by no means everywhere else), expresses something different, the aspiration to be released and distanced from finite human concerns altogether, and this is reflected in his conception of what is 'for the best'. Dr Pangloss and his metaphysically more distinguished model, Leibniz, are regarded as optimists,[39] but even in the Utopian *Republic* Plato is pessimistic about everyday life, and although these Middle Period works frequently remind us of finite and fleeting happiness, particularly through friendship, the ascent from the cave into the sunlight signals a departure from human concerns altogether.

Plato offers us in the *Republic* another model of the relation between everyday experience and the 'higher' reality. We are to imagine a line, divided into two sections. The top part corresponds to knowledge, and also, therefore, to those things that we can know; the lower part corresponds to belief, and to those things about which we can have no better than belief. These two parts are each divided again into two subsections. When we consider these subsections the emphasis is not so much on different things about which we may have knowledge or belief, but rather on more or less direct methods[40] of acquiring knowledge or belief. The lowest sub-section is said to relate to shadows and reflections, while the sub-section above relates to ordinary, three-dimensional, things. Plato can hardly think that there is a special state of mind involved simply in looking at shadows and reflections. The point is that relying on shadows and reflections is a poor or second-best way of acquiring beliefs about ordinary solid objects. The sub-sections of the upper part of the line make a similar point, one that is also expressed in the story of the cave. There is a state of mind that is a poor or second-best way of getting to know about unchanging reality. This, according to Plato, is the state of mind of mathematicians in his time.

He saw two limitations to that mathematics. One was that although it understood, of course, that its propositions were not literally true of any physical diagram—no line is quite straight, no equalities are really equal, no units are unequivocally units—nevertheless, it relied on diagrams. Moreover, it relied on unproved assumptions or axioms, and Plato takes the opportunity of describing the Guardians' education to sketch an ultimately ambitious research programme, which will derive all mathematical assumptions from some higher or more general truths, arriving ultimately at an entirely rational and perspicuous structure which in some sense depends on the self-explanatory starting point[41] of the Good. It is made quite clear that Socrates cannot explain what this will be like, not just because his hearers will not understand it but because he does not understand it himself. It involves an intellectual project and a vision that lay beyond the historical Socrates, obviously enough, but also beyond Plato when he wrote the *Republic*. In fact, it was a project that was never to be carried out on such a grandiose scale.

The reality that corresponds to the highest section of the line[42] consists of Forms, objects which are—whatever else—eternal, immaterial, unchanging, and the objects of rational, *a priori*, knowledge (which, in the *Republic*'s scheme of things, is the only knowledge there is). Commentators discuss 'the Theory of Forms', but there is really no such thing (which is why there is no question to be answered of whether or when Plato gave it up). It is more helpful to see Plato as having a general conception of a Form, in the sense of some such abstract, intellectual, object; having also a set of philosophical questions; and as continually asking how such objects might contribute, in various ways, to answering those various questions. The *Republic* represents the boldest version of the idea that one and the same set of objects could answer all those questions. Plato did not cease to think that there were abstract objects of rational understanding, existing independently of the material world, but he came to see that one and the same kind of object could not serve in all the roles demanded of it by the *Republic*.

Aristotle[43] says that Socrates was interested in questions of definition, but that Plato was the first to make Forms 'separate'. In this connection, a Form can be understood as the quality or character in virtue of which many particular things are of the same kind; and to say that it is 'separate' marks the point that the quality would exist even if there were no particulars that possessed it, as one might say that there would be a virtue of courage even if there were no courageous people. (As we shall see, Plato also wants to say that, for more than one reason, particulars cannot properly, perfectly, or without qualification instantiate Forms.)

This is the approach to Forms from the theory of meaning; in the *Republic* Plato seems to give an entirely general formulation of this idea when he says: 'Shall we start the enquiry with our usual procedure? We are in the habit, I take it, of positing a single idea or Form for each case in which we give the same name to many things.'[44]

Aristotle also says[45] that Plato, 'Having in his youth first become familiar with Cratylus and the Heracleitean doctrines (that all sensible things are always in a state of flux and there is no knowledge about them), these views he held even in later years.' In this connection, Forms are, or are very closely associated with, the objects of mathematical study. As the image of the divided line makes clear, geometers use material, particular, diagrams, but they cannot be talking directly about those diagrams, or what they say ('the line AB is equal to the line AC' and so on) would be simply untrue. They must be talking about something else, triangles formed of absolutely straight lines with no breadth. This is the approach from the possibility of *a priori* knowledge. It is in this role that Forms can also be naturally taken to be those objects of intellectual vision that the argument of the *Meno* needed as the archetypal source of the beliefs recovered in recollection.

The geometers' triangles, unlike scrawled or carpentered triangles of everyday life, are perfect. This is an idea that Plato applied to some other kinds of objects as well: a Form was a paradigm. So when a craftsman makes an artefact, his aim is to approximate to the best that such a thing could be, an ideal which, it may well be, neither he nor anyone else will ever adequately express in a particular material form. So it is with a couch in Book X of the *Republic* and a shuttle in the *Cratylus*.[46] The conceptions of a Form as a paradigm, and of a Form as a general quality or characteristic, come together with special force when there is a quality that we find in particular things, but which occurs in them in a way that is imperfect in the strong sense that our experience of them carries with it an aspiration, a yearning, for an ideal. The most powerful example of this, for Plato, is beauty.

The geometers' triangles, on the one hand, and qualities or characteristics such as courage or dampness, on the other, are all uncreated and unchanging. The world changes: damp things dry out, particular people become courageous or cease to be so. But dampness and courage and such things do not themselves change, except in the boring sense that beauty changes if at one time it characterizes Alcibiades and at a later time it does not, and this is not a change *in it* (any more than it is a change in Socrates that young Theaetetus, who is growing, is shorter than him one year and taller the next year).[47] So there is a fundamental contrast between Forms and the world in which things change, our everyday world.

Sometimes, Plato invokes Forms to explain change. This is notably so in the *Phaedo*, which uses conceptions that are hard to fit together with the discussions, particularly in the *Republic*, which emphasize the metaphysical distance between Forms and particulars. It treats Forms as though parts of them could be transitory ingredients or occupants of material things (as we speak of the dampness in the wall). It is relevant that this discussion has a very special aim, to support a curious proof of the immortality of the soul (which Plato nowhere else uses or relies on). This proof requires the indestructible Form, life, in the sense of 'aliveness', to join with a particular, Socrates, in such a way that there will be an item, 'Socrates' aliveness', which is as indestructible as the Form but as individual as Socrates. This is Socrates' soul; indeed, it is Socrates himself, when he is freed of the irrelevance of his body.[48]

When Plato says that, in contrast to the Forms, particulars in the material world are 'changing', he means more than that they are changing in time. He also means that when we say that a material thing is round or red, for instance, what we say is only relatively or qualifiedly true: it is round or red from one point of view but not another, to one observer rather than another, by comparison with one thing and not another. So what we say about material things is only relatively or qualifiedly true. Indeed, if our statements mean what they seem to say, for instance that this surface is red without qualification, then they are not true at all— not *really* true. Only what we say about Forms can be absolutely or unqualifiedly true.

This gives a broader sense in which things in the material world are imperfect compared with Forms. Only in some cases, such as beauty, does the imperfection of particular things evoke the pathos of incompleteness, of regret, indeed (given Plato's idea of recollection) of nostalgia. But in the sense that nothing is unqualifiedly or absolutely what we say it is, but is so only for a time, to an observer, or from a point of view—in that sense, everything in the material world is imperfect. In the *Republic* this contrast is expressed in the strongest terms, which we have already encountered in the image of the line. Only what is in the world of Forms 'really is'; the world of everyday perception is 'between being and not being', and is mere appearance or like a dream; only 'being' can be the object of knowledge, while the world of 'becoming' is the object of mere belief or conjecture.

There has been much discussion of what exactly Plato meant by these formulations. We should certainly try to make the best sense we can of them, but we should not expect an overall interpretation that is fully intelligible in our terms. To do so is to ignore a vital point, that, however exactly his thought developed, he himself certainly came to think that the *Republic*'s formulations would not do. There are many ways in which the later dialogues acknowledge this. Most generally, Plato came to recognize the tensions that the various approaches to the Forms, taken together, must create. The approach from the theory of meaning implies, unless it is restricted, that there should be a Form for every general term we can use, but other approaches imply that Forms, being perfect, have something particularly grand and beautiful about them. So are there Forms for general terms which stand for low and unlovely things, such as mud and hair? Again, some approaches imply that a Form itself has the quality it imparts. The Form of beauty is itself beautiful, paradigmatically so; the *Phaedo*'s theory of explanation seems to imply that the dampness in an object is indeed damp. The theory of meaning approach, on the other hand, and perhaps others, imply that this had better not be so, or we may be confronted with a regress: shall we need another Form to explain how the first Form has the properties that it has? All these are among the questions that are put to the embarrassed Socrates in the first part of the *Parmenides*.[49]

In the *Sophist*, Plato explores with very great care the complex relations between five particularly abstract concepts, which he calls 'the greatest kinds' rather than Forms—being, sameness, difference, motion and rest—and reaches subtle conclusions about the ways in which they apply to each other and to themselves. In the course of this, he distinguishes various ways in which a thing 'is' something or other, and invents powerful instruments for solving the logical and semantic problems that underlie some of the central formulations of the *Republic*. He also recognizes there, gravely dissociating himself from the admired Parmenides, that there cannot be two worlds of appearance and reality. If something appears to be so, then it really does so appear: appearance must itself be part of reality.[50] This conclusion in itself represents a direct repudiation of the detailed metaphysics of the *Republic*.

The *Theaetetus*, which offers a most powerful and subtle discussion of knowledge, develops a theory of sense perception which at least refines the *Republic*'s view out of all recognition, and on one reading, is opposed to it.[51] In the same dialogue, and in the *Sophist*, Plato advances in discussion of false belief, and of being and not being, to a point at which it is clear that many things said in the *Republic* need revision. Moreover, he goes back in the *Theaetetus* to the point acknowledged in the *Meno*, that it must be possible for one person merely to believe what another person knows. The ideas of knowledge and belief that are articulated in the *Republic* and expressed in the images of the line and the cave are controlled by consideration of subject matter, of what might be or become a body of systematic *a priori* knowledge. The *Republic* is not interested, for example, in the state of mind of someone who makes a mathematical mistake (it cannot be belief, because he is thinking about the eternal, and it cannot be knowledge, because he is wrong). This would not matter if Plato were concerned only with the nature of the sciences, but, as he recognizes, we must be able to talk about knowledge and belief as states of individual people. The ascent from the cave must be a story of personal enlightenment, if the *Republic* is to fulfil its promise of helping us to understand how to live, and this needs a psychology of belief which can bridge the metaphysical gulf between the eternal and the changing.

PLATO'S PHILOSOPHY AND THE DENIAL OF LIFE

The sharp oppositions of the *Republic* between eternal reality and the illusions of the changing material world not only left deep problems of philosophical theory; they defeated Plato's ethical purposes. The problem of how justice is to be preserved in the world was solved by the return of the Guardians to rule, unwillingly, in the cave. There is a question, touched on in the *Republic*, of why they should do this. Certainly, Plato thinks that it is better that the just and wise should rule unwillingly, rather than that those who actually want power should have it. But that must mean, *better for the world*, and Plato must acknowledge the reality of the material world to this extent, that Socrates' fate and other injustices, and the horrors described in the degeneration of the city, are real evils, which are better prevented. Although the just city (and only the just city) suits the Guardians' nature, even there the activity of philosophy is more satisfying than ruling. Returning to the cave is good for them only because it is a good thing to do.

But why is it a good thing to do, and why is it better 'for the world' that it should be ruled justly? The returning Guardians cannot abolish the cave and its apparatus, as Parsifal with the sign of the cross destroys Klingsor's magic garden. Do they release its prisoners? (Here again we meet the ambivalence between power and mere illusion.) Most of the prisoners could not be released, for the ascent to the light is reserved for those special people in whom reason is strong and who are capable of becoming Guardians themselves. But those who are not like this will at least be saved from exploitation, and they can be helped by the laws and institutions of the city not to become unjust exploiters themselves, making others and themselves miserable. So it does matter, a great deal, what happens in this world, and the sense, which it is easy to get from the *Republic*, that in being required to rule, the Guardians are displaced or sentenced to it, like intellectual imperialists in a dark place, cannot really be adequate to Plato's conception of them and of society's need for justice.

The same tensions surface, differently, in the *Gorgias*. There, Socrates asserts the paradoxes that it is better to have injustice done to one than to do injustice, and that the good man 'cannot be harmed', because the only thing that really matters to him is his virtue and that is inviolate against the assaults of the world.[52] This outlook (which was to be developed by some philosophers in later antiquity into an extreme asceticism) leaves an impossible gap between the motivations that it offers for an ethical life, and what one is supposed to do if one leads it. The motivations to justice are said to lie in the care of the soul, and, along with that, in the belief that what happens to one's body or one's possessions does not really matter; but, if we have that belief, why do we suppose, as justice requires us to suppose, that it matters whether other people's bodies and possessions are assaulted or appropriated?[53]

In the *Phaedo*, Plato seems to present in the strongest terms the idea that the good person is better off outside the world. We are told that Socrates' very last words[54], as the hemlock took its effect, were, 'Crito, we owe a cockerel to Asclepius', and since Asclepius was a god of healing, this has been taken to mean that life is a disease, a 'terrible and ridiculous "last word"', as Nietzsche put it, a 'veiled, gruesome, pious and blasphemous saying'.[55] Spinoza, equally, rejected the *Phaedo*'s suggestion that philosophy should be a 'meditation' or preparation of death, urging that it should be a 'meditation of life'. It might be said that the dialogue's disparagement of this life as opposed to the metaphysical beyond is forgivable granted the occasion. Yet that is not right either, since the end of the *Phaedo* is, hardly surprisingly, run through with a deep sorrow, and we are not supposed to think that Socrates' friends are grieving simply because they have not been convinced by the arguments for immortality. It registers, rather, that, even given immortality and the world of Forms, this world and its friendships are of real value, and that its losses are at some level as bad as they seem.

Plato's will to transcend mortal life, to reach for the 'higher', is part of the traditional image of his philosophy, and is one element in the equally traditional contrast between him and the more empirically rooted Aristotle, a contrast expressed most famously, perhaps, in Raphael's fresco in the Vatican, *The School of Athens*, which displays at its centre the figures of Plato and Aristotle, the one turning his hand towards heaven, the other downwards towards earth. In our own century, Yeats wrote:

> Plato thought nature but a spume that plays
> Upon a ghostly paradigm of things;
> Solider Aristotle played the taws
> Upon the bottom of a king of kings . . .[56]

But Plato is not always drawing us beyond the concerns of this world. Even those works in which 'the higher' is celebrated do not always take the tone of the *Phaedo*'s official message, or of the *Republic*. In the case of the *Republic*, we spoke first in terms of ascent, the journey out of the cave, but in fact it is the Guardians' return that lends its colour to the work as a whole, an impression strengthened as it goes on by the long story of social and personal decline. The world of desire, politics, and material bodies is essentially seen from above, from outside the cave, and we are left with a sense of it as denatured and unreal or as powerfully corrupting. But elsewhere, and above all in the *Symposium*, the picture really is of ascent, and the material world is seen with the light behind it, as it were, giving an image not of failure and dereliction but of promise.

The participants in the dinner party which the *Symposium* describes, talk about what *eros* is, what it is to be a lover. The lover and his desires have some relation to beauty, or beautiful things; in particular, beautiful young men. We learn more precisely what these desires are. His desire is not a desire for the beautiful, at least in an obvious sense:

> —Love is not love of the beautiful, as you think.
> —What is it, then?
> —Of reproduction and birth in the beautiful.
>
> *Symposium*, 206e

This desire itself turns out to be an expression, or form, of a desire to be immortal.

Now this provides a schema, to put it in rather formal terms, which can be filled out differently for different types of love. A man's love for a woman defines 'birth' literally; 'in', 'in association with', is sexual; and the immortality in question is genetic. A man may bring forth or generate not babies but ideas or poems, and live for ever (or at least for longer) through those. The beauty in question may now be that of a particular youth, or something more general—as we might say, youthful beauty; again, it may be beauty of soul rather than of body. There is nothing to imply that the various abstractions, as we might call them, necessarily keep step with one another. Socrates has been disposed to generate ideas and good thoughts but in association with youths who had beautiful bodies. Conversely, Alcibiades, we learn later,[57] is drawn to Socrates' beautiful soul, but he has little idea of what an appropriate birth would be.

Then Diotima gives her account of the end of the progress, to the 'final and highest mysteries of love', which she doubts that Socrates can achieve. Here, in a famous passage, the lover is said to turn to the great sea of beauty, and will come to see something 'wonderfully beautiful in its nature', which

> always is and neither comes to be nor passes away, neither waxes nor wanes; it is not beautiful in one way and ugly in another, nor beautiful at one time and not at another, nor beautiful in relation to one thing and ugly in relation to another, nor beautiful in one place and ugly in

another, as it would be if it were beautiful to some people and ugly to others . . .

Symposium, 210e–211a

and it is not embodied in any face or body, or idea, or knowledge, or, indeed, in anything at all. This culminating, ultimately fulfilling, encounter still fits the original schema. This would indeed be a worthwhile life for a man; he would bring forth, not images of virtue, but true virtue, and his relation to the Form of beauty, which is what has just been described, would be that of seeing it and being with it, words reminiscent of the language originally applied to sexual relations with a beautiful person.

Diotima's account of this progress or ascent does not imply, as some have thought, that no one ever really loves a particular person, but only the beauty in that person, or beauty itself. On the contrary, one can love a particular person in any of the various ways that count as bringing something to birth in the presence of that person's beauty. The account directly denies, in fact, that all love is love of beauty. Moreover, it does not suggest that the particulars, sights and sounds and bodies, were only seemingly or illusorily beautiful. They are not unconditionally, or unqualifiedly, or absolutely, beautiful, which is what the item of the final vision is. Indeed, Diotima can say that from the vantage point of the vision, colours and human bodies and other such things are merely 'mortal nonsense', but that is only by comparison with the vision, and it does not imply that the mortals who thought that those things were beautiful were simply mistaken, or that they were mistaken to have pursued them. The undertaking she teaches is something like a growth in aesthetic taste, from kitschy music, say, to more interesting music. It does not deny the point or the object of the earlier taste, and indeed the earlier taste is a condition of the process, which is a progress rather than the mere detection of error or the elimination of a misunderstanding.

Diotima says that the earlier pursuits were 'for the sake of' the final secrets. This does not mean that unless the ultimate state is reached the earlier states are pointless. It means that from the latter perspective we can see a point to them which they do not reveal at all to some people, and reveal only imperfectly even to those who are going about them in the right way. For those who do go about them in the right way, that imperfection is expressed in an obscure unsatisfactoriness or incompleteness in those earlier relationships, which can be traced to their failure to express adequately the desire to be immortal, to have the Good for ever. How far such a feeling may come even to those who are not going about the erotic in the right way and could never reach the vision, is something about which the earlier speeches have things to say.

All of this, certainly, expresses a discontent with the finite, and a sense of a greater splendour that lies beyond our ordinary passions, but it does so in a way that, far more than the *Republic* or the rather dismal *Phaedo*, allows those passions to have their own life and to promise more. This effect is achieved in the dialogue by the later intervention of Alcibiades, and by the earlier speeches, which are variously funny and idiosyncratic and one of which, that of Aristophanes, tells a suitably absurd and touching story about the origins of sexual attraction. The sense that the *Symposium* knows what it is talking about in its dealings with desire—in this respect it is like some other less sunny dialogues—lends colour to another comment of Nietzsche's: 'All philosophical idealism to date was something like a disease, unless it was, as in Plato's case, the caution of an over-rich and dangerous health, the fear of over-powerful senses . . .'[58]

Plato set higher than almost any other thinker the aspirations of philosophy, and, as we have seen, its hopes to change one's life through theory. Granted the distrust and even the rejection of the empirical world which do play a significant role in his outlook; granted, too, the fact that his politics are far removed from any that could serve us now, not only in time but by an unashamedly aristocratic temperament; we may ask how his dialogues can remain so vividly alive. They are, indeed, sometimes sententious, and Socrates speaking on behalf of virtue can be tiring and high-minded, just as his affectation of ignorance and simplicity, the famous 'irony', can be irritatingly coy. But their faults are almost always those of a real person. They speak with a recognizable human voice, or more than one, and they do not fall into the stilted, remote complacency or quaint formalism to which moral philosophy is so liable. In part this is because of the dialogue form. In part, it is because (as Nietzsche's remark implies) Plato is constantly aware of the forces—of desire, of aesthetic seduction, of political exploitation—against which his ideals are a reaction. The dialogues preserve a sense of urgency and of the social and psychological insecurity of the ethical. Plato never forgets that the human mind is a very hostile environment for goodness, and he takes it for granted that some new device, some idea or imaginative stroke, may be needed to keep it alive there and to give it a hold on us. A treatise which supposedly offered in reader-friendly form the truth about goodness could not do anything that really needed doing.

The dialogues are never closed or final. They do not offer the ultimate results of Plato's great enquiry. They contain stories, descriptions, jokes, arguments, harangues, streams of free intellectual invention, powerful and sometimes violent rhetoric, and much else. Nothing in them straightforwardly reports those theoretical findings on which everything was supposed to turn, and they never take the tone that now you have mastered this, your life will be changed. There are theoretical discussions, often very complex, subtle, and original. There are many statements of how our lives need to be changed and of how philosophy may help to change them. But the action is always somewhere else, in a place where we, and typically Socrates himself, have not been. The results are never in the text before us. They could not be. The passage from the *Phaedrus* from which we started was true to Plato's outlook, as it seems to me, in claiming that what most importantly might come from philosophy cannot be written down.

This does not mean that it could be written down, but somewhere else. Nor does it mean, I think, that it could not be written down but could be spoken as a secret lore among initiates. The Pythagoreans in Italy from whom Plato may have got some initial inspiration seem to have had esoteric doctrines, and some scholars have thought that the same was true of Plato's Academy, but there is not much reason to believe it. The limitations of writing do not apply only to writing. Rather, Plato seems to have thought that the final significance of philosophy for one's life does not lie in anything that could be embodied in its findings, but emerges, rather, from its activities. One will find one's life changed through doing something other than researching the changes that one's life needs—through mathematics, Plato thought, or through dialectical discussion of such things as the metaphysical problems of not being, conducted not with the aim of reaching edifying moral conclusions, but the aim of *getting it right* (particularly if one has got it wrong before, and intellectual honesty, or—come to that—a most powerful curiosity, demands that one try again).

Plato did think that if you devoted yourself to theory, this could change your life. He did think, at least at one period, that pure studies might lead one to a transforming vision. But he never thought that the materials or conditions of such a transformation could be set down in a theory, or that a theory would, at some suitably advanced level, explain the vital thing you needed to know. So the dialogues do not present us with a statement of what might be most significantly drawn from philosophy, but that is not a peculiarity of them or of us; nothing could present us with that, because it cannot be stated anywhere, but can only, with luck and in favourable surroundings, emerge. Plato probably did think himself that the most favourable surroundings would be a group of people entirely dedicated to philosophy, but clearly he supposed that reading the dialogues, thinking about them, entering into them, were activities that could offer something to people outside such a group. He acknowledged, as Socrates makes clear in the *Phaedrus*, that they could not be the vehicles of one determinate message, and it is just because they are not intended to control the minds of his readers, but to open them, that they go on having so much to offer.

It is pointless to ask who is the world's greatest philosopher: for one thing, there are many different ways of doing philosophy. But we can say

what the various qualities of great philosophers are: intellectual power
and depth; a grasp of the sciences; a sense of the political, and of human
destructiveness as well as creativity; a broad range and a fertile imagination; an unwillingness to settle for the superficially reassuring; and, in an
unusually lucky case, the gifts of a great writer. If we ask which philosopher has, more than any other, combined all these qualities—to that
question there is certainly an answer, Plato.

THE DIALOGUES

A quick reference list of Plato's dialogues that are mentioned in this book.
    E(arly), M(iddle), L(ate): represent datings. In most cases there is a fair
consensus, but some remain controversial.

Apology [E] a speech that Socrates might have given at his trial.
Cratylus [?M] on language, critically discussing certain theories of
    names.
Gorgias [E/M] on rhetoric and the good life; Socrates argues succes-
    sively with Gorgias, Polus and Callicles.
Laches [E] on courage.
Laws [L] probably Plato's last work; in twelve books, on desirable po-
    litical and social arrangements. Socrates does not appear, and the
    main speaker is 'an Athenian'.
Meno [E/M] whether virtue can be taught; Socrates invokes 'recollec-
    tion' and immortality.
Parmenides [?L] Parmenides first raises problems about Forms, and
    then gives a demonstration of dialectic.
Phaedo [M] the scene of Socrates' death; they discuss immortality.
Phaedrus [M] during a walk in the country, Phaedrus and Socrates
    have a conversation about love, beauty, poetry, philosophy and
    writing.
Philebus [L] on pleasure, but with an opening discussion of 'limit' and
    the 'unlimited'.
Protagoras [E] brilliant exchanges between Socrates and Protagoras,
    on virtue, knowledge and politics.
Republic [M] in ten books, on justice in the individual and in the city,
    and many other matters.
Socratic dialogues [E] dialogues in which the discussion does not go
    beyond the interests and methods of the historical Socrates. Besides
    the *Laches*, among those of particular interest are the *Euthyphro*,
    which discusses the relations of ethics to the gods, and the *Crito*, in
    which Socrates argues that he must stay and face the death penalty.

Sophist [L] complex and sophisticated argument in metaphysics and the philosophy of language. Socrates is present, but the argument is entirely conducted by an 'Eleatic stranger'.

Statesman (Politicus) [L] also conducted by the Eleatic stranger, the discussion develops a classificatory form of dialectic by 'division', which also appears in the *Sophist*.

Symposium [M] a dinner party, at which the guests entertain themselves with a series of speeches about love.

Theaetetus [L] exceptionally powerful and concentrated philosophical enquiry, in which three accounts of knowledge are considered and rejected; the first, in terms of perception, is the most developed.

Timaeus [?L] elaborate, if tentative, speculations about the creation of the world. Socrates is present but five-sixths of the work consists of uninterrupted exposition by Timaeus.

Notes

The standard system of reference to Plato's works is by 'Stephanus' page numbers, which denote the page and column number of a given passage in the edition of Plato published in 1578 by Henri Estienne.

The translations of the quoted passages are by myself, but they are based on the translations, by various authors, in *Plato: Complete Works*, ed. J. M. Cooper (Hackett, Indianapolis, 1997).

For help in preparing the notes and bibliography, I am grateful to Casey Perrin.

1. The ancient sources are not consistent in their dating of Plato's life. Most modern accounts date his birth some time between 429 and 427 BC. For details see Kraut (1992), p. 30 n. 1 and Guthrie (1975), p. 10.

2. A. N. Whitehead, *Process and Reality: An Essay in Cosmology*, corrected edn, ed. D. R. Griffin and D. W. Sherburne (Free Press, New York, 1978), p. 39. As Kraut (1992), p. 32 n. 4 says, perhaps rather unnecessarily, Whitehead's remark should not be taken to imply that philosophers after Plato all accepted his views as their starting point.

3. As, it should be said, many still do.

4. Thirteen Letters are among a set of works attributed to Plato in antiquity by Diogenes Laertius (3.50, cf. 3.57–62) and included in the medieval manuscripts, but whose authenticity is a matter of long and still unsettled controversy among scholars. For references see Guthrie (1975), pp. 399–401. One other work that is not strictly speaking a dialogue is the *Apology*, which is a speech that Socrates might appropriately have made at his trial.

5. But he mentions himself three times (excluding the Letters). In the *Apology* (34b, 38b) he twice says that he himself was present at the trial of Socrates, and in the second passage he is said to be among those who offered to pay a fine on

behalf of Socrates should the court accept that as a penalty. At *Phaedo* 59b the narrator of the dialogue reports that Plato himself was not present on the last day of Socrates' life, because he was ill.

6. On the historical Socrates see Vlastos (1991) and Gottlieb (1997). There is a harder question about the dialogues as evidence of what Socrates believed (the so-called 'Socratic question'): see below pp. 152, 153–56, 170.

7. We can learn a lot from the *Theaetetus*, but the second, and still more the third, sections of it are clearly designed to provide material for further discussion. This is brought out in Burnyeat (1990).

8. A good example is the final argument of the *Protagoras*: see below pp. 156–57.

9. Whatever the status of the works ascribed to Aristotle (who was forty-three years younger than Plato, was his pupil and broke away from him) they are a lot nearer to the treatise in form, and display a very different temperament.

10. The school lasted, with an unbroken line of successors, till the first century BC; the prevailing philosophy changed a lot, and was by no means always Platonic.

11. For discussion of this dialogue, see Ferrari (1987), and of this passage, chapter 7.

12. For a concise discussion of the methods and results of stylometric studies, see Brandwood (1992). Aristotle tells us (*Politics* 1264b26–7) that the *Laws* was written after the *Republic*; it is universally agreed to be late. In the case of some dialogues, there is evidence for their actual date of composition or their chronology relative to other dialogues. Several dialogues contain allusions to historical events which allow us to fix a date after which they must have been written. The *Symposium*, for example, alludes to the King's Peace of 386 BC (182b) and the Spartan division of Arcadia in 385 (193a). The *Theaetetus* begins with a conversation that takes place very shortly before the death of Theaetetus after a battle in Corinth in 369 BC (142a–b). The *Statesman* is taken to have been composed after the *Sophist* since it refers back to the *Sophist* on several occasions (257a, 258b, 266d, 284b, 286b). In what follows I use 'dating' loosely, to cover placing the dialogues in an order relative to one another.

13. The *Republic* is in 10 books, and some scholars take Book I to be significantly earlier than the other books. See Vlastos (1991) p. 248–51 for discussion.

14. Some scholars place the *Theaetetus* in Plato's Middle Period, but it must surely be associated closely with the *Sophist*. The *Statesman* is often known by its Latin name, *Politicus*.

15. See *Theaetetus*, 183e–184a, and various passages in the *Sophist* (e.g. 237a, 241b), where his central doctrine is rejected. The poem of Parmenides (*c*.515–*c*.450 BC) survives only in fragments. A translation of these, with commentary, can be found in McKirahan (1994).

16. Zeno of Elea (born *c*.490 BC), who invented famous paradoxes, including that of Achilles and the Tortoise, which supposedly show that the idea of movement is self-contradictory. For discussion, see Kirk, Raven and Schofield (1983).

17. It is worth saying that there is no hope of making adequate sense of the first part of the *Parmenides*, which is crucial to these debates, unless we can get a better grasp on the second part than most people claim to have.

18. Here, as on several other points, I am indebted to Myles Burnyeat.

19. One of the characters in the *Laches* is Melesias, the son of Thucydides—not the historian, but an Athenian politician who opposed Pericles and was banished from Athens for ten years some time around 440 BC. He is mentioned in the *Meno* (94b–e) (along with Themistocles, Aristides, and Pericles) as an example of a father who failed to teach his son (the Melesias of the *Laches*) virtue.

20. Ancient democracy was both more and less 'democratic' than modern systems: more, because all citizens could take part in political decisions; less, because there were no minority rights, it was based on slavery, and women were excluded.

21. See *Gorgias*, 515d–516d. Pericles (*c*.495–*c*.429 BC) was an Athenian statesman and the main influence on Athenian policy in the middle years of the fifth century. The noblest expression of Athenian democratic ideals is to be found in the Funeral Speech ascribed to Pericles in Thucydides' *History* (II. 34–46). To call him an unprincipled demagogue was rather like comparing Abraham Lincoln to Senator McCarthy.

22. There were of course predecessors. The fragment of Parmenides' poem (see note 15 above) is an interesting case; the emphatic inferential structure, together with the determined charmlessness of the verse, seems designed to make the point.

23. The same technique is used in the *Cratylus*; in that case, it is shown that the method of etymology can be used with equal plausibility to produce contrary results.

24. *Meno*, 75b.

25. Pindar, fragment 133.

26. *Meno*, 86a: he knows this when he is a man and when he is not a man; he is always either a man or not a man; so he knows it always.

27. *Meno*, 97a. In a world without maps, personal experience may well be the best basis of such beliefs. There is a similar but more complex example, of a jury acquiring from a specious orator what is in fact a true belief about something they did not witness, in the *Theaetetus* (200d–201c).

28. Erotic relations between older and younger men were a standard feature of Athenian life, and carried strong educational and other values. See Dover (1989) for discussion. Details of Alcibiades' life (*c*.450–404 BC) are to be found in Thucydides' *History*, books V–VIII, and Xenophon's *Hellenica*, book I.

29. *Symposium*, 210a.

30. *Gorgias*, 474c–481b.

31. *Gorgias*, 491a–495a.

32. *Republic*, 352d.

33. *Republic*, 343c. The formulation 'justice is the interest of the stronger', *Republic*, 338c.

34. *Republic*, 358b–c; 367b.

35. In *Republic* IV, 435b–444e.

36. For Plato's discussion of the inclusion of women in the education of the Guardians, see *Republic*, 451c–457c.

37. *The Tempest* V, 1, 48–50. For the application of this to art, see Stephen Greenblatt, *Marvelous Possessions* (Oxford University Press, Oxford, 1991).

38. The same point is made, contrasting such explanations with others, in the *Phaedo* (96c–98b).

39. Pangloss is usually said to expound a 'vulgarized' version of Leibniz's philosophy, but Leibniz himself, like some other mathematical and metaphysical geniuses, but unlike Plato, was capable of being ethically very crass.

40. *Republic*, 509d–511e. The relations between the sun, the line, and the cave have traditionally given rise to great controversy between interpreters.

41. *Republic*, 510b–511e. Plato's own phrase means a starting point which is not a hypothesis itself and does not depend on a hypothesis.

42. Certainly with regard to the top sub-section. It is controversial whether there are 'mathematical objects', distinct from Forms, corresponding to the sub-section below this.

43. *Metaphysics*, 987b1–13.

44. 596a. But the Greek could mean: where there is a Form, the Form and the particulars have the same name.

45. *Metaphysics*, 987a32–b1.

46. *Republic*, 596a–b, *Cratylus*, 389a–b. In the *Cratylus* passage there is nothing to imply that the Form is 'separate'.

47. *Theaetetus*, 155b–c.

48. *Phaedo*, 105b–107a. When Socrates' companion Crito asks how his friends should bury him, Socrates replies: 'In any way you like, if you can catch me and I do not escape from you' (*Phaedo*, 115c).

49. For the question whether there are Forms of mud and hair, see *Parmenides*, 130c–d; for the 'Third Man' argument, one version of the regress, 131e–132b.

50. *Sophist*, 249c–d. A related point is made in the *Philebus* (54c), where it is recognized that there can be 'a becoming into being'.

51. For a detailed discussion of two competing interpretations of the first part of the *Theaetetus*, see Burnyeat (1990), pp. 7–64, especially pp. 7–10.

52. *Gorgias*, 507 seq.

53. There is a complex Christian inheritance of this problem. It has included some heretical strains, related to Manicheanism, which took seriously the idea that it did not matter at all what happened in this life; and also the temptation, inherited by some Kantians, to suppose that what really counts as harming people is to make them less moral.

54. *Phaedo*, 118a. This interpretation, rare in antiquity, became popular in the Renaissance, and again in the nineteenth century.

55. *The Gay Science*, 340. Some of his other remarks about Plato are less interesting, such as *The Twilight of the Idols*, 'What I Owe to the Ancients', sec. 2, 'Plato was a coward in the face of reality.'

56. 'Among School Children'; the reference is to the fact that Aristotle was the tutor of Alexander the Great. The contrast between Plato and Aristotle has had a complex history, and has by no means always meant the same thing; in the seventeenth century, for instance, one thing Plato stood for was the spirit of the new mathematical science. I have said something about this in an article about Greek philosophy in Finley (1981) [= chap. 1 above—Ed.].

57. *Symposium*, 215–217.

58. *The Gay Science*, 372.

BIBLIOGRAPHY

1. General Works

For a recent collection of essays on a wide range of topics in Plato see:
Kraut, Richard, ed., *The Cambridge Companion to Plato* (Cambridge University Press, Cambridge, 1992)

Perhaps the best single volume treatment of Plato's work, and one that is particularly sensitive to the literary aspects of Plato's writing, is:
Grube, G.M.A., *Plato's Thought*, with new introduction, bibliographic essay, and bibliography by Donald J. Zeyl (Hackett, Indianapolis, 1980)

Useful for historical material, summaries of scholarly debates about dating, and discussions of textual questions, though containing very little philosophy, is:
Guthrie, W.K.C., *A History of Greek Philosophy*, Vol. 4 (Cambridge University Press, Cambridge, 1975)

The starting points for any discussion of the Socratic dialogues are:
Vlastos, Gregory, *Socrates, Ironist and Moral Philosopher* (Cornell University Press, Ithaca, 1991)
———. *Socratic Studies*, ed. Myles Burnyeat (Cambridge University Press, Cambridge, 1994)

An edition of the Greek text of the *Gorgias*, the introduction and commentary to which has much of value to offer to the reader without Greek, is:
Dodds, E. R., *Plato: Gorgias, A Revised Text with Introduction and Commentary* (Clarendon Press, Oxford, 1959)

For a translation with philosophical commentary of the *Phaedo*, see:
Gallop, David, *Plato: Phaedo*, translated with notes (Clarendon Press, Oxford, 1975)

The best short discussions of the *Symposium* are the introductions to:
Nehamas, Alexander and Woodruff, Paul, *Plato: Symposium*, translated with introduction and notes (Hackett, Indianapolis, 1989), pp. xi–xxvi
Dover, Kenneth, *Plato: Symposium*, Cambridge Greek and Latin Classics (Cambridge University Press, Cambridge, 1980), pp. 1–14

The most philosophically stimulating introduction to the *Republic* remains:
Annas, Julia, *An Introduction to Plato's Republic* (Oxford University Press, Oxford, 1981)

Further discussion of a variety of topics in the *Republic*, including the sun, the line, and the cave, can be found in:

186 • Ten

Cross, R. C. and Woozley, A. D., *Plato's* Republic: *A Philosophical Commentary* (St Martin's Press, New York, 1964)
Reeve, C.D.C., *Philosopher-Kings: The Argument of Plato's* Republic (Princeton University Press, Princeton, 1988)

An idiosyncratic but closely argued account is:
Irwin, Terence, *Plato's Ethics* (Oxford University Press, Oxford, 1995)

On the *Phaedrus*, see the imaginative study by:
Ferrari, G.R.F., *Listening to the Cicadas: a Study of Plato's "Phaedrus"* (Cambridge University Press, Cambridge, 1987)

A recent and important book-length study of the *Parmenides* is:
Meinwald, Constance, *Plato's "Parmenides"* (Oxford University Press, New York, 1991)

An excellent translation of the *Theaetetus* with a book-length, philosophically compelling introduction is:
Burnyeat, Myles, *The "Theaetetus" of Plato*, with a translation by M. J. Levett, revised by Myles Burnyeat (Hackett, Indianapolis and Cambridge, 1990)

2. *Other Works Cited in the Notes*

Brandwood, Leonard, 'Stylometry and chronology', in Kraut (1992) pp. 90–120
Dover, K. J., *Greek Homosexuality*, updated with a new postscript (Harvard University Press, Cambridge, Mass., 1989)
Finley, M. I., ed., *The Legacy of Greece: a New Appraisal* (Clarendon Press, Oxford, 1981)
Gottlieb, Anthony, *Socrates* (Phoenix/Orion, London, 1997)
Kirk, G. S., Raven, J. E., and Schofield M., *The Presocratic Philosophers*, second edition (Cambridge University Press, Cambridge, 1983)
Kraut, Richard, 'Introduction to the Study of Plato', in Kraut (1992) pp. 1–50
McKirahan, Richard D., Jr., *Philosophy before Socrates* (Hackett, Indianapolis, 1994)

ARISTOTLE

ELEVEN

Acting as the Virtuous Person Acts

This paper is not mainly directed to questions about moral realism in Aristotle, but it does end with a suggestion about that subject. It starts from a question that Aristotle raises about virtuous action, and gives what I think should have been Aristotle's answer to it, an answer which I think was also, broadly speaking, Aristotle's own answer. At the end I ask where (if anywhere) this leaves questions of moral realism in relation to such a theory.

In *Nicomachean Ethics* II.4 Aristotle raises the question of how it can be true, as he claims it to be, that someone becomes (e.g.) just by doing just things: for how can someone do virtuous things without already having the appropriate virtue? His answer is that the things done by the learner, although they are in a sense virtuous things, do not yet fully display the virtue. We may say that they are minimally virtuous things: they are not done *as* the virtuous person does them. He holds, in effect,

> (A) A (fully) V act is what a V person would do, but only if it is done as the V person does such a thing.

The conditions on an act's being done as the virtuous agent would do it are these:

(i) The agent knows (*eidôs*).
(ii) He does it *proairoumenos kai proairoumenos di' auto*: choosing and choosing for its own sake.
(iii) He is in a steady, unchangeable state.

There is a question about how much (i) imports. There are conditions of intention here that are uncontroversially relevant. In many cases, however, their relevance is to an earlier question: not whether the V act was done as a V person would do it, but whether an even minimally V act was done at all. This is what is at issue if someone tackles the armed robber believing him not to be armed, or, differently, attempts a malicious act which misfires, doing the intended victim a good turn. These matters of intention are importantly different from questions of motive. Someone who sends a cheque to the hospital to advance his reputation is not like someone who puts the cheque into the wrong envelope: he intends, with regard to the outcome, what the generous person intends—he is, after all, seeking a reputation for generosity. He certainly does not act as the generous person would act, but his failure to do so falls under condition (ii), to which we shall come later, and not under condition (i).

It may seem puzzling that Aristotle says (NE 1105b1f.) that knowledge counts for everything in relation to *technai* (arts) and for little or nothing in the case of the virtues. Surely both virtue and *technê* require one to know what one is doing? I take the point to be this. There is a sense of "knowing what one is doing" that applies both to virtue and to *technê*; if there were not, Aristotle could not make the comparison on these terms. The proper possession of a *technê* can be picked out by saying that the person in general, habitually, knows what he is doing when he chooses to exercise the *technê*[1]; a person who gets it right occasionally does know, on those occasions, what he is doing, but on other occasions does not. In the case of the virtues, it is necessary to being a V person (and, indeed, we have already seen, even to doing a minimally V action) that one knows what one is doing, in that same sense, but the state of being a V person is not picked out by saying that he is standardly or regularly in that state of knowledge.

This is fairly straightforward, and it makes sense of Aristotle's contrast. However, it has a significant consequence. Just given condition (i), one might take it to refer to some kind of moral knowledge, the presence of which distinguishes the truly V person from those who do occasional V acts, or, again, acts that are less than fully V. If you are looking at that contrast, and are disposed to express virtue in terms of knowledge, this interpretation will be attractive. But in terms of Aristotle's contrast with the craftsman, it is not inviting at all. If moral knowledge is the virtuous person's special possession, then that knowledge will make *all* the difference, and not, as Aristotle says, little or none. The knowledge mentioned in condition (i) is everyday knowledge relevant to effective intentions, as it is with *technai*.

I shall not say much about condition (iii). It is important that it can be taken to include, as well as generality over time, a requirement, in the style of Hume, of (appropriate) generality over people. The generous act must not be merely a whim; in addition, the agent's generosity will not count as the virtue if he is only generous to Lulubelle. The demand that the V person should be in the appropriate state *ametakinêtos* (unchangeably) also covers, as Sarah Broadie has well pointed out,[2] two considerations that distinguish a virtue from a *technê*: that one cannot choose to exercise it or not, and (a less familiar thought, perhaps) that it counts

---

[1] "When he chooses to exercise" already picks out a difference from the virtues, of course: one that is picked up by condition (iii), as noted below.

[2] *Ethics with Aristotle* (Oxford: Oxford University Press, 1991), 89.

against one's having virtues that one can be distracted by passion from exercising them, whereas this is not so with the *technai*: a carpenter who makes a bad job of it because of rage or sexual distraction is not shown by this to be a bad carpenter.

There are several complexities in this area that are connected with the unity of the virtues. My clumsy formulation "it counts against having virtues" was designed to contain, without developing, the point that, if one does not accept Aristotle's view about unity, it may make a difference what distraction is in question: if a man is distracted from brave deeds by lust rather than fear, he is not shown to lack courage. Further, there will be some skills (notably, some political ones) that require some virtues, above all the executive virtues of courage and self-control: I shall briefly come back to these later.

The question I want principally to discuss arises from condition (ii), specifically from the requirement that the V person chooses V things "for their own sake." My concern is with this phrase, and I shall not discuss the condition more generally (e.g. the question of how the two conjuncts are related). As Broadie says in her very helpful discussion of Aristotle's definition of virtue,[3] a virtuous disposition is expressed in choice (but not only so expressed), and this is not simply a matter of deliberation. The virtue is expressed in "reason-structured responses", such as the emotions, which link rational and non-rational aspects of the agent.

The first question is whether (ii) entails

(B) A V person chooses V acts qua V acts.

(A) and (B) together seem to make the ideas of a V act and a V person depend on each other. There is no problem just in this, but there will be a problem if it leads to vacuity. This will be so, if we cannot distinguish one virtue from another, and/or the V agent is left with no determinate content to his thoughts. Both of these threaten if (B) and no more is adopted.

But (B) is in general false, in a *de dicto* sense: courageous people rarely choose acts as courageous, and modest people never choose modest behaviour as modest. Justice is about the only case in which it clearly holds. So what might be put in place of (B)? Various alternatives might be suggested.

(a) Might the acts be chosen qua *kala* (qua fine or noble)? Aristotle repeatedly says that virtuous people act for the sake of *to kalon* (the fine or

---

[3] Particularly on the force of *proairetikê*, ibid., p. 78. On the relation of the conjuncts, see p. 87. It is worth saying that the question whether *kai* is "epexegetic" is quite complexly related to questions about the role of *proairesis* in the good life. It should be remembered that *proairesis* is not peculiar to the virtuous. See below, pp. 195–96 and note 8.

the noble), and stresses that this is something common to all the virtues.[4] Moreover, the presence of this idea to the mind of a virtuous agent would be less objectionable to Aristotle than it is to post-Christian thinkers. But this proposal does not tell us what it is to do a particular sort of V thing for its own sake. It leaves us with the problem of distinguishing the virtues, even to the extent that Aristotle needs to distinguish them. (Both Socrates and Aristotle, despite their views on the unity of the virtues, need to secure the minimal result that the names of the virtues have different senses, which they must have even if they have the same reference (as Socrates held), or (as Aristotle held) they pick out different dispositions, but those dispositions all imply and are implied by one and the same virtue, *phronêsis* (practical wisdom)).

On the present proposal, the distinctness of the virtues will be underrepresented in the agent's thought, as in (B), interpreted *de dicto*, it is too directly represented.

(b) I lay aside the suggestion that the V person's fully V act can be picked out as having been done as a result of what Broadie calls "Grand End" *proairesis*. This again would not help with the distinction of the virtues; and I accept Broadie's view that, so far as we can, we should disembarrass Aristotle of the Grand End view. In any case, even the greatest enthusiast for the Grand End View will surely not say that each fully V act is the product of a Grand End deliberation.

(c) The fully V act of the V person is an expression of *phronêsis*: it is done *ek tou orthou logou* (for the right reason). I take it that this (as opposed to the Grand End interpretation of it) is true, but there is a difficulty in supposing that it could answer this problem. First, *phronêsis* will add something to the account only if it takes us beyond the mere expression of a V disposition in a V act. Let us assume that it does so by adding the idea that the V act is the result of deliberation, actual or (let us say) appropriately understood as in the offing. Then that deliberation will offer the answer that this is the thing to do; this thing will be the V thing, and the conclusion being that of a V person, this conclusion will be appropriately related to the deliberation and to the person. But how? This is just a version of the question we are already trying to answer. Adding the fact that the V person has deliberated well (or can be seen as having deliberated well, or that there is a good deliberation in the offing) does not seem to help in answering it: it merely provides a new focus for it. What we need seems to be something, at least in central cases, about the *content* of the V person's deliberation (but not the content offered by (B)).

(d) The right answer starts from the idea that *di' auto* should be read negatively: the agent does the V thing not for the wrong reasons. This is

[4] *NE* 1115b12, 1120a23, 1122b6.

correct, but it needs positive reinforcement, in the form of an account of the kinds of reasons that appropriately go with various Vs. When developed in this direction, this can indeed lead us back to the original formulation (B). (B) is very roughly right, but only if "qua V" is read *de re*. We say that the agent did the generous (e.g.) thing because it was the generous thing to do, and we understand what this means because we understand what it is about the situation and the action that makes this action in this situation something that would seem to a generous person the appropriate thing to do. It will follow from this that the philosophical understanding of the various virtues will require some, at least, of the understanding that comes from having the virtues: which is of course what Aristotle holds.

This does imply that there is a way in which the action seems to the agent the appropriate thing to do: a way in which such an action commends itself in such a situation to a generous person. What this means is that typically there is a kind of reason or consideration present to the agent's thought that goes with the act's being of this particular V kind. One important sort of consideration involved is that which serves to dismiss alternative courses of action as variously unworthy: thus, a modest person might dismiss a course of action as vainglorious. A person with a particular V disposition will have a specific repertoire of considerations that operate for or against courses of action. He may include both kinds, positive and negative, under the label "acting for X reasons."

The V agent, then, does the V act because he thinks it is the thing to do for X reasons, where "for X reasons" is part of his thought, and the type X is tied (both positively and negatively) to the V in question. (As we have already seen in considering (B), X is only rarely the same notion as V, as it occurs in "V act": justice is the leading case in which it is.) The role of the distinctive types of reason helps to answer the question about the separation of the virtues.

We can now have non-vacuous mutual dependence:

—A V act is an act done for X reasons.
—A V person is disposed to do V acts.

This does not simply make acts primary, because "an act done for reasons" is not a type of act independent of its agent's state; it is an act done by an agent with a certain disposition. The account locates an important role of desire focused on *to kalon*, in explaining the "because" of "he did it because it was the V thing." The business of concentrating on the X reasons, allowing them to have force, can be assisted by thoughts of how it would be shameful not to. There is no reason for Aristotle to deny this, even though he seems to think that the word *"aidôs"* ("shame") relates only to a motivation of the immature (NE 1128b15f.).

There is a vital role, too, for *phronêsis*: without it, one could not reliably see what acts X reasons could lead to, or what more specific considerations might fall into the class of X reasons. We shall have to ask how much, if anything, that might imply in the direction of moral idealism. Before turning to this, however, we have to register that there are some of Aristotle's virtues for which this account does not work. These are the so-called "executive" virtues of courage and *sôphrosunê* (temperance). I shall discuss the latter in terms of "self-control", which is not Aristotelianly correct: "self-control" is *enkrateia*, a virtue that, for Aristotle, a really virtuous person does not need, and hence not strictly speaking a virtue. This, like some other views associated with the mean, seems just to represent a substantive and tedious Aristotelian ideal, which we can ignore.

The problem with courage and self-control is not just that courageous and self-controlled people do not choose acts as courageous or self-controlled; as we have seen, that is standard. The self-controlled person may reject actions as shameful, unsuitable, exploitative, etc., but his self-control is manifested not so much in that recognition—although it is partly manifested in the fact that he can achieve that recognition—as in the fact that he can carry that recognition through into action. The courageous person may (although he does not have to) reject acts as cowardly, and he may possibly do acts as *kalon*—Aristotle was happier to accept this than we are, having a more self-conscious idea of nobility.[5]

The real problem is that there is no X such that courageous or self-controlled people choose their acts for X reasons. Rather, for various other V-related X reasons, they choose acts for those reasons in the face of fear or desire: the structure of the situation is that they do those things for those reasons, although . . . We shall say that those other reasons are V-related, of course, to the extent that we sympathize with Aristotle's unity of the virtues. We could, and I believe reasonably should, say that people can display courage or self-control in doing things for reasons *not* related to some other virtue; but that does not matter much for the present question. The point is that even if we put in the V-related restriction on what counts as a reason for doing some courageous or self-controlled thing, courage and self-control still do not fit the account. This is because they will not fit Aristotle's tripartite structure, which the account is explicating: no version of (ii) applies to them.[6] Courageous or self-controlled things are not done "for their own sake", and doing them for their own

---

[5] One of the passages mentioned in note 4 above relates the general role of *to kalon* to the case of courage: "the brave man holds his position for the sake of *to kalon*: for this is the *telos* of virtue", 1115b12.

[6] It is worth saying that this result is not a product of my taking "self-control" as the executive virtue in question. On Aristotle's account of *sôphrosunê*, the point is still more obvious.

sake would be something quite special: something like doing a certain thing in a certain situation to display or develop one's courage or self-control.

If the account of virtuous action looks like this, where, if anywhere, does that leave questions of moral realism? The answer must lie in the relations of all this to *phronêsis*, a topic that has been briefly touched on before. Aristotle uses that language of knowledge and of a kind of perception in relation to *phronêsis*. Is there an element in the *phronêsis/* deliberation structure that could invite a kind of picture that might be labelled "moral realism" (MR)?

Might it come in, first, in explaining what the *phronimos* comes to know when he comes to see *what to do*? Surely not, since Aristotle gives us no reason to say that the conclusion of practical reasoning is *in itself* different when the virtues are being expressed from what it is when it is a matter of the crafts. On the contrary, the idea of a distinctive content that is introduced at this point, just when the virtues are involved in practical reasoning, is alien to Aristotle's approach, which is essentially to incorporate the account of ethics into the theory of rational action in general.

There is, of course, a tradition according to which there is in Aristotle no distinctive conclusion of practical reasoning at all: there is only the actual doing of the action. I do not want to discuss this unappealing account here: in any case, if this were correct, the suggestion I am presently considering for where we might find a place for MR would fall away altogether.

We might add, further, that conclusions about what to do can also be reached by non-moral or anti-moral agents who are presumably not in touch with any such supposed subject matter. Aristotle does not say much about the deliberative activities of such people. A description of the *akolastos* (self-indulgent), that he thinks it always appropriate to pursue the present pleasure, does not eliminate such activities: on the contrary, Aristotle says of this character, as opposed to the *akratês* (incontinent), that he *agetai proairoumenos* (is led on in accordance with his own choice), and this must imply that he arrives at deliberative conclusions.[7]

All this shows is that MR is not going to show up by considering the outcome of the *phronimos'* deliberations. Now Aristotle says that *phronêsis* is related to cleverness (*deinotês*), but he holds that *phronêsis* is not identical to this, although it cannot exist without it (NE 1144a29). *Phronêsis* is essentially connected to virtue of character: and it is important that this is not a verbal point ("treason never prospers"). The thought of the *phronimos* is structurally and materially peculiar; and this is because he

[7] NE 1146b23–24; cf. 1151a7 for an association between *kakia* (vice) and *proairesis*.

thinks of "ends"—we might say, more generally, considerations—that do not occur to other people. As Broadie points out, this capacity is part of his intelligence. He sees that certain considerations apply, are relevant, carry more weight than others. These include examples of the reasons X that are tied to the various virtues.

To some extent, one can distinguish between seeing that a statement is correct, and seeing that it is relevant to the practical situation at hand. Some of the reasons X will be simply "factual" statements ("it will embarrass her") which might be seen to be true by someone not disposed to count them as reasons in a V-linked way. But it is easy to move out of this area (consider "she needs help"), and many of the most significant reasons X—notably among the negative considerations mentioned before—will be "thick" ethical concepts ("inconsiderate", "disloyal", "shabby"), where the questions of truth and of relevance can be separated only in relation to particular cases. At a general level, those questions cannot be separated, since you cannot make the judgements without having the concept, and you have the concept only if you do count such considerations as relevant in deliberation.[8]

MR will come in, it seems to me, only if it comes in with such concepts. The *phronimos* will exercise his perception, presumably, in seeing that certain considerations of this sort apply. In so judging, he can judge something true. Equally, someone who misses the point, is obtuse, fails in *phronêsis*, may be said to have missed a truth, overlooked something, and so forth. Is this enough to speak of realism?

One might say so. However, much of what is said about realism suggests a stronger condition than this. The requirement will be not only that true judgements can be made under the concept, and that one user of the concept can point out to another that he has missed an application. It will, further, have to be true that people who do not use that concept at all are missing something—that the concept "picks up on" an aspect of the world that an attentive and interested observer should acknowledge. But this further condition does not follow from what is indisputably true about thick concepts. With regard to many of them, it is hard to accept; and it is impossible to accept it of all of them taken together (because the thick concepts of different societies are often not combinable, and we have no idea of how they might all be mapped onto one grid).

Aristotle did hold a quite strong position about such concepts: that a definitive set of them represented the best achievable human understand-

---

[8] It is important that "having the concept" here means "possessing it as one's own", where this implies being disposed to use it in judgements with which one is identified. One can understand such a concept, as an anthropologist does, without satisfying this condition.

ing of the ethical. Is Aristotle's position a version of the view which, I have just suggested, might be identified with MR? Only, I suggest, if one accepts more of Aristotle's philosophy than his ethics. For Aristotle, a certain set of thick ethical concepts, including those that define the virtues themselves, provide the best achievable human understanding of the ethical in this sense, that their intelligent use in a life that they serve to define as virtuous is the most satisfying life accessible to a human being. The set of concepts is, one might say, ethically categorical. This is not, for us, obviously the same idea as that expressed by MR (as we are presently interpreting it), which is rather that of certain concepts being cognitively categorical: one who does not use some or all of them has left an important element out of his understanding of the world. So for us, the basic Aristotelian idea, and the suggested interpretation of MR, are distinct. Aristotle himself, however, had further conceptions in the light of which those two ideas are not distinct, but come to much the same thing.

We can, in our own way, seek to remove the gap between the two ideas, by saying that the sense of "understanding the world" that is appropriate to these concepts must be that of ethically understanding the world: these concepts are, after all, hardly going to help us make a contribution to the physical or biological sciences. But our difference from Aristotle's situation is measured precisely by the fact that we need to make this point. Aristotle could see ethics as connected to biology in a way that made human flourishing, understood in terms of a rational ethical life, as straightforwardly an application to us of explanatory categories that apply to all species; you would mention this kind of flourishing in saying what kind of living thing a human being was. We do not share this picture, and it is a denial of history and of scientific change to pretend that we do.

Of course it is we, and not Aristotle, who deploy such formulae as "moral realism", and we must decide what we mean by them. We also must decide how to make the best use, in our circumstances, of Aristotle's ethics. But if we mean the kind of thing by "moral realism" that I have suggested, then even the fullest use we might reasonably make of Aristotle's ethics will not in itself lead us to MR. It would do that only if we accepted Aristotle's own account of the relation of human ethical life to everything else, and that, certainly, we cannot reasonably do.

TWELVE

Aristotle on the Good: A Formal Sketch

This paper attempts a simple formal treatment of Aristotle's discussion of the good in *Nicomachean Ethics* I 1–7 (1094 a 1–1098 a 20). Its aim is to distinguish some of the leading concepts used by Aristotle, and to examine some of the logical relations between them; with the particular purpose of establishing what premisses, granted the formal apparatus, are sufficient or necessary for some of the main conclusions supposedly established by Aristotle in this passage.

We shall use first-order predicate calculus with identity and with the modal operator "N" = "it is necessary that". Variables "x", "y", etc., will range over the arts, enquiries, actions, etc. (1094 a 1 seq) which can in the broadest sense be pursued, and which Aristotle regards as the subject matter of his enquiry into the good. We shall use one primitive predicate letter "P", which will however have two rôles, as standing for a one-place and for a two-place predicate. "Px" is to be interpreted "x is pursued"; "Pxy" is to be interpreted "x is pursued for the sake of y". In these interpretations, the terms "pursued" and "pursued for the sake of" are intended to cover a number of expressions used by Aristotle, but which, at least in the discussion under consideration, he seems to use interchangeably, such as "aims at", "is desired for the sake of", etc. Some further remarks about the interpretation of "P" will follow the next paragraph.

1094 a 1 seq gives us, a little tentatively, a statement which is presupposed throughout the discussion: that everything that is pursued is pursued for the sake of something; we may trivially add that everything pursued for the sake of something is pursued:

(1) (x) [Px ↔ (∃y) Pxy].

We may add further that if x is pursued for the sake of y, y is itself pursued:

(2) (x) (y) [Pxy → Py].

The discussion of the architectonic relations in cc. 1, 2 init. make it clear that the relation "Pxy" must be *transitive* and, for different values of x and y, *asymmetrical*:

(3) (x) (y) (z) [Pxy & Pyz → Pxz].

(4) (x) (y) [Pxy & x ≠ y → ~ Pyx].

The restriction of asymmetry to non-identical values of x and y in (4) is necessary because, as will be seen, "Pxy" is not irreflexive.

(3) and (4) clearly raise certain questions about the interpretation of "P". If, as the previous sketch of an interpretation might well suggest, it is a sufficient condition of the truth of "Pa" that a is at some time pursued by somebody, (3) and (4) will almost certainly under interpretation come out false, since it is clearly possible that Pab by somebody at some time, and Pbc by somebody else at some time, without Pac by anyone at any time. Again, it seems that it might well be the case that Pab by someone at some time, and Pba by someone else at any time, or by the same person at a different time. These difficulties, however, lie not so much in the formalization of Aristotle's discussion by means of the predicate "P", as in Aristotle's discussion itself; exactly these questions are bound to arise in any consideration of his very general method of argument. The most effective ways to avoid these difficulties are perhaps: (1) to restrict interpretation of the variables to actions *as characterized by* certain preferred descriptions—for instance by selecting characterizations of a and b in "Pab" such that it will be obvious how someone can pursue a for the sake of b, which will in general rule out "Pba" for the same characterizations of a and b; (2) to take as interpretation the dispositional pursuit-structure of one fully rational and consistent agent with a settled pattern of desires. "Fully rational" here must include an evaluational element, which is certainly inherent in Aristotle's treatment; his discussion, for instance, of things which can be pursued for their own sake is confined to things which a sane and rational man would pursue for their own sake. (This accords with his remarks on the requirements for intelligent study of his theory, 1095 b 3 seq.) It will be safe to say that Aristotle supposes all his propositions to hold for the pursuits of a thoroughly consistent *phronimos*;* some for wider classes of agents; some, being, or supposedly being, logical truths (such as (1) and (2)), for any conceivable agent. The same must hold for the interpretation of "P".

Granted that something is pursued, (1) and (2) can generate an infinite series of P-statements:

Pa;
Pab, for some b (by (1));
Pb   (by (2));
Pbc, for some c (by (1)); etc.

* Person of practical wisdom—Ed.

1094 a 20 (whatever else it states) states that such a series cannot be continued indefinitely, for the good reason that the notion of "pursuit for the sake of" would then lack content ("our desire would be empty and vain"). Nor can we stop its infinite prolongation by making it circular, i.e. by introducing some earlier term into the second argument place of some later statement. For suppose such a series

(i) Pab
(ii) Pbc . . .
(n) Pna.

Repeated applications of (3) will give from (ii) . . . (n) : Pba; but this, by (4), is inconsistent with (i). Hence we may infer, as Aristotle infers,

(5) $(\exists x)\ Px \rightarrow (\exists y)\ Pyy$.

From this, of course, we cannot infer that there is only *one* x such that Pxx, i.e.:

*(6) $(\exists x)\ Px \rightarrow (\exists y)\ [Pyy\ \&\ \sim (\exists z)\ (z \neq y\ \&\ Pzz)]$;

nor can we infer

*(7) $(\exists x)\ Px \rightarrow (\exists y)\ [(z)\ (Pz \rightarrow Pzy)]$;

for there is nothing in what has gone before to show that we may not have independent chains Pab Pbc . . . Pkk, Pmn Pno . . . Puu, with no common members.

It may be tempting to think that the two statements *(6) and *(7) are equivalent. This is not so, and since *(7), but not *(6), will be of interest in the later argument, it is worthwhile to distinguish them. The following argument will illustrate the issue:

Suppose (i) Paa.
Suppose further that for some d
   (ii) $(x)\ [Px \rightarrow Pxd]$
Then (iii) Pa (i, by 1)
   (iv) Pad (ii, iii)

Thus, it may be thought, from (i) and (iv)

   (v) a = d.

But since the argument applies equally well to any a such that Paa, we shall have derived *(6) from *(7).

The foregoing argument, however, is invalid, since it requires an extra premiss, that if something is pursued for its own sake, it cannot be pursued for the sake of something else as well:

*(8) $(x)\ [Pxx \rightarrow \sim (\exists y)\ (x \neq y\ \&\ Pxy)]$

*(8) is rejected by Aristotle, 1097 a 34. If *(8) were accepted, *(6) and *(7) would indeed be equivalent, since (*a*) the foregoing argument, with the extra premiss, would be valid, so that *(6) could be derived from *(7); (*b*) *(7) can be derived from *(6) even without the extra premiss, as follows:

(i) Suppose *(6), and $(\exists x)\, Px$;

then (ii) there is just one thing, say d, such that Pdd;

but (iii) everything that is pursued is pursued either for its own sake, or for the sake of something pursued for its own sake (by the argument of (5));

(iv) in either case, it is pursued for the sake of d (by (ii));

so (v) there is something for which everything is pursued.

Thus *(6) implies *(7).

Even the addition of *(8), however, would not make either *(6) or *(7) derivable from any of (1)–(5).

The notion contained in *(7), viz. that of something for the sake of which everything is pursued, is important for Aristotle: it is his notion of "the good, or the supreme good" (1094 a 22). We may therefore define:

(9) $SGx \leftrightarrow (y)\, [Py \to Pyx]$ Def.,

and the consequent of *(7) may be written

(10) $(\exists x)\, SGx$.

Aristotle is not yet in a position to prove (10). It might be suggested that 1094 a 1 seq. shows Aristotle to have derived (10) invalidly from (1); but this is an implausible, as well as uncharitable, interpretation of his intention, since he clearly regards (1) as certain and presupposes it throughout, but (10) is later introduced as uncertain (1097 a 22 seq.). Nor, I think, does the difficult passage 1094 a 18 seq. (the first sentence of c. 2) *have* to be taken as an attempt to infer (10) from (5) and the considerations that lead up to it. The passage runs:

If, then, there is some end of the things we do, which we desire for its own sake (everything else being desired for the sake of this), and if we do not choose everything for the sake of something else (for at that rate the process would go on to infinity, so that our desire would be empty and vain), clearly this must be the good and the chief good. [tr. Ross]

Here we have two antecedents for the same consequent, each containing a parenthesis. Let the antecedents with their parentheses be signified by 'A(a)', and 'B(b)'. Clearly (b) is offered as a *reason* for B, and (a) as a *specification* of the 'end' mentioned in A. If now B(b) were offered as a reason for A(a), we should have the invalid inference referred to. However, it is possible to take B, not as a reason for A(a), but as a consequence of it, brought in by Aristotle as suggested by the larger hypothesis A(a), and suggesting in its turn a reason for itself (b); in this case the invalid inference will not be committed. The passage is in any case confusedly expressed, and it is perhaps impossible to say exactly what it means. If so, the former interpretation is certainly not obligatory. Even if it is accepted, however, it is clear that Aristotle lays no great weight on the invalid argument.

We shall return to (10). Meanwhile, it is to be noted that Aristotle believes that there are at least four things pursued for their own sake (pleasure, honour, reason, virtue 1097 b 2, cf. 1096 b 17):

(11) $(\exists x)\,(\exists y)\,(\exists z)\,(\exists w)\,[x \neq y \neq z \neq w \;\&\; Pxx \;\&\; Pyy \;\&\; Pzz \;\&\; Pww]$

Of any such thing, it is evident that there does not have to be anything else for the sake of which it is pursued, although (*(8) being rejected) there could be. Of any such thing, Aristotle says that it is *final* (*teleion*):

(12) $TLx \leftrightarrow Px \;\&\; \sim N\,(\exists y)\,[y \neq x \;\&\; Pxy]$ Def.

1097 a 34 seq. In the same passage, Aristotle goes on to introduce the notions, at first sight surprising, of "more final" (*teleioteron*) and "most final" (*teleiotaton*). He gives in fact two applications of the former, the first to things not pursued for their own sake, the second to things that are pursued for their own sake; of these the former seems of little use, and involves the awkward consequence that something can be more final without being final. Omitting this application, his accounts of the two notions may be represented, respectively:

(13) $TLRxy \leftrightarrow TLx \;\&\; TLy \;\&\; \sim N \sim (Pyx) \;\&\; N \sim (Pxy)$ Def.;

(14) $TLTx \leftrightarrow TLx \;\&\; (y)\,[(TLy \;\&\; y \neq x) \to TLRxy]$ Def.

We may infer

(15) $(x)\,[TLTx \to (y)\,\{y \neq x \to N \sim (Pxy)\}]$

For (i) $(x)\,[TLTx \to (TLx \;\&\; (y)\{TLy \;\&\; y \neq x \to \sim N \sim (Pyx) \;\&\; N \sim (Pxy)\})]$ (by Defs.)

so (ii) $(x)\,[TLTx \to (y)\,\{TLy \;\&\; y \neq x \to N \sim (Pxy)\}]$ (by dropping consequents)

but the restriction to y's that are TL in the consequent of (ii) can be dropped, the consequent holding for non-TL y's as well: for, for any non-TL y such that Pxy, there would have to be (by the argument of (5) and by (12)), some TLz such that Pyz; whence by (3), there would be a TL z such that Pxz, contrary to (ii).

We may further infer

(16) (x) [TLTx → (y) (TLTy ↔ y = x)]

i.e. that there is at most one TLT thing. For

suppose (i) TLTa & TLTb & a ≠ b;
then   (ii) TLRab & TLRba, (by (14));
so   (iii) ~ N ~ (Pba) & N ~ (Pab) & ~ N ~ (Pab) & N ~ (Pba),
                (by (13)),

which is absurd.

We cannot infer, however, that there is at least one TLT thing:

(17) (∃x) TLTx.

(It is worth noting, in passing, that we could *not* derive this by adopting the premiss, nowhere offered by Aristotle,

*(18) (x) (y) [TLx & TLy & x ≠ y → TLRxy V TLRyx]

Since the TLR-relation is asymmetrical, as seen in the proof of (16), *(18) would allow us to derive (17) if the TLR-relation were also transitive, but it is not.)

More importantly for Aristotle's argument, we could not derive (17) from (10), if we independently accepted that. From (9) and (10) we should have

(i) (∃x) (y) [Py → Pyx]; from this *a fortiori*
(ii) (∃x) (y) [TLy & y ≠ x → Pyx].

From (ii), by the acceptable principle *ab esse ad posse valet consequentia*, we could infer

(iii) (∃x) (y) [TLy & y ≠ x → ~ N ~ (Pyx)].

(17), however, by (13) and (14), requires

(iv) (∃x) (y) [TLy & y ≠ x → ~ N ~ (Pyx) & N ~ (Pxy)],

and it is clear that the second conjunct of the consequent of (iv) cannot be provided from (i)–(iii). Moreover, (iv), and hence (17), does not imply (10), since *a posse ad esse non valet consequentia*. Thus we have the interesting negative result that the existence of an SG thing and of a TLT thing do not imply one another. Nor is this surprising, if one considers the interpretation of "N" in (12)–(14). It is clear that Aristotle regards the necessity and possibility involved in the notions there defined as intensionally connected with the specifications of the things that are final, most final, etc. Thus happiness (*eudaimonia*), which is said in fact to be most final, is so because it makes no sense, according to Aristotle, to ask of happiness, so specified, for what it is being pursued. This being so, we can see that merely from the fact that a certain thing was that for which everything was done, it would not follow that it had the further intensional property of being TLT; or conversely.

What we can show, however, is that if there is a SG thing, and there is a TLT thing, they must be one and the same:

(19) (x) (y) [SGx & TLTy → x = y].

For suppose (i) SGa
            (ii) TLTb
            (iii) a ≠ b

Then, from (i), (ii) (which implies Pb), and (10),

            (iv) Pba;

but from (ii), (iii), and (15),

            (v) N ~ (Pba).

Aristotle does in fact assert both (10) and (17). What are his reasons? For the latter, two reasons can perhaps be found. The first consists in the mere observation that happiness does possess the intensional character-istic in question, and is in fact pursued. The second is a more *a priori* reason. It seems to be Aristotle's belief that a reason or justification can be given or found for a given pursuit only in terms of some end served by the pursuit.[1] This end may, of course, lie in the pursuit itself, as has been seen (5). This can be the case with any TL thing. But Aristotle remarks that there is more than one TL thing (11). If we were merely left with the set of TL things as each providing reasons, there could be ultimately rea-sonless choices *between* pursuits, since no reason could be given for choosing what conduced to one TL thing rather than what conduced to another. If this is to be avoided, there must be some TL thing that stands in a special relation to the others, as something for which they can be pursued, but not it for them, and this will be the TLT thing.

From neither of these reasons does (10) follow, because it does not fol-low from the fact that there is one special TL thing for which the others can be pursued that they always are or should be pursued for it. It may be that Aristotle overlooked the lack of implication between (17) and (10), and falsely supposed that an argument for the first was an argument for the second. There is, however, no necessity to think this. For Aristotle gives at least one quite independent argument for (10), viz. the argument from function, 1097 b 25 seq. Moreover, even omitting this as coming

---

[1] Cf. e.g. the account of deliberation, 1112b12 seq. and its rôle in *phronesis* [practical wisdom—Ed.] 1140a24 seq.

rather late in the discussion to be more than a confirming argument, (10) might be supported merely *a posteriori* (thus 1094 a 1 seq., granted it is not an invalid derivation of (10) from (1), may be the tentative acceptance of an *endoxon* or received opinion in favour of (10)). If this is so, we may suppose Aristotle to have had independent reasons for believing in an SG thing, and in a TLT thing, and then (validly) have inferred their identity.

We may end by considering one further characterisation that Aristotle applies to the good, viz. that it should be *autarkes*, or self-sufficient. There are two senses of this term, which, though connected, are distinct, and are sufficiently distinguished by Aristotle at 1097 b 14. In the first sense, the good is *autarkes* if its possession is to the greatest extent secure, and not subject to the whims of others and similar contingencies not in the possessor's power. This is the sense that Aristotle also, and better, expresses by saying that the good should be "proper to a man and not easily taken from him" (*oikeion ti kai dusaphaireton*, 1095 b 25). In the second sense, the *autarkes* is "that which when isolated makes life desirable and lacking in nothing . . . the most desirable, not counted as one good thing among others" (1097 b 14 seq.). This account at least involves the thought that what is *autarkes* is a TL thing, and that no other TL thing can be pursued independently of it; for TL things are things pursued for their own sake by reasonable men, i.e. are worth pursuing, and besides the *autarkes* there is nothing worth pursuing. Thus we can say, as a possible definition:

(20) $\text{AUT}x \leftrightarrow \text{TL}x \,\&\, (y)\{(y \neq x \,\&\, \text{P}yy) \rightarrow \text{P}yx\}$ Def. 1.

But by transitivity (3) we can conclude that anything pursued for the sake of any of the things pursued for their own sake is also pursued for the sake of the AUT. Moreover, the AUT is pursued for its own sake; since nothing else is left, we have

(21) $(x) [\text{AUT}x \rightarrow (y) (\text{P}y \rightarrow \text{P}yx)]$.

The implication, moreover, obviously holds in the opposite direction *a fortiori*; so, by (9)

(22) $(x) [\text{AUT}x \leftrightarrow \text{SG}x]$.

In this case, by previous arguments, being AUT will be neither a necessary nor a sufficient condition of being TLT.

However, an alternative definition might be suggested in which "AUT" was expressed in terms of necessity. Thus it might be suggested that anything that satisfied Aristotle's description of AUT would be something other than which there could not *conceivably* be anything higher, i.e.

*(23) $\text{AUT}x \leftrightarrow \text{TL}x \,\&\, \text{N} \sim (\exists y)\{y \neq x \,\&\, \text{P}xy\}$ Def. 2.

This, however, would not by itself be adequate, since it leaves open the possibility, excluded by the first definition and by Aristotle, that there should be some TL thing independent of, though not superior to, the AUT. Thus what is needed is rather a combination of (20) and *(23). If we allow the principle of inference

(n) $Np \rightarrow p$,

this can be economically effected by merely adding "N" to (20):

(24) $AUTx \leftrightarrow TLx \;\&\; N \;(y)\{(y \neq x \;\&\; Pyy) \rightarrow Pyx\}$ Def. 3.

From this, using (n), we can infer as before (21); but we cannot derive the converse implication to give (22). We can infer the universal closure of *(23) by a simple argument:

Suppose that AUTa and that, contrary to *(23), for some x, say b, such that $b \neq a$, Pab. Then, by the argument of (5), there is some y, say c, such that Pcc, and Pac, either directly if $c = b$, or by transitivity. Then by (24), since Pcc, Pca. But this, by (4), is impossible, since we have Pac.

Moreover, we can clearly derive

(25) $(x) [AUTx \rightarrow (y)\{Py \rightarrow \sim N \sim (Pyx)\}]$

from (21), (which we have seen to be derivable from (24)), by the principle *ab esse ad posse*. Putting together (25) and the universal closure of *(23), obtained by the last result, we can reach

(26) $(x) [AUTx \rightarrow TLTx]$,

though the converse implication will not of course hold. Thus if the attractive definition (24) is accepted, we shall have the result that something's being AUT will imply both its being SG and its being TLT; while, as we have seen before, its being SG neither implies nor is implied by its being TLT; the most that can be established in respect of the two latter concepts alone being that if there is an SG thing and there is a TLT thing, they are one and the same.

THIRTEEN

Justice as a Virtue

I shall consider some points in Aristotle's treatment of justice in Book 5 of the *Nicomachean Ethics*, in order to raise certain questions about justice as a virtue of character. I am concerned with what Aristotle calls "particular" justice, that is to say, with justice considered as one virtue of character among others. This disposition is said to have two basic fields of application, the distributive and the rectificatory; this distinction will not concern us, and almost all the discussion can be referred to the first of this pair. Particular justice and injustice are concerned with a certain class of goods—"those which are the subjects of good and bad luck, and which considered in themselves are always good, but not always good for a particular person" (1129b3–5). These are listed at 1130b3 as honor, money, and safety: these are "divisible" goods, which are such that if one person gets more, another characteristically gets less.

From the beginning, Aristotle associates particular injustice with *pleonexia*—variously, greed, the desire to have more, the desire to have more than others: *pleonektēs ho adikos* 1129b1. This characteristic Aristotle treats as the defining motive of particular injustice:

> If one man commits adultery for the sake of gain, and makes money by it, while another does so from appetite, but loses money and is penalized for it, the latter would be thought self-indulgent rather than *pleonektēs*, while the former is unjust and not self-indulgent: this is obviously because of the fact that he gains. Again, all other unjust acts are ascribed in each case to some kind of vice, e.g. adultery to self-indulgence; deserting a fellow soldier, to cowardice; assaulting someone, to anger. But if he makes a gain, it is ascribed to no other vice but injustice. [1130a24 f.]

This passage occurs in chapter 2 where Aristotle is concerned to find the distinguishing mark of particular injustice. It seems clear that the reference to "unjust" acts is to acts that are unjust in the general sense—that is to say, roughly, wrong—and a similar interpretation is given to *adikei* at 1130a17.[1] Aristotle's point is that the way to pick out acts that are

---

[1] So commentators, e.g. Joachim and Gauthier-Jolif, ad loc.; W.F.R. Hardie, *Aristotle's Ethical Theory* (Oxford, 1968), p. 187.

unjust in the particular sense from the whole range of acts that are contrary to justice in the general sense is by reference to the motive of pleonexia (which, on any showing, is excessively restricted, at this point of the discussion, to the desire for monetary gain). This is what the passage means; but its exact conclusion is unclear, and discussions of it do not pay enough attention to the Aristotelian distinction between unjust acts and an unjust character. It is one question whether particular injustice as a vice is characterized by the motive of pleonexia; it is another question whether all acts that are unjust in the particular sense are motivated in that way. The two questions come together only if some quite complex assumptions are made, which I shall try to bring out.

Later in the book, Aristotle directly addresses the distinction between acts and character, and also applies his usual distinctions about responsibility. In chapter 8, he first considers acts done from ignorance, and makes various distinctions among these: of a person acting in this way involuntarily, he says that they act neither justly nor unjustly except *kata sumbebēkos*—they do things that merely happen to be just or unjust (1135a17–18). Beyond this, if someone acts, not out of ignorance, but also not from deliberation (*ek prohaireseōs*) and, rather, from some passion, the act will indeed be an unjust act, but the agent will not be an unjust person: *adikei men oun, adikos d' ouk estin* (1134a21, the first paragraph of chapter 6, a passage evidently displaced from its context). One who acts unjustly *ek prohaireseōs* is a person who possesses in the full sense the vice of injustice, and is fully an unjust person.

This, so far, is standard Aristotelian doctrine about bad acts and their relation to character and intention. Leaving aside acts that are involuntary through ignorance (more simply, unintentional), we can concentrate on the distinction, among intentional acts, between those that are the product of passion and later regretted, and those that are the expression of a settled disposition or vice of character.

This distinction bears a close relation, of course, to that between the *akratēs* and the *mochthēros*, but it is not exactly the same. *Akrasia* is itself a disposition, a trait of character, and as with any other bad characteristic, one can draw the distinction between someone who has this characteristic and is regularly disposed to give in to certain kinds of impulse, and someone who on some few occasions does so. We need not be concerned here to fit the *disposition* of akrasia into the account.

For the present purpose we need only a distinction between *acts*. With respect to some undesirable characteristic V, it is the distinction, among acts that are, in the relevant aspect, intentional, between:

(A) those that are V acts but are not the acts of a V person

and

(B) those that are both V and the acts of a V person.

The usual situation with the vices of character, in Aristotle's treatment, is that it will be a necessary condition of an act's being V that it is the product of some particular motive—lust, fear, or whatever.

To be put alongside this is another distinction among acts, in terms of their motives: the distinction between those that are motivated by a desire for gain, and those that are motivated otherwise. Now the distinction between (A) and (B) standardly consists in this, that (A) acts are the episodic and later regretted expressions of a motive that regularly motivates the person who does (B) acts, that is to say, the person who is V. But it is obvious that an (A) unjust act need not be motivated by desire for gain at all. To take Aristotle's paradigmatic distribution case, a person could on a particular occasion be overcome by hopes of sexual conquest, or malice against one recipient, and so knowingly make an unjust distribution, and his act would surely be an unjust act.

Another of Aristotle's claims, admittedly an obscure one, indeed leads to this conclusion. In his rather unhappy and perfunctory account of the application of the mean to justice, he says:

> . . . just action is intermediate between acting unjustly and being unjustly treated; for the one is to have too much and the other to have too little. Justice is a kind of mean, but not in the same way as the other virtues, but because it relates to an intermediate amount, while injustice relates to the extremes. [1133b3 f.]

It is not worth pursuing all the difficulties raised by these remarks, but one thing that the passage seems awkwardly to acknowledge is that if X has been unjustly treated, then someone else (chap. 11), Y, has acted unjustly toward him. But it cannot be a necessary condition of X's being unjustly treated by Y that Y be motivated by the desire for gain, rather than by lust, malice, anger, or whatever.

However, Aristotle is certainly tempted by his standard model, according to which, since pleonexia is the motive of the unjust person, (A) acts of injustice must be episodic expressions of pleonexia. This idea issues in a desperate device at 1137a1 f.:

> If (the distributor) judged unjustly with knowledge, he himself gets an unfair share of gratitude or revenge. As much, then, as if he had shared in the plunder, one who judges unjustly for these reasons gets too much. . . .

There must be something wrong in extending pleonexia to cover someone's getting more of this kind of thing. What would it be in such a case to get the right amount of gratitude or revenge?

Aristotle correctly holds:

(a) one who knowingly produces an unjust distribution acts unjustly.

He also explicitly claims:

(b) the characteristic motive of the vice of injustice is the desire for gain.

In addition, he seems disposed to accept the standard model from which it will follow that:

(c) the difference between (A) acts and (B) acts of injustice is not of motive, but only a difference in the dispositional grounding of that motive,

and the consequence of accepting all these claims is obviously false. There are acts that are unjust, and in the "particular" sense, but which are the products of fear, jealousy, desire for revenge, and so on. Moreover, they may be not just episodic expressions of motives of that kind, but rather of some related dispositional trait. The cowardly man who runs away in battle acts not only in a cowardly way, but also unfairly, and does so because of his cowardice. Unjust acts that are not expressions of the vice of injustice can thus stem from other vices. But the motives characteristic of those other vices are not the motive of pleonexia supposedly characteristic of the vice of injustice. So we cannot, granted these truths, accept both (b) and (c).

It might be said that the cowardly man's act of injustice is in fact motivated by pleonexia, the desire for gain, as well as by fear: he is aiming at an unfair share of the divisible good of safety. That description, unlike the nonsense about an unfair share of gratitude or revenge, could contain some truth. But it will not do in order to straighten out Aristotle's account of the matter, since 1130a17 f. makes it clear that pleonexia is seen as *contrasted* with such motives as fear, and not as coexisting with, or being a product of, such motives. The broader question of what pleonexia exactly is I shall come back to at the end.

(c) is one of the assumptions that I referred to earlier as needed to bring together the two questions, whether the unjust character is characterized by the motive of pleonexia, and whether all unjust acts are the product of that motive. (c) states that each unjust act must have the same motive as the unjust acts that are the product of an unjust character; and that is surely wrong. We can recognize that it is wrong, however, only because we can identify certain intentional acts as unjust in the particular sense, and can do this without referring to their motive. Indeed, we are helped by Aristotle in doing this, by his drawing our attention to such basic cases as the intentional misdistribution of divisible goods. Aristotle himself gives us a clear indication of the areas in which some unjust acts are to be found; in doing so, he also puts us in a strong position to deny, as he does not seem clearly to have done, the assumption (c).

However, the fact that some unjust acts can be located without referring to their motive does not entail that they all can be. It might be that some other unjust acts could be identified simply from their motive; in particular, by their flowing from a settled dispositional motive characteristic of the unjust character. In this case, they would not all have to be of the same types as those unjust acts that are identified independently of motive, such as misdistributions of divisible goods. They might, for instance, be acts of a sexual kind which, if motivated in a more usual way, would not be identified as having anything to do with particular injustice at all. Aristotle clearly thinks that there are acts of this kind. He associates the vice of *adikia* so closely with a certain motive (or rather, I shall suggest later, a certain class of motives), pleonexia, that he calls a person who is dispositionally motivated by that an *adikos*, and holds, in chapter 2, that any act which that person does from that motive is an act of particular injustice. Aristotle could of course go further, and hold that any act, of any kind, which is even episodically motivated by pleonexia is an unjust act in the particular sense. He would then have completed the equation of adikia and pleonexia, not only with respect to character, but with respect to acts. It is not clear to me, however, that he does hold that: chapter 2, at any rate, seems to commit him only to the view that any act of a dispositionally pleonektic man which is an expression of his pleonexia is an unjust act.

Aristotle, then, certainly equates the character-state of adikia with that of pleonexia. He certainly thinks that any act, whatever its other characteristics, which flows from that state is an unjust act. He may think, though it is not absolutely clear that he does, that any act that is even episodically motivated by pleonexia is an unjust act. He is strongly disposed to think, lastly, that any act that is an unjust act is motivated, even if only episodically, by pleonexia; but since he himself suggests some plausible ways of identifying some unjust acts independently of their motive, this is an unsound conclusion for him to hold, and insofar as he tends to hold it, it is probably because of the unsound theoretical assumption (c).

Treated in this way, adikia comes out as something rather different from anything that we would now be disposed to call "injustice." One must certainly recognise that the *dikaiosunē-adikia* scheme does not exactly match even a part of our *justice-injustice* scheme. The point, however, can also be put more critically. Since Aristotle leads us so clearly, as has already been said, to some areas in which dikaiosunē undoubtedly overlaps with justice, his dealings with the question of motive can be seen as an imperfection in his attempt to relate those areas to the virtues of character. Even in his own terms, the assumption (c), if indeed he made it, would be a mistake. His willingness, further, to equate the character state of adikia with that of pleonexia and to call an unjust act any act that arises from that state, can be seen as the other side of the same coin. In both ways his theory inclines him to think that the state of character that stands opposed to dikaiosunē must have a characteristic motive; and dikaiosunē is enough like justice to make it convenient, and perhaps even fair, to call this a mistake.

I now turn to some questions about justice and injustice as states of character, independently, to some degree, of Aristotle's treatment. I shall concentrate on the area where our concepts most clearly overlap with Aristotle's, that of distributive justice. As a way of dealing with justice as a virtue, this concentration is obviously very selective, but the general shape of the conclusions will, I believe, apply more widely. In discussing distributive justice, I will not always assume, as Aristotle does, that we are concerned with some unallocated good that is, so to speak, "up for grabs" and waiting to be distributed by some method or other to some class of recipients. We can, besides that, recognize also the case in which the good is already in somebody's hands, and the question is rather whether he justly holds it. We can extend the term *distribution* to cover such possibilities,[2] though since I am mainly concerned with justice as a virtue of character and am discussing the case of distributive justice in the interest of that concern, the case where there is no distributor will be of secondary interest.

In the distributive case, we can distinguish three items to which the terms *just* and *unjust* can be applied: a distributor (if there is one), a method, and an outcome. The question basically raised by Aristotle's treatment concerns the relation between the first of these and the other two; but it is worth saying something about the priority between method and outcome in determining what is just. Is a just outcome to be understood as one reached by a just method, or is a just method, more fundamentally, one that leads to just outcomes? At a first glance there seem to be examples that tell either way. Aristotle's own preferred examples tend to be ones in which the relevant merit or desert of the recipients is understood (at least by the distributor) beforehand, so that the basic idea is of a just outcome, namely, that in which each recipient benefits in proportion to his desert, and a just method will be, derivatively, a method that brings about that outcome. It seems different, however, if one takes a case in which some indivisible good has to be allocated among persons

---

[2] Robert Nozick, who strongly emphasizes this point in his *Anarchy, State and Utopia* (New York, 1974), calls the chapter in which this is discussed "Distributive Justice."

who have equal claims to it, and they agree to draw lots (a method that can be adapted also to cases in which they have unequal claims to it). Here the justice is not worn in its own right by the outcome of, say, Robinson, getting it, nor is it the fact that it has that outcome that makes the method just; it is rather the other way round.

This distinction is more fragile than it first looks, and it is sensitive to the ways in which the outcome and the method are described. Thus if the method is itself described as that of allocating, say, the food to the hungry, the "desert" can come to characterize the method itself, and not merely the outcome. Not all the difficulties here are very interesting; they flow from an evident indeterminacy in the notions of method and outcome. But, even allowing for the difficulties, there is a class of cases in which the justice very specially rests in the method rather than in the particular outcome. In these, when we ask "what makes it fair that A has it (or has that amount of it)?" the answer refers to a process by which A came to have the good in question, and, moreover, no characteristic of A which does not relate to that process is appropriately cited as grounding his claim to the good. This is true of Nozick's "entitlement theory,"[3] under which someone justly holds an item if he received it by an appropriate process (e.g., buying it) from someone who justly held it. Under such a theory, the process by which someone receives something is constitutive of the justice of his holding, and there is no independent assessment of the justice of the outcome at all.

This bears a resemblance, illuminating and also politically relevant, to another kind of case that also satisfies the condition for primacy of method, the case of allocation by lot. If Robinson draws the long straw, then what makes it fair that he gets the good is simply the fact that it was he who drew the straw. We may of course want to go further than that, and add that the straw-drawing was itself a method that, for instance, was agreed upon in advance. The fact that we can do this does not mean that the justice of the method ceases to be primary over the justice of the particular outcome: in explaining the fairness of Robinson's getting the good, we still essentially refer to the method. However, the point that we can, in the case of lots and similar processes, relevantly go on to say such things as that the method was agreed upon in advance, serves to bring out an important contrast with entitlement theory. In the case of lots, it is possible to ask questions about what makes the method a just or fair method.

The answers to those questions may even refer, in a general way, to outcomes. They will not refer to the particular outcome, and relative to that, the method remains primary, but some general relation of the

<hr>

[3] Nozick, *Anarchy*, chap. 7.

method to outcomes may be relevant. For instance, a familiar argument in favor of a particular method of allocating some indivisible good would be that the probability it assigned to any given person of receiving the good was the same ratio as the share which that person, under the same general criteria, would appropriately receive of a divisible good (he gets one fifth of the cake, and a one-in-five chance of getting the chess set). A similar point emerges from the fact that lot-drawing can be modified, in certain circumstances, to allow for repeated trials; for instance, earlier winners may be excluded from later draws because it is thought fairer to increase over time the chances of a given person's winning. In such ways it is possible to criticize the fairness of methods such as drawing lots, by reference to general patterns of outcome, and by applying a notion of justice to such general patterns. But this resource seems mysteriously not available with Nozick's entitlement theory, and no other considerations, it seems, can be brought to bear on the question whether established methods of transfer are fair methods. But if we are to be convinced that the favored transactions are not only just but unquestionably just, some special argument needs to be produced: it certainly does not simply follow from the truth that, relative to the particular case, the concept of "justice" applies primarily to the method and derivatively to the outcome. That is a feature which Nozick's preferred methods of transfer share with other methods of distribution, where criticism of the methods is nevertheless possible.

For our present purposes, however, the priorities of method and outcome are a secondary issue. The main question concerns the relations of either of these to the notion of a just person, and from now on I shall speak of a "just distribution" to cover both those cases in which the method would naturally be considered primary, and those in which it is more natural to pick on the outcome. The notion of a fair distribution is prior to that of a fair or just person. Such a person is one who is disposed to promote just distributions, look for them, stand by them, and so on, because that is what they are. He may also be good at inventing just distributions, by thinking of a good method or proposing an acceptable distribution in a particular case: this will be a characteristic of Aristotle's *epieikēs* (1137b34), the person who is good at particular discriminations of fairness. But even there, it is important that, although it took him, or someone like him, to think of it, the distribution can then be recognized as fair independently of that person's character. It cannot rest on his previous record that some particular distribution, which perhaps seems entirely whimsical, is just (except in the sense, uninteresting to the present question, that his past record may encourage us to believe that there are other considerations involved in the present case, known to him though invisible to us).

The disposition of justice will lead the just person to resist unjust distributions—and to resist them *however they are motivated*. This applies, very centrally, to himself. There are many enemies of fair conduct, both episodic and dispositional, and the person of just character is good at resisting them. This means that he will need, as Aristotle himself insists, other virtues as well: courage, for instance, or *sōphrosunē*. But the disposition of justice can itself provide a motive. The disposition to pursue justice and to resist injustice has its own special motivating thoughts: it is both necessary and sufficient to being a just person that one dispositionally promotes some courses as being just and resists others as being unjust.

What then is the disposition of injustice? What is it to be a dispositionally unjust or unfair person? The answer surely can only be that it is to lack the disposition of justice—at the limit, not to be affected or moved by considerations of fairness to all. It involves a tendency to act from some motives on which the just person will not act, and indeed to have some motives which the just person will not have at all. Important among the motives to injustice (though they seem rarely to be mentioned) are such things as laziness or frivolity. Someone can make an unfair decision because it is too much trouble, or too boring, to think about what would be fair. Differently, he may find the outcome funny or diverting. At the end of that line is someone who finds the outcome amusing or otherwise attractive just because it is unfair.

It is important that this last condition is not the central or most basic condition of being an unjust person. The thoughts that motivate the unjust do not characteristically use, in this upside-down way, the concepts of justice and injustice. Those concepts, however, as has just been said, do characteristically figure in the thought of the just person. It is not untypical of the virtues that the virtuous person should be partly characterized by the way in which he thinks about situations, and by the concepts he uses. What is unusual about justice is that the just person is characterized by applying to outcomes and methods, in an analogous sense, the concept under which he falls; this is itself connected with the priority of the justice of distributions over justice of character.

On this account, there is no one motive characteristic of the unjust person, just as there is no one enemy of just distributions. In particular, the unjust person is not necessarily greedy or anxious to get more for himself, and insofar as Aristotle connects injustice essentially with pleonexia, he is mistaken. The mistake can, moreover, be fairly easily diagnosed at the systematic level: the vice of adikia has been overassimilated to the other vices of character, so that Aristotle seeks a characteristic motive to go with it, whereas it must be basic to this vice, unlike others, that it does not import a special motive, but rather the lack of one.

The point is not merely that "injustice" is not the name of a motive. Beyond that, there is no particular motive which the unjust person, because of his injustice, necessarily displays. In particular, he does not necessarily display pleonexia, which, whatever else needs to be said about it, certainly involves the idea of wanting something for oneself. Not all the motives that operate against justice, and gain expression in the unjust person, fit this pattern—not even all the important ones do so.

Beyond this, however, what is pleonexia? Is it even a motive itself? To call someone pleonektēs surely does ascribe certain motives to him, but motives that are very indeterminately specified. The pleonektēs wants more, but there must be something in particular of which in a given case he wants more. But "more" than what? More than is fair or just, certainly, but he does not characteristically want it in those terms—he has no special passion for affronting justice, and, like the unjust person generally, he is not specially interested in using the concepts of justice and injustice at all. It is rather that he wants more than he has got, or that he wants more than others. Now anyone who wants anything that admits of more or less wants more than he has got, or at least more than he thinks that he has got; but when this becomes a recursive condition, it is called greediness, and that is certainly one sense of *pleonexia*. Such a person does not necessarily, or even typically, worry about comparisons with others. But in another, and probably the most important, sense of *pleonexia*, comparisons with others are the point, and the notion of having more than others is included in the motivating thought. The application to such goods as money or honor or the Nobel Prize is obvious.

The case of Aristotle's third divisible good, safety, is more difficult. To want *more safety than others* is surely an odd want, if that is its most basic intentional description; what one wants is *as much safety as possible*—enough, one hopes, to keep one safe. Of course, since safety is in the circumstances a divisible good, the steps taken to satisfy this want will involve, and may be aimed at, taking away other people's safety (pushing them out of the fallout shelter). Thus the actions involved are much the same as with cases of pleonexia, but there is still a significant difference. With the Achillean pleonektēs of honor, an essential part of his satisfaction is that others do not have what he has; but the Thersitean pleonektēs of safety does not mind how many are eventually saved, so long as he is, and for this reason, his pleonexia is a different thing. The important point is that pleonexia is not, in his case, ultimately a motive at all: he is a coward, with a keen understanding that safety is a divisible good, and no sense of justice. Thus even in some cases of the egoistic desire for a divisible good, pleonexia is not the most basic or illuminating way of characterizing what is wrong with the man who does not care about justice. The love of competitive honor, however, is essentially pleonektic, and straightforwardly directed at making sure that others do not get it instead of oneself.

The word *pleonexia* can cover both greed and competitiveness. It certainly refers to a class of motives, rather than to any single motive. Those who are pleonektic of some things are not usually pleonektic of everything: as Aristotle well knew, those who are pleonektic of honor are not necessarily pleonektic of money, and conversely; and if there is anyone who is pleonektic of safety, it is certainly not Achilles. These various motives have no doubt at all times fueled some of the most settled indifferences to justice; but it is a mistake, one that dogs Aristotle's account, to look for something other than that settled indifference itself to constitute the vice of injustice, and, having looked for it, to find it in such motives.

FOURTEEN

Hylomorphism

I take hylomorphism to be the view that the relation of soul to body
bears some illuminating resemblance to the relation of form to matter:
where *form* is a semi-technical expression, its sense illustrated by the
example of *shape*, but going beyond that example. I take it that such a
view is advanced by Aristotle. I shall not get involved in any very detailed questions about the exegesis of Aristotle's writings about this
subject. While I shall discuss one or two specific features of Aristotle's
outlook, my aim is rather to consider some general features of such a
view.

Its charm lies in its heroic Aristotelian capacity for compromise. It resists materialism, because it

(1.1) distinguishes between A and A's body,
(1.2) in particular, allows that A can cease to exist when his body
does not,
(1.3) does not imply (and probably actually excludes) physical reduc-
tivism for mental functions.

(Among these, (1.2) will need some modification in the case of
Aristotle's own view: see below.)

On the other hand, it resists dualism, which

(2.1) achieves (1.1), but only at the cost of making 'A' the name of an
immaterial item, (or some complex variant on that), which involves truth-conditions of embarrassingly heterogeneous sorts
for predications about A;
(2.2) substitutes (standardly) for the apparently common-sense truth
that A can cease to exist while his body still exists—it might in
some versions even add to that truth—the more controversial
idea that A's body can cease to exist while he still exists;
(2.3) regards the immaterial item mentioned in (2.1) as the subject of
the mental predications about A.

(How far (2.2) is regarded as an embarrassment to dualism is
of course a matter of cultural climate. It tends to be cited as an
embarrassment now.)

It is tempting to represent hylomorphism and dualism as two views about the relations of soul to body (I started this paper that way). But if that means 'the relations of *a* soul to *a* body', we should perhaps be more careful. Dualism, certainly, raises exactly that question; but it is not, perhaps, clear that hylomorphism needs, or has a place for, the idea of *a* soul. Perhaps hylomorphism might be better expressed by saying that there was no such thing as *the* soul at all. More cautiously, we should just start by saying: there are facts (such as the existence of mental functions) which make dualists speak of a soul, but which make the hylomorphist speak of *something* in terms of the relations of form and matter. That something seems to be, for example, a human being, or again, a person. (A difference between those two will concern us briefly at the end of this paper.) If the term 'soul' comes into it at all, perhaps it should come into it only in some such connection as 'having soul', such that from '*A* has soul' it cannot be inferred that there is a soul which *A* has. We shall come back to that question.

Of course Aristotle's use of 'soul' (using that only to translate *psuchē*) is not confined to the case of human beings or persons; I mentioned those because that is the case that primarily concerns us here. Aristotle thinks that any living thing can be said to have 'soul'; that this is displayed in characteristic activity; that that activity in the case of human beings includes mental activities of various kinds; and that it is a general feature of all these uses of 'soul' that we have an analogy to the relations of matter and form—or, in the generalized sense of 'form', an example of it. 'The whole *this*, Kallias or Socrates, is analogous to *this brazen sphere*' (*Metaphysics* (*Metaph.*) 1033b23); 'such and such a form in this flesh and these bones, this is Kallias or Socrates . . .' (1034a7); and we get the famous account in the *de Anima* (412a16–20):

> Since it is indeed a body of such a kind (for it is one having life), the soul will not be body: for the body is not something predicated of a subject, but exists rather as subject and matter. The soul must, then, be sustance *qua* form of a natural body which has life potentially . . .

which issues in the claim that soul is (he says, in fact, 'the soul') '. . . the first actuality of a natural body which has life potentially'.

This claim is, categorially, puzzling. For soul is said to be substance, and there are references (as here) to *a* soul, or *the* soul. Yet the claim itself does not seem to introduce any particular item for any particular soul to be. It seems to introduce something more in the nature of a fact, or, possibly, a property. This is indeed a problem, and a basic one: and there is worse to come. But let us for the moment leave the term 'soul' altogether. Let us rather consider what sort of fact might be introduced here; and then consider afterwards how, if at all, the term 'soul' might usefully be introduced.

If we make a bronze sphere, Aristotle says, we do not make the shape (he means, that is not the kind of thing it makes sense to suppose someone could make: we will leave the interesting question of whether someone could not actually invent a shape). Nor do we make the bronze (or if we do, that is not the present point). But *that there is a bronze sphere*, this we do make, he interestingly says at one point (*Metaph.* 1033b9), and this must be right: when I make something, I thereby bring about a fact. Granted that I make the thing, bring it into existence, by shaping or giving a certain character to existing stuff, this suggests the correlation of two facts:

(*a*) the fact that this matter *M* has a certain character *C*;
(*b*) the fact that there exists this particular *G*.

In our primitive case, *M* is bronze (this, particular, bronze); *C* is the spherical shape; this particular *G* is this bronze sphere, here. *C* is a general thing; two non-identical particular things can have the same *C* (1034a7: two bronze spheres are the same in form, are different in matter). The correlation of the two facts (*a*) and (*b*) seems in fact to be identity: or as near identity as you can get, one might say, granted the asymmetry that I bring about (*b*) by bringing about (*a*), and not conversely. (What sort of asymmetry is that?)

The supposed analogy of Kallias or Socrates to the bronze sphere means that there should be an (*a*)–(*b*) structure for them. If so, we need values for *M*, *C*, and *G*. At first sight, *C* seems to be *life, being alive*; *G* seems to be *man, human being*; while for *M*, Aristotle seems implicitly to offer two different suggestions in passages already quoted: *flesh and bones*, and *body*. He has a difficulty either way; the difficulties stem from at least two different sources. One is implicit in the generalization of the concept of *form* from that of *shape*; in the bronze sphere case, it is perfectly clear what it would have been for this bronze to have been made into something else, and also clear what it would be for non-bronze to be made into a sphere (though it would not have been this one). In other applications of the form/matter distinction it is notoriously more difficult to formulate the parallel possibilities.

The other, less general, level of difficulty is presented by a problem about the property of *life* in Aristotle, that it is associated intimately by him with something's even being, in the appropriate sense, a *body*. A part of the body, a finger or an eye, is only really such, and not merely bearing that name, if it is alive, and hence the body of which it is a part is alive (e.g. *Metaph.* 1035b14ff): if it is not alive it is not a part (1036b32). Certainly a body consists of hands, fingers, etc.: it follows that if it is dead, it is not really a human body. So it is not merely that a corpse is not a man (*de Partibus Animalium* 640b30f)—that would follow even from the (*a*)–(*b*) structure with 'body' for M. Rather, it is not a *body* to which life is, so to speak, added, as it is certainly bronze that is shaped.[1] Hence 'body' will not do for M. So perhaps we should retreat to 'flesh and bones'.

Now it might be said that if we read the (*a*)–(*b*) structure with this for M, we will not get the right result; perhaps adding *life* to these flesh and bones will not necessarily give us a man, as Baron Frankenstein's unfortunate experience illustrates. Aristotle will reply that the Baron's operations were not those of nature, nor was the *life* which he induced the proper form of life. But this leads us back in the direction we came from, for when we enquire more closely into the proper form of life to constitute a human being, it seems that it could constitute it only in matter of *this* sort, where that already introduces the human shape and human bodily dispositions: they, and human life, unsurprisingly, fit together.[2]

An immediate reaction to these difficulties would be to say the following. Aristotle is very insistent that a dead body is not (really) a body. Hence we cannot identify even as a body that which if it has life constitutes a human being, and if it lacks life constitutes a corpse, since a body cannot lack life. But then does that not show that we merely need another term—say, 'Body'—for that which can have life or lack it, of which life is an occurrent and not an essential property? (It might even be suggested that the term for Body in current English is 'body'). Then we can start again, with Body filling the M slot in our (*a*)–(*b*) structure.

This answer seems—as Aristotle might say—to be in one way right and in one way wrong. It is in one way wrong, because it seems to be his view that anything that can have the property of life at all must have it as an essential property: 'for living things, living is existing' (*de Anima* (*de An.*) 415b8). So there cannot be *anything*, such as our 'Body', which is one and the same thing, at one time alive, at another dead. On the other hand, he would no doubt say that the claim was right, if 'Body' was read more like a mass term, and what had to be true of it to constitute a living body was something other than the property strictly called 'life'. *This* may be what he means by 'flesh and bones'.

---

[1] A similar point has been made by John Ackrill, 'Aristotle's definitions of *psuchē*,' *Proceedings of the Aristotelian Society*, LXXIII (1972–3).

[2] There is a passage—*Metaph.* 1036b1f—which might be taken to mean that the human *form* could be realized in something other than flesh and bones, etc. But I doubt that that is what it means: Aristotle thinks it necessary that they go together, but that we can (though for this very reason we find it difficult) abstract the form from the matter. The argument is bedevilled by Aristotle's persistent difficulty with the notion of there 'being matter in the *logos*'.

Here I think that we have to admit that we have acquired a more mechanical (in a broad sense) conception of 'life' than Aristotle had:[3] the
difference between living bodies and dead ones is for us more like the
difference between going watches and stopped ones, as Descartes put it.
You have to be very resolutely Aristotelian to deny that a stopped clock,
even a clock that will never start again, is a clock, unless it is in advanced
physical dilapidation. For organic things, we have the fact that certain
kinds of functional arrest lead to very rapid irreversible decay, and this
grounds our current conception of death. But it should not obscure from
us the element of truth in the clock analogy (we may need it more under
technical change); and this should encourage us to insist on something
which Aristotle himself would have had to admit, that 'Body' cannot be
just a mass term, like 'meat'. We have a clear conception of a structured
physical thing (call it 'a Body'), which can have and then lose (we might
now say, could conceivably regain) a property which, out of deference to
Aristotle, we will not call 'life', but, say, 'working'. 'Body' is not a mass
term (we can count them, e.g.) but a Body serves as the matter, it seems,
not just of a human being, but of a human body.

Thus we get the structure: the fact that a given Body is working constitutes the existence of the (living) body of a (living) animal: when that
Body ceases to work, that animal ceases to live, and hence to exist. What
remains, the corpse, is (for a while, anyway) a Body, a non-working one.
But it is not an animal; for example, it is (in the memorable words of
Monty Python) an ex-parrot. In the case of man, it is the living animal,
the human being, that is Kallias or Socrates; in their case, moreover, to
live involves thinking and various mental functions, and it is Kallias or
Socrates who perform these functions.

But now how much have we bought with all this? Here we should
note two facts. One is the obvious fact that truths about living bodies are
extremely intimately related to truths about working Bodies. The items
are not identical, on the present view (thus it is true of the Body, but not
the body, that it will be buried); but for every truth about a given body
there is a corresponding truth about a given Body, and in many cases
they will, to put it mildly, look much the same. The second fact is that on
the hylomorphic view, mental functions are intimately connected with
what it is for a certain kind of animal to be alive: those functions are
part of what it is for it to live. This correctly emphasizes, among other
things, the various ways in which mental functions can be grounded in
physical processes and needs. The facts which lie behind this require us,
notoriously, to conjoin a variety of predications about Kallias, some of

---

[3] Myles Burnyeat has strongly argued, in an as yet unpublished paper, that for reasons
of this kind Aristotle's psychology must be incredible to us.

which relate to Kallias' mental functions, and some to his bodily functions, and some which (as hylomorphic doctrine itself may insist) there is no good reason to assign exclusively to either heading.

When these points are put together, we can see that truths about Kallias are inextricably involved with truths not just about Kallias' body, but about that Body which, when working, is his body. Moreover, we have more reason than Aristotle did to expect that for mental properties and activities in general there will be some corresponding truths about the Body. The more we have of all this, the less clear it becomes what *deep* point is effected by the insistence that Kallias and his Body are not the same thing. We have of course the one claim that gives us that result, namely that Kallias ceases to exist when his Body just ceases to work. But if the insistence on that is the only major distinguishing mark of the doctrine, it is hard to see why it should not be regarded as basically a form of (non-reductive) materialism, marked by a respectful deference to some (as a matter of fact, not all) aspects of ordinary language.

In fact, on the version of the doctrine we have been working with, some version of materialism seems immediately at hand. For we have gone a long way round to accommodate Aristotle's idea that a dead body is not strictly a body, by introducing the concept 'Body' (that which can be dead—more strictly, non-working—but existent). Kallias, on the view under discussion, is certainly not his Body; but it is not at all clear that he is not his body—which has the feature that it ceases to exist just when he does, in dying just when he does. If we have lost the basic argument that Kallias is not his body, then this version of hylomorphism seems to be *simply* non-reductive materialism. The only way to avoid that, within the present framework, would be to deny that 'body', as now defined, is fully a material concept: it is 'Body' which is that. In more modern terms, that will presumably mean that it is Body that is the subject of physical enquiry. Then what is *body* the subject of? If it is the subject of, for example, physiology, then some very odd consequences for the relations of physics and physiology will follow, or, alternatively, materialism will once more follow; while if it is the subject only of psychology, then 'body' becomes only a shadow thrown by the mental functions on to Body.

Even if we forget the body/Body distinction—which hardly in the end serves the hylomorphic cause, though Aristotle seems to need something like it—the hylomorphic view in no way helps us to get clear about the relations of the sciences of man. How could it, in so far as it implies that there are two non-identical (though related) items which are the subjects of respectively physical and psychological investigation? The supposition that there are two different sorts of items, human beings and Bodies (or bodies if the Aristotelian loop is eliminated) must, if it is taken as more than a courtesy move, merely obscure the intimate relations between the studies.

So far then, it seems to me that hylomorphism emerges as just a polite form of materialism; and while, in a way, we might be said to honour it in ordinary speech (though only in part), it is to be actually distrusted at the theoretical level. But this may be, in fact, too kind to it. The view so far sketched may be regarded, with some justice, as being less than hylomorphism, on the ground that it has so far made no reference to the soul—and surely hylomorphism makes some such reference? It does: but the effect of it seems to be to move the doctrine from the class of the unhelpful to that of the downright confused.

We have one way of introducing 'soul' on the basis of what we have got: that in which 'having soul' can represent that property of life and functioning which an animal possesses when it is alive (and hence exists). But this is, simply, a *property*, and one which all living things (at least of that sort) will share. (It is, as we saw earlier, indeed a form). Now of course, the fact that they all, alike, 'have soul' does not mean that they all have the same soul; but then we have given no use to 'same soul' at all, nor to 'a soul' or 'the soul'. That is why I said earlier that hylomorphism might be represented as denying that there was such a thing as the soul. But we might, without taking any new step, in fact admit such expressions: we can admit 'Kallias' soul' to mean just 'Kallias' life', in the sense not of Kallias' *bios* (that which gets written up in his obituary) but rather Kallias' *zōē*, as we might put it: that is, an item which exists just in virtue of Kallias being alive, as Kallias' generosity exists just in virtue of his being generous. We might even, though at some risk of being misleading, say that Kallias' soul is that by means of which he lives, perceives, and thinks (*de An.* 414a10): it would be a way of saying that he is the sort of thing whose way of being alive is one which means that in virtue of his life he thinks, etc. What we could not say at all reasonably nor with any clear sense was that it is his soul which thinks, or that it is Kallias' soul which can equally be called 'Kallias'. Yet these are things which Aristotle seems to show some temptation to say, or at least to admit as possible (*de An.* 429a10, but cf. 408b14–15; *Metaph.* 1036a, 1037a, 1043b). These ideas seem just to translate into the hylomorphic area the kind of error that Plato dualistically committed at the end of the *Phaedo*, when he thought that he had identified an (indestructible) item called 'Socrates' because he had located, roughly, Socrates' life.

There are temptations for hylomorphism which lead in this direction. For if we emphasize the non-identity of Kallias and his Body, we may want to say that what concerns us about Kallias, what Kallias is for us, is some complex function of his mental capacities. A man is a living animal who thinks; Kallias is one who thinks thus and so, who has just these memories, who thinks and feels and desires in just these highly individuated ways. So while Aristotle is committed to saying that the particularity of Kallias consists in his being soul in this flesh and these bones (*Metaph.* 1034a7), there is nevertheless a temptation to move in the direction of saying that he is *this* soul in this flesh and these bones: where what that must mean is, the faculty of thought functioning in *this* way. So that if one were more impressed than Aristotle was by certain thought-experiments about diachronic identity, one might take the further step of saying that Kallias is *this* soul in *some* flesh and bones: for if that integral individuated mental functioning is so important, then its importance might seem to outreach the material identity of the matter, especially if one thought that that material identity was to some degree conventional.

This would still fall short of Platonic or Cartesian dualism, of course: there is still no way of being Kallias without *some* flesh and bones (or some suitably organized matter, some Body). But it has shifted the weight away from the materialistic emphasis enough, perhaps, to give a sense to saying that there is 'a' soul, and calling *that* Kallias. Hylomorphism's desire for the best of all worlds does make it lean in this direction, away from the position, earlier sketched, of polite materialism. But it does not get what it wants; or rather it gets more. For the idea that Kallias is (in the sense explained) some highly individuated mental functioning expressed in some Body does not in fact yield the common-sense conclusion that Kallias is some concrete particular: it yields rather the idea that Kallias is a *type*, exemplified perhaps, as things are, in only one token, but which could have multiple tokens. And this is an idea which very rapidly drifts away from our understanding of the concept of a person (more drastically so, in some ways, than dualism does, which we should remember is a *primitive* conception).[4]

Hylomorphism earns its reputation as everybody's moderate metaphysics of mind, I believe, by in fact wobbling between two options. In one of them, *soul* does basically appear only adjectivally, and while the doctrine is, so far as I can see, formally consistent, it is only a polite form of materialism, which is cumbrous, misleading, and disposed to point in the wrong direction from the point of view of deeper theoretical understanding. It also has precisely this disadvantage of readily sliding into the

[4] Some features of *person* as a type-notion have been briefly explored in my 'Are Persons Bodies?', in *Problems of the Self* (Cambridge, 1973). The claim that dualism is a primitive notion can be defended, I think, against Richard Rorty's arguments in *Philosophy and the Mirror of Nature* (Princeton, 1980), see esp. ch I, but those arguments do demand, at the very least, an account of how any given *philosophical* dualism is supposed to be related to that primitive idea.

other view, in which *soul* tries to transcend its adjectival status, and become the bearer of personal proper names: in that form, it yields us a notion of *person* which is a type-notion. We might one day need such a notion: but it is not what hylomorphism wants, and hylomorphism itself is not well equipped to help us to understand it.

One last point. A strength of hylomorphism, particularly in its more materialistic version, is that it does point to *human being* as being a basic concept in the philosophy of mind, and, consequently, in ethics. There is much to be said for this emphasis, though I think that it can be consistently expressed independently of the most characteristic formulations of hylomorphism. The point can be illustrated if we consider another version of our (*a*)–(*b*) relation, this time in, so to speak, a higher register:

(*a*) the fact that a certain living human being has the capacity for higher mental functions;

(*b*) the fact that there exists a certain person.

A schema of this kind is implicit in some contemporary moral philosophy, the idea being that when some (biologically) living human being lacks these higher capacities, it is not a person; while it is to *persons* that we owe various basic duties (such as not killing them). Such ideas are used by, for example, Tooley,[5] who is thus encouraged to speak of humans who are not yet persons, or who have ceased to be so—infants and the senile—and to claim that they fall outside moral restrictions on killing. So far as infants are concerned the application of the doctrine seems anyway arbitrary—it turns just on where the lines of *potentiality* are drawn: Aristotle, rightly, would have regarded infants as instances of the first potentiality, which is surely the most that even Tooley can demand (if the requirements are moved too high one would be ill-advised to fall asleep). But with the irreversibly senile, and some defective human beings, this point cannot be made. The Aristotelian approach avoids this slippery slope by taking the moral categories (or these fundamental ones, at least) to apply in the first instance—though they may reach also *more* widely—to a *kind*, to which the senile undoubtedly belong. (This is a thought we undoubtedly use: the possibility is to be taken very seriously that we may not know morally how to do without it.) The gross weak-

---

[5] Michael Tooley, 'Abortion and Infanticide', *Philosophy and Public Affairs*, II, no 1 (1972), 37–65; and his book of the same title (Oxford, 1983). Tooley actually says 'An organism possesses a serious right to life only if it possesses the concept of a self as a continuing subject of experiences and other mental states, and believes that it is itself such a continuing entity'. What exactly this threatens depends on such things as what a 'serious' right might be; but it suggests that in order not to be killed, one needs not only philosophical opinions, but some philosophical opinions rather than others.

ness of the schema now under consideration is that *person* appears as a fake natural kind, assisted by the sortal grammatical character of the term 'person'. But *person* is not a natural kind, and its grammar is misleading, rather like that of 'dwarf', or 'giant': the characteristics involved in its application are in fact *scalar* characteristics, and there is a real arbitrariness in the degree or level of mental functioning which is going to qualify for one's being a 'person'. This scalar character of the underlying considerations, together with the misleading 'on-off' grammatical character of 'person', has genuine and thoroughly undesirable consequences for its use as a central concept of moral argument.

'Human being' does not share these difficulties. It cannot be impossible to make clear how 'human being' can be the foundation of what is correctly called a 'humane' ethics, without our having to adopt the misleading metaphysics of hylomorphism.

DESCARTES

FIFTEEN

Descartes' Use of Scepticism

Descartes was not a sceptic. One has to take a distant and inaccurate view of his writings to suppose that he was. One of his principal complaints against Bourdin, who produced the *Seventh Objections*, was that Bourdin seemed only to have studied the passages of the *Meditations* in which Descartes raised the doubt, and not those in which he answered or dispelled it; as he complained in his letter to Father Dinet (VII, 574), "Who has ever been so bold and shameless in calumny, that he blamed Hippocrates or Galen for having set out the causes from which illnesses arise, and concluded from that, that they have never taught anything except the method of falling ill?"

The point of reading Hippocrates or Galen was, presumably, to learn how to recover from illness, and there is a well-known asymmetry to this in the practice of philosophy, lying in the fact that the illness is in that case self-inflicted and of the same general nature as the cure. This asymmetry pressed hard on the conception of philosophy offered by "therapeutic positivism" and similar outlooks, which diagnose as the illness not merely deformations such as philosophical scepticism, but the disposition to philosophy itself. Such a program needs, and characteristically lacks, a theory of the origins and nature of the philosophical neurosis.

That same problem does not apply to Pyrrhonism, where scepticism is the cure—a cure, first of all, for an uncertainty which flows from the unsatisfiable desire for knowledge. Nor does it apply to Descartes, whose aim is precisely to replace uncertainty with knowledge. For him, scepticism was two things. It was the extreme dramatization of uncertainty, an uncertainty which, largely independent of any philosophical discipline or exercise, already existed, and which Descartes felt he had to confront. It was, second, part of his method for overcoming uncertainty and attaining knowledge.

In his mature works he presents himself as, from the beginning of his enquiry, adopting scepticism as a method. In the fourth part of the *Discourse on the Method* (VI, 31–32) he writes:

References to Descartes' writings are made, by volume and page, to the standard edition of Charles Adam and Paul Tannery (most recent edition, Paris, 1964–1975). In the case of some letters, a page reference, preceded by the letter K, has been given to Anthony Kenny, *Descartes: Philosophical Letters* (Oxford, 1970).

For a long time I had remarked that so far as practical life is concerned, it is sometimes necessary to follow opinions which one knows to be very uncertain, just as though they were indubitable . . ., but because I wanted to devote myself solely to the search for truth, I thought that it was necessary that I should do just the opposite, and that I should reject, just as though it were absolutely false, everything in which I could imagine the slightest doubt, so as to see whether after that anything remained in my belief which was entirely indubitable.

A similar introduction to the method of doubt occurs in the *First Meditation* (VII, 18):

Reason persuades me already, that I should withhold assent no less carefully from things which are not clearly certain and indubitable, as from things which are evidently false; so that if I find some reason for doubt in each of them, this will be enough for me to reject them all. It does not follow that I should have to go through them one by one, which would be an endless task; if the foundations are undermined, anything built on top of them falls down by itself, so I shall attack directly those principles which supported everything I have up to now believed.

That this is Descartes' starting point implies from the beginning a certain *control* of scepticism. He does not merely encounter scepticism as an outside force and survive it, like the knightly hero of some romance, and he does not even present himself as so doing. His tone differs in this from that of a work such as Ayer's *Problem of Knowledge*, which chronicles a series of successes by the knower against various applications of scepticism. Such a work makes it seem as though the supports and nature of scepticism could be encountered first, quite independently of the view of knowledge which will help to overcome it; and since in fact the solutions merely adopt standards of knowledge which bypass the problem (indeed, virtually constitute an assertion of customary practice), the battle seems either lost, or all the time a sham, and the supposed solutions factitious. The Cartesian, however, resembles the Pyrrhonist, in deploying a scepticism which he has intelligibly shaped to his own purposes, in the one case of satisfying the desire for knowledge, in the other of banishing it.

Descartes thought that the scepticism he deployed, though he carefully used it for his own methodical purposes, was at least as extreme as that deployed by those who called themselves sceptics. He boasted that he was the first of all to overthrow the doubts of the sceptics (*Seventh Replies*: VII, 550). In these words, as elsewhere, he construes the doubt that he constructs and overcomes as belonging to a tradition. Exactly how much he knew of that tradition and through what writers, remains, to some degree, uncertain: "I had long ago seen several books written by the Academics and Sceptics," he wrote (*Second Replies*: VII, 130), and he says in the *Seventh Replies* that the "Sect of the Sceptics still flourishes" (VII, 548–549). He seems to have been familiar with the works of Montaigne and Charron, among other sceptical writers.[1] Insofar as he deploys doubt both in that tradition and against its contemporary representatives, his doubt can be seen as preemptive. It is designed to head off any subsequent recurrence of scepticism, and his claim that he has taken doubt to its extreme, as far as any doubt could be taken, is central to his claim that what he recovers from the process is a foundation of knowledge. Thus his two claims, that he takes traditional scepticism to an extreme, and that he refutes it, are connected. If the ancient sceptics had persisted far enough in their doubt, they could have transcended it: as he puts it (letter of 1638: II, 38-K 53), "although the Pyrrhonians reached no certain conclusion from their doubts, this is not to say that no one could."[2]

The fact that doubt is used as a tool and as part of a method—the method referred to in the title of the work which is called, in correct translation, the *Discourse on the Method*[3]—radically affects the character of the doubt. It conditions the structure of the sceptical arguments themselves and prescribes a particular attitude toward them. The Method is deployed in the course of an intellectual project, which has the feature that if doubt can possibly be applied to a class of beliefs, then that class of beliefs must, at least temporarily, be laid aside. One question raised by that project is what it is for; one answer to that question is the one already implied in saying that the doubt is preemptive—namely, that if the project can generate knowledge or permit knowledge to be generated, then we know that the sceptics are wrong, who claim that such a project can generate nothing but doubt. But there is also a distinct aim, in relation to which the inquiry can be seen not just as banishing doubt and establishing the possibility of knowledge, but as concerned with the content of that knowledge, and as helping to generate the most fundamental

---

[1] For detailed discussion of Descartes' acquaintance with ancient and contemporary scepticism, see Richard Popkin, *The History of Scepticism from Erasmus to Spinoza* (Berkeley, Los Angeles and London, 1979), a revised edition of his *History of Scepticism from Erasmus to Descartes* (Assen, 1960).

[2] This point is very clearly made by Myles Burnyeat in his "Idealism and Greek Philosophy: What Descartes Saw and Berkeley Missed," in *Idealism Past and Present*, ed. G. Vesey (London, 1982), where he quotes this passage.

[3] The title of this famous work is very often mistranslated. See my *Descartes: The Project of Pure Enquiry* (Harmondsworth, 1978) (subsequently referred to as *PPE*), pp. 18–19, n. 4.

kind of knowledge, absolute knowledge. I shall come back to that wider objective later.

In the *Meditations* Descartes proceeds—and does so, it is clear, self-consciously—through three levels of doubt. The first is associated with the common illusions of the senses. Descartes uses these examples only to loosen everyday convictions in a preliminary way, and does not claim that reflection on these cases has any tendency to cast doubt on *each* case in which one thinks that one is perceiving a material object. He makes the transition to the idea that on each occasion of supposed perception one can properly think "I might be mistaken *now*" very clearly in *Discourse* Part iv, in the *First Meditation*, and also in the *Recherche de la Vérité* (X, 510 ff.), by moving from the occasional errors of the senses to the phenomenon of dreaming.

The difference between the two cases, for Descartes, consists in the fact that errors which depend on such things as bad light, distance, illness, and so forth, resist generalization, in the sense that they depend on special misleading conditions, and reflection on those conditions can arouse suspicion even at the time. But dreams take one in completely, and reflection cannot get a grip within the situation to reveal that situation as special: the beliefs one might bring to bear on it are themselves affected by dreaming.[4] In this case, correction is unequivocably retrospective. But, if it is, how does one resist the thought that one might, now, be dreaming?

Descartes' own eventual answer to that question is not totally satisfactory. The answer refers to the coherence of our waking experience under natural laws, which helps to form a general rational picture of the world in which dreaming is "placed" relative to waking. We need that picture, in fact, even to understand his introduction of dreaming in the first place (as opposed, for instance, to madness, which he notably dismisses in the *First Meditation* from the discussion of scepticism), but he does not give us the means to focus that understanding of dreaming on answering the sceptical question when it is raised on a particular occasion. This is partly because his conception of dreaming is itself inadequate.

However, his very passing reference to this problem at the end of his inquiry makes perfectly good sense in terms of what, by then, he thinks that he has achieved. Once we have acquired the well-founded picture of the world, we do not have to go back and answer every sceptical question, because we do not have to go on asking them. Having eventually come through and out of the general doubt, we are provided not only

---

[4] This is how Descartes represents the matter. He assumes that the pure intellectual power of judgment is not affected in sleep, and this assumption makes it harder for him to dispose of scepticism based on dreaming. For further discussion, see *PPE*, Appendix 3.

with answers to general and philosophical doubts, if someone still raises them, but also with methods of answering particular doubts when, in a nonphilosophical way, they present themselves. In addition to that, we will have been given the grounds of a confidence that we need not raise such doubts, nor try to answer them, when they do not present themselves in practical life or in the course of some more limited scientific inquiry. The prereflective confidence in waking experience as waking experience is in fact well founded, and the best witness to that fact, most of the time, will be that very confidence.

The distinction between everyday errors of the senses on the one hand, and dreaming on the other, is used by Descartes to mark the distinction between the undeniable fact that we are sometimes deceived, and the stronger possibility that *on any given occasion* of apparent sense-perception we may be deceived. He goes further, however, to a more radical consideration (which he recognizes to be more radical) that not only on any given occasion may one be deceived, but that it is possible that one may be deceived on every occasion and the "external world" not exist at all. In the *Meditations* he achieves this final level of doubt by invoking the fiction of the *malin génie*, the malicious demon "of the highest power and intelligence, who devotes all his efforts to deceiving me" (*First Meditation*, VII, 22).[5] This device provides a thought experiment which can be generally applied: if there were an agency which was indefinitely powerful and acted purposively and systematically to frustrate inquiry and the desire for truth, would *this* kind of belief or experience be invalidated? It is obvious how far such a conception goes beyond the old material about the illusions of the senses, and, correspondingly, how clearly removed it is from any idea that if scepticism is a rational attitude, then it is so because it is *supported* by the facts of sense-deception or of dreaming.

The fully "hyperbolical" doubt, as Descartes calls it, which is introduced with the demon, does not only permit, for the first time, the idea that every supposed sense-perception may be illusory. It also obliterates the past, and God. Moreover, it casts some shadow over the reliability of

[5] Popkin (*History of Scepticism*, pp. 180–181) interestingly speculates that the origin of this idea may lie in the famous trial at Loudun, concerned with demoniac possession. It should be noticed, however, that the trial was in 1634, three years before the publication of the *Discourse*, in which the idea does not occur. It does not appear until the *Meditations*, in 1641. The idea may go back to a passage in Cicero reporting arguments used by Academic sceptics about the powers of the gods (*Academica* II 47), though, if it does, Descartes' use of it (as of other ancient material) goes far beyond anything envisaged by the ancients themselves. E. M. Curley (*Descartes against the Skeptics* [Oxford, 1978]) points toward sources in Montaigne, but his evidence relates more to Descartes' account of God's relation to the eternal truths than to the (admittedly associated) issue of the *malin génie*.—On the Ciceronian material, see Burnyeat, "Idealism and Greek Philosophy."

purely intellectual processes. The exact extent and depth of that shadow has been extensively discussed, but the answer to the question, as we shall see later, is bound to be in a way indeterminate.

Toward the end of the *First Meditation*, Descartes says (VII, 21): "I am forced to admit that there are none of the things I used to think were true, which may not possibly be doubted, and not because of carelessness or frivolity but for sound and well-considered reasons (*non per inconsiderantiam vel levitatem, sed propter validas & meditatas rationes*)." Thus the doubt, even the hyperbolical doubt, is in some sense serious and well founded. Yet Descartes also says, and with great and repeated emphasis, that the doubt is not to be carried into everyday life, and indeed that the existence of the external world is something which "no one of sound mind ever seriously doubted" (*Synopsis* of the *Meditations*, VII, 16; cf. *Fifth Replies*, VII, 350; *Principles* i 1–3; letter of August 1641, III, 398-K 110). That judgment, moreover, is not simply retrospective, something to be recovered when one has come out at the other end; rather, it is an observation about the nature of the project.

What then are, or could be, the "sound and well-considered reasons"? This phrase gets its content from what it is contrasted with, its force being that the doubt is not a matter of "carelessness or frivolity." The reasons are systematic, arrived at as part of Descartes' sustained intellectual project: they are *validae* because *meditatae*, sound just because they are well considered. It is not that, by practical standards, the doubt is as reasonable as its opposite. It is extremely important in this connection that so little use is made of the empirical material deployed by Montaigne or Charron or indeed Sextus. "Reasons for doubt" which relied on empirical content would not, beyond an early stage, be "serious" in Descartes' context. In the empirical context, his doubts are unserious; they are serious in the context of the problem, and in that context the reasons that do the work are not those with the most empirical content, but rather the utterly abstract conception of the demon. The other considerations are helpful in the business of getting used to thinking about corporeal things (in particular) in a certain way, and that is why Descartes devoted a whole *Meditation* to those doubts, and, as he put it, reheated with some distaste the stale cabbage of the Academics and Sceptics (*Second Replies*, VII, 130).

Descartes' distance from the empirical materials of scepticism means also that the traditional Pyrrhonist claim (or weapon) of *isostheneia*, although it has an application to Cartesian scepticism, has it only in an indirect and refined way. The "equally plausible argument to the opposite effect" takes the form, in Descartes' procedure, of a consideration which removes all effect both from the original argument and from its normal contraries. There is thus no place for the states of mind which Pyrrhonists thought to be the appropriate reaction to lack of real knowledge. Those states of mind, for the Pyrrhonists, while not the conclusion of philosophical reflection, were *at* the conclusion of it; but the hyperbolical doubt could not possibly, for Descartes, have constituted the conclusion of anything.

If the Cartesian inquiry had been disappointed, there would have been no question of staying in a state of hyperbolical doubt. It would rather be a question of giving up science, and returning to an operationalist outlook and everyday standards of reasonable belief. (This is of course a point about Cartesian, as opposed to Pyrrhonist, *inquiry*. What Descartes himself would have done if so disappointed is an empty question; we are concerned with the Descartes given by his writings, and what we are given leaves no room for such a disappointment.)

It is important that, for Descartes, to fall back on everyday empirical standards of belief would be to *give up* science. Unlike Mersenne, Gassendi, and others who tried to give an operationalist style of answer to scepticism, he shared with the ancients the idea that the coherence of appearances in itself provided no foundations for a real science; and although at the practical level some bets about appearances were no doubt better than others, he thought that arguments which had pretensions to being scientific but which operated merely at the level of appearances really were subject to *isostheneia*, and were no better and no worse than one another. This attitude evidently emerged at the very beginning of his career, in the incident when he spoke against a speech by Chandoux, to the approval of Cardinal Bérulle.[6] In his mature work this attitude comes out in the belief that rival hypotheses, until properly criticized, may all share some profound and equally vitiating misconceptions—misconceptions, above all, about appearances themselves and the respects in which they may or may not be systematically misleading. The doubt is an instrument to uncover such misconceptions, and it is reflection encouraged by the doubt that leads Descartes to isolate, first in the *Second Meditation*, a nonsensory conception of matter as extension, which not only becomes the central concept of his physics but also enables him to revise radically everyday ideas about the relation of sense-perception to knowledge.

Descartes' undertaking of applying successively three levels of doubt yields, correspondingly, three levels at which our thought might be affected by error: the merely local; systematically, as in our conception of nature; and universally, the imagined result of the malicious demon. The last, which would undercut the other two altogether, is eventually shown to be baseless by appeal to the existence and benevolence of God. The

[6] See Popkin, *History of Scepticism*, pp. 174 ff., and notes, pp. 285–286.

second turns out to be real, but corrigible by the progress of the sciences. The first kind of error is at the limit, ineliminable, but it can be contained and allowed for, particularly granted the systematic understanding gained at the second level. The fact that there is need for theoretical correction of systematic prereflective error at the second level means (as Margaret Wilson rightly emphasizes)[7] that the doubt is, in a sense, correct: *we are* systematically deceived by our senses. It also illustrates the need for the sciences to be given "foundations." That does not mean that they are to be provided with axioms, from which all scientific truth can be deduced. It means that they have to be purged of false presuppositions, and put on a sound basis of method.

The *Synopsis* to the *Meditations* states quite clearly that we can doubt of all things, particularly material things, "so long as we have no foundations of the sciences other than the ones we had before." It says also (VII, 12) that the process of doubt delivers us from all sorts of prejudices; detaches the mind from the senses; and puts us finally in a situation where we no longer have any doubt about what we discover to be true. All these three are important to the method of doubt, and the first two, as we have seen, are connected. The third, Descartes' search for "something firm and enduring" (*First Meditation*, VII, 17), raises further issues. Descartes insists that no *cognitio* which can be rendered doubtful "should, it seems, be called *scientia*" (*Second Replies*, VII, 141; cf. *Fifth Meditation*, VII, 70), and this is connected by him with having a kind of reason "so strong that it cannot be knocked out by any stronger reason." In considering Descartes' emphasis on this, it is important to bear in mind the extent and chaotic character of the disagreements that obtained in the early seventeenth century, both in religious matters and in the understanding of nature. There was little effective agreement at a theoretical level and, correspondingly, little understanding of where disagreement might explicably arise. A probabilistic and corrigibilist conception of the scientific enterprise, in any specifically modern sense, did not yet exist.

Descartes' belief that there is nothing between agreed certainty and a chaotic disagreement in which anything goes is not simply or even mainly the product of reflection on the concept of knowledge. It is, rather, an effect produced jointly by the historical situation of scientific understanding in his time, and a very natural interpretation of what scientific knowledge should be. That interpretation takes scientific knowledge to be a system which represents the world as it is independently of

---

[7] Margaret Dauler Wilson, *Descartes* (London, 1978). It will be evident that I agree with Wilson when she says (p. 8) "While Descartes is, no doubt, concerned with the problem of certainty—of traditional scepticism—in its own right, he is also concerned to *use* this problem to present convincingly an anti-empiricist metaphysics, a form of (rationalist) 'scientific realism' " (emphasis in original).

any inquirer, using terms which to the greatest possible extent display that independence. This objective of *absolute* knowledge, as it may be called, is not peculiar to Descartes. Indeed, it can be seen as implicit in a natural conception of knowledge itself, and the fact that this ideal is, in particular, an ideal for scientific knowledge implies the idea that scientific knowledge peculiarly realizes, or seeks to realize, the ambitions for knowledge *tout court*. What is more peculiar to Descartes is the connection that he makes between the objective of absolute knowledge and an ideal of certainty, and that connection is the product of his historical situation, which encouraged him and others to think that if a claim to knowledge—at least, to the most basic and general kinds of knowledge— was not certain, then it must be *relative*, the product, to an undetermined degree, of one's peculiar circumstances. Those two ideas could perhaps be separated only when the existence of scientific institutions gave practical substance to the idea that claims even to the most fundamental kinds of scientific knowledge need to be tested and can be corrected. It could then be seen that a respectable claim to scientific knowledge does not need to be certain (indeed, according to some, its respectability depends on its not being so). At the same time, the methods of testing such claims, and the theories for their correction, themselves reflect the idea of absolute knowledge; and the understanding of disagreement, in particular insight into reasons that make disagreement in certain cases entirely natural, prevents disagreement generating scepticism.[8]

For Descartes, however, *scientia*, real knowledge, would have to be immune both to disagreement and to being recalled into doubt. There were two steps that Descartes had to take in order to replace disagreement,

---

[8] A striking characteristic of contemporary science, which links the various features mentioned here, is the high degree of convergence that it displays. Some philosophers, however, regard this appearance of convergence as a cultural artifact. Richard Rorty, in his *Philosophy and the Mirror of Nature* (Princeton, 1980), seems to express this view, though in a notably self-destructive way. See, e.g., pp. 344–345: "It is less paradoxical . . . to stick to the classic notion of 'better describing what was already there' for physics. This is not because of deep epistemological or metaphysical considerations, but simply because, when we tell our Whiggish stories about how our ancestors gradually crawled up the mountain on whose (possibly false) summit we stand, we need to keep some things constant throughout the story. . . . Physics is the paradigm of 'finding' simply because it is hard (at least in the West) to tell a story of changing physical universes against the background of an unchanging Moral Law or poetic canon, but very easy to tell the reverse sort of story." The force of "simply because" in this passage would repay some exegesis. The fundamental difficulty is that, if the story that Rorty tells were true, then there would be no perspective from which he could express it in this way. If, for whatever reasons, we need to describe physics as an activity of finding out how nature already is, then the correct thing for everyone to say, including Rorty, is that physics is an activity of finding out how nature already is. This is just one example of a persistent confusion in Rorty's book between what might be called empirical and transcendental pragmatism.

and scepticism associated with disagreement, with *scientia*. The first was to find a class of truths which, when they were carefully considered, commanded assent from anyone who so considered them. The second step was to provide a way of safeguarding those truths against sceptical attack at times when they were not being carefully considered: that is to say, to permit the project of acquiring knowledge to go on in a settled and cumulative manner, and not constantly be thrown off balance by recurrent sceptical doubt.

So far as the basic truths were concerned, he believed that he could identify these, and, further, that the sceptics, if not merely pretending, could never have perceived these things clearly, or they would no longer be sceptics (*Seventh Replies*, VII, 477); as he wrote to a correspondent in August 1641 (III, 434-K 119): "Certainly I have never denied that the Sceptics themselves, so long as they clearly perceive some truth, spontaneously assent to it, nor do they remain in that heresy of theirs, of doubting everything, except just in name, and possibly in intention and resolve. . . ."

Despite some mild ambiguities about the role of the will, Descartes fundamentally regards these propositions as *irresistible*. This is made clear in the *Fifth Meditation* (VII, 65, 69) and frequently elsewhere—for instance, in the *Second Replies* (VII, 145–146), and at *Principles* i 43— and he must so regard them, if the method of doubt is not to leave him with assent suspended forever. In connection with this notion of irresistibility, it is important what is meant by the idea of a proposition's being "carefully considered." It is natural to say that a proposition is irresistible if it cannot come before the mind without, in Descartes' phrase, being clearly and distinctly perceived, and thus (in these cases) believed; as Descartes says in the *Second Replies* (VII, 145–146) of the things about which we can be perfectly certain, "we cannot think of them without believing them to be true," and he there claims that we cannot doubt them without thinking of them. From those premises it follows, as he correctly points out, that we cannot doubt them. Yet it seems that there is something which counts as doubting even those propositions, so it must be possible for such a proposition to be sufficiently "before the mind" for one to entertain a doubt about it, but not be so clearly in view that one's belief in it is activated. This is not a very deep or difficult problem. All that is required is some way of referring to or indicating a proposition or idea of this kind without bringing it clearly to mind. A standard way of doing that will lie in deploying a word or sentence which expresses that idea or proposition, without, however, concentrating closely on what that word or sentence expresses. One can, granted this, entertain a doubt about an irresistible proposition, but only by not thinking about it clearly (cf. *Seventh Replies*, VII, 460, 546; to Clerselier, IX-I, 204–205).

A more serious problem, however, has been thought to arise at this point. There is no great difficulty in admitting that one can refer to an idea without clearly and distinctly perceiving it, but Descartes also (*Seventh Replies*, VII, 511) claims that many people think that they have clearly and distinctly perceived an idea when they have not done so. This is a more alarming consideration, since it suggests that the notion of irresistibility may ultimately be vacuous: it may turn out that these ideas or propositions are irresistible only because one does not count as having clearly and distinctly perceived them unless one assents to them.

However, what Descartes says need not really weaken his position. His point basically concerns a *practice* of clear intellectual concentration, and the people he has in mind are those who, while they may claim clearly to see certain truths, show by their whole practice of argument that they do not separate one item from another nor concentrate intently on any one question or consideration. When the matter is seen in this way, the decision whether an objector has clearly and distinctly considered a given proposition does not turn, vacuously, simply on the issue of whether he agrees with that proposition. The first question is whether a given person is one who in general, by careful intellectual consideration, can isolate an idea or proposition and concentrate on it. Such a capacity, Descartes believes, is innate in every nondefective human being, though it needs eliciting by practice—practice which need not involve standard academic education, and may well be impeded by it.

Two such people will, Descartes believes, almost always agree about the truth of a simple proposition if—by the ordinary criteria of concentration—they concentrate on it. If, exceptionally, they do not agree, then one of them after further concentration will eventually come to agree with the other. Descartes thought that constant disagreement and hence scepticism obtained because people addressed large and contentious issues in a confused manner, without subjecting them to analysis, and because they had not acquired practice in analyzing them into intellectually simple elements. The ability to do that is one that almost everyone displays in some familiar connections, but conventional education and styles of learning actually discourage one from applying it in the right way to the fundamental issues of scientific and metaphysical inquiry.

Thus Descartes supposed that conditions of proper concentration would produce clear and distinct perception, and clear and distinct perception would of course produce agreement. Moreover, that agreement would be agreement to *truth*. Descartes says in the *Third Meditation* (VII, 35): "I seem to be able to take it as a general rule that everything that I very clearly and distinctly perceive is true." However, the indeterminate shadow of the *malin génie* can in certain circumstances be taken to threaten this assurance, and Descartes thinks that he has eventually established it only by proving the existence of God, whose benevolent purpose as the creator of intellectual beings assures him that they cannot be mistaken in what they clearly and distinctly perceive. Since, however, the existence of God is itself proved only by reliance on clear and distinct perceptions, this claim has famously elicited the charge of circularity, first in the *Second* and *Fourth* sets of *Objections* (VII, 125, 214).

It has sometimes been asked whether Descartes regards clear and distinct perception as the *criterion* of truth. The answer to this depends on what is meant by the claim that it is such a criterion. If that claim means that the idea of a proposition's being true is the same idea as that of someone's clearly and distinctly perceiving it, then Descartes' answer is certainly "no." If it means that one can on a given occasion decide that a proposition is true on the basis of noting that one is then clearly and distinctly perceiving it, then the answer is again "no," since we are here dealing with propositions that are irresistible, and with them there is no gap between clear and distinct perception and deciding that the proposition is true: if one is actually clearly and distinctly perceiving such a proposition, by that very fact one believes it to be true. If the claim means, again, that it is itself certain as a general proposition that anything clearly and distinctly perceived is true, then indeed Descartes accepts that claim; but if it means, lastly, that no justification could appropriately be given for that general proposition, then Descartes once more rejects such a claim, since he gives precisely such a justification, in the existence and benevolence of God.

There are obviously some parallels here to ancient discussions of *katalēpsis*, just as there are some parallels with regard to the notion of irresistibility, the Stoics finding some difficulty, it seems, in saying under what conditions propositions would "drag us by the hair to assent."[9] But the fundamental difference is, of course, that the Stoic kataleptic presentations were paradigmatically some particular kinds of sense-perception. No sensory item, at least when regarded as a perception of the world rather than as a purely psychological datum, can for Descartes carry this kind of kataleptic certainty. For him, the kataleptic impression is intellectual. However, that does not exclude its giving information of reality outside the mind, for—whatever view one takes on the vexed question of the status that Descartes gives to "eternal truths" which make no claim of existence—the existence of God is thought by Descartes to be something that we can come to know through such impressions, and that is a vital feature of his system.

The Stoics have been accused[10] of not distinguishing issues of truth and

---

[9] Cf., e.g., J. M. Rist, *Stoic Philosophy* (Cambridge, 1969), pp. 133–151.

[10] See Julia Annas, "Truth and Knowledge," in *Doubt and Dogmatism*, ed. M. Schofield, M. Burnyeat, and J. Barnes (Oxford, 1980). It must be said, however, that Annas

issues of knowledge. There have, similarly, been strains in the criticism of Descartes and in the exposition of him[11] which represent him as equally running these matters together. This representation of him can be itself a reaction against the charge of circularity. It is thought, roughly, that he can be protected from the charge of getting something for nothing only if it turns out that all he gets is the coherence of knowledge.

The clearest and simplest way of representing Descartes' position, however, seems to me to free him from this charge. It is essential to Descartes' system that he supposed that he could argue from thought to independent reality, in particular to the existence of God. In the ontological proof in the *Fifth Meditation*, he argues to God's existence from the content of his idea of God, while the causal proof in the *Third Meditation* proceeds to the same conclusion from the factual existence of that idea as an item in his thought (the kind of fact guaranteed in the *cogito*). These arguments are not valid, and there is no historical reason to think that they commanded even in the seventeenth century the kataleptic assurance for which Descartes hoped. But the fault in Descartes' answer to scepticism lies in the faults of these arguments themselves and not in his general procedure. Granted those arguments, there is no reason to accuse him of confusing knowledge and truth nor of arguing in a circle.

The exact nature of the answer that Descartes gives to the charge of circularity has been much disputed.[12] Descartes certainly held that unless one knew of the existence of God, one could have no perfect assurance or *scientia* about anything; he also held that, in some sense, this point applied only with respect to conclusions which recur in memory when we are no longer attending to the arguments on which they are based. One of Descartes' strongest, and also most helpful, statements of his position occurs in the *Second Replies* (VII, 141):

> That an atheist can clearly know that the three angles of a triangle are equal to two right angles, I do not deny; I merely say that this knowledge of his (*cognitio*) is not true science (*scientia*), because no knowledge which can be rendered doubtful should, it seems, be called science. Since he is supposed to be an atheist, he cannot be certain that

does not succeed in distinguishing the two issues at all satisfactorily by means of her two questions (p. 100) "Are there any experiences whose veridicality can be guaranteed?" and "Can we know that there are any experiences whose veridicality can be guaranteed?" *Guarantee* is surely itself an epistemological notion.

[11] Most recently by H. Frankfurt in *Demons, Dreamers and Madmen* (New York, 1970). For criticism, see *PPE*, pp. 35–36, n. 2, and pp. 197 ff.; and Curley, *Descartes against the Skeptics*, pp. 104–114 and elsewhere.

[12] See *PPE*, pp. 188–207, and Curley, *Descartes against the Skeptics*, chap. 5 and references.

he is not deceived even in those things that seem most evident to him, as has been sufficiently shown; and although this doubt may never occur to him, nevertheless it can occur to him, if he examines the question, or it may be suggested by someone else, and he will never be safe from it, unless he first acknowledges God.

My own interpretation of Descartes' position, in brief summary, is as follows. His aim is to build up a systematic body of knowledge (*scientia*) which will be immune to being recalled into doubt. He starts from what he takes to be a fact, that there are some propositions which, when clearly considered, are irresistible, and are so to the sceptic himself. Among these are the proofs of the existence and benevolence of God. So long as an inquirer is clearly considering, or (in a Cartesian phrase) intuiting, any irresistible proposition, he cannot doubt it and is not open to entertaining sceptical doubts; equally the sceptic himself must, in such a moment, lay aside his doubts. But no one who is going to develop a systematic body of knowledge can spend all his time intuiting one proposition, not even that of the existence of God, and when he is not considering such a proposition, some sceptic might make him doubt it. He might doubt some particular proposition, because he is not properly considering it, or he might entertain very general or hyperbolical doubt, and indeed wonder, in the abstract, whether anything that he clearly and distinctly perceived was true. Here, according to Descartes, it makes a difference whether the inquirer believes in God—the believer has a general answer to the general doubt, while the atheist does not. The atheist can only cite some clear and distinct propositions, and get the sceptic to assent, temporarily, to those propositions. The believer, however, has a general and systematic answer to a general and systematic doubt—an answer that rests in the existence and benevolence of God. Of course, the sceptic may doubt that, but he cannot doubt it while he intuits the proofs of it. So the believer can always recall the sceptic, unless the sceptic is willfully obstinate, to considering the existence and benevolence of God, and if the sceptic concentrates on those proofs, he will believe not only those propositions themselves but also something that follows from them—namely, that clear and distinct perceptions are reliable, and hence scepticism is unjustified. If the sceptic, ceasing to intuit the proofs, then reverts to objecting merely because he is no longer intuiting, we can point out that the use of propositions one is not at that instant intuiting is a minimal structural condition on getting on at all in the acquisition of systematic knowledge, and that just as it would be unreasonable to spend all one's time rehearsing one intuition, so it would be unreasonable to spend all one's time rehearsing the proofs of the general answer to scepticism, an answer which we nevertheless possess.

This interpretation of Descartes' answer involves three distinctive features of his position, besides his crucial acceptance of the proofs of God. One is his distinction between the situation in which one is actually intuiting an irresistible proposition and that in which one is merely remembering that one has done so; this has the consequence, of course, that one can entertain a doubt at the latter time which is impossible at the former. Another is the distinction between particular doubts about particular propositions, and the general doubts of the sceptic, at the limit of which is Descartes' own ultimate and hyperbolical doubt. The third feature is an element very characteristic of Descartes' general outlook which has nevertheless been neglected by commentators.[13] This is a pragmatic consideration, to the effect that the aim is to get on and construct *scientia*, engage in an ongoing scientific inquiry, and that it is *practically* unreasonable to spend one's time repeatedly answering scepticism. If scepticism can be answered, at the general level required by the hyperbolical doubt, then there are other things to do, and we have an assurance that we can do them. The sceptic has no reasonable claim, in terms of practical reason, to make us spend time on going round and round his problems, rather than making genuine progress (as we are now assured that we can) with the problems of science.

Descartes thought that he had put us in a position, once and for all, to have that assurance. He probably also thought that it was worthwhile for each of us, or at least some of us, to relive the process of doubt and recovery from it that is enacted so vividly in the *Meditations*, but he did not suppose that it was sensible to spend too much time on such inquiries. He not only converted scepticism from being an obstacle to metaphysical inquiry to being a tool of it, but characteristically placed both scepticism and metaphysical inquiry as essentially preliminaries relative to the real business of scientific investigation.

[13] Curley's interesting treatment (*Descartes against the Skeptics*) rightly draws attention to the requirement that the sceptic should have to bring forward some grounds for doubt, a requirement which the classical sceptics accepted: it underlies, as Curley points out, the idea of *isostheneia*. He then bases his construction of Descartes' argument on the principle that what counts as a ground for doubt at one stage of the proceedings may not still count as one at a later stage. However, unless one appeals to a pragmatic dimension of the exchange with the sceptic, there is nothing to stop him from recalling the argument to an earlier stage. Curley's treatment is based, in effect, on the idea that a proposition can acquire more strength in the course of Descartes' inquiry, so that more strength will be needed in any consideration that could raise a doubt against it. But the claim that a given proposition has acquired a given degree of strength can itself have a doubt brought against it, which will be removed only by going back and intuiting the proposition and its supports once more. So the pragmatic dimension is needed, against constant recursion; and once we have that dimension, we do not need, for this problem at least, such an elaborate account as Curley offers of what a reason for doubt at any given stage needs to be.

SIXTEEN

Introductory Essay on Descartes' *Meditations*

'I would not urge anyone to read this book except those who are able and willing to meditate seriously with me', Descartes says to his readers in the Preface, and he makes it clear that he means the *Meditations* not to be a treatise, a mere exposition of philosophical reasons and conclusions, but rather an exercise in thinking, presented as an encouragement and a guide to readers who will think philosophically themselves. Its thoughts, correspondingly, are presented as they might be conducted by its author— or rather, as though they were being conducted at the very moment at which you read them. Indeed, the 'I' who is having these thoughts may be yourself. Although we are conscious, in reading the *Meditations*, that they were written by a particular person, René Descartes, and at a particular time, about 1640, the 'I' that appears throughout them from the first sentence on does not specifically represent that person: it represents anyone who will step into the position it marks, the position of the thinker who is prepared to reconsider and recast his or her beliefs, as Descartes supposed we might, from the ground up.

This 'I' is different, then, from the 'I' that occurs in the *Replies* to the *Objections*. In the *Replies*, Descartes speaks straightforwardly for himself, and the 'I' represents the author of the *Meditations*. The 'I' in the *Meditations* themselves represents their narrator or protagonist, whom we may call 'the thinker'. Of course the author has to take responsibility for the thinker's reflections. He takes responsibility both for the conduct of them and for their outcome, where that includes the beliefs to which we shall have been led if we are persuaded by the arguments, and also the improved states of mind that the author expects us to reach by following his work. But the author is not answerable for every notion entertained by the thinker and for every turn that the reflection takes on the way. The series of thoughts has an upshot or culmination, reached in the Sixth Meditation, and some of the thinker's earlier thoughts have been overcome and left behind in the process of reaching that final point.

Some of those who submitted the *Objections* found it hard to follow the working out of this idea, and to see how far the thinker had got at various points in the process of reflection. It is still hard today, and commentators' discussions of the *Meditations* often take the form of asking how much at a given stage Descartes takes himself to have established.

In such discussions, it is *Descartes* and his intentions that come into question; the modern objectors address themselves, if less directly than the objectors whose texts appear in this volume, to the author. It was, after all, Descartes who gave the thinker the directions he follows. There is a suggestion implicit in the beginning of the work that the thinker does not know how it will all turn out: but that is a fiction.

To say that it is a fiction is not necessarily to say that in terms of the work itself it is untrue. This might have been a work in which the thinker's fictional ignorance of how his reflections would turn out was convincingly sustained. To some extent it is so, and to that extent, one of the gifts offered to the reader by this extraordinary work is a freedom to write it differently, to set out with the thinker and end up in a different place. The rewriting of Descartes' story in that way has constituted a good deal of modern philosophy.

However, it would be wrong to suggest that the *Meditations* offers no more than an invitation to philosophical reflection, by asking some questions and showing one way in which they might be answered. We are expected, rather, to sense the author's guiding hand throughout. Modern readers may take this for granted too easily, because they underestimate Descartes' intention to engage the reader in the argument. They may think of the *Meditations* as just a device that Descartes chose to get across the opinions that we now find ascribed to him in histories of philosophy. It is, certainly, a device for convincing us, but it is more than that, because it aims to convince us by making us conduct the argument ourselves.

The first readers of the *Meditations* may have felt the author's guiding presence for a different reason, that they were conscious of a kind of writing that it resembled. It was, and remains, a very unusual work, and there had never been a work of philosophy presented in such a form before. But there did exist, familiarly, works of religious meditation, and Descartes' book self-consciously resembles them. Like many of them, it is ostensibly divided between days of contemplation and, again like them, it encourages and helps the reader to overcome and get rid of misleading and seductive states of the soul, so as to arrive at an understanding of his or her own nature and of a created being's relations with God.

Those who wrote religious meditations were acting as guides to a spiritual discipline. Descartes' work gives his readers guidance in an intellectual discipline, and helps them to discover in themselves pure intellectual conceptions—of matter, of mind and of God—from which they will be able to form a true and unclouded understanding of the world. The inquiry in which he leads them does indeed yield a conviction of the existence of God. There is no reason at all to suppose that Descartes was insincere in these religious affirmations (though theories that ascribe to him complex strategies of deceit have a strange capacity to survive). What is true is that the thoughts that lead to these conclusions are not in the least religious in spirit, and God's existence is established as a purely metaphysical conclusion. Anything to do with a religious life or, indeed, with any distinctively religious aspects of life, will have to come in after Descartes' reflections are over. The *Meditations*, though they have an analogy to traditional meditations that belong to the religious life, assuredly do not belong to it themselves.

A still greater difference lies in the authority with which the two kinds of works were offered. The authors of religious meditations claimed authority from their own experience, but also, most often, from a religious office. Descartes does not suppose that his right to claim a reader's attention lies in any sacramental, traditional or professional position. His authority to show us how to think lies only in this, that he has himself, as he supposes, uncovered methods of simple, clear-headed and rational inquiry which all reasonable people can conduct if they clear their minds of prejudice and address themselves in a straightforward way to the questions. No special training, no religious discipline, no knowledge of texts or of history is needed in order to do this. He was disposed to think, in fact, that such things could be an actual obstacle.

His justification for believing that his readers had these powers, if only they could use them, is to be found in the *Meditations* themselves. If we follow Descartes to the end of them and accept his considerations, we shall have come to a conception of ourselves as rational, immaterial selves born with pure intellectual ideas and a capacity for reasoning which enable us to grasp in basic respects the nature of the world. Each of us does indeed exist in some kind of union with a particular physical body. '*My* body', one says, and Descartes took this phrase to register a profound truth, that what one truly is, is a mind 'really distinct' from the body. We need sensory information provided through the body not only to survive in the material world, but to find out particular scientific laws. But our own nature, the existence of God and indeed the most abstract structural features of the physical world itself can be discovered, Descartes supposed, by directed intelligence and rational insight.

Among these things we discover, when we direct our intelligence in the right way, is that we are beings who are capable of making just such discoveries, and we gain insight into the way in which we can make them. So we discover also how the *Meditations*, a work of pure reflection aiming to free us from error and to help us understand these basic matters, can succeed. Its end lies in its beginning, not just because its author knows how the thinker will come out, but in the philosophical sense that if we undertake to follow its method of inquiry, our doing so, Descartes supposed, is justified by our being the kind of creatures that it finally shows us to be.

The method deployed and invoked in the *Meditations* works, to an important degree, through argument, clear chains of reasoning. This tells us something of how to read the book. We are asked to argue, not merely through it, but with it. Because of this, it is specially appropriate that the book was associated, at its first publication, with *Objections* and *Replies*. Descartes had some political motives in having the *Objections* assembled, as he also did in dedicating the book to the Sorbonne. He wanted to have his work accepted by the religious authorities. For the same reason, he did not welcome all the *Objections* that were collected by his friend Mersenne, who organised the enterprise, being embarrassed in particular by those of the English sceptic and materialist Hobbes. But whatever the strategy of the publication, it was true to the spirit of the work, as Descartes clearly believed, that it should appear together with arguments attempting to refute it or defend it.

If we are to read the *Meditations* properly, we must remember that the thinker is not simply the author. We must not forget that the work is a carefully designed whole, of great literary cunning, and that it rarely lays out arguments in a complete or formal way. But this does not mean that it is not sustained by argument, or that arguing with it is inappropriate. It means only that we must read it carefully to find out what its arguments are, and what Descartes is taking for granted. If we reflect on what he is taking for granted or asking us by implication to accept, we are doing part of what he invited us to do, when he asked us to meditate with him.

A question of what he is taking for granted presents itself right at the beginning. 'Reason now leads me to think', he writes in the First Meditation,

> that I should hold back my assent from opinions which are not completely certain and indubitable just as carefully as I do from those which are patently false. So, for the purpose of rejecting all my opinions, it will be enough if I find in each of them at least some reason for doubt. And to do this I will not need to run through them all individually ... Once the foundations of a building are undermined, anything built on them collapses of its own accord; so I will go straight for the basic principles on which all my former beliefs rested.

Why does reason now lead him to think this? Everyone is engaged in trying to get information about matters of concern to him; some, such as Descartes, are involved in the sciences and want to arrive at systematic and reasoned beliefs about nature. But no one ordinarily supposes that the rational way to start on these things is to throw away or lay aside all the information one thinks one already has. Descartes thinks not only that this is the right course for him, but that it is self-evidently the right course for him. Why should he think this? Why should doubt seem the path to knowledge, if there is a path to knowledge at all?

We must notice first that the approach is not supposed to be applied to the ordinary affairs of life. Descartes makes that point over and over again, saying for instance that we must distinguish between 'the actions of life' and 'the search for truth'; and in the *Synopsis* to the *Meditations* he is prepared to use such a distinction even to define what counts as serious: 'no sane person has ever seriously doubted these things'. He does not mean that the results of his reflections will not affect ordinary practice or the conduct of the sciences. On the contrary, this is what he hopes they will do, setting the sciences, for instance, on the right path. Nor does he think that these reflections are a trivial way of passing the time. They cannot be that, if eventually they could have these practical and scientific effects. He may think that it is particularly his own, the author's, use of the Doubt that will have those effects, but he also believes that it is a worthwhile exercise for any of us, once in a lifetime, to take temporarily the position of the thinker of such reflections, and this will not be a trivial undertaking, either. Indeed, he himself said that the meditation to which he invited us in the Preface was itself, in its own way, 'serious'.

When Descartes says that the thoughts deploying the Doubt are to be separated from practical life, and in that sense (but only in that sense) are not 'serious', he is defining a special kind of intellectual project which by its nature can be conducted only if it is separated from all other activities. In ordinary life, when we want the truth on a subject, we pursue it, necessarily, in a context of other things that we are aiming to do, including other inquiries we need to make. The pattern of our inquiries is formed by many constraints on how we can spend our time and energies, and by considerations of what we risk by failing to look into one thing or spending too long looking into another. These constant and often implicit calculations of the economics of inquiry help to shape the body of our beliefs; and they have the consequence that our beliefs, while they aim at truth, will, inevitably, only partly achieve it. Descartes conceived of a project that would be *purely* the search for truth, and would be unconstrained by any other objectives at all. Because it temporarily lays aside the demands of practical rationality, it has to be detached from practice; and because it is concerned with truth and nothing else, it has to raise its requirements to the highest conceivable level, and demand nothing less than absolute certainty.

The search has to take place out of this world, so to speak, and its nature, its internal purpose, explains why this should be. But there is still a question about its external purpose. Why should Descartes or anyone else, once in a lifetime, take time out of the world to pursue this project? Descartes can commend it to us in more than one way, but his own principal reason is that he is looking for what he calls, at the start of the First Meditation and in many other places, 'foundations' of knowledge. To serve this purpose, the Doubt has to be methodical. A refusal to take things for granted that might be doubtful is part of Descartes' general intellectual method, which he had introduced in his earlier work *The Discourse on the Method*; the Doubt is an extreme application of that idea, conditioned by the circumstances of the special project, the radical search for certainty. The Doubt is deployed for defined purposes, and from the start it is under control.

It was not a new idea that scepticism might be used for its beneficial effects. Sceptics in the ancient world, Pyrrhonians and others, had advocated such techniques for their own purposes; their teachings had been revived since the Reformation, and sceptical views were in the air at the time that Descartes wrote. Some of his critics complained that material he deployed, for instance about the errors of the senses, was old stuff. But Descartes could rightly reply that while scepticism was no new thing, his use of it was indeed new. When the Pyrrhonians deployed sceptical considerations, it was in order to calm and eradicate an unsatisfiable urge for knowledge; and it was rather in this spirit, sixty years before the *Meditations*, that Montaigne had written. But Descartes' aim was precisely the opposite, to use scepticism to help in acquiring knowledge, and to bring out from a sceptical inquiry the result that knowledge was, after all, possible. The Doubt served that purpose by eliminating false conceptions; and the fact that it was possible to use it in this way and then overcome it gave the fundamental reassurance that a proper science would have nothing to fear from the doubts of the sceptics. Descartes' Doubt was to be both revelatory and pre-emptive.

'Foundations of knowledge' can mean more than one thing. Descartes has often been thought to be searching for foundations in the sense of axioms from which the whole of knowledge or, more particularly, the whole of science, might be deduced, as in a geometrical system. In fact, this is rarely his concern, and it does not represent his understanding of what a completed science would be like. Historians classify Descartes as a 'rationalist', but this should not be taken to mean that he supposed mere rational reflection to be enough to establish scientific conclusions. He was a rationalist, rather, in his views about the origins of scientific *concepts*. He thought that the terms in which physics should describe the world were given to rational reflection, and he supposed them to be, in fact, purely mathematical. It was only by empirical investigation and experiment, however, that we could discover which descriptions, expressed in those terms, were true of the actual world.

Basically, the Doubt provides foundations for knowledge because it helps to eliminate error. Descartes' aim was not so much to find truths from which all scientific knowledge could be deduced, but rather to identify false or doubtful propositions which were implied by our everyday beliefs and so made those beliefs themselves unreliable. One belief of this kind was that objects in the external world had just the qualities that they seem to have, such as colour. The Doubt helped in eliminating this very general error, which could then be replaced by the sound conviction that objects, in themselves, had only the properties ascribed to them by mathematical physics. Once this corrected view had been laid bare and found indubitable in the process of orderly reflection, it could from then on serve as a sound foundation of our understanding of the world.

Proceeding in this way, Descartes could indeed 'go straight for the basic principles on which all my former beliefs rested'. The workings of the Doubt are adjusted to these aims. In its most extreme, 'hyperbolical', form, the Doubt is embodied in the fiction that a malicious demon, 'of the utmost power and cunning has employed all his energies in order to deceive me'. This device provides Descartes with a thought-experiment that can be generally applied: if there were an indefinitely powerful agency who was misleading me to the greatest conceivable extent, would *this* kind of belief or experience be correct? Thinking in these terms, Descartes is led to identify whole tracts of his ordinary experience he may lay aside, so that he suspends belief in the whole of the material world, including his own body.

It is significant, however, and characteristic of the way in which the *Meditations* unfolds, that Descartes does not start his sceptical inquiry with this extreme device. We are invited to get used to sceptical thinking gradually, by considering first more familiar and realistic occasions of error. He starts with illusions of the senses, in which we mistake the shape of a distant tower, for instance, or suppose a straight stick, partly in water, to be bent. Such examples remind us that we can be mistaken, and that even by everyday canons the world need not really be as it presents itself to our perception. There is little in these cases, however, to encourage the more generally sceptical idea that on any given occasion when we take ourselves to be perceiving something, we may be mistaken. He thinks that we are led to that further and more radical idea by reflection on the 'errors of our dreams'. The phenomenon of dreaming creates a more general and more puzzling scepticism because, first, it is true (or at least the sceptic pretends that it is true) that anything we can perceive we can dream we perceive; and, second, there is no way of telling at the time of dreaming whether we are dreaming or not. So it seems that at any moment I can ask 'how do I know that I am not dreaming now?', and find it hard to give an answer. But what I can do, at any rate, if the question has occurred to me, is to 'bracket' these experiences, and not commit myself on the question of whether they are waking experiences which are reliable, or dreams which are delusive.

Once I am prepared to do this, I am well started on the sceptical journey. So far I have reached only the distributive doubt, *on any occasion I may be mistaken*, but reflecting on the possibility that I can have a set of experiences that do not correspond to anything real, I am nearly ready to take the step, with the help of the malicious demon, to the final and collective doubt, *I may be mistaken all the time*. In his description of what dreams are Descartes already lays the ground for what is to come. In the Sixth Meditation he says that he did not believe that what he seemed to perceive when he was dreaming came 'from things located outside me'. In an everyday sense, certainly, that description of a dream must be correct. But the description has acquired some large implications by the time I reach the last Meditation, and, having accepted the 'real distinction' between mind and body, understand that my body is itself something 'outside me'.

Every step in the sceptical progress should be questioned. It is at the beginning that all the seeds are sown of the philosophical system that has come to life by the end of the *Meditations*. To take just one example of questions that the thinker's reflections invite, do these facts about dreaming, even if we accept them, really lead to the conclusion that I can never know whether I am awake? Why, in particular, does the thinker take dreaming so seriously for his purposes, and not madness? He simply dismisses the deranged people who think that their heads are made of earthenware, or that they are pumpkins, or made of glass. Perhaps Bourdin, the author of the Seventh Objections, makes a good point in suggesting that the two conditions should be treated together. There is of course this difference, that the mad are assumed unable to conduct the meditation at all: the thinker turns away from them, treats them in the third person, because they cannot join him and the reader in thinking through these things, whereas we who are the readers have dreams, as the thinker has. But is this enough of a difference? Descartes and his thinker cannot speak to us *when we are dreaming*. Descartes seemingly thinks that if we are sane, we can be sure that we are, even though mad people cannot tell that they are mad. So why should the fact that when we are dreaming, we cannot tell that we are, imply that we cannot be sure we are awake when we are awake? There may be an answer to that question; but we should not let the argument from dreams go by until we have considered what it might be.

The *Meditations* use the Doubt to lead out of the Doubt into knowledge and a correct conception of things. In doing that, they do not merely provide a sounder conception: they show that we can reach such a conception, and demonstrate that knowledge is to be had. The foundations that Descartes believes himself at the end to have discovered are also foundations of the *possibility* of knowledge. That is why the scepticism of the *Meditations* is pre-emptive. Descartes claimed that he had taken the doubts of the sceptics farther than the sceptics had taken them, and had been able to come out the other side.

The rebuttal of scepticism depends on the existence of a God who has created us and who is 'no deceiver'. If we do our own part in clarifying our thoughts (as the thinker does in the *Meditations*) and we seek the truth as seriously as we can, God will not allow us to be systematically mistaken. However hard we think about these matters, however much we clarify our understanding of what an 'external' world might be, we are left with a conviction that there is such a world—a conviction so powerful that it needed the extreme device of the malicious demon temporarily to displace it. It would be contrary to the benevolence and the trustworthiness of God that this conviction should be untrue.

It is essential that we should have done our own part. God cannot be expected to underwrite confused conceptions which have not been carefully examined. If we do not accept a sound intellectual discipline, we deceive ourselves and are responsible for our errors. (This is one way in which Descartes thinks that the will is involved in belief.) Equally, God's benevolence does not guarantee us against every error, but only against general and systematic error. We remain liable to occasional mistakes, such as those of defective perception and also those of dreams, which before these reassurances seemed to offer a sceptical threat. Particular errors are caused by our bodily constitution, and it is not surprising that we should be subject to them. The sceptics' threat was that our entire picture of things might be wrong: now we have an assurance, because God is no deceiver, that this cannot be so.

But have we? Those who offered *Objections* were only the first among many to doubt whether Descartes' argument succeeds, even in its own terms. In the course of the *Meditations*, the sceptic has been allowed to cast doubt, it seems, even on the convictions that ground the belief in God. This doubt must be resisted, but how, in resisting it, can we appeal to the existence and nature of God, without arguing in a circle? Descartes' answer to this objection emphasises that a doubt about the proofs of God, and their implications for the validation of our thoughts, can be entertained only when one is not actually considering them. At the time they are clearly considered, these proofs are supposed to be as compelling as any other basic certainty—that I cannot think without existing, for instance, or that twice two is four. So when the sceptic professes to doubt the proofs of God, or any other such certainty, it can be only because he is not actually considering them at that time. All one can do is to refer him back to them; if he does properly consider them, he will, then, be convinced.

All this Descartes clearly says, but it is a little less clear what he expects us, and the sceptic, to make of it. His idea may be this, that if the sceptic reverts to his doubts when he has stopped thinking clearly about the proofs, we have earned the right by then simply to forget about him. He is merely insisting that we go on giving the answer—an answer we indeed have—to one question, his question, instead of getting on with our scientific inquiries or other practical activities, rather as though we were required to spend all our time out of the world with the thinker. We have offered all the justifications we could in principle offer, and now have the right to see the dispute as one about how to spend our time. If the sceptic were still to offer some basis for his doubts, it seems that it could now lie only in the idea that intellectual concentration was itself the enemy of truth: that you are more likely to be right about these matters if you do not think carefully about them than if you do. This idea is denied by the procedures of the sceptic, as well as by those of Descartes' thinker; in starting on the *Meditations* themselves, or any other inquiry, we implicitly reject it.

Modern readers will want to consider how exactly Descartes answers the problem of the 'Cartesian Circle', and whether his answer, in his own terms, is a good one. Few of them, however, will accept those terms, or agree that the theological foundation he offers for science and everyday belief is convincing. Descartes was very insistent that science itself should be thoroughly mechanistic and should not offer explanations in terms of God's purposes or any kind of teleology. In this, he was one of the major prophets of the seventeenth-century scientific revolution. Yet his justification of the possibility of such a science itself lay in God, and in a kind of teleology, a conviction that the world cannot be such that our desire to know must be ultimately misguided or frustrated. Perhaps we still have some version of that conviction, but if so, it is not for those reasons, and it could not be used to provide foundations for science.

To Descartes' contemporaries, it seemed much more obvious that God existed and was no deceiver than that natural science was possible. Neither the successes nor the institutions of modern science yet existed. For us, science is manifestly possible, and because it is so, the demand is less pressing than it seemed to Descartes that it should be justified from the ground up. We may feel happier than he did to live without foundations of knowledge. But that must leave us open to questions of how that can be so. We need to know what the science that is so manifestly possible, is.

Does it describe a world that is there anyway, independently of us? What does this question itself mean? How do we, with our thoughts and our bodies, fit into our picture of the natural world? We cannot do with Descartes' *Meditations* everything that he hoped to achieve with them himself, but there remain many good reasons to accept his invitation to them.

SEVENTEEN

Descartes and the Historiography of Philosophy

Discussing, some years ago, different ways of approaching the thought of Descartes, I made a broad distinction between two activities that I labelled 'the history of ideas' and 'the history of philosophy'.[1] The two are distinguished in the first place by their product. The history of ideas yields something that is history before it is philosophy, while with the history of philosophy it is the other way round. In particular, the product of the history of philosophy, being in the first place philosophy, admits more systematic regimentation of the thought under discussion. The two activities can be distinguished also by having rather different directions of attention. The history of ideas, as I intended the distinction, naturally looks sideways to the context of a philosopher's ideas, in order to realize what their author might be doing in making those assertions in that situation. The history of philosophy, on the other hand, is more concerned to relate a philosopher's conception to present problems, and is likely to look at his influence on the course of philosophy from his time to the present.

It is obvious that these two activities cannot be totally separated from one another, and each needs to some extent the skills of the other. It would be a mistake, however, to suppose that the distinction is simply baseless, or that the best possible historical approach to a philosopher would consist in an ideal fusion of these two activities. There is more than one reason why this cannot be so. One is that the best possible history of ideas is likely to show that the philosophy did not in fact mean in contemporary terms what subsequent philosophy has most made of it. But, apart from that, the kinds of sensibility needed for the two activities are bound to yield partly incompatible products, in rather the way that Impressionism, by exploring as intensely as possible the surface effects of light, was thereby debarred from giving as much information about structure as was accessible to some other styles of painting.

I have said that the approach associated with what I called 'the history of philosophy' is marked out both by a concern that its product should be in good part philosophy, and also by an interest in diachronic influence (a dimension which the phrase itself, of course, particularly sug-

[1] B. Williams, *Descartes: The Project of Pure Enquiry*, preface.

gests). It is important, however, that these two points do not simply, or always easily, go together. One way of putting the philosophy of the past to use in present terms is to neglect or overlook, to some extent, the history that lies between that philosophy and the present day, and to reconsider the philosophy in partial independence from its actual influence. It has been a particular speciality, in fact, of the analytic history of philosophy to approach the philosophy of the past in this way. At its extreme, this activity could take the form of triumphant anachronism, as when it used to be said, in the heyday of analytic confidence, that we should approach the works of Plato as though they had appeared in last month's issue of *Mind*. The claim that it did actually proceed in this way is now one of the standard charges associated with the demonized image of analytical history of philosophy.

Other charges against analytical history of philosophy are that it suffers from the limitations of analytic philosophy itself, in considering only a narrow range of philosophical interests; and that it neglects the literary dimension of philosophical works, so that—in the case of some of them, at least—it misses a good deal of what can be got from them even philosophically. Finally, there is the charge of its obtrusive cockiness, the condescension with which earlier writers are treated to instruction by current philosophical methods, and are reproved for their errors—errors to which they have been committed, typically, by the way in which analytical philosophy interprets them. All these charges are certainly true, in the sense that there are very many works in this style to which one or more, and often all, of the charges can justly be applied. I shall not discuss all the charges here.[2]

The first of the charges, however (and, to some extent, the last), raises the question not only of how such activities should be conducted, but of why. The idea of treating philosophical writings from the past as though they were contemporary is, at the limit, simply unintelligible. If one abstracts entirely from their history—including in this both the history of their context and the history of their influence—one has an obvious problem of what object one is even supposed to be considering. One seems to be left simply with a set of words in some modern language (which, in many cases, have been generated by a translator), and one associates with these words whatever philosophical notions they may carry with them today. This activity has no title to being history of any sort. But even when the activity is less arbitrary than this suggests, there remains a question of its point. The point of any history, one might suppose, is to achieve some distance from the present, which can help one to understand the present.

---

[2] I have said something about the literary character of some philosophical works in B. Williams, *Shame and Necessity*, 13–14.

The more extreme forms of analytical history of philosophy addressed themselves to removing that distance altogether, and in doing so lost the title to being any pointful form of historical activity. In these extreme forms, they owed their existence only to the fact that something called 'the history of philosophy' appeared in the syllabus, and they provided a philosophical activity to fill this place.

However it may have been in earlier years, these very extreme forms of the analytical history of philosophy do now belong to the demonology of the subject, and are rarely to be found in inhabited places in the daylight. There is a good deal of history of philosophy that uses analytical techniques, and yet is genuinely and non-arbitrarily historical; it is still history of philosophy in my terms, which is to say that its product is to an important extent philosophy. To justify its existence, it must maintain a historical distance from the present, and it must do this in terms that sustain its identity as philosophy. It is just to this extent that it can indeed be useful, because it is just to this extent that it can help us to deploy ideas of the past in order to understand our own. We can adapt to the history of philosophy a remark that Nietzsche made about classical philology: 'I cannot imagine what [its] meaning would be in our own age, if it is not to be untimely—that is, to act against the age, and by so doing to have an effect on the age, and, let us hope, to the benefit of a future age.'[3] One way in which the history of philosophy can help to serve this purpose is the basic and familiar one of making the familiar seem strange, and conversely, but it needs to learn how better to do this. We should bear in mind this well-known aim of history—and specifically of a history that aims in some part to be philosophy—in turning, now, to some more specific questions about Descartes.

It used to be true (and may still be so) that the guide to the Panthéon in Paris would say at one point of the tour: 'Ici, mesdames et messieurs, vous voyez le tombeau du plus grand philosophe français, Jean-Jacques Rousseau.' One wonders what he would say if, as very nearly happened, Descartes' body had also ended up in the Panthéon. Indeed, there are rather more similarities between the two than the usual descriptions allow. Both are marvellous writers, both are extremely self-consciously original, both have been massively influential, and, despite having very different attitudes towards antiquity, they have both centrally contributed to a distinctively modern consciousness. In these last respects, moreover, each of them presents problems to the history of ideas and to the history of philosophy: each of them has had an influence that owes a great deal to gigantic misunderstandings, and each has been made use of in

[3] F. Nietzsche, 'History in the Service or Disservice of Life', in *Unmodern Observations*, ed. William Arrowsmith (New Haven: Yale University Press, 1990), 88.

ways neither of them could, needless to say, either have foreseen or have tolerated. Going back to their original context, and to the influences on them, may indeed help to remove those misunderstandings, but at the same time it raises the question, in each case, of the thinker's originality.

In neither case is the originality to be denied—it is a question rather of its nature. With both of them, it is a matter of conscious self-presentation; it is not the more nearly naïve originality of Frege or of C. S. Peirce. In Descartes' case, this raises two questions. The first is where the idea of such a self-presentation came from. Descartes' methodological and metaphysical turn towards himself has been associated often enough with such influences as Augustine and Montaigne, but they do not provide enough to explain his presentation of his project as a way of life. The modes of 'self-fashioning' that Stephen Greenblatt has discussed in relation to the Renaissance consciousness[4] are perhaps relevant to the idea that Descartes had formed of what he was to do, an idea formed, of course, while he was pursuing the life of a soldier. In the words of Ausonius which he recalled, 'Quod vitae sectabor iter?', it is important that the word is *iter*, not *via*: there is a journey to be made.

The second question concerns what we might find in Descartes if we removed the 'misunderstandings' that have so immeasurably contributed to and formed his influence. In asking this question, I am not looking for an understanding of Descartes that is free of later presuppositions, which benefits from no hindsight. Clearly, there could be no such thing. It is a question, rather, of its not benefiting from *this* hindsight, or the presuppositions peculiarly associated with our inherited history of philosophy. (This is one way in which we can aim to make the familiar strange again.) As things are, the history of ideas and the history of philosophy, applied to Descartes, are likely to yield, respectively, one of two types of understanding, one purely historical, and the other largely anachronistic. The history of ideas quite properly invites us to learn about late scholastic influences and the syllabus at La Flèche, or introduces us to problems that were encountered in developing an adequate mechanics of inertia. The history of philosophy, on the other hand, speaks in terms of how one can develop a non-transcendental epistemology starting from scepticism. The first of these two activities, the history of ideas, certainly has nothing wrong with it, but, in itself, it does not yield much philosophy that can help us in reviving a sense of strangeness or questionability about our own philosophical assumptions. It may be, simply and quietly, what it seeks to be, about the past. The history of

[4] S. Greenblatt, *Renaissance Self-Fashioning* (Chicago: University of Chicago Press, 1980).

philosophy, very often, does no more to release us from our preconceptions, for the different reason that it is merely constructed out of our preconceptions. The important thing about these two approaches is not that one is historical in relation to Descartes, while the other is anachronistic. The point, rather, is that neither of them, as things are, helps us to use Descartes to gain what Nietzsche called an 'untimely' perspective on our philosophical concerns. The first fails to do so because it does not, in itself, yield philosophy; the second yields philosophy, but only too much of the time it yields *our* philosophy.

Any philosopher who is likely to be of interest now to the history of philosophy is going to raise questions of this kind. But such questions are specially raised by Descartes, because he makes a unique claim to the suspect title 'the founder of modern philosophy'. At least two difficulties attach to this title, and to Descartes' relation to it. One of them is closely connected to the matter I mentioned before, of Descartes' self-presentation. A difficulty in getting behind this title is that Descartes seems to have arranged things, in particular his presentation of himself, in order to invite such a title; to a greater extent than many philosophers, Descartes is the architect of his own reputation and, by the same token, responsible for some of the misunderstandings that have attached themselves to that reputation.

A more general difficulty lies in the shifting content of the idea of 'modern philosophy' and of what could count as being its founder. 'Modern philosophy' used to mean *our* philosophy, but perhaps that is no longer true: some would say that 'modern' now signified only a period in the history of philosophy, a period that is closed or is closing. Perhaps it makes less difference than one might suppose to the present discussion whether one accepts that description or not. Even if the 'modern philosophy' that Descartes founded is taken to be the philosophy to which our discussions still contribute, Descartes' relation to it has for a long time been problematical or contested. The view which takes the philosophy of language rather than epistemology as the heart of philosophy has already for a long time relegated Descartes to the role of anti-hero, and has replaced him with Frege in the position of the founder of legitimate modern philosophical activity. This view itself, of course, has various ways of using Descartes, with the result that he remains part of the discourse of philosophy. One important use is indeed in the role of anti-hero: his works (or a few of them) are read (or partly read) as the most challenging and informatively misleading example of what is to be rejected.

Even in this role, however, he is rather paradoxically used. Those who have wanted to displace epistemology, and in particular a concern with scepticism, from a central place in philosophy have in many cases claimed to be interested in diagnosing the apparent attractions of the problem; they have wanted to replace attempts to answer it with an understanding of why we are tempted into it. Descartes is typically wheeled out as an example of one who indulged himself in trying to answer the problem of scepticism, but not so much, it seems, as someone from whom we can learn about the temptations to get into it. He is typically presented, in his brief appearance at the beginning of philosophy courses, as one who simply had a weakness for scepticism, or perhaps for mathematical certainty; or a brief expedition is made into the history of ideas to bring back an externalist explanation in terms of seventeenth-century Christian apologetics.

This obviously does little good for the understanding of Descartes or of scepticism, and it is fairly damaging to a sense of philosophy itself and of its history. If one presents Descartes as the founder of modern philosophy, and as seized by the problem of scepticism; if the problem of scepticism is said to be interesting not for its solution, but for the motives that lead to it; and if Descartes is not represented as displaying any interesting motive for it, but is diagnosed as being trapped in history, or (as it is more usually explained) in whatever misconception particularly impresses the teacher as providing the source of scepticism: a student will reasonably conclude, not only that Descartes is a fool, or at least that he has been overtaken by history, but, more damagingly, that a subject which not only has him as its founder but thinks it important that one should now read the works of such a founder cannot be a very serious subject. Descartes' own approach to his problems had better be presented as adequate to our own interest both in them and in him.

Not every view of Descartes as part of present philosophy need treat him as an anti-hero. He can be taken to be the founder of a modern philosophy to which we still belong in virtue of more general characteristics of his work that we strive to share: that it claims to persuade by argument and the fact that its starting-point (unlike its conclusions) is not religious. This view of Descartes depends, like the anti-hero view, on interpreting it so as to make a particular kind of sense as philosophy. It depends, that is to say, on the activity that I called 'the history of philosophy'. But, equally, those who wish to detach themselves from 'modern philosophy', leaving Descartes as the founder of a certain period in philosophy's history, cannot do without the activity of interpreting him in ways that result in a set of philosophical claims. Their style of doing this is likely to lean more heavily in the direction of interpreting his philosophy in terms of a set of supposed influences. The need to separate the activities the writers would like us to pursue from something now delimited as having been 'modern philosophy' requires them to identify a set of recent philosophical activities, the activities of 'modern philosophy', precisely as having been influenced by Descartes.

This post-modern approach, as it may be called, typically runs the risk of a split consciousness. On the one hand, it has to take the history of philosophy seriously enough to constitute a tradition; it has to detect enough continuity of concerns and assumptions to support the claims of influence. On the other hand, if it looks closely enough, it will, of course, find that the influence has worked, and the tradition been constituted, through misunderstanding. The writers it invokes will, at the very least, have made partial and selective use of earlier writers, since that is what creative writers, philosophers or not, of course do with the writers they read. Now the recognition of these facts need not destroy the image of the tradition; it may merely constitute it as a tradition of misunderstanding. But it has a damaging effect on the use that the post-modern critic can make of the tradition. The better its writers are understood, the less it looks as though they necessarily hang together as the 'modernity' that the critic wants to get beyond. Ironically enough, his own typical emphasis on contingency should make him less contented with the Hegelian classifications that define his own historical position.

He may say that he need not, after all, take his own historical position too seriously. The constitution of the 'modern' tradition, with Descartes as its founder, may figure simply as a ludic trope, which gains a certain edge from the fact that its members, including Descartes himself, usually do not seem, when they are more closely examined, to be doing quite what the story of the tradition requires them to be doing. But the only point of the ludic, at least as deployed in the history of philosophy, is to disturb and unsettle, and the effect of taking the tradition of modernity as given, with Descartes as its founder, can only be deeply settling and undisturbing, since it confronts us exactly with what we thought we had already. Our sense of our situation will be unsettled only when we come to see Descartes and the other supposed contributors as stranger than they seem while they are still regarded as the constituents of that tradition.

What was called in the original distinction 'the history of philosophy' is essential to any activity that is going to give a philosophical point to writing historically about philosophy. That point is going principally to be found in the possibility of the past philosophy's being untimely, and helping to make strange what is familiar in our own assumptions. In order to do this, the history of philosophy must be separated from two tendencies with which it has often been associated. On the one hand, it cannot treat its object as though it were merely contemporary, without losing the point of historical distance altogether. On the other hand, it cannot be identified with the history of influence, the progressive exploitation of original writing in one or more philosophical traditions; this, again, destroys strangeness, by following a path which necessarily lands us at precisely the place we are at. What we must do is to use the philosophical materials that we now have to hand, together with historical understanding, in order to find in, or make from, the philosophy of the past a philosophical structure that will be strange enough to help us to question our present situation and the received picture of the tradition, including those materials themselves.

HUME

EIGHTEEN

Hume on Religion

Hume died on 25 August 1776, and his burial took place four days later. In the words of his biographer, E. C. Mossner: 'A large crowd had gathered in St. David Street to watch the coffin being carried out. One of the crowd was overheard to remark, "Ah, he was an Atheist." To which a companion returned: "No matter, he was an *honest* man." '

Both statements, with the slightest of qualifications, seem to have been true. The qualification is to the first statement; if 'atheist', is taken to imply, as it often is today, 'dogmatic atheist', one who is prepared to assert with certainty that no sort of God or religious principle exists, this Hume was not. However, he fell not very far short of it, and was certainly an atheist by, say, Christian standards: about the non-existence of the Christian God, it seems clear that he felt no doubts. But there was some dimension of religious belief, in some pretty tenuous sense, about which he seems to have remained in a sceptical or agnostic position; and one problem in interpreting Hume on religion is to determine exactly how much or how little he was prepared to regard even as a matter of doubt.

The problem arises in part from the manner in which Hume approaches the subject—in the blend of irony and caution with which he writes about it. The caution was motivated by the religious temper of the times. Even in the liberal-minded Edinburgh of the 1750s and after, there were still certain conventions about the way in which religion, and in particular, of course, Christianity, could properly be discussed, and it was incumbent on those expressing doubts to cover their attacks with some semblance of conformity. Indeed, Hume was persuaded by his friends that his *Dialogues concerning Natural Religion*—which is his greatest work on religion—could not be prudently published in his lifetime at all; and it is interesting to find him in the last few weeks of his life anxiously making dispositions to ensure that it would in fact be published after his death. In this climate, the irony that was natural to Hume's temper was of good service in assisting the demands of caution. He employs, as Kemp Smith has pointed out in his invaluable edition of the *Dialogues*, much the same methods of covering his tracks as did the French sceptic Bayle, from whom Hume learnt a lot. One such method was to claim that one was criticising not Christianity, but superstitious perversions of it; another was to claim that in destroying pretensions to rational argument in support of religious doctrines, one was only making way for Faith, on which they should properly rest. Kant, of course, who was much influenced by Hume's destructive arguments, was later to claim that this was what he was doing—'removing Reason to make room for Faith'. The difference is that he meant it, and Hume and Bayle did not.

The irony, however, does not operate only in the direction of caution. For just as in the *Treatise*, Hume cannot resist expressing himself in a manner designed to upset his conventional readers. It is these two, opposite, uses of irony, I think, one in the direction of prudence and one against it, that have enabled many interpreters in the past to suppose that Hume had more positive religious belief than in fact he did. For it all depends on which side of the irony you take the more seriously.

The central case of these doubts is his *Dialogues concerning Natural Religion*. This dialogue has three speakers: Demea, an orthodox Christian believer of traditional views, who is prepared to advance an *a priori* argument for the existence of God; Cleanthes, a more moderate believer, who rests his case on the Argument from Design; and Philo, a sceptic who seeks to subvert the force of both the arguments, and in particular devotes his efforts to refuting the Argument from Design, with which most of the work is concerned. The conversation between these persons is narrated, moreover, by a speaker who says that he agrees with Cleanthes, the moderate believer. This structure has in the past led defenders of Hume's orthodoxy to suppose that Hume himself rejected Philo's sceptical arguments: in much the same way, perhaps, as in the *Treatise*, philosophical doubts about the existence of the material world are rejected as strained and unnatural, as trying to run against the unavoidable force of natural belief. On this interpretation, it is in the person of Philo that Hume speaks ironically, to shock, and in the persons of Cleanthes and the narrator, the moderate orthodox, that he speaks directly.

But this interpretation, it would now generally be agreed, is wrong: the irony is the other way round. Kemp Smith has shown that it is the sceptical views of Philo that most closely express Hume's own. Indeed, we know from his life that he rejected Christian doctrines. He was brought up in a Calvinist household—not the most narrow and repressive of such households as could be found in Scotland in those times, but rigorous enough. In his late 'teens he worked his way out of these beliefs, and—he explicitly states in a letter—never returned to them, nor to any form of Christianity. When he was dying, indeed, he calmly reaffirmed his disbelief in orthodoxy and the after-life to Boswell, who egregiously took the occasion to exhort him to reconsider his views. In private correspondence, he uses the word 'Christian' as a mild term of abuse: he said of Rousseau, when he had too late discovered what Rousseau was like, 'he has a hankering after the Bible, and is indeed little better than a Christian in a way of his own'; and in 1765 he described the English as 'relapsing fast into the deepest stupidity, Christianity and ignorance'. Particularly in the earlier years of his adult life, he was strongly anti-clerical, even though later he became friends with various Moderate divines in Edinburgh.

Apart from these biographical evidences, it can be seen from Hume's theories that he could not have held that sceptical doubts about God's existence were in the same position as sceptical doubts about, for instance, the existence of the external world. It is of the essence of Hume's position that those latter doubts run against nature: that one *cannot* doubt the existence of material bodies, except perhaps for very brief periods in a very unnatural state of mind. But he does not regard the belief in religion as in this sense natural or inevitable at all. He does indeed think that it has natural roots, in the sense that a naturalistic account can be given of why people believe in religion, and this he attempted to give in the work called *The Natural History of Religion*. But this is a different matter; and it is notable that he did not believe, as did many apologists of his own and later times, that religious belief was a *universal* phenomenon among mankind.

While it is certain that Hume did not regard religious belief as natural, in his special sense of that term—that is, as something which human nature, by its very constitution, must embrace—there are certain obscurities in his account of it. Here it is best, perhaps, to look first at the theory of *The Natural History of Religion*. His basic thesis in this work is that polytheism is an earlier belief than monotheism, the latter arising only by a later process. The source of the original polytheism he locates in men's incomprehension and fear of various circumstances that affect them: because of the unknown and hidden causes of such things as droughts, tempests, sickness and so forth, men are primitively led to posit a collection of independent personal agencies to account for these things. In advancing this view that polytheism was primary, Hume is implicitly criticising thinkers of a Deist temper, as well as some of the orthodox, who supposed that primitive man had already an apprehension of the universe as designed and created by a single designer. On the contrary, this he supposes to be a belief that arises afterwards; roughly, he thinks that one god gets advanced over the others because of emulation in praising and admiring him; and that when he is established as *the* God, men find reasons, such as the Argument from Design, to prove his existence.

Not only does Hume think that polytheism is primary over monotheism; he also believes—or claims to believe—that it is superior. He has two reasons in particular for this. First, polytheism is more tolerant: the Greeks and Romans, for instance, were always prepared to assimilate other people's gods. Monotheism, on the other hand, by its very nature tends to intolerance and absolutism. From this greater tolerance of polytheism, Hume is disposed to infer, in general, its greater benevolence; but since he himself mentions the polytheistic Mexicans for the barbarism of their practices, this seems hardly a valid inference. The second reason for the superiority of polytheism is that it does less violence to reason. This is not because it is more reasonable; on the contrary, it is a complete muddle of inconsistent myths and absurd superstitions. The point is that just because it is so, it does not admit of any serious attempt to rationalise it. The trouble with monotheism is that it encourages men to rationalise religion, to try to make a philosophical and theological system out of it, and *so long as the religion preserves its dogmas*, this can only lead to doing violence to reason itself; one is led into an endless path of pseudo-reasoning, which is worse, because more corrupting and dishonest, than the primitive confusions of polytheism.

Hume is not, of course, recommending polytheism; he thinks that no reasonable and civilised man would dream of accepting it. Here we meet a distinction important to Hume's account of religion; a fairly commonplace eighteenth-century distinction between the vulgar and the sophisticated. The vulgar perhaps need a religion: if so, polytheism may well be better, as doing less harm. The sophisticated may well do without one: the trouble is that the religion they may be tempted to embrace may be even worse than the primitive one. Here also, and in some ways parallel, is a distinction that Hume makes between superstition and fanaticism. By the first he means an assemblage of mythical beliefs, such as those of polytheism, which may do little harm; by the latter, the proselytising zealotry of religions such as Christianity, which he thinks is straightforwardly pernicious.

Hume has been criticised for his one-sided selection of the phenomena of religion. He emphasises over and over again the power of religion to lead men into persecution, unreason, and hatred; he says little, it has been pointed out, on the power of religion to induce love, charity or steadfastness. This is indeed true. But here we have to remember Hume's moral theory, by which men have a natural tendency to sympathy and benevolence. If then, religious men act benevolently, they do not so act because of religion—they so act because they are men. It is persecution and hatred that need the explanation, and religion only too often provides it. Now this is obviously a very limited and inadequate account of the effects of religious belief—just as, we may add, the story about men's fears of the unknown is an inadequate account of its origins. In both cases, the limitations lie in the general body of Hume's philosophy: in the one case, in his moral psychology, in the other, in a limited empiricist theory about the origins of belief. Hume, like Bertrand Russell in our own time, is too amiable and optimistic a man really to understand religion.

I have mentioned Hume's distinction between the attitudes of the vulgar and of the sophisticated to religion; and I have pointed out that in his view one form of sophisticated religion was worse than the vulgar superstitious sort. Is there then no way in which sophisticated monotheism is superior to other religious beliefs? It would seem from the previous account that there was not. Yet it does seem that there is one sense in which sophisticated monotheism may be nearer in Hume's view to *something* which it would be perverse or unwise to deny: he indeed says that the excesses of fanatical monotheism illustrate the maxim, *corruptio optimi pessima*, the worst of things is the corruption of the best. What, then, is the best? What is this something that may be left over when the bad accretions of religion are stripped away?

To find this, we must look at the *Dialogues concerning Natural Religion*; and particularly, granted the previous claim that the speeches of Philo represent Hume, at those speeches. Now Sir Leslie Stephen said that the *Dialogues* was the first sustained philosophical criticism of the Argument from Design. I do not know for certain whether this is true; what is certain is that, in a slightly different sense, it is the last—after it there did not need to be another. Although the Argument from Design lingered on through the nineteenth century, and even to the present time, Hume undermined it in a through-going and definitive manner. The essence of the Argument, as used in Natural Theology—that is, as an argument actually to prove the existence of the Christian God—is that it is a type of empirical argument, an argument from effect to cause. Hume's objections add up to saying that as such an argument, it does not work. For first, in positing a cause for an observed effect, one is not justified in positing more in the cause than is strictly necessary to produce the effect, and this the Argument does, by positing an infinite, omniscient, etc. being as the cause of what may well be, for all we know, a finite world. Again, the argument assumes that the only cause of organisation, such as we see in the world about us, can be intelligence. But this is quite gratuitous; in our experience we see organisation proceeding from many principles other than intelligence, as for instance, animals from animals and plants from plants; why should we not as well assume the creator of the world to have been some animal or vegetable, rather than a mind? Indeed, the supposition of mind as the first cause is particularly gratuitous, since on every hand we see mind proceeding from matter, but not matter from mind. More generally, there is a fundamental fault in the argument. It is an argument from analogy; but arguments from analogy depend upon repeated occurrences of the instances to which they apply. But in this special case, this condition cannot be satisfied: we only have one world to argue about. Hence any analogy employed must be extremely weak, if it has any strength at all. All this is consistent with Hume's views on empirical inference, and they are certainly appropriate, for it was in a special application of empirical inference that the argument was supposed to have its strength.

There is a further point. The Argument from Design was supposed to show not merely the existence of a designer, but his benevolence. Here Hume thought that the evidence was not merely too weak to bear the conclusion, but, in some respects, downright opposed to it. While granting the beauty and fitness of final causes in nature, which move our thoughts towards a designer, Philo adds: 'But there is no view of human life or of the condition of mankind, from which without the greatest violence, we can infer the moral attributes, or learn that infinite benevolence, conjoined with infinite power and infinite wisdom, which we must discover by the eyes of faith alone'. And when Cleanthes replies that no doubt what seems inconvenient and terrible in human life seems so only because of our ignorance of some Divine plan, Philo replies with one of Hume's most important observations in this connexion: that while such considerations might serve to *reconcile* the state of man's life with Divine benevolence, if the latter were independently proved, they certainly cannot assist us to *prove* this benevolence from the state of man's life.

Apart from this further application of the criticism of the analogical argument, Hume has in any case an *a priori* reason for disbelieving in God's moral attributes. On his moral theory, moral attributes are derived from human nature, and only make sense in relation to it—our ideas of moral goodness are necessarily ideas of human goodness, and could not conceivably be applied to a non-human, infinite being. Indeed, in a letter to Francis Hutcheson, with whose moral theory his own had much in common, he criticises him for inconsistency in supposing that moral attributes could be applied to the Deity.

After all this, little seems to be left of the Argument from Design, or indeed of the Christian conception of God. Hume indeed thinks that the very idea of praying to God, or in the ordinary sense, worshipping him, must be inappropriate, for not only does it involve regarding God as like a man, but as like a not very admirable type of man: 'To know god', he makes Philo say, 'is to worship him. All other worship is indeed absurd, superstitious and even impious.' But now, what God? Well, Hume throughout the *Dialogues* is certainly impressed by the existence of the regulated final causes of nature; and he does sum up Philo's position by allowing him to assent to the 'somewhat ambiguous, at least undefined proposition, that the cause or causes of order in the universe probably bear some remote analogy to human intelligence'. This is the most that he thinks a reasonable man can assent to; and what is certain is that anything which might be called religion based on this proposition should have no prayer, no worship, no institutions, and no effect on moral conduct. The vague shadow of a possible religious belief is so remote that it could have no effect.

Hume was a sceptic, not a materialist. This was one reason why he objected, as he did, to the dogmatic tone of the French *philosophes*. For him, the ultimate causes of things remained necessarily mysterious; we know enough, he thought, to know that most things said about God must be false and inappropriate, and we can see further that attempts to argue to his existence must be useless. But we do not know what the ultimate origin of anything is, and cannot—we do not know enough to—exclude the possibility that something rather like an intelligence might—just conceivably—have something to do with it. One suspects that he had another reason for his objections to the *philosophes*, which was that they got too excited about the non-existence of God. He smelt the odour of a negative fanaticism, and any fanaticism, for Hume, was as bad as any other. Consistently with his philosophy, it would be the human effects of unbelief, as of belief, that would concern him most.

SIDGWICK

NINETEEN

The Point of View of the Universe: Sidgwick and the Ambitions of Ethics

Sidgwick's book *The Methods of Ethics* was first published in 1874, and he took it, with substantial alterations, through five editions, and partly through a sixth. It has been recently described as 'a systematic treatise on moral philosophy, examining in detail a far wider range of topics than any previous book on the subject, and setting new standards of precision in wording, clarity in exposition, and care in argument'.[1] It is not merely an historical monument. After a period of fairly resolute neglect, it is now beginning once again to be admired and, it may even be, to some extent read. It bears a very real intellectual relation to modern Utilitarianism and to certain of its problems. There are difficulties not only about Utilitarianism, but about the very project of a systematic ethical theory, which emerge with special clarity from the pages of Sidgwick's book, particularly because Sidgwick was in various ways both more and less conscious of them than modern writers have been. It is the relevance of Sidgwick's book to a large and still very pressing question, the possibility of ethical theory, that I shall discuss.

Of course Sidgwick was not only famous for this book, or for his other work in philosophy. Born in 1838, he had an interest from his undergraduate days in enquiries into supernatural phenomena, and he played an important part in the early history of the Society for Psychical Research founded to pursue on a supposedly scientific basis what Sidgwick sometimes called his 'ghostological' interests. He felt in a way which was perhaps peculiar to his time, and indeed rather specially peculiar to Cambridge, that séances in darkened and stuffy sitting-rooms, with heavily unconscious ladies who might be hoped at least to hear voices from the departed and, with exceptional good luck, to extrude some ectoplasmic embodiment of them—that these undertakings could

This is substantially the text of the Henry Sidgwick Memorial Lecture 1982, delivered on 18 February. I am grateful to the Principal and Fellows of Newnham College for their invitation to give the lecture. I believe that it may be the first Sidgwick lecture to be concerned with Henry Sidgwick himself.

[1] J. B. Schneewind, *Sidgwick's Ethics and Victorian Moral Philosophy* (Oxford: Clarendon Press, 1977), p. 1.

have some relevance to the truth of the Gospels (cf. Schneewind, p. 31). This might seem to many people now an error of judgement, as indeed it seemed at the time to Christians of other persuasions, but certainly Sidgwick's part in the revealing history of that strange subject was substantial.

Another substantial and certainly more securely beneficent claim to fame was the very large part that he played in the foundation of Newnham College. In addition to his own large expenditure of effort, time and money on this project, his wife, Eleanor Mildred Balfour, the sister of the Prime Minister, was the College's second Principal. In his ethical theory, as we shall see, there is a rather notable tension between on the one hand Utilitarian principles which could lead to radical change, and on the other hand an application of those principles serving in good part to justify the *status quo*. That tension emerges particularly in passages of considerable unease about sex and the character and motives of women in contrast to men. It is notable too that in *The Methods of Ethics*, the issue of women's rights gets no mention at all, though it was of course famously a salient feature of the political and social thought of his Utilitarian forebear, John Stuart Mill. But in practice Sidgwick was energetic to admirable ends in this respect. We must be grateful that he had no disposition to share, nor even to regard as Utilitarianly valuable, a kind of conventional outlook which was expressed—I am afraid one has to admit, rather splendidly expressed—in a letter from W. B. Yeats to Katherine Tynan in 1889:

> [If women go through] 'the great mill called examinations', they come out with no repose, no peacefulness, their minds no longer full of secluded paths and umbrage-circled nooks, but loud as chaffering market places. Mrs Todhunter is a great trouble mostly. She has been through the mill and has got the noisiest mind I know. She is always denying something.[2]

There was quite a strong tendency, at least in liberal circles, to regard Sidgwick as rather saintly. This was a response in particular to his intellectual honesty, to be found both in the marked scrupulousness of the argument of *The Methods of Ethics*, and also in his resignation of his Fellowship because he could not subscribe sincerely to the Thirty-Nine Articles. That impression of saintliness, however, had about it an unremovable Victorian quality which laid it open to question by those of the next generation. Maynard Keynes wrote to his friend Swithinbank about Sidgwick's Memoir in 1906, six years after Sidgwick's death:

[2] Quoted in Frank Kermode, *Romantic Image* (London: Fontana, 1971), p. 64.

Have you read Sidgwick's Life? It seems to be the subject of conversation now. Very interesting and depressing and, the first part particularly, very important as an historical document dealing with the mind of the period. Really—but you must read it yourself. He never did anything but wonder whether Christianity was true and prove that it wasn't and hope that it was. He even learnt Arabic in order to read Genesis in the original, not trusting the authorised translators, which does seem a little sceptical. And he went to Germany to see what Ewald had to say and fell in love with a professor's daughter, and wrote to his dearest friends about the American Civil War.

I wonder what he would have thought of us; and I wonder what we think of him. And then his conscience—incredible. There is no doubt about his moral goodness. And yet it is all so dreadfully depressing—no intimacy, no clear-cut crisp boldness. Oh, I suppose he was intimate but he didn't seem to have anything to be intimate about except his religious doubts. And he really ought to have got over that a little sooner; because he knew that the thing wasn't true perfectly well from the beginning. The last part is all about ghosts and Mr. Balfour. I have never found so dull a book so absorbing.[3]

Yet Keynes and his friends, of course, had another saint of their own, and one equally involved in moral philosophy. Keynes had written to Lytton Strachey just a month before:

I am studying Ethics for my Civil Service.

It is *impossible* to exaggerate the wonder and *originality* of Moore; people are already beginning to talk as if he were only a kind of logic-chopping eclectic. Oh why can't they see!

How amazing to think that we and only we know the rudiments of a true theory of ethic; for nothing can be more certain than that the broad outline is true. What is the world doing? It does damned well bring it home to read books written before P. E. I even begin to agree with Moore about Sidgwick—that he was a wicked edifactious person.[4]

In so far as this is not just about Moore's personality, it is about 'P. E.', the famous book that he had produced in 1903, *Principia Ethica*, a book still a great deal more read than *The Methods of Ethics*—or at least parts of it are, the wrong parts in fact. There are some merits, certainly, that it

[3] R. F. Harrod, *The Life of John Maynard Keynes* (London: Macmillan, 1951), pp. 116–17.

[4] *Ibid.*, p. 114.

has of a kind inconceivable in Sidgwick's work, and which chiefly compelled Keynes's admiration: an intense conversational tone, at certain
points, an immediate persuasive presence. Sidgwick never sounds like
that.

But in other respects, especially in argument, *Principia Ethica* is not as
admirable a book as *The Methods of Ethics*. In fact, despite some fundamental differences in their conclusions, a good deal of it actually comes
from Sidgwick, with Moore simply ignoring a number of difficulties
which Sidgwick, usually rightly, thought that he had identified. Certainly
it was not any theoretical merit of *Principia Ethica* in comparison to *The
Methods of Ethics* that should have persuaded Keynes that it was the
more valuable work. Nor, really, should it have been that Moore's work
was the more spiritually radical. It certainly seemed so: both in the values that it espoused, and in the way it went on about them, it was a good
deal less dauntingly earnest than Sidgwick—but that was due in good
part to a change in time and temper. As Keynes's remarks themselves
show, there was no more *doubt* in the world of *Principia Ethica* than in
that of *The Methods of Ethics*—and perhaps in certain ways less doubt—
about the solid foundations of the whole enterprise.

It is a standard criticism of *The Methods of Ethics* that it is extremely
boring. Roy Harrod wrote (p. 76): 'I remember Alfred Whitehead telling
me that he had read *The Methods of Ethics* as a young man and found it
so stodgy that he had been deterred from ever reading any books on
ethics since'. Defenders of Sidgwick these days have a tendency to reply
to this charge in the general style of the libel lawyer, to the effect that
first, it isn't true, and second, if it is true it is justified by his unflashy
concern to get things right in detail. The truth is, first, that a lot of it
is boring; second, not all of it is. There are distinct moments of tension
which grow out of passages of that very boredom. One might say indeed
that the overwhelming Englishness of this book extends even to a similarity to a cricket match, which has the very sophisticated feature that
one can only appreciate the significant detail of the monotony that lies
before one at a given time because one understands remote and hypothetical moments of excitement which might grow from it. Third, the fact
that a lot of *The Methods of Ethics* is boring is not the most important
fact about it. It is not even the most important negative fact about it, because what is most deeply wrong with it emerges in the most interesting
bits. Yet, nevertheless, it is still true that there is something revealing
about the boringness, and that it has a certain quality which constitutes a
quiet sustained comment on what is wrong with the work.

Here we have to recall one or two points about how the book is shaped.
The 'methods of ethics' to which the title refers are Egoism, Intuitionism
and Utilitarianism. As Sidgwick admits, to call Egoism a method of *ethics*

at all may seem rather misleading, since pure Egoism is easily contrasted with the very idea of an ethical outlook. But Sidgwick makes it entirely clear what he is talking about, and it is in fact one of the best features of his undertaking. Like Plato and Aristotle, of whom he said that 'through a large part of the present work' their influence had been 'greater than that of any modern writer',[5] he regarded the fundamental question of ethics as 'in what way is it reasonable or rational to live?'—a question to which Egoism might conceivably turn out to provide the answer. If some moral or distinctively ethical (in the narrower sense) answer to that question is to be adopted, then it has to work its passage against Egoism as much as against alternative answers of the moral, non-Egoistic, sort.

The task of adjudicating by reason alone between the claims of Egoism and those of morality was one which Sidgwick was not to claim that he had achieved.[6] He was left with the suspicion that it could be achieved only by appealing to religious principles, and those were principles which he neither thought it appropriate to introduce into a science of ethics—which he conceived, distinctively and rather originally, in a secular light—nor was himself prepared to put sufficient faith in.

What he did feel had been achieved by The Methods of Ethics was a demonstration that at any rate the moral option should take the form of the Utilitarian theory. In arriving at this conclusion he engaged in an extensive survey of commonsense morality, in which he set out a good deal of everyday moral thought, or at any rate those conclusions and arguments that might find favour with what he variously calls educated, cultivated, intelligent or morally sensitive persons. The main emphasis of this is to point out the doubtfulness, unclarity, and uncertainty of much of this thought, and the difficulty of deriving its conclusions from any clear and limited set of principles.

It is the aim of deriving these conclusions from such principles that gives the point to the label that Sidgwick attaches to the section of the book in which he surveys commonsense morality. It is the section that is supposed to display the method of 'Intuitionistic ethics'. It is important in trying to follow Sidgwick's thought to see what this label does and does not imply. Some writers on ethics, including some later than Sidgwick and indeed Moore himself, made rather a lot of the notion of intuition, as being a particular kind of mental capacity for discerning fundamental

---

[5] Henry Sidgwick, The Methods of Ethics, 7th edn (London: Macmillan, 1907; reissued 1962), pp. 375–6.

[6] Chiefly because the task must be impossible. However, the difficulties that Sidgwick encounters are certainly heightened by confusions in the distinctively hedonistic part of the theory. See in particular the footnote on pp. 499–500.

ethical truths; and arguments about the existence or possibility of a power of that kind have taken up quite a lot of room in the literature of moral philosophy. They have been concerned, so to speak, with the theory of moral knowledge. However, Sidgwick is actually not very interested in this aspect of the question, which he regards as part of the 'psychology' of ethics—and in not being very interested in it he is importantly followed by some contemporary writers such as, notably, Rawls.

In talking about 'Intuitionism' Sidgwick is concerned chiefly with a method—the method, roughly, that takes the reflective or even the relatively unreflective convictions of everyday moral thought and uses them to arrive at basic and supposedly certain moral truths or, again, to reach conclusions about unfamiliar cases. However, there are some important ambiguities in how ambitiously such a method is to be taken. At its least ambitious, it looks much like going on as people generally go on—using some cases to think about others, and not being immensely surprised if, as Aristotle always held and the results of Sidgwick's reflections illustrate, there are no very definite, clear and exceptionless moral principles to be found in everyday thought.

Sidgwick, however, finds this a reproach to commonsense morality; though, as we shall see later, it may be that he finds it a reproach to that morality only if commonsense morality is seen in a certain light, as selfsufficient. He quite certainly finds it a reproach to any *theory* which tries to derive from that morality a set of clear, definite and certain moral principles which will be specific enough to decide uncertain cases. The outlook that claims to do that he calls *dogmatic Intuitionism.*[7] He is less clear than he might be about what its success would consist in, but he is clear that it fails.

However, there is another, higher, level of Intuitionism of which Sidgwick takes a different view. This, he says, 'springs from the demand to find some deeper explanation of why conduct commonly judged to be right is so: while accepting the morality of common sense as in the main sound, it still attempts to find for it a philosophical basis which it does not itself offer'. He equates with that the aim of getting one or more principles 'more absolutely and undeniably true and evident, from which the current rules might be deduced, either just as they are commonly received or with slight modifications and rectifications' (p. 102).

The conclusion that Sidgwick eventually arrives at is that this task can in fact be carried out—the task, that is to say, of starting from received

---

[7] Schneewind has usefully discussed the problems that arise because Sidgwick actually approaches the discussion of dogmatic intuitionism through some considerations about perfectionism. Sidgwick's discussion certainly involves his own 'thin' view of moral dispositions, criticized below.

moral opinion, justifying and explaining a good deal of it in terms of some more general principles and applying those same general principles as a way of criticizing some other parts of received opinion which do not coherently hang together with the rest. This he thinks can be done, but he thinks it can be done only through the principles of Utilitarianism. Indeed, in the end he thinks that the contrast between Intuitionism and Utilitarianism is wrongly drawn, since the only way of correctly carrying out the Intuitionist objective is by reference to Utilitarianism, and the only justification of Utilitarianism itself is, as we shall see, dependent upon certain general principles which are intuitive. One difficulty of the book is that it is formed by a distinction between the Intuitionistic method and the Utilitarian method, which at an ultimate level Sidgwick eventually rejects.

I think that it is this structural feature of the book, the fact that its design is not actually very well adjusted to its conclusions, that helps to make some of it so boring, in particular this survey of commonsense opinion. There are other reasons as well. It is a general feature of the book that the account of commonsense morality is very linear, lacking any sense of the possibility of alternative moral traditions or the idea that certain moral outlooks of cultivated contemporary opinion might represent interests less broad than those of society or mankind as a whole. His discussion for instance of the ethics of making a financial profit out of persons who are in a disadvantaged situation is one example where the notion of *commonsense* itself demands to be examined in ways in which Sidgwick never examines it. The discussions of sexual morality, again, though they do get mildly more adventurous as we move from Intuitionism to Utilitarianism, continue to make fairly uncritical use of a notion of purity which is no doubt part of what Bloomsbury found oppressive and stuffy.

The lack of any non-moral perspective on the morality of his time is a feature of the work in general. The structural failing that I mentioned before comes out rather in this, that the only example of a theoretical structuring of everyday morality that we are in the end given in the book is the Utilitarian example itself. When Sidgwick is discussing, in the Intuitionist section of the book, an Intuitionist method which is, at that point, supposedly *distinct* from Utilitarianism, there is no fixed set of expectations against which commonsense opinions are being tested for coherence, definiteness and completeness. We are constantly reminded that there are various kinds of cases to which commonsense seems not to provide an absolutely clear and unambiguous answer. But we need some account of what kind of Intuitionist theory is, as an ideal, in question; and in the absence of that we have no guiding sense of how far we should be disappointed by the absence of these clear and unambiguous answers. Without the guiding notion—and also without, as I have said, any sense of the possibility that social or economic causes might have played some part in all this—the trail of inconclusive commonsense considerations and unresolved commonsense questions is bound to leave a rather dispiriting impression.

While Sidgwick criticized those who wanted to draw up a rational morality distinct from Utilitarianism, it is very important that he nevertheless shared their aspiration to a rational morality. The aim of throwing 'the morality of commonsense into a scientific form' (p. 338) was his aim too, and he shared with those Intuitionists the desire to be able to answer moral questions of judgement with a 'clear and accepted principle' (p. 249 *et al.*) It is very revealing of his own outlook that he asks, just before starting on his treatment of Utilitarianism (p. 406), 'If we are not to systematize human activities by taking universal happiness as their common end, on what other principles are we to systematize them?'.

In 1864, ten years before the publication of *The Methods of Ethics*, he had written (Schneewind, p. 44): 'I will hope for any amount of religious and moral development, but I will not stir a finger to compress the world into a system, and it does not at present seem as if it was going to harmonise itself without compression'. Yet in *The Methods of Ethics*, he certainly came to think that a system was needed which would ideally possess properties of clarity, reflectiveness and consistency, and would be such as to command the general agreement of unprejudiced people. The notion that that is what moral philosophy should produce, and that it is that which gives it power to combat the irrational, the merely personal and the merely habitual, is one which is still very powerfully with us.

No such system can be derived, Sidgwick concludes, by the Intuitionistic method, so long as that method is regarded as operating at a fairly low level of generality, merely considering everyday principles of action or everyday models of virtuous conduct. The consequences of that, we have been shown by the long survey of commonsense opinion, are too often conflicting, unclear and inconclusive. However, if we move to a higher level of generality, there are some principles which when he reflects on them Sidgwick finds to possess geometrical certainty, and which he believes can command universal assent. This is the level of what, as we just saw, he calls 'philosophical Intuitionism', where intuition is required to deliver to us only propositions of a very abstract and general kind, which will need interpretation in order to give us definite resolutions of our moral difficulties. He offers us three such fundamental principles. They appear in fact in a variety of formulations, and a great deal of effort could be spent on discussing how those various formulations relate to one another. That, however, does not matter for our present purpose.

The first principle is closely related to that familiar item, the Golden Rule 'Do to others as you would have them do to you': one of Sidgwick's formulations is 'If a kind of conduct that is right (or wrong) for me is not right (or wrong) for someone else, it must be on the ground of some difference between the two cases, other than the facts that I and he are different persons'.

The second of Sidgwick's basic principles is a substantive principle of prudence: what it says is that it is rational to pursue 'one's good on the whole' where 'on the whole' implies that we should have an 'impartial concern for all parts of our conscious life', and 'Hereafter *as such* is to be regarded neither less nor more than Now'. Sidgwick explains (p. 381):

> It is not of course meant that the good of the present may not reasonably be preferred to that of the future on account of its greater certainty: or again, that a week ten years hence may not be more important to us than a week now through an increase in our means or capacities of happiness. All that the principle affirms is that the mere difference of priority and posteriority in time is not a reasonable ground for having more regard for the consciousness of one moment than for that of another.

One consequence of this principle is that 'a smaller present good is not to be preferred to a greater future good (allowing for difference of certainty)'.

This principle of impartiality over all the times of one's life is an interesting example of what Sidgwick wants from an intuitive principle, since it is certainly not tautological, and many people find it completely self-evident. Indeed, it is fair to say that almost everybody who agrees with it finds it completely self-evident. However, the trouble is that the world also contains a group of people, distinguished perhaps from the first on grounds of temperament, who find it to an equal degree self-evidently false. I personally am convinced that whatever merits such a principle of impartial prudence may have, it is certainly not a mere derivation from the notion of practical rationality, and does require the introduction of a special attitude towards one's own life and one's own future. Whether this is so, is a large and interesting question, which I cannot take any further here. The one remark I would make about it is that Sidgwick's own discussion of it, and indeed almost all the extensive discussion of it in the recent literature, has taken for granted a large falsehood, namely that the length of time over which this prudence is to be exercised—the extent of one's conscious life—is something that is given independently of one's own prudential or other practical reasoning: it is not a matter for one's own control. This is consistent for Sidgwick, who, at least in

The Methods of Ethics, unquestionably accepts, without any comment at all, a prohibition on suicide. Others who do not subscribe to that restriction should for this reason, as well as for a number of others, take another look at that assumption.

The third of Sidgwick's basic principles which supposedly attract assent from all reflective persons lands us unambiguously in the territory of morality. He writes (p. 382):

> So far we have only been considering the 'Good on the Whole' of a single individual, but just as this notion is constructed by comparison and integration of the different 'goods' that succeed one another in the series of our conscious states, so we have formed the notion of Universal Good by comparison and integration of the goods of all individual human—or sentient—existences. And here again, just as in the former case, by considering the relation of the integrant parts to the whole and to each other, I obtain the self-evident principle that the good of any one individual is of no more importance, from the point of view (if I may say so) of the Universe,[8] than the good of any other . . . and it is evident to me that as a rational being I am bound to aim at good generally—so far as it is attainable by my efforts—not merely at a particular part of it.

This, then, yields a principle of universal benevolence that 'each one is morally bound to regard the good of any other individual as much as his own, except in so far as he judges it to be less when impartially viewed, or less certainly knowable or attainable by him'.

'Accordingly', Sidgwick writes, 'I find that I arrive, in my search for really clear and certainly ethical intuitions, at the fundamental principle of Utilitarianism' (p. 387). Sidgwick does in fact think that there remains one further task to be performed, in order to demonstrate that the set of principles which he has identified uniquely determines Utilitarianism as the ethical theory capable of systematizing our moral intuitions—that is the identification of what in this argument has been called universal good with universal happiness. This is, for a rather technical reason, more of a problem for Sidgwick than it is for a modern theorist at a comparable point in the argument. Though Sidgwick's views on the subject of happiness are quite complex, he fundamentally believes, in the tradition of Bentham and Mill, that happiness is to be interpreted in terms of pleasure—and pleasure is a subject on which he has some complex views. However, a modern Utilitarian is more likely to interpret the ultimate end to which the tradition gives the name 'happiness' in terms of satisfaction of desires or some such notion as rational preference.

---

[8] The phrase recurs at p. 420 without the apology.

When it is seen in these terms, Sidgwick's three premises do seem to deliver Utilitarianism virtually immediately. When, motivated by universal benevolence, we are concerned with the good of each person, we are required to be concerned with the very same thing that each of those persons has to be concerned with prudentially in his own case, so it will precisely be something like each person's objectives or rationally organized set of preferences that will become the raw material of the additive sum of universal good. Indeed, the fact that what we are concerned with is already assumed to be an additive sum, and that universal good is understood already as something that can be globally assessed in some such way, shows how far Sidgwick's three axioms already determine that the system which is going to satisfy these conditions will be a kind of Utilitarianism. It should also make us wonder once more how far the axioms do have to be accepted as rationally inescapable.

I shall come back to saying something about the merit of the axioms—in particular the last one, which is the one which both distinctively delivers morality, and also delivers this distinctive morality. However, there is one more very important thing to be said first about the way in which Sidgwick actually proceeds to apply the Utilitarian system at which he has now arrived. It is extremely distinctive of his system: it is what enables him, more than anything else, to reconcile his system with large areas of commonsense morality; and it is what very particularly brings out, in my view, a basic fault not only in his results but also in his approach. This is Sidgwick's insistence, perfectly correct in itself, that it cannot be a desirable result of a moral system that it should imply that actions should always be taken as the result of conscious rational calculation whether it be of prudence or of universal good. It had been an old objection to Utilitarianism that it could lead to a denial of all natural affections and the stifling of impulse and spontaneity in the interests of a calculative spirit directed to universal good. As Schneewind has well shown, this objection was in fact aroused much more by Godwin than it was by Bentham; Godwin's ferociously rational determination to respect almost any consideration other than those that an ordinary human being would find compelling did considerable damage to the image of Utilitarianism, as well as being something that Godwin, even when he adopted more moderate views in his later years, could never live down. This problem Sidgwick both saw and took resolute steps to avoid. He saw that from the point of view of Utilitarianism it must simply be an empirical question what motivations actually lead to the greatest good; and, in particular, whether the motivation of thinking about the greatest good is likely to lead to the greatest good. The Utilitarian consciousness, then, is itself made a problematical item about which it is necessary to think, and it is at least perfectly possible—and Sidgwick clearly regards it as true—that the Utilitarian consciousness should not, at least in many departments of life, be over-encouraged. Indeed, this is not just a point about the Utilitarian consciousness, although it very strongly applies to that: it is a point about the rationality of deliberation altogether. As Sidgwick puts it (p. 345) the dictates of reason ought always to be obeyed, but it does not follow that the dictation of reason is always a good.

From these considerations Sidgwick can offer a Utilitarian account of various values, particularly of such things as dispositions of character and action, which are often thought of as having an intrinsic or non-Utilitarian value. They include such things as the disposition to tell the truth, to be loyal to one's friends, to feel a particular affection and concern for one's own children, and other such items. Such an account plays quite a large role in carrying out the task that Sidgwick assigns to Utilitarian theory, of explaining and also in some sense justifying various parts of commonsense morality which might at first glance not seem to be of Utilitarian inspiration, and which indeed had not seemed to the Intuitionists to be of that inspiration, since they were constantly cited as counter-examples to the Utilitarian outlook. The values of justice, of truth-telling, of spontaneous affection, and so forth, were all items which it seemed the thorough-going Utilitarian would not endorse. But if it is not only permissible but indeed (according to Sidgwick) very important to consider the Utilitarian value of a state of affairs in which people have those dispositions, then the Utilitarian justification could extend much further than had at first been thought.

The business of giving these explanations or justifications is, in Sidgwick, conducted in a slightly desultory way and, in a manner which is shared by large numbers of later Utilitarian writers, he makes pretty cavalier use of what are supposed to be evident matters of fact, which in some cases may invite much the same doubt as the dispositions or rules that they are being invoked to justify. His account of the double standard in sexual morality, to revert to an earlier example, not surprisingly makes use of some fairly ideological material about the differences between the sexes, as well as appealing to such notions as 'the contagion of unchastity' (p. 452). In pursuing his project of uncovering what he calls the 'unconscious Utilitarianism' (p. 454) of commonsense morality—a phrase which itself raises some extremely pressing issues in the philosophy of social explanation—he is also sometimes guilty of a mistake which, again, turns up in later writers; this is to infer that, because considerations of utility or the greater happiness are quite often used in order to resolve a conflict between two other values, it then follows that those values must all the time be directly or indirectly expressions of the end of utility or the greatest happiness. This simply does not follow.

But the most interesting problems that arise from Sidgwick's treatment lie not so much in these standard features of the Utilitarian enterprise, but rather in the view his theory requires us to take of these various dispositions themselves. Unsurprisingly, Sidgwick has to treat these dispositions, when he is talking about them theoretically, in a very instrumental way, and the arguments that he produces about them are very linear. The dispositions are regarded just as devices for generating certain actions, and those actions, in the end, as the means by which practical reason produces certain states of affairs, those that most minister to universal good. That is what those dispositions look like when seen from the outside, from the point of view of the teleological Utilitarian consciousness. But it is not what they necessarily or usually seem like from the inside; and indeed what the Utilitarian argument may very well yield is the conclusion that they should *not* seem like that from the inside. Certainly it is empirically possible, and on the lines of Sidgwick's argument it must be true, that the dispositions will do the job which the Utilitarian theory has assigned to them only if the agents who possess those dispositions do not see their own character purely instrumentally, but rather see the world from the point of view of that character. Moreover, those dispositions require them to see other things in a non-instrumental light. Though Utilitarianism usually neglects the fact, they are dispositions not simply of action, but of belief and judgement; and they are expressed precisely in ascribing intrinsic and not instrumental value to various activities and relations such as truth-telling, loyalty and so on. Indeed, if Sidgwick is right in saying that the Utilitarian theory explains and justifies larger areas of everyday morality than had been supposed by the Intuitionists, and that he has succeeded in his project of reconciling Utilitarianism and Intuitionism by explaining in Utilitarian terms some of the phenomena on which the Intuitionists were most insistent—if that is so, then it *must* be that in the actual world the dispositions do present themselves to their possessors, and also present other features of the world, in this non-instrumental light. It was these possessors who, just because they had these dispositions, were so strongly disposed to reject Utilitarianism and insist on the intrinsic value of these actions and ends other than universal good.

It follows that there is a deeply uneasy gap or dislocation in this type of theory between the spirit that is supposedly justified and the spirit of the theory that supposedly justifies it. The gap is not very clearly perceived, if at all, by Sidgwick, nor, in my view, is its significance fully or at all adequately understood by later theorists who have adopted very much Sidgwick's position. In both Sidgwick's case and theirs, there is a distinction which has the effect of disguising from them this very deep area of difficulty: a distinction between theory and practice. That distinction, though regularly used, remains remarkably unexamined in this tradition of philosophy; and in fact I believe that if it is examined, it will be found to have, in these connections, virtually no saving power at all.

There is, first, the question of the practice of the theorist himself. The theorist may be presumed—at least as a first presumption—to possess the dispositions of which at a theoretical level he also possesses the Utilitarian justification. So in his mind at least the consciousness that goes with these dispositions, that they are directed to objects of intrinsic value, has to coexist with the consciousness of their justification, that both they and the objects to which they are directed have no intrinsic but only instrumental value. The conditions of this supposed coexistence are by no means easy, and they are hardly ever in Utilitarian writers made clear.

Sidgwick's failure to confront them is illustrated by the rather famous passage in which he discusses something which from a Utilitarian point of view he is certainly right to discuss, namely whether the Utilitarian theory is itself something which should be made known. He has been discussing exceptions to the general rules:

> . . . the Utilitarian may have no doubt that in a community consisting generally of enlightened Utilitarians, these grounds for exceptional ethical treatment would be regarded as valid; still he may, as I have said, doubt whether the more refined and complicated rule which recognises such exceptions is adapted for the community in which he is actually living; and whether the attempt to introduce it is not likely to do more harm by weakening current morality than good by improving its quality. Supposing such a doubt to arise, . . . it becomes necessary that the Utilitarian should consider carefully the extent to which his advice or example are likely to influence persons to whom they would be dangerous: and it is evident that the result of this consideration may depend largely on the degree of publicity which he gives to either advice or example. Thus, on Utilitarian principles, it may be right to do and privately recommend, under certain circumstances, what it would not be right to advocate openly; it may be right to teach openly to one set of persons what it would be wrong to teach to others; it may be conceivably right to do, if it can be done with comparative secrecy, what it would be wrong to do in the face of the world; . . . These conclusions are all of a paradoxical character: there is no doubt that the moral consciousness of a plain man broadly repudiates the general notion of an esoteric morality, differing from that popularly taught; and it would be commonly agreed that an action which would be bad if done openly is not rendered good by secrecy. We may observe, however, that there are strong Utilitarian reasons for maintaining generally this latter common opinion; . . . Thus the Utili-

tarian conclusion, carefully stated, would seem to be this; that the opinion that secrecy may render an action right which would not otherwise be so should itself be kept comparatively secret; and similarly it seems expedient that the doctrine that esoteric morality is expedient should itself be kept esoteric. Or if this concealment be difficult to maintain, it may be desirable that Common Sense should repudiate the doctrines which it is expedient to confine to an enlightened few. And thus a Utilitarian may reasonably desire, on Utilitarian principles, that some of his conclusions should be rejected by mankind generally; or even that the vulgar should keep aloof from his system as a whole, in so far as the inevitable indefiniteness and complexity of its calculations render it likely to lead to bad results in their hands. (pp. 489–90)

On this kind of account, Utilitarianism emerges as the morality of an élite, and the distinction between theory and practice determines a class of theorists distinct from other persons, theorists in whose hands the truth of the Utilitarian justification of non-Utilitarian dispositions will be responsibly deployed. This outlook accords well enough with the important colonial origins of Utilitarianism. This version may be called 'Government House Utilitarianism'. It only partly deals with the problem, since it is not generally true, and it was not indeed true of Sidgwick, that Utilitarians of this type, even though they are theorists, are prepared themselves to do without the useful dispositions altogether. So they still have some problem of reconciling the two consciousnesses in their own persons—even though the vulgar are relieved of that problem, since they are not burdened with the full consciousness of the Utilitarian justification. Moreover, Government House Utilitarianism is unlikely, at least in any very overt form, to commend itself today.

A more popular version now is to identify the required distinction between theory and practice as a distinction between the *time* of theorizing and the *time* of practice, and to use that notion, deployed in moral philosophy by Butler, of the 'cool hour' in which the philosophically disposed moralist reflects on his own principles and practice. There are problems, no less severe, with that model—problems which in fact become deeper and deeper the more that, in some appropriate cool hour, one thinks about them. There is the relatively straightforward artificiality of supposing that the thorough commitment that is required to the values of friendship, truth or whatever it may be, can merely alternate, on a timetable prescribed by calm or activity, with an alien set of reflections. At a rather more interesting level, the model implies an extremely naïve conception of what is going on in the cool hour itself. It is assumed that it is the cool activity of theorizing that will display to oneself the true value of one's own dispositions and reactions, where I mean by their 'true' value, the value that they really have for one. Should that be different from the value that one really believes that they have, when one is not reflecting on the value that one believes they have? The idea that cool and articulated reflection must be authoritatively revealing about one's structure of values is not itself a very sophisticated belief. Moreover, it can be seen as performing a function.

Utilitarians standardly present everyday unschooled moral reactions as at least presenting a problem of justification, and as running a serious risk of turning out, when unmasked, to be mere prejudices which should be dismissed in the light of Utilitarian reason. But it is at least as plausible, and the history of the subject very strongly suggests that it is true, that the theoretical reasonings of the cool hour are themselves only sustained and directed by some sense of the moral shape of the world as provided by the everyday dispositions. The belief that one can look at all one's dispositions from the outside, from the point of view of the universe, and that so doing is embodied in a cool hour of personal reflection, is a misrepresentation of that cool hour. What that hour does for one may be not to allow one to assume the point of view of the universe, but rather to disguise the fact that the affections and perceptions that mean most to one may well be not only contingent but also essentially incapable of being made totally transparent to oneself.

A suspicion related to that emerges, too, if one turns away now from the state of consciousness of the Sidgwickian theorist, to the result of his theorizing. Here we must remember what the objections to unreconstructed Intuitionism were, and how it was to be a demand on ethical theory that conflicts, inconsistencies and unclarities in everyday thought should be resolved and some clear principle provided for answering these questions. We left aside at that point the question of why these intellectual improvements were required. The question might indeed scarcely seem worth asking: its answer would generally be supposed to lie, at least to an important extent, in the improvement of practice. If our practice can be related to a more complete and coherent ethical theory, then the questions which in practice (or at very least in the more reflective parts of practice) demand and do not receive an answer—how, for instance, to extend some recognized principle to a new kind of case—can receive some rational resolution. Yet on Sidgwick's account of the matter it is just very unclear, at the end of the enterprise, how far we have actually advanced towards these objectives.

There is more than one reason for this. First of all, our general unclarities and conflicts and our sense of divergent claims are quite certainly related to the dispositions of action and judgement which we actually possess. Indeed, in his treatment of dogmatic Intuitionism, Sidgwick makes it repeatedly clear how that is so—it is just these various virtues, and various moral ideals related to them, that fail to yield determinate results in various places where he hopes for such results. Yet in the end we learn that it does actually serve the ends of universal good that we should have these dispositions, and that they should be expressed in the field of practice. But if so, then it is for universal good that we should live in a world which presents itself in at least quite a lot of these ways as raising conflict and divergence of sentiment.

To put it another way, these dispositions turn out to be a very valuable element in the world of practice. But that means that divergences of sentiment and various kinds of conflict that flow from those dispositions are themselves part of the world of practice, and the answers that they demand have to come from impulses which are part of the situation as it is actually experienced in the world of practice. It follows that a theory which stands to practice as Sidgwick's theory does cannot actually serve to eliminate and resolve all conflicts and unclarities in that world of practice, though *they* are the conflicts that were complained of when the method of Intuitionism was unfavourably reviewed.

It is some consciousness, perhaps, of this point that encourages another feature of Sidgwick's treatment—again a feature which is displayed in the work of later Utilitarians: namely, that it seems not to matter very much if the immense calculation of additive satisfaction cannot actually be carried out. 'We have to observe', Sidgwick writes (p. 439), 'that the difficulties which we found in the way of determining by the Intuitional method the limits and relative importance of these duties are reduced in the Utilitarian system to difficulties of Hedonistic comparison'. In fact, we are not given many examples, and it is hard to see how we could be, of how those Hedonistic comparisons do actually resolve those conflicts. It seems rather that it is that fact itself, the very idea that those conflicts and obscurities have been reduced to Hedonistic comparison, that provides the intellectual comfort. It seems that the theorist has certain expectations of how practice should respond to theory, and then finds that they are better satisfied by a certain kind of *theory* than they ever could be by any concrete experience of practice.

Some of the problems presented by Sidgwick's Utilitarianism and its need for a dissociation between theory and practice, are peculiar to such a Utilitarianism. Other schemas for ethical theory might at least satisfy one test which, as we have seen, Sidgwick's notably and confessedly failed (though he seems not to have regarded it as a failing), the test of being *open*; the requirement, that is to say, that if the theory in question governs the practice of a given group, then it must be possible for everyone in that group to know that it does. Rawls's theory, for instance, reasonably introduces, and itself passes, this test. Yet there are warnings and, I believe, finally negative lessons to be learnt from Sidgwick's theory by ethical theories in general, even those less extravagantly evasive than his.

Here we have to go back to Sidgwick's third axiom, the principle of impartiality which stated that from the point of view of the universe the good of any individual is equally valuable. Of course, Sidgwick himself, as we have already explained, immediately sets about to reverse this emphasis, as soon as we get to practice:

> . . . each one is morally bound to regard the good of any other individual as much as his own, except in so far as he judges it to be less when impartially viewed, or less certainly knowable or attainable by him. I before observed that the duty of Benevolence as recognised by common-sense seems to fall somewhat short of this. But I think it may be fairly urged in explanation of this that *practically* each man even with a view to Universal Good, ought chiefly to concern himself with promoting the good of a limited number of human beings, and that generally in proportion to the closeness of their connection with him. (p. 382)

The model is that I, as theorist, can occupy, if only temporarily and imperfectly, the point of view of the universe, and see everything from the outside, including myself and whatever moral or other dispositions, affections or projects, I may have; and from that outside view, I can assign to them a value. The difficulty is, however, as we have already seen, that the moral dispositions, and indeed other loyalties and commitments, have a certain depth or thickness: they cannot simply be regarded, least of all by their possessor, simply as devices for generating actions or states of affairs. Such dispositions and commitments will characteristically be what gives one's life some meaning, and gives one some reason for living it; they can be said, to varying degrees and variously over time, to contribute to one's practical or moral identity. There is simply no conceivable exercise that consists in stepping completely outside myself and from that point of view evaluating *in toto* the dispositions, projects and affections that constitute the substance of my own life.

It is significant that this is not just the point, analogous to an important truth in the philosophy of science, that the Cartesian stance or Archimedean fulcrum is impossible, and that one can only evaluate some beliefs on the basis of others. That is indeed true, and its analogue in moral thought, that some values are needed to evaluate other values, is also true. But *that* point has already been allowed for in Sidgwick's theory. There is one evaluative disposition that one takes to the point of view of the universe—or, perhaps one could say, finds waiting there, since it is the same for everyone. That is, simply, the disposition of impartial benevolence—or perhaps, in other versions of ethical theory, some other very general principle of impartiality. But that does not meet the real point, which lies rather in a *disanalogy* with the philosophy of science. Even though one cannot reconstruct a scientific body of belief starting totally from outside it, nevertheless it is an aim, in reconstructing it, to free one's view of the world to the maximum degree from perspectives peculiar to one's historical or local situation—to correct for observer's bias, and indeed to try to see the universe from the point of view of the universe, that is to say from no distinctive point of view at all. Some contemporary philosophers of science will say, of course, that this objective is actually impossible, but certainly it has been a basic aim of science, and if it is impossible, even as a limiting ideal, then of course so much the worse for any supposed analogy to it in ethical theory. But, whether it is possible or not, the analogy to it presents an insoluble problem to ethical theory. For, I agree with Sidgwick, such a theory must aim to be a theory for practice, and to be closely related to reasons for action. It cannot be a reasonable aim, with regard to that purpose, that I or any other particular person should take as the ideal view of the world—even if one then returns from it to one's self—a view from no point of view at all. My scientific theory, if I have one, is, as a scientific theory (as opposed to a personal achievement, or a possible means to entry to the Royal Society), only incidentally *mine*: if it is true, which is what it seems to be, then anyone else's true theory will to that extent be the same thing. But my life, my action, is quite irreducibly mine, and to require that it is at best a *derivative* conclusion that it should be lived from the perspective that happens to be mine is an extraordinary misunderstanding. Yet it is that idea that is implicitly contained in the model of the point of view of the universe.

Sidgwick rightly emphasized, as I have said, the conception of ethics as part of the theory of rational conduct. He also held that ethical theory should yield objective truths about what is ultimately valuable. That is not an aspect of his thought which I have emphasized or examined on this occasion. A full enquiry into the possibility of ethical theory, of course, would have to consider what now can be done with such a claim. But I hope that I have at any rate not begged the question against it—I have, if you like, implicitly allowed it to Sidgwick. Yet on that very showing, deep holes reveal themselves in Sidgwick's account, and an extensive indeterminacy appears in the relations that are supposed to hold between theory and practice.

The thoroughness and care of Sidgwick's work will only support the belief that this is neither a superficial feature of his outlook, nor one due only to its peculiarities. My own view is that no ethical theory can render a coherent account of its own relation to practice: it will always run into some version of the fundamental difficulty that the practice of life, and hence also an adequate theory of that practice, will require the recognition of what I have called deep dispositions; but at the same time the abstract and impersonal view that is required if the theory is to be genuinely a *theory* cannot be satisfactorily understood in relation to the depth and necessity of those dispositions. Thus the theory will remain, in one way or another, in an incoherent relation to practice. But if ethical theory is anything, then it must stand in close and explicable relation to practice, because that is the kind of theory it would have to be. It thus follows that there is no coherent ethical theory.

The fact that Sidgwick's theory so clearly and significantly fails in these respects follows, I believe, simply from the fact that it is so clear and significant an example of an attempt at an ethical theory.

NIETZSCHE

TWENTY

Nietzsche's Minimalist Moral Psychology

NIETZSCHE, WITTGENSTEIN AND THE EXTRACTION OF THEORY

Nietzsche is not a source of philosophical theories. At some level the point is obvious, but it may be less obvious how deep it goes. In this respect, there is a contrast with Wittgenstein. Wittgenstein said repeatedly, and not only in his later work, that he was not to be read as offering philosophical theory, because there could be no such thing as philosophical theory. But his work was less well prepared than Nietzsche's was to sustain that position posthumously. There is more than one reason for this.[1] Wittgenstein thought that his work demanded not only the end of philosophical theory but the end of philosophy—something associated, for him, with the end of his demands on himself to do philosophy. That association, of the end of philosophical theory with the end of philosophy, does not deny the idea that if there is to be philosophy, it will take the form of theory; indeed, it readily reinforces that idea. Moreover, the topics on which Wittgenstein wanted there to be no more philosophy— the topics, for him, of philosophy—were traditional topics of academic philosophy. It is not surprising that those who continue theoretical work on those topics still look for elements in Wittgenstein's work itself from which to construct it.

No doubt many who do this lack a suitable irony about what they do to Wittgenstein's texts, but their attitude is not in any important sense a betrayal: less so, in fact, than the attitude of those who think that Wittgenstein did bring to an end philosophical theory on those topics, and themselves sustain an academic activity that consists of reiterating that very thing. Among those who think that there is room for ongoing philosophical theory on those topics, and that Wittgenstein contributed to it, someone owes Wittgenstein an account of why he had ceased to see that this was so. But such an account might be given, and we might come to understand that if Wittgenstein could no longer see the edifice of an

---

[1] Even when we leave aside the point that there is only one work by Nietzsche (*The Will to Power*) that is not a work by Nietzsche, whereas the later works of Wittgenstein are, as whole books, very variably his.

intellectual subject, his sightlessness was not that of Samson, but rather that of Oedipus at Colonus, whose disappearance left behind healing waters.

Wittgenstein's posthumous texts, though not designed to express or encourage theory, are not actually mined against its extraction. With Nietzsche, by contrast, the resistance to the continuation of philosophy by ordinary means is built into the text, which is booby-trapped not only against recovering theory from it, but, in many cases, against any systematic exegesis that assimilates it to theory. His writing achieves this partly by its choice of subject matter, partly by its manner and the attitudes it expresses. These features stand against a mere exegesis of Nietzsche, or the incorporation of Nietzsche into the history of philosophy as a source of theories. Some think that these features stand against the incorporation of Nietzsche into philosophy as an academic enterprise altogether, but if that is meant to imply the unimportance of Nietzsche for philosophy, it must be wrong. In insisting on the importance of Nietzsche for philosophy, I mean something that cannot be evaded by a definition of 'philosophy'. In particular, it cannot be evaded by invoking some contrast between 'analytic' and 'continental' philosophy. This classification always involved a quite bizarre conflation of the methodological and the topographical, as though one classified cars into front-wheel drive and Japanese, but besides that and other absurdities of the distinction, there is the more immediate point that no such classification can evade the insistent continuities between Nietzsche's work and the business of what anyone calls philosophy. At least in moral philosophy, to ignore them is not simply to adopt a style, but to duck a problem.

I agree with a remark made by Michel Foucault in a late interview, that there is no single Nietzscheism, and that the right question to ask is 'what serious use can Nietzsche be put to?' One serious use is to help us with issues that press on any serious philosophy (in particular, moral philosophy) that does not beg the most basic of its own questions. Nietzsche will not help if he is taken to impose some one method on us. I have already said that I find his texts securely defended against exegesis by the extraction of theory; but it does not follow, and it is important that it does not follow, that when we are trying to put him to serious use our philosophy should contain no theory. This is because the insistent continuities between his questions and our business run in both directions. Some of the concerns to which he speaks are going to be better met—that is to say, met in a way in which we can better make something of them—by quite other styles of thought, and perhaps by some theory that comes from elsewhere; certainly not by theoretical, or again anti-theoretical, incantations supposedly recovered from Nietzsche himself.

NATURALISM AND REALISM IN MORAL PSYCHOLOGY

There is some measure of agreement that we need a 'naturalistic' moral psychology, where this means something to the effect that our view of moral capacities should be consistent with, even perhaps in the spirit of, our understanding of human beings as part of nature. A demand expressed in such terms is perhaps accepted by most philosophers, apart from some *anciens combattants* of the wars of freewill. The trouble with this happy and extensive consensus, however, and no doubt the condition of it, is that no-one knows what it involves. Formulations of the position tend to rule out too much or too little. The position rules out too much if it tries reductively to ignore culture and convention; this is misguided even on a scientific basis, in the sense that to live under culture is a basic part of the ethology of this species.[2] It rules out too little if it includes many things that have been part of the self-image of morality, such as certain conceptions of moral cognition; a theory will scarcely further the cause of naturalism in this sense if it accepts as a basic feature of human nature the capacity to intuit the structure of moral reality. It is tempting to say that a naturalistic moral psychology explains moral capacities in terms of psychological structures that are not distinctively moral. But so much turns on what counts as explanation here, and what it is for a psychological element to be distinctively moral, that it remains persistently unclear whether the formula should be taken to be blandly accommodating, or fiercely reductive, or something in between.

The difficulty is systematic. If a 'naturalistic' moral psychology has to characterise moral activity in a vocabulary that can be applied equally to every other part of nature, then it is committed to a physicalistic reductionism that is clearly hopeless. If it is to describe moral activity in terms that can be applied to something else, but not everything else, we have not much idea what those terms may be, or how 'special' moral activity is allowed to be, consonantly with naturalism. If we are allowed to describe moral activity in whatever terms moral activity may seem to invite, naturalism excludes nothing, and we are back at the beginning. The trouble is that the very term 'naturalism' invokes a top-down approach, under which we are supposed already to know what terms are needed to describe any 'natural' phenomenon, and we are invited to apply those terms to moral activity. But we do not know what those terms may be, unless they are (uselessly) the terms of physics, and this leads to the difficulty.

---

[2] I discuss this point at greater length in 'Making sense of humanity', in *Making Sense of Humanity and Other Philosophical Papers 1982–1993* (Cambridge: Cambridge University Press, 1995), chap. 7.

In this quandary, we can find in Nietzsche both a general attitude, and some particular suggestions, that can be a great help.[3] I shall say something later about what I take some of his suggestions to be. The general attitude has two relevant aspects, which have to be taken together. First, to the question 'how much should our accounts of distinctively moral activity add to our accounts of other human activity?' it replies 'as little as possible', and the more that some moral understanding of human beings seems to call on materials that specially serve the purposes of morality—certain conceptions of the will, for instance—the more reason we have to ask whether there may not be a more illuminating account that rests only on conceptions that we use anyway elsewhere. This demand for moral psychological minimalism is not, however, just an application of an Occamist desire for economy, and this is the second aspect of the Nietzschean general attitude. Without some guiding sense of what materials we should use in giving our economical explanations, such an attitude will simply fall back into the difficulties we have already met. Nietzsche's approach is to identify an excess of moral content in psychology by appealing first to what an experienced, honest, subtle, and unoptimistic interpreter might make of human behaviour elsewhere. Such an interpreter might be said to be—using an unashamedly evaluative expression—'realistic', and we might say that what this approach leads us towards is a realistic, rather than a naturalistic, moral psychology. What is at issue is not the application of an already defined scientific programme, but rather an informed interpretation of some human experiences and activities in relation to others.

Such an approach can indeed be said to involve, in Paul Ricoeur's well-known phrase, a 'hermeneutics of suspicion'. As such, it cannot compel demonstratively, and does not attempt to do so. It invites one into a perspective, and to some extent a tradition (one marked by such figures as Thucydides, for instance, or Stendhal, or the British psychologists of morals whom Nietzsche described as 'old frogs'), in which what seems to demand more moral material makes sense in terms of what demands less. The enterprise can work, however, only to the extent that the suspicion it summons up is not a suspicion of everything. Writers on Nietzsche typically pay most attention to his claims, or what appear to be his claims, that every belief about the relations of human beings to reality is open to suspicion, that everything is, for instance, an interpreta-

[3] It will be obvious that Nietzsche's interest is located by the present discussion mostly in terms of his more 'sceptical' works, rather than in (for instance) his ideas of self-overcoming. This is not to deny that they, too, can have their uses. In any case, there is no hope of getting anything from his redemptive aspirations without setting them against his accounts of familiar morality.

tion. Whatever may need to be said at that level, it is equally important that when he says that there are no moral phenomena, only moral inter-pretations,[4] a *special* point is being made about morality. This does not mean that we should simply forget, even in these connections, the larger claims. We need to get a deeper understanding of where these points of particular suspicion are to be found, and it may be helpful to work through larger claims on a path to getting a grasp on more limited claims. This is particularly so if we bear in mind that 'claim', for Nietzsche, is in fact rarely the right word. It is not only too weak for some things he says and too strong for others; we can usefully remember, too, (or perhaps pretend) that even when he sounds insistently or shrilly expository, he is not necessarily telling us something, but urging us to ask something.

In the rest of this chapter, I shall try to assemble some of Nietzsche's suggestions about a supposed psychological phenomenon, that of will-ing. I shall leave aside many interesting things that Nietzsche says about this concept, in particular about its history. My aim is to illustrate, through a schematic treatment of this central example, the way in which a method of suspicion—the search, one might almost say, for a culprit— can help us to achieve a reduced and more realistic moral psychology.

ILLUSIONS OF THE SELF

Speaking seriously, there are good reasons why all philosophical dog-matizing, however solemn and definitive its airs used to be, may nev-ertheless have been no more than a noble childishness and tyronism. And perhaps the time is at hand when it will be comprehended again and again *how little* used to be sufficient to furnish the cornerstone for such sublime and unconditional philosophers' edifices as the dog-matists have built so far; any old popular superstition from time im-memorial (like the soul superstition which, in the form of the subject and ego superstition, has not even yet ceased to do mischief): some play on words perhaps, a seduction by grammar, or an audacious gen-eralization of very narrow, very personal, very human, all too human facts.[5]

The general point that Nietzsche makes here (one shared with Wittgen-stein, and indeed J. L. Austin, about the extraordinary lightness of philosophical theories) is directed to a particular idea, that the ego or

---

[4] Nietzsche, *Beyond Good and Evil*, translated by Walter Kaufmann (New York, 1966), 108.

[5] *ibid.*, Preface. The reference to Lichtenberg, below, is at section 17.

self is some kind of fiction. Later in the same book he follows Lichtenberg in criticising the *cogito* as the product of grammatical habit. Elsewhere, he makes a similar point more specifically about action. He
quotes a sceptic:

> 'I do not in the least know what I am doing. I do not in the least know
> what I ought to do.' You are right, but be sure of this: *you are being
> done* [*du wirst getan*], in every moment. Mankind at all times has mis-
> taken the passive for the active: it is their constant grammatical mis-
> take.[6]

Many ideas might be drawn from this complex, some of them uninviting; for instance, that we never really do anything, that no events are actions. More interestingly, Nietzsche can be read as saying that *action* is a
serviceable category of interpretation, but a local or dispensible one; this
seems to me hardly less implausible, but some have accepted it.[7] If people perform actions, then they perform them because they think or perceive certain things, and this is enough to dispose, further, of a crude
epiphenomenalism that might be found in some of Nietzsche's sayings—
perhaps in his suggestion that all action is like willing the sun to rise
when the sun is just about to rise.

Nietzsche's doubts about action are more usefully understood, I suggest, as doubts not about the very idea of anyone's doing anything, but
rather about a morally significant interpretation of action, in terms of
the will. The belief in the will involves, for him, two ideas in particular:
that the will seems something simple when it is not; and that what seems
simple also seems to be a peculiar, imperative, kind of cause.

> Philosophers are accustomed to speak of the will as if it were the best-
> known thing in the world . . . But . . . [w]illing seems to me to be above
> all something *complicated*, something that is a unit only as a word—
> and it is precisely in this one word that the popular prejudice lurks,
> which has defeated the always inadequate caution of philosophers.[8]

---

[6] Nietzsche, *Daybreak*, translated by R. J. Hollingdale (Cambridge: Cambridge University Press, 1982), 120. The passage about the sunrise, mentioned below, is also from *Daybreak*, 124.

[7] E.g. Frithjof Bergmann, 'Nietzsche's critique of morality'. Bergmann includes 'individual agency' (along with such items as selfhood, freedom, and guilt) in a list of concepts al-
legedly special to our morality; he takes himself (wrongly, I think) to be following Clifford
Geertz in the claim that it was not known in traditional Bali. Similar errors have been
made about the outlook of Homeric Greece: see below, note 10. The idea that *action*, in
our ordinary understanding of it, is a dispensable and indeed mistaken conception is shared
by a very different kind of philosophy, eliminative materialism; in that case for scientistic
reasons.

[8] Nietzsche, *Beyond Good and Evil*, 19. The whole section is relevant.

He goes on to explain that what is called 'willing' is a complex of sensations, thinking, and an affect of command. He points to the consequences of our being both the commanding and the obeying party, and of our 'disregarding this duality'.

> Since in the great majority of cases there has been an exercise of will only when the effect of the command—that is, obedience; that is, the action—was to be *expected*, the appearance has translated itself into the feeling, as if there were a *necessity of effect*. In short, he who wills believes with a fair amount of certainty that will and action are somehow one; he ascribes the success, the carrying out of the willing, to the will itself, and thereby enjoys an increase of the sensation of power that accompanies all success.

What exactly is the illusion that Nietzsche claims to expose here? It is not the idea that a certain experience is a sufficient cause of an action. He does indeed think that the experiences involved in 'willing' do not reveal, and may conceal, the shifting complex of psychological and physiological forces that lies behind any action, the constant, unknown, craving movements that make us, as he puts it, a kind of polyp.[9] But it is not that the experience sets itself up as the cause. Rather, the experience seems to reveal a different kind of cause, and suggests that the cause does not lie in any event or state of affairs—whether an experience of mine or otherwise—but in something that I refer to as 'I'. Such a cause seems to be related to the outcome only in the mode of prescription, through an imperative; and since this stands in no relation to any causal set of events, it can seem to bring about its outcome *ex nihilo*.

Of course, any sensible theory of action, which allows that there is indeed action, and that thoughts are not merely epiphenomenal in relation to it, will have to allow that my consciousness of acting is not the same as a consciousness that a state of mine causes a certain outcome. This follows merely from the point that the first-personal consciousness which one has when involved in action cannot at the same time be a third-personal consciousness of that very involvement. But the first-personal consciousness which an agent necessarily has does not in itself have to lead to the kind of picture that Nietzsche attacks; action does not necessarily involve this understanding of itself.[10] The picture is a special

---

[9] Nietzsche, *Daybreak*, 119.

[10] This is clearly illustrated by the treatment accorded by some scholars to the Homeric conception of action; not finding in Homer this picture of action, they have thought that the archaic Greeks either had no idea of action, or had an imperfect one, lacking the concept of the will. I discuss this and related misconceptions in *Shame and Necessity*: see in particular chapter 2.

one, particularly associated with a notion such as 'willing', and when it is present, it is not merely a philosophical theory of action, but can accompany many of our thoughts and moral reactions. So where does it come from, and what does it do?

Part of Nietzsche's own explanation is to be found in the course of one of his most famous passages:

> For just as the popular mind separates the lightning from its flash, and takes the latter for an *action*, for the operation of a subject called lightning, so popular morality also separates strength from expressions of strength, as if there were a neutral substratum behind the strong man, which was *free* to express strength or not to do so. But there is no such substratum; there is no 'being' behind doing, effecting, becoming; 'the doer' is merely a fiction added to the deed—the deed is everything. The popular mind in fact doubles the deed; when it sees the lightning flash, it is the deed of a deed: it posits the same event first as cause and then a second time as its effect.[11]

There are two helpful ideas in this account. One is that the picture under attack involves a kind of double counting. The self or I that is the cause is ingenuously introduced as the cause *of an action*. If my agent-self produces only a set of events, it may seem that I shall not have enough for my involvement in the action: I shall be at best the 'pilot in a ship' to which Descartes referred. The doubling of action also follows from the idea that the mode of causation is that of command. Obedience to a command consists of an action; but commanding is itself an action. The self can act (at one time rather than another, now rather than earlier) only by doing something—the thing it does, willing; but, for more than one reason, what it brings about in this way seems itself to be an action. In making action into something that introduces an agent-cause, the account has a powerful tendency to produce two actions.

The second helpful thought to be recovered from Nietzsche is that such a peculiar account must have a purpose, and that the purpose is a moral one.

The Target of Blame

The purpose of the account can be read from the way in which it associates two ideas, which contribute to its incoherence and together com-

---

[11] Nietzsche, *The Genealogy of Morals*, translated by Walter Kaufmann and R. J. Hollingdale (New York, 1967), First Essay, section 13.

pound it. One idea is that there is a metaphysically special unit, a real action, unlike anything else that can be individuated among the world's processes. The other is that this stands in an unmediated relationship—something like being an effect *ex nihilo*—to something of quite a different kind, again unique—a person, or self, or agent. There is an idea that needs items standing in just such a relation: it is a certain purified conception of blame.

Blame needs an occasion—an action—and a target—the person who did the action and who goes on from the action to meet the blame. That is its nature; as one might say, its conceptual form. In the real world, it does not need these things in the pure and isolated form implied by the account of the will. The Homeric Greeks blamed people for doing things, and whatever exactly went into their doing so, it was not all this. Rather, this version of the occasion and the target will be demanded by a very purified conception of blame, a conception seemingly demanded by moral justice. It is important that the mere idea of just compensation does not make this demand, nor every idea of responsibility. If A has been damaged by B's careless action, B may be held responsible for the loss and reasonably required to compensate A, though the loss to A formed no part of what B willed. A very exact concentration on B's will, and the purely focussed conception of blame that goes with it, are demanded not merely by responsibility or demands in justice for compensation, but by something more specific.

It is not hard to find an explanation of the more specific demand. It lies in the seeming requirement of justice that the agent should be blamed for no more and no less than what was in his power. What the agent brought about (and for which, in the usual order of things, he may be asked to provide compensation) may very well be a matter of luck, but what he may be strictly (as these conceptions say, 'morally') blamed for cannot be a matter of luck, and must depend in a strict and isolable sense on his will. It is appropriately said that what depends on his will is what is strictly *in his power*: it is with regard to what he wills that the agent himself has the sense of power in action to which Nietzsche refers. As agents, and also as blamers under justice, we have an interest in this picture.

The needs, demands, and invitations of the morality system are enough to explain the peculiar psychology of the will. But there is more that needs to be said about the basis of that system itself. Nietzsche himself famously suggested that a specific source for it was to be found in the sentiment of ressentiment—a sentiment which itself had a historical origin, though hardly one that he locates very precisely. I shall not pick up the historical aspect, but I think it is worth suggesting a brief speculation about the phenomenology of focussed blame, which is a close enough relation to Nietzsche's 'genealogy', perhaps, to be a version of it.[12]

If there is a victim with a complaint for a loss, there is an agent who is to blame, and an act of that agent which brought about the loss. The anger of the victim travels from the loss to the act to the agent; and compensation or recompense given by the agent will acknowledge both the loss and the fact that he was the cause of the loss. Suppose the agent brings about a harm to the victim, and does so intentionally and voluntarily; where 'intentionally and voluntarily' is not supposed to invoke the special mechanisms of the will, but merely means that the agent knew what he was doing, wanted to do it, and was in a normal state of mind when he did it. Suppose that the agent is not disposed to give compensation or reparation, and that the victim has no power to extract any such thing from him. In refusing reparation, the agent refuses to acknowledge the victim or his loss; it is a peculiarly vivid demonstration of the victim's powerlessness.

These circumstances can give rise, in the victim or in someone else on behalf of the victim, to a very special fantasy of retrospective prevention. As victim, I have a fantasy of inserting into the agent an acknowledgement of me, to take the place of exactly the act that harmed me. I want to think that he might have acknowledged me, that he might have been prevented from harming me. But the idea cannot be that I might in some empirical way have prevented him: that idea presents only a regret that it was not actually so and, in these circumstances, a reminder of humiliation. The idea has to be, rather, that I, now, might change the agent from one who did not acknowledge me to one who did. This fantasied, magical, change does not involve actually changing anything, and it therefore has nothing to do with what, if anything, might actually have changed things. It requires simply the idea of the agent at the moment of the

---

[12] A Nietzschean genealogy typically combines, in a way that analytical philosophy finds embarrassing, history, phenomenology, 'realistic' psychology, and conceptual interpretation. The historical stories, moreover, strikingly vary from one context to another. Some of Nietzsche's procedures are to be seen specifically in the light of Hegel's *Phenomenology*, and of his recurrent amazement that there could have been such a thing as Christianity. Some are certainly less helpful than others. But the mere idea that we need such elements to work together is surely right. We need to understand what parts of our conceptual scheme are, in what degree, culturally local. We understand this best when we understand an actual human scheme that differs from ours in certain respects. One, very important, way of locating such a scheme is finding it in history, in particular in the history of our own scheme. In order to understand that other scheme, and to understand why there should be this difference between those people and ourselves, we need to understand it as a human scheme; this is to understand the differences in terms of similarities, which calls on psychological interpretation. Very roughly speaking indeed, a Nietzschean genealogy can be seen now as starting from Davidson plus history.

action, of the action that harmed me, and of the refusal of that action, all isolated from the network of circumstances in which his action was actually embedded. It involves precisely the picture of the will that has already been uncovered.

Much can grow from this basic feeling. It lays the foundation for the purest and simplest construction of punishment, and it is very significant how the language of retribution naturally deploys teleological notions of conversion, education, or improvement ('teaching him a lesson', 'showing him') while insisting at the same time that its gaze is entirely retrospective and that, inasmuch as it is purely retributive, it does not look to actual reform.[13] But the construction is at least as much at work when it is not a question of any actual punishment, but only of the purely moral conceptions of guilt and blame, and it then involves a further abstraction; it introduces not only retribution's idea of retrospective causation, but morality's idea of an authoritative but sanctionless law, of a judgement that carries no power besides that judgement itself.

CONCLUSION

This is, of course, only a sketch of a possible account, drawn (fairly directly) from Nietzschean materials. The most important feature of it, for the present purpose, is its structure. We start with a supposed psychological phenomenon, willing, associated with the conception of the self in action. The phenomenon seems recognizable in experience, and it seems also to have a certain authority. Its description already presents difficulties and obscurities, but proposals merely to explain it away or to ignore it seem typically to have ignored something important, even to leave out the essence of action. Reminded both that different pictures of action have been held in other cultures and that the notion of action itself is less than transparent, we can be helped to see that the integrity of action, the agent's genuine presence in it, can be preserved without this picture of the will—indeed, can only be preserved without it. The process by which we can come to see this may be complex and painful enough for us to feel, not just that we have learned a truth, but that we have been relieved of a burden.

Since the picture is neither coherent nor universal, yet has this authority, we need to ask where it comes from and what it does. It is not itself

---

[13] A particularly illuminating example is Robert Nozick's discussion of retributive punishment in *Philosophical Explanations* (Oxford: Oxford University Press, 1984), 363ff. His heroic attempt to express what pure retribution tries to *achieve* (as opposed to what, in actual fact, it does) reveals, it seems to me, that there is no logical space for it to succeed.

manifestly tied to morality, offering rather a picture of voluntary action in general, but there is a moral phenomenon, a certain conception of blame, which it directly fits. This conception, again, is not universal, but is rather part of a special complex of ethical ideas which has other, and related, peculiar features. The fit between the special psychological conception and the demands of morality enables us to see that this piece of psychology is itself a moral conception, and one that shares notably doubtful features of that particular morality itself. In addition to this, we may be able to supply some further psychological conceptions which help us to understand the motivations of this particular form of the ethical. Those conceptions, as presented by Nietzsche under the name of ressentiment, certainly lead out of the ethical altogether, into the categories of anger and power, and it cannot be a matter simply for philosophy to decide how much those categories will explain. Other explanations may be needed, and it may be that they will prove to be more basically linked to notions of fairness, for instance. But in laying such explanations against one another, and in diagnosing the psychology of willing as a demand of the morality system itself, we shall be following a distinctively Nietzschean route towards the naturalisation of moral psychology.

TWENTY-ONE

Introduction to *The Gay Science*

The Gay Science is a remarkable book, both in itself and as offering a way into some of Nietzsche's most important ideas. The history of its publication is rather complex, and it throws some light on the development of his thought and of his methods as a writer. He published the first edition of it in 1882. In that version, it consisted of only four books, and had no Preface, though it did have the 'Prelude in Rhymes'. A second edition appeared in 1887, which added a fifth book, the Preface, and an Appendix of further poems. This is the work as we now know it, and which is translated here.

Between the two editions of *The Gay Science*, Nietzsche wrote two of his best-known works, *Thus Spoke Zarathustra* (1883–5) and *Beyond Good and Evil* (1886); the last section of Book Four of *The Gay Science* (342)[1] is indeed virtually the same as the first section of *Zarathustra*. So the complete *Gay Science* brackets these two books, which are different from it and from each other. (*Zarathustra*, which is a peculiar literary experiment in a rhetoric drawn from the Bible, was once one of Nietzsche's most popular works, but it has worn less well than the others.) Book Five of *The Gay Science* anticipates, in turn, some of the themes of another famous book which was to follow in 1887, *On the Genealogy of Morality*, which is again different in tone, sustaining a more continuous theoretical argument.

The Gay Science is a prime example of what is often called Nietzsche's 'aphoristic' style. It consists of a sequence of sections which are not obviously tied to one another except, sometimes, in general content, and which do not offer a connected argument. The second half of Book Three, in particular, consists of many very short paragraphs of this kind. Elsewhere, however, there are longer passages, and in fact the arrangement of the shorter sections is not as fortuitous as it may look. It is often designed to gather thoughts which will, so to speak, circle in on some central theme or problem.

In his earlier works, Nietzsche had moved gradually towards this style. He had been appointed in 1869 as a professor of classical philol-

---

[1] References to *The Gay Science*, and to other works by Nietzsche, are to numbered sections.

ogy at the University of Basle, at the extraordinarily early age of twenty-four. He served in this position for ten years, resigning in 1879 because of the ill health which was to persist throughout his life. (The last letter he wrote, when in 1889 he broke down into insanity and a silence which lasted until his death in 1900, was to his distinguished colleague at Basle, Jacob Burckhardt, in which he said that he would rather have been a Swiss professor than God, but he had not dared to push egoism so far.) In his years at Basle he published first *The Birth of Tragedy*, which has the form, if not the content or the tone, of a treatise, and a set of four long essays collected as *Untimely Meditations*. In 1878–9 he brought out two books forming *Human, All Too Human*, followed in 1880 by a further part called 'The Wanderer and his Shadow', and in these writings he moved from continuous exposition and argument to setting out a sequence of thoughts which were not necessarily tied discursively to their neighbours, a style that allowed him to approach a question from many different directions. In *Daybreak*, which came out in 1881, the style is fully developed. As late as 25 January 1882 he still referred to what were to be the first books of *The Gay Science* as a continuation of *Daybreak*; by June they had acquired their separate title.

When he made that decision, he sensed that Book Four, which is called 'Sanctus Januarius' and invokes the spirit of the New Year, might be found obscure, and he was anxious about whether his correspondent, Peter Gast, would understand it. He knew that this was not just a set of penetrating, perhaps rather cynical, *aperçus*. 'Aphorism', the standard term which I have already mentioned, implies too strongly that each is supposed to be a squib, or a compact expression of a truth (often in the form of an exaggerated falsehood) in the style of the French writers La Rochefoucault and Chamfort, whom Nietzsche indeed admired, but whom he did not simply follow in giving a self-conscious exposé of some human failing, foible or piece of self-deception. There is a certain amount of that, particularly in the earlier books, but he was very aware of the risk that such aphorisms run of sliding from the daring through the knowing to the self-satisfied (it is not merely cynicism that he intends when he says in 379 that 'we are artists of contempt'). His ambitions are deeper; the effect is meant to be cumulative, and its aim is more systematically subversive. A philosopher who had a similar intention, though in totally different connections, is the later Wittgenstein, and Nietzsche might have called the sections of this book, as Wittgenstein called the paragraphs of his manuscripts, 'remarks'.

His remarks cover very various subjects. Many of them touch on what may be called moral psychology, and sometimes he does claim to detect an egoistic origin of some ethically approved reaction (as he does, for example, in the shrewd observation about magnanimity and revenge at section 49). The search for the 'shameful origin' of our moral sentiments was later to become an important principle of his genealogical method. But he is very clear that mere reductionism, the readily cynical explanation of all such attitudes in terms of self-interest, is a mistake. Partly this is because he does not think that self-interest is an individual's basic motive anyway, and this book contains some quite complex, if unresolved, reflections on that question, in particular when he considers whether the virtues have a value for the individual who possesses them, or for the group. But, more broadly, Nietzsche thinks that the reductive spirit itself can be in error, a form of vulgarity (3), and that the 'realists' who congratulate themselves on having the measure of human unreason and self-deception are usually themselves in the grip of some ancient fantasy (57).

Above all, it is simply not enough, in Nietzsche's view, to 'unmask' some supposedly honourable sentiment or opinion and leave it at that. 'Only as creators can we destroy', he very significantly says (58). What things are *called* is fundamentally important, but a conventional set of names—as we may say, an interpretation—can be replaced only by another, more powerful, interpretation. When we say that one interpretation is more powerful than another, it is vitally important what counts as 'power'. It is often said that Nietzsche explains everything in terms of power. This says something about the way in which he saw these problems, but it is wrong if it is supposed to state his solution to it. The point is very clear in *On the Genealogy of Morality*. There he tells a story of how a certain outlook or interpretation, embodying metaphysical illusions, came into existence as a psychological compensation for the weakness of people who were powerless, and how this outlook triumphed over the conventionally strong and their view of the world. The question must be, how could this have come about? What was the source of this new power? There had to be *something to* this new way of describing the world which accounted in naturalistic terms for its triumph, and Nietzsche fully accepts this, even if he does not have a very rich vocabulary of social explanation in which he can discuss what it might be. 'Let us . . . not forget', he goes on in section 58 of *The Gay Science*, 'that in the long run it is enough to create new names and valuations and appearances of truth in order to create new "things"'. Indeed, but this immediately raises the question, one to which Nietzsche returned in many different connections: what must someone do to 'create' new names?

The words 'The Gay Science' translate the German title 'Die Fröhliche Wissenschaft'. No one, presumably, is going to be misled by the more recent associations of the word 'gay'—it simply means joyful, light-hearted, and above all, lacking in solemnity (section 327, on taking things seriously, says something about this). 'Science' has its own difficulties. The word 'Wissenschaft', unlike the English word 'science' in its modern use, does not mean simply the natural and biological sciences—they are, more specifically, 'Naturwissenschaft'. It means any organized study or body of knowledge, including history, philology, criticism and generally what we call 'the humanities', and that is often what Nietzsche has in mind when he uses the word in the text (it is often translated as 'science', for want of a brief alternative). But in the title itself there is an idea still broader than this. It translates a phrase, 'gai saber', or, as Nietzsche writes on his title page, 'gaya scienza', which referred to the art of song cultivated by the medieval troubadours of Provence, and with that, as he explains in *Beyond Good and Evil* (260), it invokes an aristocratic culture of courtly love. As he made clear, this association comes out in the fact that the book contains poems. But the title has other implications as well. One—particularly important to understanding this book and Nietzsche more generally—is that, just as the troubadours possessed not so much a body of information as an art, so Nietzsche's 'gay science' does not in the first place consist of a doctrine, a theory or body of knowledge. While it involves and encourages hard and rigorous thought, and to this extent the standard implications of 'Wissenschaft' are in place, it is meant to convey a certain spirit, one that in relation to understanding and criticism could defy the 'spirit of gravity' as lightly as the troubadours, supposedly, celebrated their loves. This is why the original publisher could announce at the beginning of the book that it brought to a conclusion a series of Nietzsche's writings (including *Human, All Too Human* and *Daybreak*) which shared the aim of setting out 'a new image and ideal of the free spirit'.

He said that it was the most personal of his books, meaning that in part it was explicitly about his own life: some of it is like a diary. It is not irrelevant that the 'gai saber' belonged to the south of Europe, to the Mediterranean. Nietzsche spent much of his time in the last years of his working life in Italy (in places such as those he praises in sections 281 and 291), and he was very conscious of the contrast between overcast German earnestness and Southern sun and freedom, an idea which had a long literary history and had been most famously expressed, perhaps, in Goethe's *Italian Journey*. That is a recurrent contrast in *The Gay Science*, but, as so often with Nietzsche, it is not one contrast, and his reflections on the German spirit in philosophy and religion are specially nuanced in this book, for instance in his discussion (357) of 'What is German?'

Nietzsche's general reflections, here as elsewhere, have some recurrent weaknesses. There are cranky reflections on diet and climate. His opinions about women and sex, even if they include (as at 71) one or two shrewd and compassionate insights into the conventions of his time, are often shallow and sometimes embarrassing; they were, biographically, the product of an experience which had been drastically limited and disappointing. However, what is most significant for his thought as a whole is the fact that his resources for thinking about modern society and politics, in particular about the modern state, were very thin. The point is not that he was opposed to a free society, equal rights, and other typically modern aspirations (though he certainly was, as section 377, for instance, makes clear). In fact, Nietzsche has by no means been a hero exclusively of the political Right, and many radical, socialist and even feminist groups in the last century found support in his writings.[2] This was possible just because the deeply radical spirit of his work was combined with a lack of effective political and social ideas, leaving a blank on which many different aspirations could be projected. His clearly aristocratic sympathies are, in political connections, not so much reactionary as archaic, and while he has many illuminating things to say about the religious and cultural history of Europe, his conception of social relations owes more to his understanding of the ancient world than to a grasp of modernity. The idea of nihilism which is so important in his later works is undeniably relevant to modern conditions, but his discussions of such subjects as 'corruption' (in section 23 of this book) borrow a lot from the rhetoric of the Roman Empire and the disposition of its writers to praise the largely imaginary virtues of the vanished Republic.

The Gay Science marks a decisive step beyond the books that came before it because it introduces two of what were to become Nietzsche's best-known themes, the Death of God and the Eternal Recurrence. The idea that God is dead occurs first at 108, in association with the image of the Buddha's shadow, still to be seen in a cave for centuries after his death. This is followed at 125 by the haunting story of a madman with a lantern in the bright morning, looking for God. He is met by ridicule, and he concludes that he has 'come too early', that the news of God's death has not yet reached humanity, even though they have killed him themselves. This idea recurs in more literal terms in 343, the first section of Book Five (published, we may recall, five years later). The death of God is identified there as the fact that 'the belief in . . . God has become unbelievable': this, 'the greatest recent event', is beginning to cast its shadow across Europe. Once this event is fully recognized, it will have

---

[2] A very interesting study in this connection is Steven E. Ascheim, *The Nietzsche Legacy in Germany 1890–1990* (Berkeley: University of California Press, 1992). A helpful discussion of Nietzsche's political thought is Bruce Detwiler, *Nietzsche and the Politics of Aristocratic Radicalism* (University of Chicago Press, 1990). Mark Warren, in *Nietzsche and Political Thought* (Boston: MIT Press, 1988), well brings out the limitations of Nietzsche's social ideas, but is over-optimistic in thinking that if his philosophy were true to itself, it would offer a basis for liberalism.

incalculable consequences, in particular for European morality. Some of these consequences will be melancholy, and indeed elsewhere Nietzsche struggles with the question of what act of creation, by whom, might overcome the emptiness left by the collapse of traditional illusions. But here the news brings, at least in the short term, only joy, a sense of daybreak and freedom, the promise of an open sea: 'maybe there has never been such an "open sea" '.

Nietzsche continued to think that the death of God would have vast and catastrophic consequences. But on the account that he himself gave of Christian belief and its origins (in this book and in *Beyond Good and Evil*, but above all in *On the Genealogy of Morality*), should he really have thought this? He believed that the faith in the Christian God, and more generally in a reassuring metaphysical structure of the world, was a projection of fear and resentment, representing a victory of the weak over the strong. That metaphysical belief has died; it has been destroyed, as Nietzsche often points out, by itself, by the belief in truthfulness—and we shall come back to that—which was itself part of the metaphysical faith. But how much difference should he expect its death to make? He shares with another nineteenth-century subverter, Marx (with whom he shares little else), the idea that religious belief is a consequence, an expression of social and psychological forces. If those forces remain, and the Christian expression of them collapses, then surely other expressions will take its place. If need secretes thought, and the need remains, then it will secrete new thoughts.

Indeed, Nietzsche does think this: he thinks that liberalism, socialism, Utilitarianism and so on are just secularized expressions of those same forces. But he thinks that they are too manifestly close to the original, and that our growing understanding that the world has no metaphysical structure whatsoever must discredit them as well. The death of God is the death of those gods, too. He has a particular contempt for benign freethinkers who hope to keep all the ethical content of Christianity without its theology: George Eliot is the unlucky target when the point is spelled out very clearly in *The Twilight of the Idols* (the section called 'Expeditions of an Untimely Man'). But that is not the most important point. Even if the content of our morality changes noticeably, as for instance attitudes towards sex have done in recent times, much more basic and structural elements of it, its humanitarianism and its professed belief in equal respect for everyone, are in Nietzsche's view too bound up with the mechanisms that generated Christianity, and will inevitably go the same way that it has gone. It is too soon, surely, to say that he was wrong.

For Nietzsche himself there was another dimension as well, one immediately connected with his own values. He saw the unravelling of Christianity as part of the phenomenon that he called European nihilism, the loss of any sense of depth or significance to life. The world might conceivably avoid destruction and overt hatred by organizing a pleasantly undemanding and unreflective way of life, a dazed but adequately efficient consumerism. Nietzsche probably did not think that such a society could survive in the long run, but in any case he could not reconcile himself to such a prospect or regard it as anything but loathsome. Contempt was one of his readier emotions, and nothing elicited it more than what he sometimes calls 'the last man', the contented, unadventurous, philistine product of such a culture. This book, like all his others, makes it clear that any life worth living must involve daring, individuality and creative bloody-mindedness. This is indeed expressed in the 'gaiety' of its title. Gaiety can encompass contentment, as it does on New Year's Day at the beginning of Book Four, but when that is so, it is a particular achievement and a piece of good luck. Gaiety is not itself contentment, and while it rejects solemnity and the spirit of gravity, it does so precisely because it is the only way of taking life seriously.

Nietzsche has been thought by some people to have had a brutal and ruthless attitude to the world; sometimes, perhaps, he wished that he had. But in fact, one personal feature which, together with his illness and his loneliness, contributed to his outlook was a hyper-sensitivity to suffering. It was linked to a total refusal to forget, not only the existence of suffering, but the fact that suffering was necessary to everything that he and anyone else valued. 'All good things come from bad things' is one of his fundamental tenets: it signals his rejection of what he calls 'the fundamental belief of the metaphysicians, *the belief in the opposition of values*' (*Beyond Good and Evil*, 2). This is, for him, a principle of interpretation, but it presents itself in the first instance simply as a fact, which he thought no honest understanding of the world could evade. If a sense of the world's achievements and glories—art, self-understanding, nobility of character—cannot in common honesty be separated from the knowledge of the horrors that have been involved in bringing these things about, then there is a question that cannot, Nietzsche supposed, simply be ignored: whether it has all been worth it.

Thinkers in the past have supposed that the question could be answered, and answered positively. Leibniz, with his famous doctrine that this is the best of all possible worlds, believed in a cosmic cost-benefit analysis which would vindicate God's mysterious management. Hegel had told a progressive metaphysical story of the historical development of freedom and reason, which represented the horrors as all dialectically necessary to the eventual outcome, so that we could be sure that none of them was meaningless. Neither of these fantasies, Nietzsche reasonably thought, could be taken seriously in the late 19th century. Nor, he came to think, could one take altogether seriously someone who answered the same question, but in the negative. In his earlier years he had been very impressed, as Wagner was, by the philosophy of Schopenhauer, and his references to Schopenhauer in this book are mostly respectful (more so than those to Wagner), but he came to be very sceptical about Schopenhauer's so-called pessimism, which had been expressed in the judgement (for instance) that the world's 'non-existence would be preferable to its existence'.[3] 'We take care not to say that the world is worth *less*', he says at 346:

> The whole attitude of man . . . as judge of the world who finally places existence itself on his scales and finds it too light—the monstrous stupidity of this attitude has finally dawned on us and we are sick of it.

Nietzsche recognizes that his own *Birth of Tragedy* had been full of the Schopenhauerian spirit. Taken in that spirit, the question of 'the value of life', he came to think, had no answer and was indeed not a question. Yet it did not simply go away, because there remained what seemed to Nietzsche, at least, to be a fact, that anyone who really understood and held in his mind the horrors of the world would be crushed or choked by them. That fact left, if not a question to be answered, at least a problem to be overcome. Nietzsche presents the problem, and his way of overcoming it, in the form of the thought-experiment of the Eternal Recurrence, which appears for the first time in *The Gay Science*.[4] In the startling words of 341, what would you think if a demon told you that everything in life would recur over and over again eternally? How would you answer the question 'Do you want this again and innumerable times again?'? This question, Nietzsche says, 'would lie on your actions as the heaviest weight'. It tests your ability not to be overcome by the world's horror and meaninglessness. There is no *belief* which could 'justify the world': confronted with the question of its value, or rather with the replacement for that question, which is the prospect of being crushed by the consciousness of what the world is like, the only issue is (as Nietzsche also puts it) whether one can say 'yes' to it, and the test of that is whether seriously and in the fullest consciousness you could will that the course of everything should happen over and over again, including not just its pain and cruelty and humiliation, but also its triviality, emptiness and ugliness, the last man and everything that goes with him.

[3] *The World as Will and Representation*, trans. E.F.J. Payne (2 vols., New York: Dover, 1969), vol. II, chapter 46, p. 576.

[4] The *phrase* 'eternal recurrence' occurs first at 285, but in a more limited connection, of recognizing that there is no perpetual peace, but only (as the pre-Socratic philosopher Heraclitus taught) a cycle of war and peace.

This is an entirely hypothetical question, a thought-experiment. It is not a matter, as I read him, of Nietzsche's believing in a *theory* of eternal recurrence. The idea (which does not occur in *Beyond Good and Evil* or *The Genealogy of Morality*) appears in *Zarathustra* in a form similar to that of *The Gay Science*, and Nietzsche mentions its importance in *The Twilight of the Idols* and in *Ecce Homo* (the intellectual autobiography that he wrote on the verge of insanity). There are some places in which it is treated as a theoretical idea, but they are largely confined to his unpublished notes (his *Nachlass*), some of which, particularly from his last years, were published in *The Will to Power*, which is not a book by Nietzsche at all, but a selection from these notes tendentiously put together by his sister.

But if the idea of the Eternal Recurrence is a thought-experiment, how can answering its question lie on our actions 'as the heaviest weight'? If it is a mere fantasy, then how can 'willing' the Eternal Recurrence cost one anything at all? It seems as simple as saying 'yes'. But one has to recall that in facing the question one is supposed to have a real and live consciousness of everything that has led to this moment, in particular to what we value. We would have to think in vivid detail, if we could, of every dreadful happening that has been necessary to create Venice, or Newton's science, or whatever one thinks best of in our morality. Then we would have not simply to say 'yes', but to say 'yes' and mean it. That does not seem exactly weightless. What perhaps does less work in the thought-experiment is the element, which Nietzsche certainly thought essential to it, of *eternity*. If there is anything in this test at all, why would willing one recurrence not be enough? If you could overcome the 'nausea', as Zarathustra repeatedly puts it, of the prospect that the horrors and the last man and all the rest will come round again *even once*, and say 'yes' to it, you would have taken the essential step: could willing all those further recurrences cost you very much more?

There is another, very natural, reaction to the problem, which is almost everyone's reaction: to forget about it. One can forget that the horrors exist, and also, if one has a taste for metaphysical consolations, that God is dead. The narrator of Scott Fitzgerald's *The Great Gatsby* says of Tom and Daisy that they 'retreated back into their money and their vast carelessness, or whatever it was that held them together', and that is, roughly speaking, the remedy that the 'last man' finds for Nietzsche's problem. David Hume spoke of 'carelessness and inattention' as the only remedy for sceptical doubts; but that is not the same, because Hume thought that sceptical doubts were *unreal*. Nietzsche knew that the considerations we all forget were not unreal, and he held obstinately to an idea of truthfulness that would not allow us to falsify them. In this book, he calls on honesty and intellectual conscience at 319 and (as we shall see) at 344; at 284 he speaks of those who have to have an argument against the sceptic inside themselves—'the great self-dissatisfied people'. In *The Anti-Christ* (50), at the very end of his active life, he wrote:

> Truth has had to be fought for every step of the way, almost everything else dear to our hearts, on which our love and our trust in life depend, has had to be sacrificed to it. Greatness of soul is needed for it, the service of truth is the hardest service.—For what does it mean to be *honest* in intellectual things? That one is stern towards one's heart, that one despises 'fine feelings', that one makes every Yes and No a question of conscience!

The value of truthfulness embraces the need to find out the truth, to hold on to it, and to tell it—in particular, to oneself. But Nietzsche's own dedication to this value, he saw, immediately raised the question of what this value is. We have taken it for granted, he thinks, and we have seriously misunderstood it: as he says in *Beyond Good and Evil* (177), 'Perhaps nobody yet has been truthful enough about what "truthfulness" is.'

Section 344 of *The Gay Science* (the second section of Book Five) gives one of Nietzsche's most important and illuminating statements of this question:

> This unconditional will to truth—what is it? Is it the will not to let oneself be deceived? Is it the will *not to deceive*? For the will to truth could be interpreted in this second way, too—if 'I do not want to deceive *myself*' is included as a special case under the generalization 'I do not want to deceive'. But why not deceive? But why not allow oneself to be deceived?

The reasons for not wanting to be deceived, he goes on to say, are prudential; seen in that light, wanting to get things right in our intellectual studies and in practical life will be a matter of utility. But those considerations cannot possibly sustain an *unconditional* value for truth: much of the time it is more useful to believe falsehoods. Our belief in the unconditional will to truth

> must have originated *in spite of* the fact that the disutility and dangerousness of 'the will to truth' or 'truth at any price' is proved to it constantly. 'At any price': we understand this well enough once we have offered and slaughtered one faith after another on this altar! Consequently, 'will to truth' does *not* mean 'I do not want to let myself be deceived' but—there is no alternative—'I will not deceive, not even myself'; *and with that we stand on moral ground.*
> . . . you will have gathered what I am getting at, namely, that it is still a *metaphysical faith* upon which our faith in science rests—that

even we knowers of today, we godless anti-metaphysicians, still take *our* fire, too, from the flame lit by the thousand-year-old faith, the Christian faith which was also Plato's faith, that God is truth; that truth is divine . . .

The title of the section is 'In what way we, too, are still pious'. The idea is developed further in Book III of *On the Genealogy of Morality*, where the 'ascetic ideal' which has received an unflattering genealogical explanation is discovered to lie at the root of the will to truth, which powered the need to discover that very explanation. But that does not overthrow the will to truth: 'I have every respect for the ascetic ideal *in so far as it is honest!*' (III. 26).

The 'unconditional will to truth' does not mean that we want to believe any and every truth. It does mean that we want to understand who we are, to correct error, to avoid deceiving ourselves, to get beyond comfortable falsehood. The value of truthfulness, so understood, cannot lie just in its consequences, as Nietzsche repeatedly points out. Earlier in this book (121), he says that various beliefs may be necessary for our life, but that does not show them to be true: 'life is not an argument'. Already in *Human, All Too Human* (517) he had noted: *Fundamental Insight*: There is no pre-established harmony between the furthering of truth and the well-being of humanity.' Again, in *Beyond Good and Evil* (II) he says that we must understand that there are some judgements which 'must be *believed* to be true, for the sake of preservation of creatures like ourselves, though they might, of course, be false judgements for all that'.

Truth may be not just unhelpful, but destructive. In particular the truths of Nietzsche's own philosophy, which discredit the metaphysical world, can (as we have seen) destructively lead to nihilism if they come to be accepted. In the *Nachlass* (*The Will to Power* 5) there is a revealing note, which mentions the way in which the idea of truthfulness has turned against the morality which fostered it, and ends with the remark:

This antagonism—not to esteem what we know, and not to be *allowed* any longer to esteem the lies we should like to tell ourselves—results in a process of dissolution.

In what ways are we 'not allowed' to esteem these lies? To some degree, Nietzsche thought that this was already in his time a historical or social necessity: that, at least among thoughtful people, these beliefs simply could not stand up much longer or have much life to them. It is a good question whether this was right, indeed whether it is right today—particularly when we recall the secularized, political, forms which are now taken, as Nietzsche supposed, by the same illusions. What is certainly true is that Nietzsche took it to be an *ethical* necessity, for himself and anyone he was disposed to respect, not to esteem these illusions. He did think that there were things which, even for honest and reflective people, could rightly compensate in some ways for the loss of the illusions; it is in this spirit that he remarks elsewhere in the *Nachlass* (*The Will to Power* 822) 'We possess *art* lest *we perish of the truth.*' He does not mean that we possess art in place of the truth; he means that we possess art so that we can possess the truth and not perish of it.

There continue to be complex debates about what Nietzsche understood truth to be. Quite certainly, he did not think, in pragmatist spirit, that beliefs are true if they serve our interests or welfare: we have already seen some of his repeated denials of this idea. A more recently fashionable view of him is that he shared, perhaps founded, a kind of deconstructive scepticism to the effect that there is no such thing as truth, or that truth is what anyone thinks it is, or that it is a boring category that we can do without. This is also wrong, and more deeply so. As we have seen, Nietzsche did not think that the ideal of truthfulness went into retirement when its metaphysical origins were discovered, and he did not suppose, either, that truthfulness could be detached from a concern for the truth. Truthfulness as an ideal retains its power, and so far from truth being dispensable or malleable, his main question is how it can be made bearable. Repeatedly Nietzsche—the 'old philologist', as he called himself—reminds us that, quite apart from any question about philosophical interpretations, including his own, there are facts to be respected. In *The Anti-Christ* (59) he praises the ancient world for having invented 'the incomparable art of reading well, the prerequisite for all systematic knowledge', and with that 'the *sense for facts*, the last-developed and most valuable of all the senses'. At the beginning of *On the Genealogy of Morality*, he tells us that 'the English psychologists' should not be dismissed as old, cold, boring frogs; rather, they are brave animals,

> who have been taught to sacrifice desirability to truth, every truth, even a plain, bitter, ugly, foul, unchristian, immoral truth . . . Because there are such truths—

He keenly detects elements in our intellectual structures which we mistake for truths. In *The Gay Science* he stresses the importance of 'a law of agreement', which regulates people's thoughts and provides intellectual security (76). He stresses the historical, indeed the continuing, importance of these conceptions, but he does not think that they are the truth, or that they are immune to the discovery of truth. They are *contrasted* with the truth, and the question is, what will emerge from a battle between them and a growing awareness of the truth: as he asks at 110, 'to what extent can truth stand to be incorporated?'

In his earliest writings about truth and error, Nietzsche sometimes spoke as though he could compare the entire structure of our thought to the 'real' nature of things and find our thought defective. It is as though the business of using concepts at all falsified a reality which in itself was—what? Formless, perhaps, or chaotic, or utterly unstructured. Later, he rightly rejected this picture, with its implication that we can somehow look round the edge of our concepts at the world to which we are applying them and grasp it as entirely unaffected by any descriptions (including, we would be forced to admit, the descriptions 'formless', 'chaotic', and so on).[5] There are passages in *The Gay Science* where it is unclear whether he is still attached to this picture. He discusses fictions, the practice of regarding things as equal or identical or mathematically structured when they are not so or only approximately so (110, 121). He is making the point, certainly, that mathematical representations which are offered by the sciences are in various ways idealizations, and this is entirely intelligible. There is greater ambiguity when he suggests that nothing is really 'identical' or 'the same'. To take an example: the concept 'snake' allows us to classify various individual things as 'the same animal', and to recognize one individual thing as 'the same snake'. It is trivially true that 'snake' is a human concept, a cultural product. But it is a much murkier proposition that its use somehow *falsifies* reality—that 'in itself' the world does not contain snakes, or indeed anything else you might mention. Nietzsche came to see that this idea of the world 'in itself' was precisely a relic of the kind of metaphysics that he wanted to overcome. As a remark in the *Nachlass* puts it (*The Will to Power* 567): 'The antithesis of the apparent world and the true world is reduced to the antithesis "world" and "nothing".'

It is less than clear, and also well worth considering, how far the formulations of *The Gay Science* still commit him to the murky metaphysical picture. Some of the same problems affect another idea which appears in the book, and which was to be important in works he wrote after it, the idea of 'a perspective'. Our interpretative outlook, our particular 'take' on the world, is modelled on the analogy of a literal, visual, perspective, and this analogy has two implications: that we understand that there can be alternative perspectives, and, importantly, that these will be alternative perspectives *on the same reality*. In later works, Nietzsche is often less than definite about what is involved in this second

[5] This is well argued by Maudemarie Clark, *Nietzsche on Truth and Philosophy* (Cambridge University Press, 1991).

implication, but he is very clear about the first implication, and indeed urges us to combine perspectives, or move between them, which shows that we not only know *that* there are other perspectival views, but that we know what some of them are. In *The Gay Science*, he seems on the very edge of stepping into this problem. Section 299, for instance, suggests that we can make use of different perspectives. But at 374, where he says 'we cannot reject the possibility that it [the world] includes infinite interpretations', the idea of the 'alternatives' seems to remain an entirely abstract possibility: 'we cannot look around our corner'.

The 'Greeks were superficial—out of profundity', he says in the Preface (and he repeated the remark later, in the epilogue to *Nietzsche contra Wagner*). But the Greeks in their time could straightforwardly display a delight in surfaces and appearances which was indeed profound. That is not possible for us, after so much history: any such attitude for us will be a different and more sophisticated thing, and it will represent an achievement. At the very end of the book, he returns to the gaiety of the gay science, and calls up the ideal of 'a spirit that plays naively, i.e. not deliberately but from overflowing abundance and power, with everything that was hitherto called holy, good, untouchable, divine . . .' This might seem even inhuman in comparison to conventional forms of seriousness, that is to say, solemnity,

> and in spite of all this, it is perhaps only with it that *the great seriousness* really emerges; that the real question mark is posed for the first time; that the destiny of the soul changes; the hand of the clock moves forward . . .

Then he adds, at the end of that section, '. . . the tragedy begins.' But immediately there comes the last section of all, *Epilogue*, in which the spirits of his own book tell him to stop these gloomy noises, these 'voices from the crypt, and marmot whistles'. 'Nicht solche Töne!' they cry in an echo of Schiller's *Ode to Joy*, 'Not such sounds!' He says he will give them something else—the poems, presumably, with which he ends the book. But he does so with a final question, and it is a question which he wanted his readers to ask themselves not just at the end of this book, but throughout it and indeed throughout all his books—'Is that what you *want?*'

TWENTY-TWO

"There are many kinds of eyes"

"There are many kinds of eyes", he says in the *Nachlass* [WP (*The Will to Power*)540](1885); "Even the sphinx has eyes—and consequently there are many kinds of 'truths', and consequently there is no truth." Here "there is no truth" can mean that there is no one truth, and that is one thing that he means. But in another, and significant, remark from the *Nachlass* [WP 616](1885/6), the same phrase reappears in the company of what seems to be an uneasy suggestion that there both is and is not something that is being falsified by all these views of it:

> That the value of the world lies in our interpretation (that inter-pretations other than merely human ones are perhaps somewhere possible—); that previous interpretations have been perspectival val-uations by virtue of which we can survive in life, i.e. in the will to power, for the growth of power; that every elevation of man brings with it the overcoming of narrower interpretations; that every strength-ening and increase of power opens up new perspectives and means believing in new horizons—this idea permeates my writings. The world with which we are concerned is false, i.e. is not a fact but a fable and approximation on the basis of a meagre sum of observa-tions; it is 'in flux', as something in a state of becoming, as a falsehood always changing but never getting near the truth—for there is no 'truth'.

"The world with which we are concerned": there is a question of quite what this means, a question that can come up as a question of transla-tion. Cf BGE (*Beyond Good and Evil*) 34: "Why couldn't the world that concerns us be a fiction?"—("die Welt, die uns etwas angeht"), which is near to "so far as we have anything to do with it" or "it is our business."

There is, once again, certainly something awkward in putting together the idea that all these interpretations are false, that the world which they variously construct is a fable or, again, an approximation, with the idea that there is nothing for them to falsify or to approximate to. But we should read these words in the light of what comes before them. It is clear, first, that we should hold on to the first implication of the idea of a perspective that I mentioned before, that we can recognize that there are many perspectives, and know what some of them are. Nietzsche's idea of

an interpretation or perspective is not transcendental in anything like the Kantian sense—in a sense, that is to say, in which it provided the form of anything that we could regard as experience. If our perspective were such a thing, we could not have the idea of there being more than one of them, and then, as Donald Davidson has rightly argued, we could not have the idea of there being even one of them. Nietzsche is concerned with a recognizable multiplicity of perspectives, and that implies a multiplicity of recognizable perspectives.

A perspective or interpretation here is a large-scale world-view or system of values, something in virtue of which we or others can survive in life. We know about some of them, and those we can compare, not indeed with a true world of values which could be grasped independently of anyone's perspective, but at least with each other and with our own. There can be indefinitely many such outlooks. In many cases we can grasp them only as abstract possibilities, and cannot grasp what they might contain. They might belong, as Nietzsche suggested in the passage just quoted, to creatures who were not even human. In their case, we would have only the most limited and utterly abstract grasp on the idea that their outlook, as we have to call it if we are to sustain the idea at all, is trying to do the same kind of thing as our own. But it would have to imply this much at least, that they had a conscious and in some degree reflective social life, which required them to make sense of their circumstances. We have very little grasp on what such a life might be, except by thinking of it in human terms (as the thin fantasies of science fiction repeatedly make clear). Much more important, though, for Nietzsche and for us, is that there are *human* perspectives and interpretations which we can only poorly grasp. No doubt some of them lie in the past, and our inability to grasp them is a matter of ignorance and a failure of understanding. But this is a contingent matter: Nietzsche thinks that there are past outlooks into which we do have insight, such as those of the ancient Greeks. What really concerns him are outlooks which are beyond us because they are ahead of us and lie in the future.

As he often says, much of Nietzsche's philosophy, including his critiques of the past and the present, is in the interest of the future.

[NB the sub-title of BGE: *Vorspiel einer Philosophie der Zukunft.* Does that mean: a philosophy which is about, or is concerned with, the future (which is how Alexander Nehamas reads it)? Or does it mean: a philosophy that will come about in the future? The double Wagnerian echo surely suggests the latter.]

And who will do the creating? Nietzsche did not have much conception of politics. He had some political opinions, of an aristocratic character; he had a well-known dislike of socialism, liberalism, equality, democracy and so on. But as Mark Warren has well argued, he had not the faintest idea of the nature of a modern state.[1] His general political conceptions, such as they were, were largely drawn from the ancient world and were not so much reactionary as archaic. Indeed, he had a poor sense not just of the modern state but of a modern society: it might even be said, of any society at all. He was supported in this by a tendency, presumably derived from German Idealism, to move freely between social and historical categories on the one hand, and psychological categories on the other: GM (*The Genealogy of Morality*) itself is a puzzling exercise in this. However that may be, his models of overcoming and transforming *our* values, which is his most enduring concern, tend to be personal, individualistic, occasionally heroic. Often the undertaking is regarded as an expression simply of a personal endeavour, like that of an artist; sometimes it takes on an historically transformative note, as though the individual's feat of transvaluation will itself change society. With regard to "creating new names", he leaves us for the most part with an image of some solitary figure bringing new values into existence, an image which, brought into relation to a transformation of society, is bound to have a certain pathos about it.

The question is not whether Nietzsche's ideals for a transformed society, to the extent that he had any, are something that we are likely to accept. The point is that this individualistic or artistic way of conceiving creation through destruction, particularly when it is applied to social transformation, is not true to much else that Nietzsche believed. It implies an heroic transcendence of social and historical conditions by the creator, and this belies one of his thoughts: we do not make our thoughts out of nothing; they come in part from what is around us, and we have a very poor grasp, for the most part, of what their source may be. It also implies, if dimly, that society might be transformed, not just by such an heroic creation, but in the very terms that the creator invented, and this belies another of his thoughts: what ideas actually do is not under the control of their creators, and is rarely what their creators intend. Their ideas may help to shape other people's aims, but they are more deeply at the mercy of those other people's needs, and of opaque historical contingency.

Thoughts of this kind underlie Nietzsche's use of the idea that new perspectives and new interpretations involve an increase in power. It is not—and this is vitally important—that an increase in power can serve as a *criterion* of what interpretation or outlook we should adopt. We do not survey a range of perspectives or sets of values and choose one by considering the extent to which it will increase our power. There is a memorable sentence in the *Nachlass*: "Das Kriterium der Wahrheit liegt

[1] Mark Warren, *Nietzsche and Political Thought* (Cambridge, Mass., 1988).

in der Steigerung des Machtgefühls [The criterion of truth lies in the increase of one's sense of power]" [WP 534 (1887/8)]. This contains two errors: that this could be the way to express relations between truth and power, and also—perhaps more significantly—that an increase in power, in a sense adequate to Nietzsche's purposes, could be the criterion of anything.

There is more than one reason why this must be a mistake. One is that, as I just said, we cannot adequately imagine or understand a new perspective or interpretation, in this very broad sense, until it has come about. Another is that we cannot anticipate its power: indeed, we cannot understand in advance what kind of power it will create, what new forms of life it will make possible, or how those forms of life could express human vitality—just as the ancients could not have foreseen the distinctive shape of that world the creation of which GM claims to describe, a world centered on Christianity; nor could they have understood how that utterly strange thing could come to represent a new way of giving life a meaning. Hegel already saw that all such things can only be understood backwards, but Hegel believed that we can see behind us because we are higher on the historical mountain of progressive freedom and reason. Nietzsche precisely does not believe this, but for him, all the more, there is no way in which, in these fundamental respects, the understanding of life can get ahead of life itself. There is a marvellous line of Goethe's *Faust*, which is quoted more than once by Wittgenstein: "Im Anfang war die Tat [In the beginning was the deed]". It is never, so far as I know, quoted by Nietzsche, but it might well have been.

I have said that Nietzsche basically overcame the temptation to try to look round the side of our representations of the world and say that they were all false in relation to the undescribed world at the other end of the comparison. In this sense, I believe, he overcame metaphysics. But, at the same time, I think we can see why he could still feel the pull of saying, as he does in various remarks I have mentioned, both that our interpretations are all untrue, and that there is nothing for them to be untrue to. He is thinking here, as I have said, of large-scale interpretations of the world and value-systems that go with them. These interpretations include historical narrations which help us to make sense of those values—accounts of how human beings came to be where they are now: an account for instance of Enlightenment, moral progress, the rise of modern ideas of freedom. These stories carry with them, or have done so up to now, a demand for closure, embodied in the two ideas that there is one true set of values to which we are, with luck, moving closer, and that there is one correct narrative of how we came to be where we are.

This yields a tension or conflict. On the one hand it seems that we must have some such ideas if these values, this perspective, are to be *ours* at all. On the other hand, knowledge of our history and an understanding of human activities grasped from that history, tell us at a reflective level that these claims to closure are not true. Nietzsche is nothing if not reflective: he represents reflection carried to the point at which he recognizes that reflection itself and the self-consciousness of modernity can weaken or destroy the power to live confidently. In this respect, as he also knew, he is in a battle with his own philosophy.

He succeeded, or perhaps we should say, he is now in the process of succeeding, in seeing what a world of new values would be like, Im Anfang war die Tat—and when he said [TI (*Twilight of the Idols*)] that he philosophized with a hammer, he meant, as he said, that he was testing the wheels, not building a new vehicle. It is not just a question of whether we can foresee a world beyond ours. There is also a question of why we should recognize it as an improvement, as a higher alternative to the life we have. The power it will embody will not reveal itself as recommending it until it is a power that someone already possesses.

Nietzsche was in fact keener in some ways on laying out the qualities of people who might make a new interpretation, create new names, than he was on the impossible task of laying out the content of a future interpretation. Central to those qualities was indeed truthfulness: a truthfulness that respects truths which, as we saw, he is prepared to call "facts"—truths which remain true even though there is no "one truth" about what can give human life a meaning—truths which are indeed what show that there is no such one truth. Why is this quality so important to him?

One reason lies in the other implication, which I mentioned earlier, of the perspective metaphor: that these perspectives are interpretations or views of one reality. They cannot be various views of the "one truth" about human life, of the reality which does not exist. What they are, however—and I leave aside the extra-terrestrial possibilities—are all views *of human life*, and that is identified through a whole set of truths, including, very significantly, truths of history. Moreover, it is only those "plain, bitter, ugly, foul, unchristian, immoral" truths that can make us understand where we are now, and what our problem is.

But doesn't that mean that there is one narrative that Nietzsche has to regard as correct, or correct as far as it goes: the narrative of how the old illusions died, the narrative, as he might put it, of God's death? What we might call: the negative narrative of Enlightenment. I think the answer to that question has to be "yes". But do we need to hold on to that narrative? Some of us would be more disposed than Nietzsche was to say that, unless we face the world truthfully, any hope for a better politics will be doomed. That is not an entirely instrumentalist answer, because we have to believe in truthfulness in itself if we are to hold on to those truths: here as so often, intrinsic values have their uses. But it does imply that it is not just at a technical level that we need to understand the world if we are to make a difference to it which we might recognize as an improvement. Moreover, it is a condition of our understanding the future as in a sense *our* future: it will not be us, but surely we must think of it as the life of people bound to us by the continuation of that narrative. We might think, too, that this understanding that the old metaphysical picture of the world was a fiction is one thing, at least, that has been achieved by all this suffering, and it would be pitiful if it were to be thrown away.

But Nietzsche will certainly remind us that if it needs to be thrown away, then it will be. Perhaps people will come to forget all this, and live under some new conception of the "one truth", some new illusions. Or perhaps they will not have such a picture, nor know that they do not, nor remember that people once did and then lost it: they will not have any need to believe in any meaning to life at all. The last man will take over the world. Then that is what will have happened. To many of us, as to Nietzsche himself, that would be a final falling away. But here we do find ourselves, with him, on moral ground. Like Wittgenstein and freewill.

TWENTY-THREE

Unbearable Suffering

Nietzsche wrote:

> Was eigentlich gegen das Leiden empört, ist nicht das Leiden an sich, sondern das Sinnlose des Leidens. [What actually arouses indignation over suffering is not the suffering itself, but the senselessness of suffering.]

And again:

> [Der Mensch] *litt* am Probleme seines Sinns. Er litt auch sonst, er war in der Hauptsache ein *krankhaftes* Tier: aber *nicht* das Leiden selbst war sein Problem, sondern dass die Antwort fehlte für den Schrei der Frage "*wozu* leiden?" Der Mensch, das tapferste und leidgewohnteste Tier, verneint an sich *nicht* das Leiden: er *will* es, er sucht es selbst auf, vorausgesetzt, dass man ihm einen *Sinn* dafür aufzeigt, ein *Dazu* des Leidens. Die Sinnlosigkeit des Leidens, *nicht* das Leiden, war der Fluch, der bisher über der Menschheit ausgebreitet lag.[1] [[Man] *suffered* from the problem of what he meant. Other things made him suffer too, in the main he was a *sickly* animal: but suffering itself was *not* his problem, but the fact that there was no answer to the question he screamed, "Suffering for *what*?" Man, the bravest animal and most prone to suffer, does *not* deny suffering as such: he *wills* it, he even seeks it out, provided he is shown a *meaning* for it, a *purpose* of suffering. The meaningless of suffering, *not* the suffering, was the curse which has so far blanketed mankind.]

Of course this is not just Nietzsche's thought: in various forms, it has been a recurrent idea in Western philosophy. I shall not try to sketch any of that history, or to place the idea in the context of Nietzsche's thought, but, as with many other questions, I do want to start from Nietzsche. I find the leading edge of these problems in his understanding of what they were, and also in his foresight of what they would come to be— and, to some extent, of what they would cease to be.

I am particularly concerned with two questions raised by these texts. First, what is "Sinn" or the lack of it? What is missing when people

---

[1] *Zur Genealogie der Moral*, II 7, III 28.

encounter "das Sinnlose des Leidens"? Does "Sinn" necessarily imply a purpose, as might be suggested by "ein Dazu des Leidens"? What kinds of purpose? Or could "Sinn" imply no more than an explanation or cause of suffering?

Second, what is it that you can do with suffering if it has "Sinn", a meaning, and cannot do if it has not? Throughout this paper, as its title implies, I shall describe what you can supposedly do with meaningful suffering as "bearing" it, but it is important that this is simply a label. The question is, what relevantly counts as "bearing" it? In the second of the passages I have quoted, Nietzsche says that man "verneint an sich nicht das Leiden"—he does not "repudiate" it, as the English translators put it: he does not say 'no' to it, or reject it. One might say that he accepts it. But what is it to do this?

In the same work, Nietzsche says:

> Jeder Leidende nämlich sucht instinktiv zu seinem Leid eine Ursache; genauer noch, einen Täter, noch bestimmter, einen für Leid empfänglichen *schuldigen* Täter.[2] [[E]very sufferer instinctively looks for a cause of his distress; more exactly, for a culprit, even more precisely for a *guilty* culprit who is receptive to distress.]

This is the well-known operation of *ressentiment*. This process gives, in a way, a meaning to suffering, namely a cause or explanation of it, but by itself it does not make it any easier to bear. In particular, it does not reduce in any way the reaction of indignation, which is naturally implied by "empört" in the first quotation I gave. On the contrary: finding a blameworthy cause of one's suffering precisely provides an object for indignation. What may bring some relief to the suffering is the further elaboration of *ressentiment* which lies in the fantasy punishment of the agent cause. Inasmuch as this process makes suffering more bearable, it is this further meaning, the fantasy of revenge or retribution, that does so. Mere recognition of a cause, in particular an agent cause, cannot do this; if anything, it makes the suffering worse. This is very obvious when the "unbearable" quality of the suffering is experienced precisely through reactions of indignation or resentment.

Nietzsche also says, and in the same place as that first quotation:

> Aber weder für den Christen, der in das Leiden eine ganze geheime Heils-Maschinerei hineininterpretirt hat, noch für den naiven Menschen älterer Zeiten, der alles Leiden sich in Hinsicht auf Zuschauer oder auf Leiden-Macher auszulegen verstand, gab es überhaupt ein solches *sinnloses* Leiden. [[B]ut neither for the Christian, who saw in

[2] III 15.

suffering a whole, hidden machinery of salvation, nor for naïve man in ancient times, who saw all suffering in relation to spectators or to instigators of suffering, was there any such *senseless* suffering.]

and also:

"Jedes Übel ist gerechtfertigt, an dessen Anblick ein Gott sich erbaut": so klang die vorzeitliche Logik des Gefühls—und wirklich, war es nur die vorzeitliche? ["All evil is justified if a god takes pleasure in it": so ran the primitive logic of feeling—and was this logic really restricted to primitive times?]

Here suffering might seem to get its meaning from a divine purpose—or we might say, more precisely, from a purpose that involves a divine interest. It cannot be enough, however, to give suffering a meaning for the sufferer—in a sense that makes it more bearable for him—merely that *some purpose or other* is served by the suffering: for instance, as we have already seen, if my suffering serves the purpose of some other and hostile agent, this merely makes things worse for me. The most obvious contrast with my suffering's serving someone else's purpose is that it should serve *my* purpose, but the possibility that a divine purpose should make sense of my suffering shows that this in itself is too simple. What gives my suffering a meaning for me need not be directly my own purpose, but rather a purpose that I acknowledge, or which has authority over me, or is, in some way, a purpose *for* me.

It is a quite complex question, what it is for a purpose to fill this role. The case of primitive religion that Nietzsche discusses shows that it need not be a matter of conscious thought or reflection. At that level, people may simply be "taking for granted" (or something implying even less conscious acknowledgement than that) that there are powers or purposes over them. The situation changes if the believers are taken to be more reflective than this. But if they are, relevantly, more reflective, we must not assume that the effect must be that the purpose is one which they *reflectively choose* to acknowledge as having authority over them. To make that assumption is to accept a Kantian ideal of autonomy, and with it a dichotomy between the will and the understanding, which in these connexions is mistaken: neither in the case of finding explanations, nor in considering what to do, can one choose what makes sense to one.

So far, then, we have one relevant sense in which suffering might have a meaning: that it has an appropriate relation to a purpose that has authority for the sufferer. We shall come back to that formula, but let us first turn in the direction of the second question that I identified: what is it for suffering, when it has a meaning, to be (as I put it) "bearable"?

The first thing that must be said and never forgotten throughout the discussion is that some suffering simply is unbearable. It can break people. This is true of physical pain, as is well known to torturers and to those who send agents into the risk of being tortured. Suffering may be such that, even when you are utterly identified with the purpose for which you are suffering, you would give *anything* for it to end. The same can be true of such things as losing a child in a struggle in which, once again, one thoroughly believes. The idea that meaning, or purpose, or understanding, or even, perhaps, a true philosophy could make all suffering bearable is a lie, whether it is told by by recruiting sergeants or by ancient sages. Our question is confined to a limited class of cases, in which what one thinks or believes or takes for granted may make a difference to one's being broken or not.

If there is a space in which one may bear the suffering or find it unbearable, what will the difference between these two things be? I do not think that the thought we are looking for is best caught by saying that if, in such a case, the suffering has a meaning, this makes it less painful—that "meaning" is an analgesic. There are some cases in which something like this is true, such as the cases of intense and purposeful activity in a battle. ("By God, Sir," the Duke is said to have said to his fellow officer, "your leg has gone"; "By God, Sir," he replied, "it has".) If people sustain better the deprivations of a siege when they see a point in doing so, this means in part that they suffer less from it. But pharmacology is an empirical science, and, to the extent that meaning is an analgesic for a given kind of suffering, this will be a matter basically of contingent fact. This need not imply that, in such cases, meaning can be offered straightforwardly as a recipe for a cure: there may be some meanings (such as the fantasies of *ressentiment*) that can operate on suffering only unconsciously. But the analgesic model does imply that, with some kinds of suffering, looking for an analgesic can usefully take the form of looking for meaning, and this cannot be right, above all because I cannot choose what will make sense to me.

This is so even in the simplest possible case, in which an action makes sense to an agent because he has chosen to do it in the light of reasons that he has.[3] Even in this case, although I choose the action, I do not choose that it make sense to me: that is a matter of my reasons, my desires, my on-going projects, and I do not choose all of them.[4] The pharmacological model fails, because the "meaning" cannot be seen in a

---

[3] It is worth saying, perhaps, that "in the light of reasons that he has" is not redundant: people can choose to do things that do not make sense to them at all.

[4] I discuss the idea of events, processes and actions "making sense" to people, and argue for the unity of the idea over the agent's and the interpreter's perspectives, in *Truth and Truthfulness* [Princeton U.P., 2002], chapter 10, section 1.

therapeutic light, simply as an efficient cause of making suffering more bearable, in particular by diminishing it. The suffering, rather, becomes a different thing because the experience of it is structured by the meaning, and if this is so, while there may be some sense in which the suffering becomes less because it is bearable, this is not really the main point.

So what is the relation between suffering and meaning, in virtue of which suffering that has a meaning may be more bearable? We cannot merely say that suffering can become bearable if it makes sense to the sufferer or is a necessary part or consequence of what makes sense to him. One reason for this we have already seen. The suffering may make sense to him just because it is explicable or has an intelligible cause, and simply knowing the cause, as in the case of the agent who arouses *ressentiment*, does not make the suffering bearable. Similarly if we know the causation of the plague, this does not make the incidence of the plague any more bearable, except in the sense that it may help one to control it so that there is less suffering. There can be confusion here because in traditional discussions of these questions an explanation was often taken to be a teleological explanation. But if that kind of explanation supposedly yielded meaning in the relevant sense, this was not just because it was an explanation, but because it introduced a purpose, and not merely someone's arbitrary purpose, but rather one that was the purpose of the universe (or something like that), and so was supposed to have authority for everyone insofar as they were rational.

Leaving aside, now, divine or cosmic purposes, we should look more closely at the cases in which a purpose has authority for the sufferer because it is involved in a project that expresses a purpose of the sufferer's own. It is indeed important that it should have authority, and it is not enough for this that it should simply be some purpose or other of the agent's. It might be an arbitrary purpose, a merely chosen goal, and his identification with it might be very brief or superficial. It might be, at the limit, no more than his purpose in a given action. This may be enough to make (limited) sense of the agent's action, but it is not enough to make sense of his suffering; if it is to do that, the purpose will have to make sense to him in some larger context of life. Some creative undertaking, or relationship, or commitment to a political cause may work like this. Call such a thing, just as a label, a project of that person: for the person who has the project, it makes sense of his life or of part of his life. Suffering that is involved as a necessary means or constituent of such a project will make sense of the suffering, and that indeed can make it more bearable (always within the limits, that some suffering just is unbearable). As I said before, it may not in a simple sense act as an analgesic. But there is the important difference between there being and there not being a meaning, that when the suffering is meaningless, there is no thought associated with the awfulness except the intense desire that it should stop, while this cannot be the only thought when there is a meaning, because one wants, and very seriously so, the success of the project in which the suffering is involved, and a realistic hold on the world in which the project is being expressed can help one to hold on to that thought.

Some may think that these formulations are excessively goal-directed. Various traditional counsels have suggested that the way to make life bearable lies in the direction of *ataraxia*, the refusal of identifications and projects (except, of course, that project itself). But this line of thought in fact represents a different idea. Indeed, one might say that it belongs to a different world. It is not making a suggestion, opposed to Nietzsche's, about what might make suffering bearable, namely that it should be meaningless rather than meaningful: rather, it is suggesting a way of reducing suffering altogether, through not caring about contingencies and attachments. It is, in its simplest form, an analgesic recipe. Moreover, to the extent that such an undertaking does connect to the line of thought I have been exploring, it is not contrary to it. For what is the sage who is dedicated to *ataraxia* going to make of the sufferings that he cannot avoid? What will help him to bear them with equanimity is not the blankly negative idea that they are meaningless. What will help him, rather, is the idea, so far as he can keep it going, that they are *unimportant*, and this implies that something else is more important: notably, the conception of the self as something to which attachments and contingencies, even the contingency of its own existence, are indifferent. This conception itself is not going to be empty or purely formal, but will be supported by some further idea, for instance that the self expresses itself most appropriately by being at one with unchanging necessities. If such an idea helps to make suffering bearable, it does so by indeed providing meaning, if not to suffering itself, to a life that contains such suffering as one cannot oneself eliminate from it. In this connection, as in others, the familiar consideration that ridding oneself of projects is itself a project offers a lot more than a purely dialectical point.

If suffering can be made bearable by a project that makes sense of it, what is to be made of cases in which such a project does not succeed? The first thing to say is that there are ways of not succeeding other than, in the narrowest sense, failing. In discussing elsewhere the imaginary or at least highly schematized case of an artist (I called him Gauguin) who threw up his existing life and commitments to develop his painting, I distinguished two ways in which such a project might come to nothing. It might never really be put to the test: thus Gauguin might have fallen ill and died on the way to Tahiti. Alternatively, it might be put to the test and fail, as it would have done if Gauguin did everything he might do to develop his work but in the end neither he nor anyone else thought that it was worth much. In that case, one might say that his project had been refuted, while in the first case it had merely been negated.[5]

In which of these cases, we can rather ingenuously ask, would his suffering be more bearable? If it is meaning that makes suffering more bearable, then (assuming of course that he is conscious of the negation) it looks as though the case of negation should be the more unbearable, because the suffering that he experiences if he is aware that his project has been irreversibly stalled is not related to that project in a way that makes sense of the suffering. Suffering in the course of a life that makes sense does not itself necessarily make sense, and there could be a special bitterness in the absurdity of his having thrown up everything for the sake of a venture which came to a halt in this meaningless way. By contrast, suffering associated with the refutation of his project does seem to make sense, in precisely the terms in which the project itself made sense—the answer "no" is, after all, an answer to the original question. Yet surely the suffering brought about by definitive failure, by refutation, might be harder to bear? The clear sense that he destroyed his earlier life and commitments for something that was firmly shown to be an illusion could readily be more painful than the sense that, after all, he was never to know.

Looked at in this way, the connexion between meaning, and the suffering's being bearable, might seem to be the wrong way round. But I do not really think that this is so. The suffering of the person whose project is refuted has meaning only in the inadequate sense that it has an explanation which is provided by the failure of the project. This does not imply that his life now has a meaning—it was precisely the meaning of his life (we are assuming) that was destroyed in the refutation of the project. Yet it is *now* that he is suffering. A person, by contrast, whose project is merely negated, for whom it disappears through an external contingency, may sustain an image of how things might have been otherwise and with that, perhaps, the idea that his life to this point made at least some sense in having been directed to this purpose. The person whose project has been refuted may of course be sustained by a hope that something else may take its place, but then it will be quite another project, the search for a replacement, that will be giving his life some meaning.

In neither of these cases, or in any other, is philosophy telling people what they should feel. (It is amazing in how many ways it has tried, and still tries, to do so.) Rather, in reflecting on such cases we may see how we can use Nietzsche's thought the other way round: imagining someone who suffers for such reasons and bears it, we can ask what new sense it is that his life is now finding for itself.

---

[5] "Moral Luck", in the book with that title [Cambridge University Press, 1981]; see in particular p. 27.

R. G. COLLINGWOOD

TWENTY-FOUR

An Essay on Collingwood

Three Reasons for Talking about Collingwood

My first reason for discussing R. G. Collingwood is to right, in a small way, a genuine injustice, and a disservice to the history of Oxford philosophy, which consists in the virtual obliteration of him from the collective local consciousness. In a book which appeared in 1958 entitled *English Philosophy since 1900*,[1] there is no reference to Collingwood at all.

Second, he differed in his whole approach to philosophy from his contemporaries: the pupils of Cook Wilson (as he was himself) and others, whom Collingwood called "the realists", such as Prichard, Joseph, and, in Cambridge, Moore. He represented himself in his *Autobiography* (1939) as very isolated from them, and indeed rejected by them. It has been suggested by David Boucher, in a useful biographical essay,[2] that Collingwood somewhat exaggerated this. Certainly any isolation can only have been increased by the *Autobiography* itself, which is a fascinating and often brilliant book—"strangely conceived, but instructive," Santayana said of it—but was written under conditions of stress and bitterly attacked the realists, in particular suggesting in its closing paragraph that "the minute philosophers of my youth, for all their profession of a purely scientific detachment from practical affairs, were the propagandists of a coming Fascism".

His intellectual connections were notably with Italy, particularly through his friend Guido de Ruggiero. There is historical disagreement how far he was influenced by Croce and Gentile (though he certainly disowned the latter as a worthwhile philosopher when he became a Fascist). He shared with them (significantly) an influence of Vico. Much of his special approach lay in his sense of history. He was himself a historian, and unusually—today, unthinkably—worked professionally in both philosophy and in ancient history.

Born in 1889, he went to University College and took Mods and Greats, graduating in 1912. He became the Philosophy Fellow at Pem-

---

[1] G. J. Warnock, *English Philosophy since 1900*, Oxford University Press 1958.

[2] "The Life, Times, and Legacy of R. G. Collingwood" in *Philosophy, History and Civilization: Interdisciplinary Perspectives on R. G. Collingwood*, edd. D. Boucher, J. Connelly & T. Modood, University of Wales Press, 1995.

broke College, and in 1927 he was appointed University Lecturer in Philosophy and Roman History. When he had written three books in ancient history, culminating in *Roman Britain* (1932), he was appointed Waynflete Professor of Metaphysical Philosophy in 1935. From this deep historical experience, he formed significant views on the philosophy of history; the history of philosophy; and the interpenetration, as he supposed, of the history of thought and the study of metaphysics. All of this was unusual. The philosophy of history, because practically no-one studied it. The history of philosophy, because practically no-one really did it, although they said that they did. And the interpenetration of the history of thought and metaphysics, because it was entirely original. No-one in Oxford and few in Britain and America have been so impressed by the significance of history as Collingwood, except for Berlin, who has acknowledged Collingwood's influence; and it is significant that Berlin, whose conception of what philosophy is was rather influenced by positivism, gave up philosophy (at least, as he himself identified the subject) in favour of the history of ideas.

The third reason for considering Collingwood is that he had original and some good ideas. He also had some bad ones, and many of his interesting ideas tend to be expressed in a confusing way. Partly this was because much of his significant work was produced towards the very end of his life when he was ill. He resigned from his chair in 1941 because of failing health, having had a breakdown in 1932 and repeated strokes from 1938. He died in January 1943, aged 53. Leaving aside two early philosophical works, he published *An Essay on Philosophical Method* in 1933, of which he said that it was "my best book in matter; in style, I may call it my only book". But he said this in his *Autobiography*, which was published in 1939, when he had produced in addition only *The Principles of Art*, in 1938. The *Essay on Metaphysics* came out in 1940, and *The New Leviathan* in 1942; he left a lot of material, which was edited by T. M. Knox (who was thought by most people to be an unfortunate choice), and published as *The Idea of Nature* (1945) and *The Idea of History* (1946).

STYLE

However, the problems of Collingwood's philosophy for those with a concern for sound analytical book-keeping are not only due to the circumstances in which some of it was written. Collingwood's contempt— and contempt was a sentiment which he quite often expressed—for the "minute philosophers" meant that he simply did not try to write philosophy in the way that was favoured by them (and is still favoured by most of us some of the time and some of us all of the time), a way which aims to head off any ambiguity or any implication which some reader, perhaps a very perverse reader, might improperly take up: a style, that is to say, which seeks precision by total mind control, through issuing continuous and rigid interpretative directions.

The *Essay on Philosophical Method* is in fact mostly a dull and dated book, full of what are likely to seem now unhelpful distinctions and assimilations, but it does contain a marvellous section at the end about philosophical style, called "Philosophy as a Branch of Literature".

> Every piece of philosophical writing is primarily addressed by the writer to himself. Its purpose is not to select from among his thoughts those of which he is certain and to express those, but the very opposite: to fasten upon the difficulties and obscurities in which he finds himself involved, and try, if not to solve or remove them, at least to understand them better.
>
> . . . The philosophers who have had the deepest instinct for style have repeatedly shrunk from adopting the form of a lecture or instructive address, and chosen instead that of a dialogue . . . or a meditation . . . or a dialectical process where the initial position is modified again and again as difficulties in it come to light.
>
> The prose-writer's art is an art that must conceal itself and produce not a jewel that is looked at for its own beauty but a crystal in whose depth the thought can be seen without distortion or confusion; and the philosophical writer in especial follows the trade not of a jeweller but of a lens-grinder. He must never use metaphors or imagery in such a way that they attract to themselves the attention due to his thought; if he does that, he is writing not prose but, whether well or ill, poetry; but he must avoid this not by rejecting all use of metaphors and imagery, but by using them, poetic things themselves, in the domestication of prose: using them just so far as to reveal thought, and no further.[3]

THE HISTORY OF PHILOSOPHY

Collingwood thought that philosophical writing laid certain responsibilities on the reader—a kind of patience; a postponement, though not a refusal, of criticism; and imagination, to grasp what the writer's problem

---

[3] *An Essay on Philosophical Method* 209–214.

might be. Moreover, he had a general principle, which we shall come back to, that any assertion only made sense as an answer to a question, and that you could not understand what was being said by an author unless you understood—this did not imply, explicitly formulate—the question that he was trying to answer.

This had particular implications for the practice of the history of philosophy. Peter Strawson, talking about Paul Grice, quoted with approval a remark of Grice's, which he claimed all Oxford philosophers would agree with, that we "should treat great but dead philosophers as we treat great and living philosophers, as having something to say to *us*". Collingwood would have agreed with this, so long as it is not assumed that what the dead have to say to us is the same sort of thing as the living have to say to us. He would not have agreed, that is to say, with Ryle's frequent injunction to treat something written by Plato, for instance, as though it had come out in *Mind* last month. Collingwood insisted, correctly, that the questions being answered by Plato and Hobbes, for instance, were not the same, and that you literally could not understand them unless you understood this. The "realists" had very little sense of this; and some of the most instructive (as well as enjoyable) pages in the *Autobiography* are those in which he addresses their methods.

> . . . so, in ethics, a Greek word like *dei* cannot be legitimately translated by using the word "ought", if that word carries with it the notion of what is sometimes called "moral obligation". Was there any Greek word or phrase to express that notion? The "realists" said there was; but they stultified themselves by adding that the "theories of moral obligation" expounded by Greek writers differed from modern theories such as Kant's about the same thing. How did they know that the Greek and the Kantian theories were about the same thing? Oh, because *dei* (or whatever word it was) is the Greek for "ought".
>
> It was like having a nightmare about a man who had got it into his head that *triêrês* was the Greek for "steamer" . . .[4]

If Collingwood had not been so ignored, it might not be necessary, as I am afraid it is, to remind people of this now. It might also not have been necessary to rediscover for oneself that the point of reading philosophers of the past is to find in them something different from the present—and that is not just a historical but a philosophical discovery. That much is true, even if we do not share the view which Collingwood evidently held, that there are no permanent problems of philosophy at all. It is not immediately clear why he held this, and the question is related to some

---

[4] *Autobiography* 63 following. The whole chapter is very worthwhile.

matters we shall come to later. It is worth saying now that it would follow from something that Collingwood did favour, a historicist application of a kind of holism, which may come from Vico, a tendency to think
of an age as having an overall character.

Related to that, we do not, in order to sympathise with Collingwood's
admirable outlook on the history of philosophy, have to share his very
radical view, which he came to hold at the end of his life, about the historical character of metaphysics, something that I shall come to in the
last section of these remarks.

RECOVERING THE PAST

The "realists" or "minute philosophers", having misidentified Plato's or
Leibniz's question, could announce that the philosopher had answered it
wrongly. It was less obvious on Collingwood's own view what it was for
Plato or Leibniz to have answered their own questions rightly or
wrongly. In the *Autobiography*[5] he ties himself into something of a knot
about this:

> If Leibniz was so confused in his mind as to make a complete mess of
> the job of solving his problem, he was bound at the same time to mix
> up his own tracks so completely that no reader could see quite clearly
> what his problem had been. For one and the same passage states his
> solution and serves as evidence of what the problem was. The fact
> that we can identify his problem is proof that he has solved it: for we
> can only know what the problem was by arguing back from the solu-
> tion.

On the same page, he says that this does not mean that the question
"was Plato right to think as he did on such and such a question?" must
be left unanswered. This would be as "lunatic" as to suppose that it was
part of history that the Greek admiral Phormio acted as he did, but not
part of history that he beat the Corinthians by doing so. There is more
than one thing questionable about this analogy; but the present point is
that Collingwood, in deploying the analogy, seems to leave himself and
us in the position that there can be an answer to the question "was Plato
right to think as he did on such and such a question?", but only if the
answer is "yes".

Now we could certainly deal with this by nudging Collingwood into a
more reasonable position (though, remembering Collingwood's remarks
about the dialectical character of philosophical writing, we should prob-

[5] *Autobiography* 69–70.

ably say: more reasonable than the position he has reached at this stage of the argument). We do not have to assume that the philosophical writer has "made a complete mess" of the job. Nor need we assume that the only access to his problem is by arguing back from the solution. In fact, Collingwood would not disagree; and he did think that one relied on other parts of the text, and other texts, and other evidence, for the reconstruction of a question in the history of thought. So we are not locked in the paradox which we just glimpsed. But rather than simply taking on board these sensible modifications and qualifications, we should perhaps look at the question of why Collingwood might have been pushed in the direction of the paradox in the first place.

Here we need to address a broader doctrine that Collingwood held about historical understanding more generally. Probably Collingwood's most famous remark is "all history is the history of thought". History he held was "the history of *res gestae*, the actions of human beings done in the past".[6] The activity described in relation to the history of philosophy, of determining the writer's question and his answer to it, applies quite generally to understanding past action: to understand what an agent did, we have to understand what his question was, and what thought he had in answering it. The question "Why did Caesar cross the Rubicon?" is, if a properly historical question, to be taken as: "What did Caesar think, as a result of which he crossed the Rubicon?". Moreover, there is no way in which Caesar's thought can be identified entirely from the outside; for the historian to answer the question, he has to have Caesar's thought—the very same thought—himself. "Thought can never be mere object. To know someone else's activity of thinking is possible only on the assumption that this same activity can be re-enacted in one's own mind. In that sense, to know 'what someone is thinking' (or 'has thought') involves thinking it for oneself."[7]

This is the most famous of Collingwood's views, and the only one that I recall being discussed in the Oxford of the 1950s (except, very occasionally, some things that he had said about the philosophy of art, which I shall not discuss). There were several reasons for this being so. There was not much work being done on the philosophy of history, and Collingwood was very saliently one of the few recent and local contributors to it. Moreover, one of the few who was working on it, and the most senior, was W. H. Walsh, who had Idealist sympathies which inclined him at least to take Collingwood seriously. But most did not take him all that seriously, and the final reason for Collingwood being discussed at

---

[6] *The Idea of History* 9.
[7] *The Idea of History* 288; compare *Autobiography* 112 (about Nelson).

that time was that the re-enactment thesis provided a convenient and seemingly rather dotty version of the kind of thing that a sensible empiricist-style account of history would want to avoid.

As Patrick Gardiner has said in a recent article,[8] a lot of this criticism was based on misunderstanding. One basis of the misunderstanding was to suppose that the re-enactment thesis proposed a method; but, as Gardiner says, this is not the main point: "the question at issue is not so much one of the techniques the historian uses in his search after knowledge and understanding as one of what *constitutes* such knowledge and understanding when he has it".[9]

Another source of misunderstanding was a reading of the relation of thought and action in Collingwood in dualistic terms. This really was gratuitous: indeed, Collingwood emphasised the expression of thought in action, and in *The New Leviathan* he diagnosed dualistic errors in Descartes and was saluted for doing so by Ryle, Collingwood's successor as Waynflete Professor, in his inaugural lecture.[10]

With the removal of these misunderstandings, we can be freed from the idea that what is at issue is some form of diachronic and self-confirming telepathy. Evidence is needed, and interpretation of action and circumstance help the historian to a situation in which he can re-enact the thought.

Three other objections to Collingwood's account of history are worth rather more consideration.

Collingwood's typical insistence that re-enactment is involved in, and central to, *any* historical understanding, together with the thesis which that implies, that the subject matter of all history is individual action, unduly narrows the scope of history. This criticism seems to me unanswerable. Collingwood's view goes with a dislike of causes as opposed to reasons, something that is expressed, for instance, in his deeply eccentric attack on Thucydides for having turned history (which Herodotus had

---

[8] "Interpretation in History: Collingwood and Historical Understanding" in Anthony O'Hear ed., *Verstehen and Humane Understanding* (Royal Institute of Philosophy Supplement 41, Cambridge UP, 1996), 109–119.

[9] Page 114, Gardiner's emphasis. There are passages in which it is clear that this is what Collingwood means, although his formulation is misleading: e.g. *The Idea of History* 282 ". . . what kind of knowledge has [the historian]?: in other words, what must the historian do in order that he may know [his facts]?"—A similar distinction between method and constitution may be relevant to contemporary discussions in the philosophy of mind (not primarily concerned with understanding the past) about the supposed distinction between "simulation theory" and "theory theory".

[10] "Philosophical Arguments," in Gilbert Ryle, *Collected Papers* Vol. 2 (London: Hutchinson; New York: Barnes & Noble, 1971), chap. 14.

initiated) into something different, namely social science.[11] It will be enough to say that history potentially involves, and often puts into the foreground, the understanding of actions in such terms.

A second objection is that the thesis may be thought to be, to use one of Collingwood's words, "lunatic": on his account, it seems, the historian, in his moment of understanding Caesar, will be trying to cross the Rubicon, or doing the nearest thing he can to doing that. But Collingwood had an answer to that, an answer which, he claimed, it took him a great deal of trouble to get right.[12] This was the idea of "encapsulation", which depends on the point that the context in which the historian re-enacts the past thought—the context of the "real life" of the historian— is quite different from, and conflicts with, the presuppositions of that thought being appropriate. Having the thought, the re-enactment, is simulation, thinking in someone else's person. The content of the thought, if the attempt has been successful, is the same as that of the past agent's thought, but it occurs in the biography of the historian only in quotes or, as it were, indented.

There are two things that we should *not* say here. One is that the content is not asserted but entertained. The reason for not saying this is that the distinctions between assertion, entertaining, questioning and so on *recur* within the re-enactment itself. Nor should we say that the historian is "pretending" to think the thought. Pretending to x implies that one is not x-ing (or, at the very least, that one is not intentionally x-ing).[13] This is why not all dramatic acting is pretending; and it is very relevant, in the context of the present question, to think of dramatic acting which consists of improvisation.

A useful comparison is with another application of *Verstehen*, the ethnographer's stance. The ethnographer in the field can come to think as the people think with whom he is living, and he can enact their judgements and deliberations in his own person. But at the end of the line, these are not *his* thoughts. The difference from the historian is that the ethnographer may *lose* the end of the line: he may find it hard to come back to his regular life and may, as it used to be said, "go native". The historian cannot do that, unless he goes mad; the end of the line, at

---

[11] *The Idea of History* 28–31. The same bias comes out in the very poorly considered attack on psychology in part II of *Essay on Metaphysics*, which apart from anything else offends against Collingwood's own canons of how to read a text.

[12] *Autobiography* 112.

[13] In this I side, in a famous disagreement, with Anscombe and against Austin. J. L. Austin, "Pretending", and G.E.M. Anscombe, "Pretending", *Proceedings of the Aristotelian Society*, Supplementary Volume 32 (1958), now in J. L. Austin, *Philosophical Papers*, and G.E.M. Anscombe, *The Collected Philosophical Papers of G.E.M. Anscombe*, vol. 2, respectively.

which those thoughts which he thinks are not his thoughts, is all the time immediately in front of him.

The third problem with Collingwood's position concerns irrational or mistaken thoughts. William Dray, a philosopher who has done a lot to keep Collingwood's approach alive in the philosophy of history, referring to "empathy" theories in history, has said "one cannot re-think a practical argument one knows to be invalid".[14] In one sense, this seems to be wrong, and it can be met by appealing again to encapsulation. I can move in and out of an enactment, just enough to control it with my own sense of reality; we may compare, in the ethnographic case, the complex ambivalences of a modern investigator's approach to traditional magic. However, this only applies when I have identified the "invalid practical argument". It is a different question if I cannot get to the point of recognising anything as the practical question or reasoning which was the agent's; and this parallels, of course, the problem that we have already met in discussing the history of thought in the narrower sense, the problem of interpreting a radically confused text.

One, straightforward, thing to say is that there simply is a problem about interpreting a radically confused text, action, or set of actions. However, the problem is not as bad as it sounds, because there is a gradation from the intelligible, through things that are intelligibly confused, to that which is unintelligible. That last judgement does not simply return us to a situation in which, paradoxically, we are not in a position to make that very judgement. Precisely because there are such gradations, we can understand that something is unintelligible, without having to understand it.

However, this applies only to (relatively) particular cases—at most, certain *sorts* of texts, actions, and persons. It cannot apply generally—or rather, we should say, in order to keep open a significant area of discussion, *too* generally. We can understand a given text or action only in terms of a local set of conventions, possibilities and significances. It is what it is, means what it does, because of what it is possible to mean in those historical and social circumstances. (This reminds us again that re-enactment is not a kind of intuitive telepathy: it is based on knowing a lot about how things went there.) In understanding those circumstances themselves, how things went there, we do not have the same possibilities of detecting error or irrationality, because there is no further set of considerations which provide enough leverage to enable us to make the separation implicit in claiming *both* that we understand what is going on, *and* that we see in the light of this understanding that it is confused or

[14] *Philosophy and History: A Symposium,* ed. Sidney Hook (New York, 1963), page 113; quoted by Patrick Gardiner, page 118.

irrational. At some level of generality—and we should stress, again, in order to keep that area of discussion open, that we do not yet know what level of generality—we get to a point at which it is a condition on our understanding of what is going on that it should make sense under our interpretation, in such a way that it does not come out as seriously confused or irrational. As Collingwood rather marvellously said: "We call them the Dark Ages, but all we mean is that we cannot see".[15]

Collingwood considered history rather than social understanding more generally, for instance ethnography, but *this* idea is of course familiar. It is the idea of what is sometimes called a principle of charity, but we should reject that name in relation to Collingwood, as for ourselves, because of its entirely inappropriate suggestions of condescension. But we should also be careful with the title which is sometimes now more favoured, "the principle of humanity",[16] because that too strongly suggests a universalism of rationality, or (rather) a universalism of fairly determinate levels of rationality, applying to human beings as such. Collingwood, with his strongly historicist outlook, was very suspicious of such an idea. It must be true that Collingwood, or any other hermeneutical thinker (not that he used that expression, so far as I know), will need to make some universal assumptions about human beings in order to render the historicism, the historical varieties of experience, intelligible as varieties of human experience; but the essential question is, how determinate and specific those universal assumptions are taken to be.

At any rate, since we are dealing with Collingwood, let us label the principle "the principle of constructive re-enactment" (PCR). We can now see an answer to the question we noticed earlier, why Collingwood backed himself into the seeming paradox of there being only one answer to the question "Was Plato right to think what he thought on a certain question?", namely the answer "yes". The reason is, I suggest, that with regard to really great thinkers such as Plato and Leibniz, Collingwood took it that the PCR applied to them directly and not just to the background in which they wrote. Collingwood was disposed to think that such writers were the only philosophers worth reading anyway, or at least, the only ones worth reading for their own sakes, as opposed to their providing evidence for the belief system of their time. And to them, with a few sensible modifications and qualifications, Collingwood thought that the PCR applied directly.

It is important that there are at least two different—and in some degree, opposed—reasons why this might be so. One is that such writers

---

[15] *The Idea of History* 218.
[16] The title is owed to Robin Grandy.

embody or express in a particularly intense and deep way the general assumptions of a period or epoch. The other is that they create new assumptions, help to bring into being new canons of what it is for theory or practice to make sense.[17] It looks in a way as though Collingwood ought really to favour the first option, a description of Plato or Leibniz, in terms of expressing rather than creating assumptions. However, there is a problem in even stating this question because, on Collingwood's last and most intriguing views about the nature of philosophy, it is hard to say what such philosophers were doing at all, in particular to the extent that they were doing metaphysics. It is this question that I shall now turn to.

METAPHYSICS AND PRESUPPOSITIONS

We need first to look back at the method of question and answer. Collingwood said[18] that Bacon, in his epigram to the effect that the scientist must "put Nature to the question", laid down the true theory of experimental science. It contained the idea that the enquirer must take the initiative, deciding what he wants to know, and formulating this in the form of a question, and "he must find means of compelling nature to answer, devising tortures under which she can no longer hold her tongue". *Mutatis mutandis*, Collingwood thought that this also contained the true theory of historical method. Equally, the historian must be active, having a question to which he needs an answer. Passive history Collingwood calls "scissors and paste history", the mere assemblage, with some critical mutual adjustment, of what the records have happened to leave to us. In archaeology, it was mere rummaging around, trying to find something. As he interestingly says,[19]

"Let us see what we can find out about this site" is no more a "question", as I understand that term, than are such pseudo-questions as "What is knowledge?", "What is duty?", "What is the *summum bonum*?", "What is art?". Like them, it is only a vague portmanteau phrase covering a multitude of possible questions, but not precisely expressing any of them.

In *The Idea of History* Collingwood illustrates the idea with the straightforward example of a detective story in the English mode, where

---

[17] If one has an attachment to the idea of genius (as I think Collingwood did not, particularly), one can see this distinction as corresponding either to two theories of genius, or to two types of genius.

[18] *The Idea of History* 269.

[19] *Autobiography* 122.

the Poirot-like figure gets the right answers because he asks the right questions. Collingwood took himself to have used such methods in his archaeology. (Indeed, critics of that work have said that Collingwood only too readily interpreted what he found as the answer to his question.) In the *Autobiography*, he gives a rather famous account of how, in the First World War, he developed the idea because he had to walk each day to work past the Albert Memorial, and came to ask himself whether, in finding it loathsome to an incomprehensible degree, he was simply failing to understand the world from which it came and in which it was admired. In that work,[20] further, he discussed these ideas in terms of what he called "a logic of question and answer", but there is no reason to follow him in this, particularly given the ill-advised and arrogant remarks he offered there about what is ordinarily called "logic".

What matters for the present question is the elaboration of his ideas about question and answer that Collingwood introduced in the *Essay on Metaphysics*.[21]

There, Collingwood lays down the following theses in a rather formal style. (It will be obvious, e.g. in relation to the first, that they have to be understood to some degree as legislating about the notions involved.)

(1) Every statement is made in answer to a question.
(2) Every question involves a presupposition.

This means that the presupposition makes it a pointful, answerable question; indeed, makes it a determinate question. (It will be obvious that the identity of a question is not determined by purely linguistic means: one can ask the same question in different linguistic ways, and a different question by using the same words.)

(3) The logical efficacy of a supposition does not depend on the truth of what is supposed, or even on its being thought true, but only on its being supposed.

A supposition has "logical efficacy" in relation to a question if it causes (as Collingwood incautiously puts it) a question to arise: for instance, "this mark on a stone is an intentional inscription" has logical efficacy in relation to the question "what does it mean?".

(4) A presupposition is relative or absolute: relative if it stands to one question as presupposition and to another as answer; absolute if, for all questions to which it is related, it stands only as presupposition and not as answer.

[20] 33, 42.
[21] *Essay on Metaphysics* 23 seq.

From this it follows

(5) Absolute presuppositions are not propositions, in the sense of what is stated.

(5) does not mean that absolute presuppositions cannot be formulated or verbally expressed. It may be, possibly, that they do not have to be verbally expressed, but they certainly can be. To deny this would be inconsistent with many things that Collingwood says, for instance with the question[22] "Is this presupposition relative or absolute?". What "proposition" means is something that can be responsibly claimed to be true on the basis of proof, demonstration, verification, empirical evidence, etc.;[23] that is impossible in relation to an absolute presupposition because, if it could be verified, it would be the answer to a question.

This is illustrated by Collingwood's discussion of Mill on the principle of causation or the uniformity of nature. Such a principle was an absolute presupposition of science as Mill understood it, but Mill took, in typical positivist fashion, as Collingwood put it, a supposition for a proposition and got himself into a false position by trying to demonstrate it.

But metaphysics is the science of absolute presuppositions. Metaphysics does not propound (as defensible truth claims, that is to say) absolute presuppositions any more than natural science does, and it could not do so. It does propound a certain kind of proposition, to the effect that certain absolute presuppositions are in fact presupposed. Thus all metaphysical questions and propositions are *historical*, and metaphysics deals with a class of historical facts.[24]

A historical reminder is in place at this point. A. J. Ayer's *Language, Truth and Logic* had been published in 1936, and Collingwood took it and its dismissal of the old gang of "realists" seriously. When Collingwood heard Prichard and Joseph complaining about the book and saying that it should never have been published, he said "Gentlemen, this book will be read when your names are forgotten".[25] But he thought that positivism's "anti-metaphysics" was misconceived, and that it was based on such things as a childishly resentful attitude to ethics or religion, supported by a fear that metaphysics was "malicious" towards science (a phrase of Russell's, from *Mysticism and Logic*). This was a misunderstanding, even if it was explicable why the positivists should have taken metaphysics to be an enemy of science: on their misconception of

---

[22] Allowed at page 40.

[23] This point is made by Rex Martin in an article "Collingwood's Claim That Metaphysics Is a Historical Discipline", in *Philosophy, History and Civilization*, at page 207.

[24] *Essay on Metaphysics* 49, 61–62.

[25] Quoted by Boucher, op. cit. note 36.

it, metaphysics would have been an enemy of science, though not in the way that they supposed.[26] If metaphysics is what Collingwood says it is, the "historical study" of absolute presuppositions, then there are no objections to its status.

But is this account acceptable, or even fully intelligible? The first objection is an obvious one: why *historical*? Doesn't *our* metaphysics address itself to *our* absolute presuppositions? In a sense, Collingwood does not mind about this. The present, he says, "is the recent past",[27] and the kind of "metaphysical analysis", as he calls it, which serves to disentangle absolute presuppositions is very much the same with regard to the past and the present. Indeed, this is what you would expect from the re-enactment doctrine: to say that thinking about our presuppositions is like thinking about other people's is less surprising when one recalls that understanding other people's thoughts in the past involves thinking them yourself in the present.[28] These suppositions, importantly, are always in flux. Our present presuppositions are a transmutation of the past, and they are in course of transmutation towards the future. There are always "internal strains" in the "constellation of absolute presuppositions" at any given time. Metaphysical analysis can present those presuppositions and, presumably, the tensions between them, and this activity can be applied to one's own case. We may suppose that some of such arguments might look like trying to establish one absolute presupposition at the expense of another; if that is so, then, on Collingwood's view, that will be simply appearance, or alternatively some absolute presupposition has turned into a relative one.

However, there remain problems about the content of absolute presuppositions. The historical context I have mentioned, of replying to positivism, only serves to underline that problem. Consider some sentence "S" which might traditionally be taken to express some metaphysical claim, the content of which is unverifiable. It is not much of an answer to the positivist to claim that the following is a historical, verifiable proposition: We (or someone else) presuppose absolutely the content of "S". To interpret this historical proposition we need to know what relation to what is involved in presupposing the content of "S", and if the content of "S" is *ex hypothesi* suspect, this looks fairly daunting. It is important that this problem remains even if one is less worried than the positivists were by, specifically, verification.

Collingwood does not offer any general guidance as to how the content of absolute presuppositions is to be identified. The one example

---

[26] There is a sparkling paragraph on this theme at *Essay on Metaphysics* page 169.

[27] *Essay on Metaphysics* 70.

[28] This point does not entail the view, rejected by Martin, op. cit. page 216, that recovering or coming to know an absolute proposition is just an exercise of re-enactment.

with which he takes particular trouble, "God exists", does not help very much. The existence of God is an absolute presupposition for thinking done by Christians,[29] and as such it cannot be proved. A thinker, addressing himself to "God exists" as a metaphysical proposition, will put in the "metaphysical rubric" which yields a proposition to the effect that we presuppose in our thinking that God exists. Collingwood continues,[30] "If 'God exists' means [sic] 'somebody believes that God exists' (which is what it must mean if it is a metaphysical proposition) it is capable of proof . . . historical proof ". He then points out that an archetypal proof of God's existence in the Christian tradition is the Ontological Proof, which indeed derives "God exists" from somebody's believing that God exists.

This may be a spectacular *tour de force*, but if it achieves anything, it achieves it only for this very peculiar case. Indeed, Collingwood's wider discussion of this case itself suggests that the content of absolute propositions, in its relation to the thinking of which they are the absolute presuppositions, can diverge a great way from the apparent semantic content of an absolute presupposition as verbally expressed. The presupposition that God exists is expressed, for instance, in our treating nature in our science as a unitary system.

So, two problems remain: that of identifying the content of absolute presuppositions, and of specifying the relation that they have to the thinking or activities of enquiry and so forth of which they are the presuppositions. Those two problems come together in the question already mentioned, of how an agent or group of agents are supposed to be related to what, when it is said that they presuppose a given absolute presupposition.

COLLINGWOOD AND WITTGENSTEIN

I think that this represents a genuine problem. It is the version in Collingwood's philosophy of a very real problem that presents itself to any philosophy which, like his, is hermeneutical and non-foundationalist. The problem concerns the relation between the discursive formulation of ideas or assumptions, on the one hand, and, on the other, practices and the description of practices. This is part of the question of how a *reflective* account of a practice, in particular of a practice of enquiry, can be given. Collingwood does not think that people can typically state the absolute presuppositions of their activities, and he makes a special point of saying that an absolute presupposition cannot be discovered by

[29] *Essay on Metaphysics* 186.
[30] *Essay on Metaphysics* 188.

introspection.[31] He does not think that people engaged in a practice necessarily or typically can be best described as *believing* the absolute presuppositions of their activities; the discursive formulation in which
something is presented as an absolute presupposition and looks superficially like something that could be believed or asserted, is a particular
representation of an understanding which is implicit in and recovered
from reflection on that practice.

Collingwood often speaks in terms of practices and changes of practices in a revealingly holistic way. In an interesting discussion of
progress, he discusses a change in fishing methods between generations.
The older generation will think that the old method is better than the
new "not out of irrational prejudice, but because the way of life which
it knows and values is built round the old method, which is therefore
certain to have social and religious associations that express the intimacy of its connection with this way of life as a whole".[32] In *The Essay
on Metaphysics*,[33] he speaks of a certain "natural piety", in Wordsworth's
phrase, which could help the metaphysician simply to recognise facts—
things simple and familiar, visible to the eyes of a child, and perhaps
hidden from clever men because they are too clever. He saluted Samuel
Alexander for expressing in an unassuming way such an outlook. Such
things are not matters of proof or argument, not even of belief. The
idea that the world is responsive to magic, for instance, is not a proposition which is refuted: "As long as you believe in a world of magic, that
is the kind of world in which you live".[34] (And this can be taken as suggesting what, if anything, might count as "a belief in" a world of
magic.)

Since absolute presuppositions structure practices; since they are not
propositions in the sense of things believed; and since Collingwood's examples, though not his own account, suggest a difficulty in identifying
their discursive formulations; then perhaps Collingwood should have
acknowledged more than he did in this connection what in relation
to Wittgenstein is called the primacy of practice, and the strength of
Goethe's phrase, quoted more than once by Wittgenstein: *Im Anfang
war die Tat*, in the beginning was the deed. Other resemblances to
Wittgenstein, with regard to meaning as use, and the necessary expression of thought in action, have been noted by various writers.[35]

I should like to end, not by suggesting a *compte rendu* of relations between the two thinkers, but by mentioning one or two considerations

[31] *Essay on Metaphysics* 188.
[32] *The Idea of History* 325.
[33] Chapter XVII, 172 seq.
[34] *Essay on Metaphysics* 194.
[35] See Boucher, op. cit. note 42 for references.

which Collingwood encourages us to bear in mind in these connections, more perhaps than Wittgenstein does.

(a) The account of metaphysics helps to bring out, though it does not solve, the question of the relations of reflection, and hence of philosophical reflection, to practice, and the status of discursive formulations of assumptions recovered from practice. Some Wittgensteinians seem to think that the primacy of practice means the primacy of descriptions of practice, and this, certainly, is a mistake, one that Wittgenstein himself did not make. However, for more than one reason (including, perhaps, the "realist" origins of his own philosophical formation, and his ongoing fear that the activity of philosophy itself was pathological), Wittgenstein did not spend much time on considering how reflective descriptions of practice might be related to practice itself.

(b) Wittgenstein largely ignored history, and disliked science. Collingwood respected science and based his entire philosophy on history. This at once places science as one activity among others, and reminds us of genuine and pervasive cultural variation. It therefore gives us richer resources for combating a stupid scientism in philosophy, since it invites one to think about the cultural role of science among other forms of understanding. At the same time, it provides a concrete sense of variations between actual "forms of life". The emphasis on history, again, also emphasises (a), since it adds to our reflections a sense of that variation.

(c) Collingwood's emphasis on historical change and constant tension in absolute presuppositions counteracts a danger which is implicit in talking in holistic terms about ways of life, the danger of falling into assumptions of functional coherence. Those assumptions simply install at the general cultural level Collingwood's paradox of the necessary rationality of a correctly interpreted text. I said before that Collingwood applied his principle of constructive re-enactment to whole systems and very great writers, rather than to every text or action taken particularly. However, while this is true, it is qualified by the emphasis on change. One has to make, not just a system, but a movement between various stages of systems, intelligible, and one thing that makes this possible is that in its earlier stage the system of thoughts, understandings or practices was in fact not fully coherent, but was under tension.[36] Wittgensteinian accounts of social understanding have, notoriously, tended to favour a static picture of a fully functioning and coherent system.[37]

[36] This is, of course, a fundamental Hegelian principle. Beyond this important point, I do not suppose that Collingwood was a very Hegelian thinker, but to argue this would require a longer treatment, in particular of Collingwood's understanding of progress, and the extent to which he was in some sense, unlike Hegel, a relativist.

[37] Peter Winch's *The Idea of a Social Science and Its Relation to Philosophy* (London: Routledge & Regan Paul, 1958) was an early and influential example of this tendency.

(d) There is a well-known problem to be found in writers about these questions, particularly in Wittgenstein, which lies in their evasive use of "we", which may be taken in an inclusive sense, as implying universalistic preconditions on interpretation and intelligibility; or, in a contrastive sense, under which "we", here and now, are distinct from others elsewhere and elsewhen, who lived in other and different intelligible human formations. Collingwood has a good deal to offer on this set of questions. He himself tended to a radical historicism which played down, as I have said, the idea of permanent philosophical problems, and does not make much of assumptions which may be necessary in order to identify any way of life as a human way of life at all. He is helped, however, here once again by his emphasis on history, where continuity and change permit a developmental, diachronic understanding which is not offered by the blankly ethnographic case—still less by the purely imaginary and schematic ethnographic case which is favoured by Wittgenstein, the relation of which to "us" tends to be thoroughly ambiguous.

To consider, as Collingwood did, the case of history, and in particular the history of the Western world, is, of course, not a substitute for considering also the hermeneutical problems raised by ethnographic and similar studies. But it is, in itself, a deeply important case. Moreover, it is the case which is implicated very deeply in our attempts to understand the ethnographic case as well, and in our attempts to determine the relations between cultural variation and some universal assumptions about human nature (assumptions which, as we have seen, are necessary if we are going to be able to understand the notion of cultural variation itself). For it is a lively question, how far "our" understanding (and that is meant to preserve every ambiguity of "we") of the ethnographically exotic, of cultural variation, and hence of the humanly universal, itself indelibly carries with it assumptions drawn from our cultural experience as historically understood.

No adequate philosophical enquiry into interpretation can eventually ignore these questions, and so it must itself be informed by a historical sense. Collingwood reminds us of that fact; he reminds us of the problem and its importance; and, besides offering philosophical writing which in twentieth-century British philosophy is unrivalled in its brilliance, gives us fruitful lines of enquiry into that problem.

WITTGENSTEIN

TWENTY-FIVE

Wittgenstein and Idealism

1 Solipsism and the *Tractatus*

Tractatus 5.62 famously says: 'what the solipsist *means* is quite correct; only it cannot be *said* but makes itself manifest. The world is *my* world: this is manifest in the fact that the limits of *language* (of that language which alone I understand) mean the limits of my world.' The later part of this repeats what was said in summary at 5.6: 'the limits of my language mean the limits of my world'. And the key to the problem 'how much truth there is in solipsism' has been provided by the reflections of 5.61:

> Logic pervades the world; the limits of the world are also its limits.
>
> So we cannot say in logic 'the world has this in it, and this, but not that'.
>
> For that would appear to presuppose that we were excluding certain possibilities, and this cannot be the case, since it would require that logic should go beyond the limits of the world; for only in that way could it view those limits from the other side as well.
>
> We cannot think what we cannot think; so we cannot think what we cannot *say* either.

Now Wittgenstein says that 'there is no such thing as the self that thinks and entertains ideas' (5.631), and this item is presumably the same as what at 5.641 he perhaps loosely, but comprehensibly, calls 'the human soul with which psychology deals'—that is to say, the item that does not really exist, the thinking and knowing soul *in* the world, is an item which people look for there as the subject of the phenomena with which psychology deals. In this interpretation I think I am substantially in agreement with P.M.S. Hacker in his book *Insight and Illusion: Wittgenstein on Philosophy and the Metaphysics of Experience* (OUP, 1972), which I have found helpful on these questions. There are, however, respects in which I would put the position rather differently from him. Hacker, as against Black and others, says that what Wittgenstein does is to deny the existence of a knowing self *in* the world, and denies it, moreover, on Humean grounds[1] to the effect that it cannot be encoun-

---

[1] Hacker, p. 59.

tered in experience. At the same time, Wittgenstein, under Schopen-hauerian influence, does believe in the existence of another, metaphysical or philosophical self, which is 'the limit of the world, not a part of it' (5.632, 5.641), and in some such sense he really is a solipsist; only that of course cannot be said, but merely manifests itself. Since Wittgenstein denies the first of these selves and in some way or other accepts the second, he cannot mean them to be the same thing.

Granted the intensely paradoxical and ironical character of Wittgenstein's thought here, one is in any case in expounding it going to be choosing between different kinds of emphasis. But I would enter two qualifications to Hacker's account. First, as regards the negative movement against the knowing self, it is not just an unsuccessful Humean search that we are dealing with. Wittgenstein says:

> There is no such thing as the subject that thinks or entertains ideas.
>
> If I wrote a book called *The World as I Found It*, I should have to include a report on my body, and should have to say which parts were subordinate to my will, and which were not, etc., this being a method of isolating the subject, or rather of showing that in an important sense there is no subject; for it alone could not be mentioned in that book. (5.631)

He adds, just before the analogy of the visual field, which I shall not consider (5.633): 'where *in* the world is a metaphysical subject to be found . . .?' This seems to me to say, not just that there was something we were looking for and which turned out not in fact to be in the world—which is Hume's tone of voice, though the full content of Hume's negative discovery is not to be found in his failing to find something which he might have found, either. Rather Wittgenstein says: that which I confusedly had in mind when I set out to look is something which could not possibly be in the world. Hacker's emphasis is: there is one specification, which is the specification of a possible empirical thing, and to that nothing as a matter of fact corresponds; but there is a quasi-specification of a non-empirical thing to which something does, in a way, correspond. But rather, what we first looked for was never a possible empirical thing. For it had to satisfy the condition of being something *in* the world as I experience it and yet at the same time necessarily there whenever anything was there, and there could not be anything which did that. This is why Wittgenstein can explain his thought in this connection by saying (5.634) that no part of our experience is at the same time *a priori* (the phrase translated 'at the same time' is important here). Thus Wittgenstein's thought is, as Hacker indeed says, very like Kant's criticism of the Cartesian *res cogitans*.

The other qualification affects the other half of the argument. We cannot in any straightforward sense say that there is, or that we can believe in, or accept, a metaphysical, transcendental, self instead; for neither *what* it is, nor *that* it is, can be said, and attempts to talk about it or state its existence must certainly be nonsense. That is why, as we have already seen, the non-occurrence of a subject in the book of *The World as I Found It* means that 'in an important sense there is no subject'. The sense in which it *is* a limit, also means that *at* the limit, it is not anything at all (5.64):

> Here it can be seen that solipsism, when its implications are followed out strictly, coincides with pure realism. The self of solipsism shrinks to a point without extension and there remains the reality co-ordinated with it.

Indeed, granted this, I find puzzling why Wittgenstein can say (5.641) that there really is a sense in which philosophy can talk about the self in a non-psychological way. But I take this to mean that philosophy can talk about it in the only way in which by the end of the *Tractatus*, we find that *philosophy* can talk about anything: that is to say, not with sense.

Whatever exactly we make of that, we can recover from the *Tractatus* discussion of the self and solipsism three ideas which will be particularly important as points of reference in what follows: that the limits of my language are the limits of my world; that there could be no way in which those limits could be staked out from both sides—rather, the limits of language and thought reveal themselves in the *fact that* certain things are nonsensical; and (what follows from the first two, but is an important point to emphasise) that the 'me' and 'my' which occur in those remarks do not relate to an 'I' *in* the world, and hence we cannot conceive of it as a matter of empirical investigation (as the *Tractatus* is fond of putting it, a matter of 'natural science') to determine why my world is this way rather than that way, why my language has some features rather than others, etc. Any sense in which such investigations were possible would not be a sense of 'my', or indeed, perhaps, of 'language', in which the limits of my language were the limits of my world.

It may seem that these ideas are foremost among those that Wittgenstein abandoned in his later work, and that they, and the forms of puzzlement which gave rise to them, were particular objects of the criticisms of the *Investigations*. In a sense that is true, and Hacker devotes a good deal of his book to explaining how the later interest in such things as the impossibility of a private language and the necessity for public criteria is related to a long-term project of exorcising solipsism—exorcising it even from some vanishing and unsayable transcendental redoubt. The later arguments about oneself and others are designed (among other things) to remove the need even to try to point, hopelessly, in a solipsistic direction. That need certainly exists in the *Tractatus*. The well-charted moves in the later work from 'I' to 'we' mark one and the most evident attempt to banish that need; equally the emphasis in the later work on language's being an embodied, this-worldly, concrete social activity, expressive of human needs, as opposed to the largely timeless, unlocated and impersonal designatings of the *Tractatus*—that emphasis also can naturally be thought of as a rejection of the transcendental and Schopenhauerian aspects of the earlier work: the *transcendentales Geschwätz*, the 'transcendental twaddle' as Wittgenstein wrote to Engelmann in a different context in 1918 (quoted by Hacker, p. 81).

But the question is not as simple as this, and my chief aim will be to suggest that the move from 'I' to 'we' was not unequivocally accompanied by an abandonment of the concerns of transcendental idealism. To some extent, the three ideas I mentioned are not so much left behind, as themselves take part in the shift from 'I' to 'we': *the shift from 'I' to 'we' takes place within the transcendental ideas themselves.* From the *Tractatus* combination (as Hacker justly puts it) of empirical realism and transcendental solipsism, the move does not consist just in the loss of the second element. Rather, the move is to something which itself contains an important element of idealism. That element is concealed, qualified, overlaid with other things, but I shall suggest that it is there. I shall suggest also that this element may help to explain a particular feature of the later work, namely a pervasive vagueness and indefiniteness evident in the use Wittgenstein makes of 'we'.

2   Solipsism and Idealism

Hacker says (p. 59) that an aim of his book is 'to show that the detailed refutation of solipsism and hence of idealism, which Wittgenstein produced in the 1930s and incorporated, in low key, in the *Investigations*, is directed against views which he himself held as a young man'. A refutation 'of solipsism and *hence* of idealism': this is a connexion of ideas, not immediately self-evident, which Hacker makes throughout. Thus at p. 214:

> The solipsist claimed that the present moment is unique, that he is privileged, that it is always he who sees, that what he has when he sees is unique, that his seeing is exceptional, that 'this' is incomparable.

Each move is illegitimate. The illegitimacy of each move damns not just solipsism, but phenomenalism and indeed any form of idealism.

Yet it is not at all obvious that everything which could pointfully be called a form of idealism, or indeed which has been so called by the history of philosophy, would necessarily be refuted by arguments which, by undermining a private language, removed the supposed privileged first-person immediacies which are the basis of solipsism, whether expressed or presupposed.

To phenomenalism, which Hacker mentions, such criticism can indeed be extended, and it may help towards the business of sketching a kind of idealism to which that criticism does not extend, if we first consider one or two points about phenomenalism. Phenomenalists used stoutly to hold that it was a crass misunderstanding to regard their theory as any form of idealism. If they were right at all in holding that, clearly their denial applies at best only to non-transcendental idealism—which we may call, following Kant, *empirical* idealism, and which we can define for our present purposes as a form of idealism which regards the existence of the material world as dependent on minds which are themselves things *in* the world, empirical beings whose existence or non-existence is a matter of contingent fact.[2]

In fact, it is not clear that phenomenalism even manages to avoid being that. The question of whether it does or not, turns on the issue of the status of the hypothetical observers whose equally hypothetical sense-data constitute the content, under phenomenalist translation, of statements about unobserved portions of the material world. If *they* are regarded as empirical items, then there may be a difficulty about phenomenalism's steering clear of empirical idealism. For if it is to do that, and so maintain its professed stance as a realist theory at the empirical level, then it must be able to translate into its language any comprehensible *empirical* proposition which denies the mind-dependence of material objects: thus phenomenalists are happy to translate into their language, as they hope, propositions saying that there were rocks, etc. in certain spaces before there were any observers of them. But what about the following proposition, which seems to be a comprehensible and indeed true empirical proposition in the material object language: 'Even if there were not any observers, certain material objects would exist'? If phenomenalist observers are empirical items, the question of their existence is an

---

[2] This definition excludes Berkeley's completed theory from being an example of empirical idealism. Yet clearly Kant was right in distinguishing Berkeley's views from transcendental idealism. We need not, for the present purpose, pursue the important distinctions which are needed here.

empirical question—the same empirical question, indeed, as is raised by the antecedent of that conditional. Thus the phenomenalist translation of that conditional must be of the form: if P were not the case, then if P were the case, then Q, and it is not, to say the least of it, clear that that is satisfactory.

If that cannot be made satisfactory, then phenomenalism cannot adequately represent in its terms a proposition which constitutes a basic empirical denial of mind-dependence. It will be thus a form of empirical idealism. But even if we dispose of that, phenomenalism will still be a kind of transcendental idealism. Suppose that we eliminate the antecedents of the phenomenalist sentences which merely hypothesise the existence of observers, and which are there just as a universal condition of the analysis. Thus we make the so-called existence of observers a redundant condition on the occurrence of sense-data. Then genuinely empirical statements about the existence or non-existence of observers, such as the antecedent of the material object statement we considered just now, can be translated into the phenomenalist language: in some such form, presumably, as statements of the existence of Humean aggregations of sense-data. Then the sense-data which are the raw materials of the phenomenalist translations (including those sense-data aggregations of which constitute the empirical existence of observers) will not, as such, have a subject, and it is obvious from what has just been said why they cannot, as such, have a subject. The only candidate for a subject recognisable to phenomenalism will be the empirical observer, but his existence has now been represented as the contingent aggregation of items which already, and even outside such an aggregation, have the character of sense-data. As Carnap said in the *Logische Aufbau*, '*das Gegebene ist subjektlos*', the given has no subject.

But it is still the *given*: and unless phenomenalism is to surrender its basically epistemological way of introducing one to these items, and its references to their being, or being related to, *observations*, they must remain items of which we have been given no adequate grasp unless they are in *some* sense mental. Neutral monism perhaps attempted to drop that implication, but to the limited extent that it progressed in that attempt, it seems not to leave one with any adequate bearings on the items in question at all. But then, while no form of mind-dependence of the world can be truly asserted *in* the phenomenalist language, the fact that its raw materials are of this character, and the fact that it is basically *the* language,[3] these facts *show* that the world is mental. We cannot say (ex-

---

[3] I shall not try to discuss how that second fact is to be understood. For the closely related point that the 'two languages' version of phenomenalism is not neutral about reality, cf. J. L. Austin, *Sense and Sensibilia* (Oxford, 1962), pp. 60–1.

cept empirically and falsely) that the world is the world of experience: rather, its being the world of experience conditions everything we say. That is what it is for phenomenalism to be a form of transcendental idealism, a form which indeed is liable to the same objections as Wittgenstein, faced with solipsism, made to such things as the empiricist theory of meaning. Those objections are directed to starting with supposed first-person immediacies, and phenomenalism incurs them because that in terms of which it represents the world cannot be understood except in terms of first-person immediacies.

Thus phenomenalism is one or another form of idealism, and in either form is exposed, as much as solipsism, to the later Wittgenstein arguments. But, to turn away now from phenomenalism, must anything which could be called idealism have this character? Hacker, as I have mentioned, assumes that it is so. His reason for that emerges when he says (p. 216) that 'idealism in most of its forms'—that is his one qualification—is just a half-hearted form of solipsism which has not been thought through with the consistency of solipsism; thus also he refers (p. 71) to Schopenhauer's 'glib dismissal' of solipsism. Idealism is regarded just as a kind of aggregative solipsism. That is indeed ridiculous,[4] but if the idea that the limits of *my* language mean the limits of *my* world can point to transcendental solipsism, then perhaps there is a form of transcendental idealism which is suggested, not indeed by the confused idea that the limits of *each* person's language mean the limits of *each* person's world, but by the idea that the limits of *our* language mean the limits of *our* world. This would not succumb to the arguments which finished off solipsism, for those arguments are all basically about the move from 'I' to 'we', and that, in this version, has already been allowed for.

I think that there is such a view implicit in some of Wittgenstein's later work. To see what such a view will be like, we can try to follow an analogy between this, first-person plural, view, and the first-person singular transcendental view which we have already touched on. First and most basically it is essential that the proposition that the limits of our language mean the limits of our world should be taken neither as a blank tautology, nor as an empirical claim. It would be a mere tautology if it meant something like: whoever are meant by 'we', it is going to be true that what we understand, we understand, and what we have heard of and can speak of, we have heard of and can speak of, and what we cannot speak of, we cannot speak of. Certainly. But the singular versions of those truisms were not just what was meant when it was said originally

---

[4] Cf. Moore's objection to what he supposed to be a consequence of egoism in ethics: *Principia Ethica* (Cambridge, 1903), p. 99.

that the limits of my language meant the limits of my world. Nor, in that original case, did we intend an *empirical* thought, in which I both take myself as something in the world and make it depend on me. That is precisely what we left behind in distinguishing transcendental from empirical idealism. Now, we do not mean the plural analogue of that empirical monomania, either, and that is one way in which our statement is not an empirical statement.

There are other, and important, ways in which it is not an empirical statement. Thus the claim that the limits of our language mean the limits of our world might be construed empirically in this way, by taking *language* narrowly, to refer to one's system of communication, its grammatical categories, etc., and *world* widely, to mean how in general the world appears to one, and the general framework of comprehension one applies to things; then, taking 'we' relatively to various linguistic groups, one would have the hypothesis, perhaps to be ascribed to Whorf, that the way things look to different groups profoundly depends on what their language is like. I shall come back to certain relativist questions raised by such theories. For the moment the aim is just the general one of illuminating by contrast the non-empirical character of an idealist interpretation of our slogan. If we are dealing with a genuinely empirical theory of this 'Whorfian' sort, then a given group's language should provide some sort of an empirical explanation, if only a very weak one, of its way of looking at the world. Connectedly, we could explain some particular person's way of looking at the world, or some aspect of that, by reference to the language group he or she belonged to. But all that cancels the force of the essentially first-personal, even though plural, formulation we are dealing with. An idealist interpretation will not be served by anything that merely puts any given 'we' in the world and then looks sideways at us. Under the idealist interpretation, it is not a question of our recognising that we are one lot in the world among others, and (in principle at least) coming to understand and explain how *our* language conditions *our* view of the world, while that of others conditions theirs differently. Rather, what the world is for us is shown by the fact that we can make sense of some things and not of others: or rather—to lose the last remnants of an empirical and third-personal view—in the fact that some things and not others make sense. Any empirical discovery we could make about our view of the world, as that it was conditioned by our use of count-words or whatever, would itself be a fact which we were able to understand in terms of, and only in terms of, our view of the world; and anything which radically we could not understand because it lay outside the boundary of our language would not be something we could come to explain our non-understanding of—it could not become clear to us what was wrong with it, or with us.

Here, in the contrast with a mere tautology and, very basically, in the contrast with an empirical view, we can begin to see an analogy between the plural view and the original first-person singular transcendental view. But still; why *idealism*? Enough reason, I think, is to be found in the considerations, rough as they are, which we have already put together, and which will serve also to tie those to certain identifiable concerns of the later Wittgenstein. Since the fact that our language is such and such, and thus that the world we live in is as it is, are, as presently construed, transcendental facts, they have no empirical explanation. Anything that can be empirically explained, as that certain external features of the world are this way rather than that, or that we (as opposed to the Hopi Indians, or again as opposed to cats) see things in a certain way, or deal with things in one way rather than another—all these fall *within* the world of our language, and are not the transcendental facts. In particular, in the sense in which we are now speaking of 'our language', there could be no explanation of it, or correlation of it with the world, in sociological terms, or zoological, or materialistic, in any of the several current senses of that expression. Indeed there could not be an explanation of it which was 'idealistic', in the *explanatory* sense of that term often used, e.g. by Marxist writers, of an explanation given in terms of conditioning ideas or thoughts, for there are no ideas or thoughts outside it to condition it. However, while we could not explain it in any of those ways, we could in a way make it clearer to ourselves, by reflecting on it, as it were self-consciously exercising it; not indeed by considering alternatives—for what I am presently considering can have no comprehensible alternatives to it—but by moving around reflectively inside our view of things and sensing when one began to be near the edge by the increasing incomprehensibility of things regarded from whatever way-out point of view one had moved into. What one would become conscious of, in so reflecting, is something like: *how we go on*. And *how we go on* is a matter of how we think, and speak, and intentionally and socially conduct ourselves: that is, matters of our experience.

As phenomenalism, regarded as a form of transcendental idealism, gave everything in terms of something mental, though in the only sense in which it could say that everything was mental, that statement was false; so *our* language, in this sense in which its being as it is has no empirical explanation, shows us everything as it appears to our interests, our concerns, our activities, though in the only sense in which we could meaningfully say that they determined everything, that statement would be false. The fact that in this way everything can be expressed only via human interests and concerns, things which are expressions of mind, and which themselves cannot ultimately be explained in any further terms: that provides grounds, I suggest, for calling such a view a kind of *idealism* (and not of the stupid 'aggregative' kind). The history of post-Kantian philosophy might in any case lead one to expect that there would be a place for such a view.

3   RELATIVISM

We have here, in a vague sketch, the outline of a view. I have not yet offered any grounds for the claim that Wittgenstein held it. In fact, I am not going to claim anything as strong as that he held it. It seems to me that both the nature of the view, and the nature of the later Wittgenstein material, make it hard to substantiate any unqualified claim of that kind. I offer this model and its implied connection with the earlier work as a way of looking at and assessing that later material. But I will offer some considerations which suggest that the influence of the sort of view I have sketched is to be felt in the later work, and that reference to it may help to explain some curious and unsatisfactory features of that work. In particular it may help us to understand the use that Wittgenstein makes of 'we'. To reach any understanding on that matter, we have to approach it through the uninviting terrain of relativism.

In trying to distinguish a little while ago the transcendental version of 'the limits of our language mean the limits of our world' from an empirical version, I suggested one possible empirical version which I cavalierly labelled the Whorfian hypothesis, to the effect that language (narrowly construed) conditioned world-view (broadly construed). That was useful as an example (whether or not it represents the views of Whorf). It contains, we should now notice, three different elements. The first is that it takes language in a narrow sense, and the second is that it offers language in that sense as the explanation of the world-view. The third feature is that what are explained, or would be if there were a true such theory,[5] are various different world-views, held by different human subgroups: there is more than one lot to call themselves 'we'. Now that of course follows from the first two points, since language in the narrow sense differs in the supposedly relevant respects between human groups. But, while still offering an empirical theory, one could drop the first point and keep the second and third: thus one would suppose that there were empirical explanations of differences in local world-view, but they did not lie in differences of language in the narrow sense.

---

[5] The references to the theory, like the references to Whorf, just function as a stand-in or dummy in the argument. I do not go into the difficulties that surround such a theory, such as that of independently characterising its explanandum.

Now as to the first point, I take it that Wittgenstein was not very interested, in these connections, in language in the narrow sense, and that he characteristically uses the term 'language' in a very extensive way, to embrace world-view rather than to stand in narrow and explanatory contradistinction to it. Hence his notoriously generous use of the expression 'language-game'; hence also, in the converse direction as it were, the tendency to use 'form of life' to refer to some quite modest linguistic practice. As Putnam[6] has justly said, '(the) fondness (of Wittgensteinians) for the expression "form of life" appears to be directly proportional to its degree of preposterousness in a given context'. The narrower sense of 'language' seems not to be an important factor in any explanations Wittgenstein would want to consider for variations of world-view between human groups. The question arises, then, of whether he is interested in any explanations at all.

I think in fact he is not basically interested in such explanations, and for a reason which I shall suggest ties up with our central question. Nevertheless at times he says things which would *prima facie* not rule out the possibility of explanation. At least, he thinks that a different way of looking at and talking about the world might become comprehensible in terms of different *interests*:

> For here life would run on differently.—What interests us would not interest *them*. Here different concepts would no longer be unimaginable. In fact, this is the only way in which *essentially* different concepts are imaginable. (*Zettel*, 388)

Suggestions of a similar kind are to be found in the neighbourhood (378, 380), and in the preceding fragment a hint at a more specific kind of explanation might be detected (though hardly one which justifies what sounds like a tone of mild daring):

> I want to say an education quite different from ours might also be the foundation for quite different concepts. (387)

In the work *On Certainty*, again, we have the recognition that a 'language-game' changes over time (256), and the model of the river (96 seq.), in which some hardened propositions can form the bank, which guides other more fluid propositions, but over time new bits may accumulate and old bits be swept away—this offers the *fact* of diachronic change, and it does not exclude, even if it does not encourage, the possibility of explaining such change. Thus both over time and over social space, variety and change are possible, and, so far as this goes, presum-

---

[6] *Language, Belief and Metaphysics*, ed. Kiefer and Munitz (SUNY Press, 1970), p. 60.

ably we might have some explanations of that variety and change. Other ways of seeing the world are not imaginatively inaccessible to us; on the contrary, it is one of Wittgenstein's aims to encourage such imagination. We can consider alternatives, as in the examples I have already mentioned—and there are of course many more in which he suggests how people with different interests and concerns might describe, classify, and see the world differently from us. Thus the different world-pictures, as so far introduced, are not inaccessible to one another. Those who had one picture might come to see the point (in terms of interests, etc.) of another picture, and also perhaps come to understand why those who had it, did so. In that light, they could reflect also on their own world-picture, and understand, perhaps, something of why they had it. Thus in speaking of these various languages or world-pictures, it looks as though we are *not* speaking of things to which their subjects are, in terms of the idealism we have discussed, transcendentally related.

Now none of this yet implies anything about the *evaluative* comparability of different world-pictures. We have said that they are accessible to one another, to some extent, but that does not say anything, or anything much, about whether one could compare them with regard to adequacy. With regard, moreover, to those elements in the world-picture which purport to be truth-carrying, nothing has yet been determined about whether there is some objective basis from which one 'we' could come to recognise the greater truth of what was believed by another 'we'. But in fact, as is well known, Wittgenstein tends to say things which cast great doubt on that possibility, and not least in his last work. Thus *On Certainty* says (94):

> I do not get my picture of the world [*Weltbild*] by satisfying myself of its correctness; nor do I have it because I am satisfied of its correctness. No: it is the inherited background against which I distinguish between true and false.
>
> 95. The propositions describing this world-picture might be part of a kind of mythology. And their role is like that of rules of a game; and the game can be learned purely practically, without learning any explicit rules.

And, revealingly, *On Certainty*, 298:

> 'We are quite sure of it' does not mean just that every single person is certain of it, but that we belong to a community which is bound together by science and education.

There are many remarks, again, which claim such things as that reasons can be given only within a game, and come to an end at the limits of the game (*Philosophische Grammatik*, p. 55), that our mode of representation is a language-game (*Philosophical Investigations*, p. 50), that 'grammar' cannot be justified (*Philosophische Bermerkungen*, p. 7), and that the language-game is not reasonable or unreasonable, but is there, like our life (*On Certainty*, 559). Nor is there any doubt that Wittgenstein included in the force of these remarks the kind of language-game which one human group might pursue and another lack. Thus in *On Certainty*, once more:

> 609. Suppose we met people who did not regard that (sc. the propositions of physics) as a telling reason. Now, how do we imagine this? Instead of the physicist, they consult an oracle. (And for that we consider them primitive.) Is it wrong for them to consult an oracle and be guided by it?—If we call this 'wrong' aren't we using our language-game as a base from which to *combat* theirs?

> 610. And are we right or wrong to combat it? Of course there are all sorts of slogans which will be used to support our proceedings ...

> 612. I said I would 'combat' the other man,—but wouldn't I give him *reasons*? Certainly; but how far do they go? At the end of reasons comes *persuasion*. (Think of what happens when missionaries convert natives.)

Now none of this, nor its negation, will follow from the idea just of different human groups empirically co-existing with different world-pictures which are (in the earlier, unambitious, sense) accessible to one another. Nor does it follow from a view or set of views which I have not so far mentioned, but which I shall come back to briefly at the end of these remarks, namely the view which has been charted by Dummett in much recent work, to the effect that *truth* must be replaced by, or interpreted in terms of, the notion of *conditions which justify assertion*. This view I shall summarily call Wittgenstein's constructivism. While constructivism must bring enquiry and speculation to a halt in what we have been trained to perceive as an adequate ground, this entails nothing about what different human groups may or may not have been trained to perceive as such a ground, nor about what they could be trained to perceive as a ground, nor about what they would find it natural to do when confronted with conflicts with what they think they already know. Constructivism might tell us something about *human* knowledge, not about that of narrower groups.

The relativist elements which have been added to this scene are extra, and do not follow from the rest. But once they are there, they have a curious and confusing effect backwards (so to speak) on the rest. For it will be remembered that one consideration that I used in characterising a transcendental interpretation of 'the limits of our language mean the limits of our world' was that the features of our language, so conceived, were not a matter of empirical explanation; and hence, conversely, that when we were dealing with what could be empirically explained, we had no such transcendentally isolated item. But if we add the relativist views, it looks as though the question, whether something is empirically explicable or not, is itself relative to a language; for such explanation, and *a fortiori*, particular forms of scientific explanation, are just some language-games among others. Thus our view of another world-picture, as something accessible, and empirically related, to ours, may just be a function of our world-picture; as, of course, may our supposed understanding of signs coming from the other group that they have the same feeling. Thus we lose hold at this level on the idea that they are *really* accessible. Once that alarm has broken out, we may indeed even begin to lose the hard-earned benefits of 'we' rather than 'I'. For if our supposed scientific understanding of the practices of other groups is to be seen merely as how those practices are *for us*, and if our experience of other forms of life is inescapably and non-trivially conditioned by our own form of life, then one might wonder what after all stops the solipsist doubt, that my experience which is supposedly of other individuals and the form of life which I share with them, cannot fail to be an experience only of how things are *for me*.

The point can be put also like this, that there is the gravest difficulty (familiar from certain positions in the philosophy of the social sciences) in both positing the independent existence of culturally distinct groups with different world-views, and also holding that any access we have to them is inescapably and non-trivially conditioned by our own world-view. For the very question from which we started, of the existence and relative accessibility of different world-views, becomes itself a function of one world-view. In fact what we have here is an exact analogue, at the social level, of aggregative solipsism.

So far as the social sciences are concerned, it is worth mentioning a certain view which is held by some followers of Wittgenstein, and which perhaps receives confused encouragement from the area we are considering. This is a view to the effect that it is possible to understand and at least piece-meal explain other outlooks, so long as the understanding is internalist and the explanation non-causal.[7] To suppose that that followed from general epistemological considerations at the level we are considering would be a muddle, representing something like aggregative solipsism (at the social level). For if relativist inaccessibility has taken

---

[7] Itself, of course, an idealist view, in what I earlier called the 'explanatory' sense of the term.

over, then there are only two options: either one is submerged in, identical with an original member of, the other social system, in which case one has no explanations at all (except its own, if it happens to be self-conscious); or else one is necessarily bringing to it one's own conceptual outlook, in which case that will be no less so if what one is bringing is *Verstand* and Gestaltist redescription, than if one is bringing causal explanation. Of course, there may be other good reasons for preferring the former type of explanation, but the project cannot just follow from some relativist story about the plurality of human language-games, as seems sometimes to be supposed.

The relativist elements introduce a persistent uncertainty in the interpretation of 'we', which not only makes the application of Wittgenstein's views unclear, but makes it unclear what kind of views they are. His references to conceptual change and to the different outlooks of different groups have a persistent vagueness which leaves it unclear how much room there is supposed to be for explanation. I earlier mentioned various cases in which Wittgenstein at least seemed to leave room for the possibility of explanation. But the range or determinacy of the explanations he left room for were, so far as the suggestions offered there went, exceedingly low—thus Wittgenstein referred sometimes in the weakest terms to what other people might find interesting, or related their practice in some broadly functional way to their interests. In some part, no doubt, these features of the work are owed to Wittgenstein's hatred of the cockiness of natural science, something which seems to me not easy in his case to distinguish from a hatred of natural science. His use of Gestaltist illumination can stun, rather than assist, further and more systematic explanation; to adapt a remark of Kreisel's,[8] when the child asks why the people on the other side of the world don't fall off, many would give an explanation in terms of gravity acting towards the centre of the earth, but Wittgenstein would draw a circle with a pin man on it, turn it round, and say, 'now *we* fall into space'.

Beyond that, however, the difficulties we have now run into raise the question of whether Wittgenstein is really thinking at all in terms of actual groups of human beings whose activities we might want to understand and explain. I think the answer to that is basically 'no'; we are not concerned so much with the epistemology of differing world-views, still less with the methodology of the social sciences, as with ways of exploring our world-view. We are concerned with the imagination, and the vaguely functionalist remarks we noticed before are not the sketch of an

---

[8] G. Kreisel, 'Wittgenstein's Theory and Practice of Philosophy', *British Journal for the Philosophy of Science*, xi (1960), pp. 238–52. Kreisel's own use of the point goes further than anything suggested here, and in a rather different direction.

explanation, but an aid to the imagination, to make a different practice a more familiar idea to us, and hence to make us more conscious of the practice we have. Seen in this light, the alternatives are not the sort of socially actual alternatives, relativistically inaccessible or not, which we have been discussing, nor are they offered as possible objects of any kind of explanation. Rather, the business of considering them is part of finding our way around inside our own view, feeling our way out to the points at which we begin to lose our hold on it (or it, its hold on us), and things begin to be hopelessly strange to us. The imagined alternatives are not alternatives *to* us; they are alternatives *for* us, markers of how far we might go and still remain within our world—a world leaving which would not mean that we saw something different, but just that we ceased to see.

4 NON-RELATIVIST IDEALISM

Relativism, then, is not really the issue. While the 'we' of Wittgenstein's remarks often looks like the 'we' of our group as contrasted with other human groups, that is basically misleading. Such a 'we' is not his prime concern, and even if one grants such views as the 'justified assertion' doctrine, the determination of meaning by social practice and so on, all of that leaves it open, how much humanity *shares* in the way of rational practice. Nor is it just a question of a final relativisation of 'we' to humanity. We cannot exclude the possibility of other language-using creatures whose picture of the world might be accessible to us. It must, once more, be an empirical question what degree of conceptual isolation is represented by what groups in the universe—groups *with* which we would be in the universe. If they are groups with which we are in the universe, and we can understand that fact (namely, that they are groups with a language, etc.), then they also *belong* to 'we'. Thus, while much is said by Wittgenstein about the meanings *we* understand being related to *our* practice, and so forth, that *we* turns out only superficially and sometimes to be one *we* as against others *in* the world, and thus the sort of *we* which has one practice as against others which are possible in the world. Leaving behind the confused and confusing language of relativism, one finds oneself with a *we* which is not one group rather than another in the world at all, but rather the plural descendant of that idealist *I* who also was not one item rather than another in the world.

But if that is the kind of *we* one is concerned with, it would, again, not follow (at least from this very general level of consideration) that any limit could be placed in advance on the scientific understanding of human practice and human meanings. For if we empirically differ from other groups in the universe with regard to the world-picture we have, then it might be possible to find an explanation of that difference, in terms of our differing evolution, our situation in different environments in the universe, or whatever. But if we could do that for ourselves (that is, humanity) if there turned out to be others to compare ourselves with, then it could not be impossible, though it might be harder, to do it for ourselves without our knowing of others, or without there being others. Even if we, humanity, were the only lot in the world, a transcendental idealism of the first-person plural could not rule out in itself the possibility of an empirical or scientific understanding of why, as persons who have evolved in a particular way on a particular planet, we have the kind of world-picture we have—even though such an explanation would, once more, have to lie within the limits of our language, in the only sense of 'our' in which they would mean the limits of our world. But if all that is possible, there is little left of the thought that those limits are *limits* at all: it might turn out with this sort of idealism, too, that 'when its implications are followed out strictly, it coincides with pure realism'.

Yet when that was so in the *Tractatus* case, the work itself, notoriously and professedly, tried nevertheless to go beyond it. I will end by suggesting that the later work may be seen also as trying to do that, or rather not preventing itself from doing that, with its own elements of a pluralised idealism. This concerns what I earlier called the 'constructivism'. This has many roots, particularly in the theory of knowledge, which I shall not try to say anything about. But a central thought it contains is one that can be put by saying that our sentences have the meaning we give them, and from that some important consequences are supposed to follow, with regard to their logic not being able to determine reality beyond, so to speak, what was put into it in the first place. Relatedly, the notion of 'truth' is to be replaced by, or interpreted in terms of, an appeal to the conditions which have been determined to be appropriate for the assertion of a given sentence.[9] But it is not easy to see, at least at first, how if this set of views is not a triviality, which has no important consequences at all, it can avoid having quite amazing consequences. For consider the following argument-schema, which I have discussed in a slightly different form elsewhere:[10]

     (i) 'S' has the meaning we give it.
     (ii) A necessary condition of our giving 'S' a meaning is Q.
ergo   (iii) Unless Q, 'S' would not have a meaning.

[9] See M. Dummett, 'Wittgenstein's Philosophy of Mathematics', *Phil. Rev.* (1959), reprinted in his *Truth and Other Enigmas* (London: Duckworth, 1978).

[10] 'Knowledge and Meaning in the Philosophy of Mind', *Phil. Rev.*, lxxv (1966), reprinted in *Problems of the Self* (Cambridge, 1973).

(iv) If '*S*' did not have a meaning, '*S*' would not be true.
ergo   (v) Unless *Q*, '*S*' would not be true.

It looks as though there should be something wrong with this argument, since any number of substitutions for *Q* in (ii) which relate to human existence, language use, etc., make it true for any '*S*' one likes, and since (i) is supposedly true for any '*S*', and (iv) for any true '*S*', we can get the truth of any true '*S*' dependent on human existence, etc.; that is, prove unrestricted idealism. Now on some traditional views, there is no need to find anything wrong with the argument in order to avoid this, since (i) will be taken to be true just in case " '*S*' " names a sentence, and in that case (v) can be harmlessly true, as meaning "Unless *Q*, '*S*' would not express a truth", and that of course will not entail: Unless *Q*, not *S*. But it is not obvious that for later Wittgensteinian views, and in particular for the theory of justified assertion, we can so easily drive a line between the sentence '*S*' expressing the truth, and what is the case if *S*. Wittgenstein does indeed sometimes speak in these connections as though he were talking simply about the sentences of natural languages, and produces some very odd results, as at *PI*, I, 381:

How do I know that this colour is red?—It would be an answer to say: 'I have learnt English'.

which is a translation of

Wie erkenne ich, daß diese Farbe Rot ist?—Eine Antwort wäre: 'Ich habe Deutsch gelernt'.

But at least that is a case of someone's *knowing* something, and the difficulties, though revealing, are comparatively superficial. But if we are considering what would be true if . . ., and if we are to replace the notion of truth-conditions with that of assertion-conditions, and if we are to grant, what Wittgenstein surely holds, that for anything to have come to be an assertion-condition for a given sentence involves certainly a human practice, and perhaps a human decision; then something has to be done if we are to avoid even empirical idealism. The obvious thing to do is to regard talk about what would be the case if there were no human beings, language, etc., as talk about what *would* justify the assertion of certain sentences which we do understand (of which the assertion-conditions are fixed). That banishes the empirical idealism, since it removes any reference to convention-fixing from the hypothetical unpopulated scene, nor does it record any piece of convention-fixing. But it would give reason to reflect that any given supposition is determinate only because, on the theory, there is at some point a decision to count certain conditions as adequate for assertion. That reflection is more radical, and is meant to be more radical, than the banal thought in standing back from a sentence describing a non-human event, that if there were no human events there would be no such sentence. The point comes out rather in the thought that the determinacy of reality comes from what we have decided or are prepared to count as determinate:

> We have a colour system as we have a number system. Do the systems reside in *our* nature or in the nature of things? How are we to put it?—*Not* in the nature of things. (*Zettel*, 357)

The diffidence about how to put it comes once more from a problem familiar in the *Tractatus*: how to put a supposed philosophical truth which, if it is uttered, must be taken to mean an empirical falsehood, or worse. For of course, if our talk about the numbers has been determined by our decisions, then one result of our decisions is that it must be non-sense to say that anything about a number has been determined by our decisions. The dependence of mathematics on our decisions, in the only sense in which it obtains—for clearly there cannot be meant an empirical dependence on historical decisions—is something which shows itself in what we are and are not prepared to regard as sense and is not to be stated in remarks about decisions; and similarly in other cases. The new theory of meaning, like the old, points in the direction of a transcendental idealism, and shares also the problem of our being driven to state it in forms which are required to be understood, if at all, in the wrong way.

Bernard Williams:
Complete Philosophical Publications

Books

Williams also wrote many essays on opera and many pieces of occasional jour-
nalism. The former will be published together as a book in due course. The
latter, several of which are of a philosophical cast, are included in a select bibliography entitled "Bernard Williams: Writings of Political Interest" in *In the Beginning Was the Deed*, referenced below.

Morality: An Introduction to Ethics. New York: Harper & Row, 1972. Har-
    mondsworth: Penguin, 1973. Cambridge: Cambridge University Press, 1976;
    Canto edition, with new introduction, 1993.
    German translation: *Der Begriff der Moral*. Leipzig: Reclam, 1978.
    Romanian translation: *Introducere in etica*. Bucharest: Editura Alternative,
    1993.
    French translation: see *La fortune morale* (1994).
    Italian translation (of the Canto edition): *La moralità: un'introduzione all'et-
    ica*. Rome: Einaudi, 2000.
    Polish translation: *Moralność: Wprowadzenie do etyki*. Warsaw: Fundacia
    Aletheia, 2000.
Problems of the Self: Philosophical Papers 1956–1972. Cambridge: Cambridge
    University Press, 1973.
    German translation: *Probleme des Selbst*. Leipzig: Reclam, 1978.
    Spanish translation: *Problemas del yo*. Mexico City: Universidad Nacional
    Autónoma de México, 1986.
    Italian translation: *Problemi dell'io*. Milan: Il Saggiatore, 1990.
A Critique of Utilitarianism. In *Utilitarianism: For and Against*, by J.J.C. Smart
    and Bernard Williams. Cambridge: Cambridge University Press, 1973.
    German translation: *Kritik des Utilitarismus*. Frankfurt am Main: Kloster-
    mann, 1979.
    Spanish translation: *Utilitarismo: pro y contra*. Madrid: Tecnos, 1981.
    Italian translation: *Utilitarismo: un confronto*. Naples: Bibliopolis, 1985.
    French translation: *Utilitarisme: le pour et le contre*. Le Champ Ethique.
    Geneva: Labor et Fides, 1997.
Descartes: The Project of Pure Enquiry. Harmondsworth: Penguin; Hassocks:
    Harvester Press, 1978. Reprinted with a new introduction by John Cotting-
    ham, London: Routledge, 2005.
    German translation: *Descartes: Das Vorhaben der reinen philosophischen Un-
    tersuchung*. Frankfurt am Main: Athenaeum, 1981.

Spanish translation: *Descartes: el proyecto de la investigacion pura.* Mexico City: Universidad Nacional Autónoma de México, 1995.

Moral Luck: Philosophical Papers 1973–1980. Cambridge: Cambridge University Press, 1981.

German translation: *Moralischer Zufall.* Königstein: Hain, 1984.

Italian translation: *Sorte morale.* Milan: Il Saggiatore-Mondadori, 1987.

Spanish translation: *La fortuna moral.* Mexico City: Universidad Nacional Autónoma de México, 1993.

Ethics and the Limits of Philosophy. London: Fontana Books; Cambridge: Harvard University Press, 1985.

Italian translation: *L'etica e i limiti della filosofia.* Bari: Laterza, 1987.

French translation: *L'éthique et les limites de la philosophie.* Paris: Editions Gallimard, 1990.

Japanese translation: *Ikikata ni tsuite tetsugaku wa nani ga Ieru ka.* Tokyo: Sangyoutosho K.K., 1993.

Spanish translation: *La etica y los limites de la filosofia.* Caracas: Monte Avila Editores, 1997.

German translation: *Ethik und die Grenzen der Philosophie.* Hamburg: Rotbuch Verlag, 1999.

Shame and Necessity. Sather Classical Lectures, vol. 57. Berkeley and Los Angeles: University of California Press, 1993.

French translation: *La honte et la nécessité.* Presses Universitaires de France, 1997.

German translation: *Scham, Schuld und Notwendigkeit.* Polis, vol. 1. Berlin: Akademie Verlag, 2000.

La fortune morale. Paris: Presses Universitaires de France, 1994. (= *Morality* + selections from *Problems of the Self*, *Moral Luck*, and *Making Sense of Humanity*.)

Making Sense of Humanity and Other Philosophical Papers 1982–1993. Cambridge: Cambridge University Press, 1995.

Der Wert der Wahrheit. Translated by Joachim Schulte. Vienna: Passagen Verlag, 1998.

Plato: The Invention of Philosophy. London: Phoenix/Orion, 1998. Reprinted in *The Sense of the Past* (2006), details below.

Ile wolnośći powinna mieć wola? Warsaw: Fundacia Aletheia, 1999. (= Polish translation of selected papers.)

Truth and Truthfulness: An Essay in Genealogy. Princeton: Princeton University Press, 2002.

German translation: *Wahrheit und Wahrhaftigeit.* Frankfurt am Main: Surhrkamp, 2003.

Italian translation: *Genealogia della verità: storia e virtù del dire il vero.* Rome: Fazi Editore, 2005.

French translation: Paris: Editions Gallimard, 2005.

In the Beginning Was the Deed: Realism and Moralism in Political Argument. Edited by Geoffrey Hawthorn. Princeton: Princeton University Press, 2005.

The Sense of the Past: Essays in the History of Philosophy. Edited by Myles Burnyeat. Princeton: Princeton University Press, 2006.

Philosophy as a Humanistic Discipline. Edited by A. W. Moore. Princeton: Princeton University Press, 2006.

BOOKS EDITED

(With A. C. Montefiore.) *British Analytical Philosophy*. London: Routledge, 1966.
  Italian translation: *Filosofia analitica inglese*. Rome: Lerici, 1967.
(With A. K. Sen.) *Utilitarianism and Beyond*. Cambridge: Cambridge University Press, 1982.
  Italian translation: *Utilitarismo e oltre*. Milan: Il Saggiatore, 1984.

ARTICLES

In general, does not include references to reprints of articles, except in

  [PS]: *Problems of the Self*
  [ML]: *Moral Luck*
  [MSH]: *Making Sense of Humanity*
  [IBD]: *In the Beginning Was the Deed*
  [SP]: *The Sense of the Past*
  [PHD]: *Philosophy as a Humanistic Discipline*

"Tertullian's Paradox." In *New Essays in Philosophical Theology*, edited by Anthony Flew and Alasdair Macintyre. London: SCM Press, 1955. [PHD]
"Personal Identity and Individuation." *Proceedings of the Aristotelian Society* 57 (1956–57). [PS]
"Metaphysical Arguments." In *The Nature of Metaphysics*, edited by D. F. Pears. London: Macmillan, 1957. [PHD]
"Pleasure and Belief." *Proceedings of the Aristotelian Society*, suppl. vol. 33 (1959). [PHD]
"Descartes." In *A Dictionary of Philosophy and Philosophers*, edited by J. O. Urmson. London: Hutchinson, 1960.
"Personal Identity and Bodily Continuity—a Reply." *Analysis* 21 (1960). [PS]
"Mr Strawson on Individuals." *Philosophy* 36 (1961). [PS]
"The Individual Reason." *The Listener*, November 16, 1961.
"Democracy and Ideology." *Political Quarterly* 32 (1961).
"The Idea of Equality." In *Politics, Philosophy and Society*, edited by Peter Laslett and W. G. Runciman. Oxford: Blackwell, 1962. [PS and IBD]
"Aristotle on the Good: A Formal Sketch." *Philosophical Quarterly* 12 (1962). [SP]
"La certitude du *cogito*." In *Cahiers du Royaumont*, vol. 4. Paris: Editions de Minuit, 1962.
  English text: "The Certainty of the *Cogito*." In *Descartes: A Collection of Critical Essays*, edited by W. Doney. New York: Doubleday, 1967.

"Freedom and the Will," with a Postscript. In *Freedom and the Will*, edited by D. F. Pears. London: Macmillan, 1963.

"Imperative Inference." *Analysis*, suppl. vol. 23 (1963). [*PS*]

"Hume on Religion." In *David Hume: A Symposium*, edited by D. F. Pears. London: Macmillan, 1963. [*SP*]

"Ethical Consistency." *Proceedings of the Aristotelian Society*, suppl. vol. 39 (1965). [*PS*]

"Morality and the Emotions." Inaugural Lecture, Bedford College, London, 1965. Reprinted in *Morality and Moral Reasoning: Five Essays in Ethics*, edited by J. Casey. London: Methuen, 1971. [*PS*]

"Imagination and the Self." British Academy Annual Philosophical Lecture, 1966. [*PS*]

"Consistency and Realism." *Proceedings of the Aristotelian Society*, suppl. vol. 40 (1966). [*PS*]

"Descartes." In *The Encyclopedia of Philosophy*, edited by P. Edwards. New York: Macmillan and Free Press; London: Collier-Macmillan, 1967.

"Hampshire, S. N." In ibid.

"Rationalism." In ibid.

"Knowledge and Meaning in the Philosophy of Mind." *Philosophical Review* 79 (1968). [*PS*]

"Has 'God' a Meaning?" *Question* 1 (1968).
  German translation: "Der unverzichtbare Gehalt des christlichen Glaubens." In *Glaube und Vernunft*, edited by N. Hoerster. Munich: Deutsche Taschenbuch Verlag, 1979. Leipzig: Reclam, 1985.

"Descartes' Ontological Argument: A Comment." In *Fact and Existence*, edited by J. Margolis. Oxford: Blackwell, 1969.

"Existence-Assumptions in Practical Thinking: Reply to Körner." In ibid.

"Philosophy." In *General Education: A Symposium on the Teaching of Non-Specialists*, edited by Michael Yudkin. Harmondsworth: Penguin, 1969.

"The Self and the Future." *Philosophical Review* 79 (1970). [*PS*]

"Are Persons Bodies?" In *The Philosophy of the Body: Rejections of Cartesian Dualism*, edited by S. Spicker. Chicago: Quadrangle Books, 1970. [*PS*]

"Genetics and Moral Responsibility." In *Morals and Medicine*. London: BBC Publications, 1970.

"Deciding to Believe." In *Language, Belief, and Metaphysics*, edited by H. E. Kiefer and M. K. Munitz. Albany: State University of New York Press, 1970. [*PS*]

"The Temporal Ordering of Perceptions and Reactions: Reply to O'Shaughnessy." In *Perception: A Philosophical Symposium*, edited by F. Sibley. London: Methuen, 1971.

"Conversation on Moral Philosophy." In *Modern British Philosophy*, edited by B. Magee. London: Secker and Warburg, 1971.

"Knowledge and Reasons." In *Problems in the Theory of Knowledge*, edited by G. H. von Wright. The Hague: Martinus Nijhoff, 1972. [*PHD*]

"The Analogy of City and Soul in Plato's *Republic*." In *Exegesis and Argument: Studies in Greek Philosophy. Essays Presented to Gregory Vlastos*, edited by

E. N. Lee, A.P.D. Mourelatos, and R. M. Rorty. The Hague: Martinus Nijhoff, 1973. [*SP*]

"The Makropoulos Case: Reflections on the Tedium of Immortality." [*PS*]

"Egoism and Altruism." [*PS*]

Remarks in *The Law and Ethics of AIDS and Embryo Transfer*. CIBA Foundation Symposium 17. Amsterdam: Elsevier/North-Holland, 1973.

"Wittgenstein and Idealism." In *Understanding Wittgenstein*, edited by Godfrey Vesey. Royal Institute of Philosophy Lectures 7. London: Macmillan, 1974. [*ML* and *SP*]

"The Truth in Relativism." *Proceedings of the Aristotelian Society* 75 (1974–75). [*ML*]

"Rawls and Pascal's Wager." *Cambridge Review*, February 28, 1975. [*ML*]

"Persons, Character and Morality." In *The Identities of Persons*, edited by A. Rorty. Berkeley and Los Angeles: University of California Press, 1976. [*ML*]

"Utilitarianism and Moral Self-Indulgence." In *Contemporary British Philosophy*, edited by H. D. Lewis. Ser. 4. London: Allen & Unwin, 1976. [*ML*]

"Moral Luck." *Proceedings of the Aristotelian Society*, suppl. vol. 59 (1976). [*ML*]

"The Moral View of Politics." *The Listener*, June 3, 1976.

"Thinking about Abortion." *The Listener*, September 1, 1977.

"Linguistic Philosophy." In *Men of Ideas*, edited by B. Magee. London: BBC Publications, 1978.

"Politics and Moral Character." In *Public and Private Morality*, edited by Stuart Hampshire. Cambridge: Cambridge University Press, 1978. [*ML*]

Introduction to Isaiah Berlin, *Concepts and Categories: Philosophical Essays*. London: Hogarth Press, 1978.

Conclusion to *Morality as a Biological Phenomenon*, edited by Gunther Stent. Berlin: Dahlem Konferenzen, 1978. Berkeley and Los Angeles: University of California Press, 1980.

[With David Wiggins.] Introduction to *Ethics, Value and Reality: Selected Papers of Aurel Kolnai*. London: Athlone, 1978.

"Another Time, Another Place, Another Person." In *Perception and Identity: Essays Presented to A. J. Ayer, with His Replies to Them*, edited by G. Macdonald. London: Macmillan, 1979. [*ML*]

"Conflicts of Values." In *The Idea of Freedom: Essays in Honour of Isaiah Berlin*, edited by A. Ryan. Oxford: Oxford University Press, 1979. [*ML*]

"Internal and External Reasons." In *Rational Action: Studies in Philosophy and Social Science*, edited by T. R. Harrison. Cambridge: Cambridge University Press, 1979. [*ML*]

"Political Philosophy and the Analytical Tradition." In *Political Theory and Political Education*, edited by M. Richter. Princeton: Princeton University Press, 1980. [*PHD*]

"Moral Obligation and the Semantics of 'Ought'." *Proceedings of the Fifth Kirchberg Wittgenstein Conference*, 1980.

Revised version: " 'Ought' and Moral Obligation." [*ML*]

"L'éthique et la philosophie analytique." *Critique* (Paris), August–September 1980.

"Philosophy." In *The Legacy of Greece: A New Appraisal*, edited by M. Finley. Oxford: Oxford University Press, 1981. [*SP*]

"Justice as a Virtue." In *Essays on Aristotle's Ethics*, edited by A. Rorty. Berkeley and Los Angeles: University of California Press, 1981. [*ML* and *SP*]

"Practical Necessity." In *Philosophical Frontiers of Christian Theology: Essays Presented to Donald Mackinnon*, edited by S. Sutherland and B. Hebblethwaite. Cambridge: Cambridge University Press, 1982. [*ML*]

"Cratylus' Theory of Names and Its Refutation." In *Language and Logos: Studies in Ancient Greek Philosophy Presented to G.E.L. Owen*, edited by M. Schofield and M. Nussbaum. Cambridge: Cambridge University Press, 1982. [*SP*]

"The Point of View of the Universe: Sidgwick and the Ambitions of Ethics." Henry Sidgwick Memorial Lecture, 1982. *Cambridge Review*, May 7, 1982. [*MSH* and *SP*]

"Evolution, Ethics, and the Representation Problem." In *Evolution from Molecules to Men*, edited by D. S. Bendall. Cambridge: Cambridge University Press, 1983. [*MSH*]

"Space Talk: The Conversation Continued." (Comment on B. Ackerman's *Social Justice in the Liberal State*.) *Ethics* 93 (1983).

"Descartes' Use of Skepticism." In *The Skeptical Tradition*, edited by Myles Burnyeat. Berkeley and Los Angeles: University of California Press, 1983. [*SP*]

"Professional Morality and Its Dispositions." In *The Good Lawyer: Lawyers' Roles and Lawyers' Ethics*, edited by David Luban. Maryland Studies in Public Philosophy. Totowa, NJ: Rowman and Allenheld, 1983. [*MSH*]

"Präsuppositionen der Moralität." In *Bedingungen der Möglichkeit: "Transcendental Arguments" und Transcendentales Denken*, edited by E. Schaper and W. Vossenkuhl. Stuttgart: Klett-Cotta, 1984.

"The Scientific and the Ethical." In *Objectivity and Cultural Divergence*, edited by S. Brown. Royal Institute of Philosophy Lectures 17. Cambridge: Cambridge University Press, 1984. [Shortened version of chapter 8 of *Ethics and the Limits of Philosophy*.]

"Morality, Scepticism and the Nuclear Arms Race." In *Objections to Nuclear Defence: Philosophers on Deterrence*, edited by N. Blake and K. Pole. London: Routledge, 1984.

"Formal and Substantial Individualism." *Proceedings of the Aristotelian Society* 85 (1984–85) [*MSH*].

"Theories of Social Justice—Where Next?" In *Equality and Discrimination: Essays in Freedom and Justice*, edited by S. Guest and A. Milne. Archiv für Rechts- und Sozialphilosophie 21. Stuttgart: F. Steiner, 1985.

"Ethics and the Fabric of the World." In *Morality and Objectivity: A Tribute to J. L. Mackie*, edited by T. Honderich. London: Routledge, 1985. [*MSH*]

"What Slopes Are Slippery?" In *Moral Dilemmas in Modern Medicine*, edited by M. Lockwood. Oxford: Oxford University Press, 1985. [*MSH*]

How Free Does the Will Need to Be? The Lindley Lecture, 1985. Lawrence: University of Kansas Press, 1986. [*MSH*]

"L'intervista di *Politeia*: Bernard Williams." *Politeia* (Milan) (Winter 1986).

"Formalism and Natural Language in Moral Philosophy." In *Mérites et limites des méthodes logiques en philosophie*, edited by Jules Vuilleman. Paris: J. Vrin, for Fondation Singer-Polignac, 1986.

"Types of Moral Argument against Embryo Research." In *Human Embryo Research: Yes or No?* London: Tavistock Publications, for the CIBA Foundation, 1986. Reprinted in *BioEssays* 6 (1987).

"Hylomorphism." *Oxford Studies in Ancient Philosophy* 4 (1986). *Festschrift* for J. L. Ackrill, edited by Michael Woods. [SP]

Introduction to René Descartes, *Meditations on First Philosophy with Selections from the Objections and Replies*, edited by J. Cottingham. Cambridge: Cambridge University Press, 1986. [SP]

"Reply to Simon Blackburn" (review of *Ethics and the Limits of Philosophy*). *Philosophical Books* 27 (1986).

Comments on Amartya Sen's Tanner Lectures, 1985, in Amartya Sen, *The Standard of Living*. Cambridge: Cambridge University Press, 1987.

"The Primacy of Dispositions." In *Education and Values: The Richard Peters Lectures*, edited by Graham Haydon. London: University of London Institute of Education, 1987. [PHD]

"Descartes." In *The Great Philosophers: An Introduction to Western Philosophy*, edited by B. Magee. London: BBC Publications, 1987.

"The Structure of Hare's Theory." In *Hare and Critics: Essays in Moral Thinking*, edited by Douglas Seanor and N. Fotion. *Festschrift* for R. M. Hare. Oxford: Oxford University Press, 1988. [PHD]

"Formal Structures and Social Reality." In *Trust: Making and Breaking Cooperative Relations*, edited by Diego Gambetta. Oxford: Blackwell, 1988. [MSH]

"What Does Intuitionism Imply?" In *Human Agency: Language, Duty, and Value. Philosophical Essays in Honor of J. O. Urmson*, edited by J. Moravscik and C.C.W. Taylor. Stanford: Stanford University Press, 1988. [MSH]

"Evolutionary Theory: Epistemology and Ethics." In *Evolution and Its Influence*, edited by Alan Grafen. Herbert Spencer Lectures, 1986. Oxford: Clarendon Press, 1989. [MSH]

"Dworkin on Community and Critical Interests." *California Law Review* 77 (1989).

"Modernita e vita etica." In *Etica e vita quotidiana*. Bologna: Biblioteca del Mulino, 1989.

English text: "Modernity and the Substance of Ethical Life." [IBD]

"Voluntary Acts and Responsible Agents." Hart Lecture, Oxford, 1987. *Oxford Journal of Legal Studies* 10 (1989). [MSH]

"Social Justice: The Agenda in Social Philosophy for the Nineties." *Journal of Social Philosophy* 20 (1989).

"Internal Reasons and the Obscurity of Blame." *Logos* 10 (1989). [MSH]

Reply to the President. *Proceedings of the Aristotelian Society* 90 (1989–90).

"Who Might I Have Been?" In *Human Genetic Information: Science, Law and Ethics*. CIBA Foundation Symposium 149. Chichester: John Wiley & Sons, 1990.

Revised version: "Resenting One's Own Existence." [MSH]

"Notre vie éthique." (Extract from the preface to the French translation of *Ethics and the Limits of Philosophy*.) *Esprit*, November 11, 1990.

"The Need to Be Sceptical." *Times Literary Supplement*, February 16, 1990.

"Making Sense of Humanity." In *The Boundaries of Humanity: Humans, Animals, Machines*, edited by James Sheenan and Morton Sosna. Proceedings of Stanford University Centennial Conference, 1987. Berkeley and Los Angeles: University of California Press, 1991. [*MSH*]

"Saint-Just's Illusion: Interpretation and the Powers of Philosophy." *London Review of Books*, August 29, 1991. [*MSH*]

"Subjectivism and Toleration." In *A. J. Ayer: Memorial Essays*, edited by A. Phillips Griffiths. Berkeley and Los Angeles: University of California Press, 1992. [*PHD*]

"Must a Concern for the Environment Be Centred on Human Beings?" In *Ethics and the Environment*, edited by C.C.W. Taylor. Oxford: Corpus Christi College, 1992. [*MSH*]

"Pluralism, Community and Left Wittgensteinianism." *Common Knowledge* 1 (1992). [*IBD*]

Introduction to Plato's *Theaetetus*, translated by M. J. Levett, revised by Myles Burnyeat. Indianapolis: Hackett, 1992. [*SP*]

"Moral Incapacity." *Proceedings of the Aristotelian Society* 92 (1992–93). [*MSH*]

"Nietzsche's Minimalist Moral Psychology." *European Journal of Philosophy* 1 (1993). [*MSH and SP*]

"Who Needs Ethical Knowledge?" In *Ethics*, edited by A. P. Griffiths. Royal Institute of Philosophy Lectures, 1992. Cambridge: Cambridge University Press, 1993. [*MSH*]

"Moral Luck: A Postscript." In *Moral Luck*, edited by Daniel Statman. Albany: State University of New York Press, 1993. [*MSH*]

"Les vertus de la vérité." In *Le respect*, edited by C. Audard. Paris: Editions Autrement, 1993.

"Pagan Justice and Christian Love." In *Virtue, Love and Form: Essays in Memory of Gregory Vlastos*, edited by Terence Irwin and Martha C. Nussbaum. Edmonton: Academic Printing and Publishing, 1994. [*SP*]

"Descartes and the Historiography of Philosophy." In *Reason, Will and Sensation: Studies in Descartes's Metaphysics*, edited by John Cottingham. Oxford: Oxford University Press, 1994. [*SP*]

"The Actus Reus of Dr Caligari." *Pennsylvania Law Review* 142 (May 1994). [*PHD*]

"Replies." In *World, Mind and Ethics: Essays on the Ethical Philosophy of Bernard Williams*, edited by J.E.J. Altham and Ross Harrison. Cambridge: Cambridge University Press, 1995.

"Ethics." In *Philosophy: A Guide through the Subject*, edited by A. C. Grayling, Oxford: Oxford University Press, 1995.

"Identity and Identities." In *Identity: Essays Based on Herbert Spencer Lectures Given in the University of Oxford*, edited by Henry Harris. Oxford: Oxford University Press, 1995. [*PHD*]

"Acts and Omissions, Doing and Not Doing." In *Virtues and Reasons: Philippa Foot and Moral Theory. Essays in Honour of Philippa Foot*, edited by Rosalind Hursthouse, Gavin Lawrence, and Warren Quinn. Oxford: Oxford University Press, 1995. [*MSH*]

"La philosophie devant l'ignorance." *Diogène* 169 (Paris: Editions Gallimard, 1995).
 English text: "Philosophy and the Understanding of Ignorance," in the corresponding English edition of *Diogenes* (Oxford: Berghahn Books). [*PHD*]

"Acting as the Virtuous Person Acts." In *Aristotle and Moral Realism*, edited by Robert Heinaman. Keeling Colloquium 1, 1994. London: UCL, 1995. [*SP*]

"A Further Introduction." In *The Blackwell Companion to Philosophy*, edited by N. Bunnin and E. P. Tsui-James. Oxford: Blackwell, 1996.

"Truth in Ethics." In *Truth in Ethics*, edited by Brad Hooker. Oxford: Blackwell, 1996.

"Censorship in a Borderless World." Faculty Lecture 16, Faculty of Arts and Social Sciences. Singapore: National University of Singapore, 1996.

"Values, Reasons, and the Theory of Persuasion." In *Ethics, Rationality and Economic Behaviour*, edited by Francesco Farina, Frank Hahn, and Stefano Vannucci. Oxford: Oxford University Press, 1996. [*PHD*]

"The Politics of Trust." In *The Geography of Identity*, edited by Patricia Yaeger. Ann Arbor: University of Michigan Press, 1996.

"Toleration: An Impossible Virtue?" In *Toleration: An Elusive Virtue*, edited by David Heyd. Princeton: Princeton University Press, 1996.

"History, Morality and the Test of Reflection." In Christine Korsgaard with others, *The Sources of Normativity*, edited by Onora O'Neill. Cambridge: Cambridge University Press, 1996.

"Truth, Politics and Self-Deception." *Social Research* 63, no. 3 (Fall 1996). [*IBD*]

"*The Women of Trachis*: Fictions, Pessimism, Ethics." In *The Greeks and Us: Essays in Honor of Arthur W. H. Adkins*, edited by R. B. Louden and P. Schollmeier. Chicago: University of Chicago Press, 1996. [*SP*]

"La tolérance: question politique ou morale?" *Diogène* 176 (Paris: Editions Gallimard, 1996).
 English text: "Toleration: A Political or Moral Question?," in the corresponding English edition of *Diogenes* (Oxford: Berghahn Books). [*IBD*]

"Dallo stato di natura alla genealogia." *Studi Perugini* 2 (1996).

"Shame, Guilt and the Structure of Punishment." *Festschrift* for the Margrit Egner-Stiftung Prize. Zürich, 1997.

"Stoic Philosophy and the Emotions: Reply to Richard Sorabji." In *Aristotle and After*, edited by R. Sorabji. Bulletin of the Institute of Classical Studies, Supplement 68. London: Institute of Classical Studies, School of Advanced Study, University of London, 1997.

"Forward to Basics." In *Equality*, edited by Jane Franklin. (Discussions of the Report of the Commission on Social Justice, 1997.) London: IPPR, 1997.

"Plato against the Immoralist." In *Platons Politeia*, edited by Otfried Höffe. Berlin: Akademie Verlag, 1997. [*SP*]

"Moral Responsibility and Political Freedom." *Cambridge Law Journal* 56 (1997). [*PHD*]

"Berlin, Isaiah." In *Routledge Encyclopedia of Philosophy*, edited by Edward Craig. London: Routledge, 1998.

"Virtues and Vices." In ibid.

"Did Thucydides Invent Historical Time?" Jahrbuch 1996–97, Wissenschaftskolleg zu Berlin. Berlin: Nicolaische Verlagsbuchhandlung, 1998. Revised version: *Representations* 19 (2001).

Foreword to Angelika Krebs, *Ethics of Nature*. Berlin: Walter de Gruyter, 1999.

"Tolerating the Intolerable." In *The Politics of Toleration in Modern Life*, edited by Susan Mendus. Edinburgh: Edinburgh University Press, 1999. Durham: Duke University Press, 2000. [*PHD*]

"In the Beginning Was the Deed." In *Deliberative Democracy and Human Rights*, edited by Harold Hongju Koh and Ronald C. Slye. New Haven: Yale University Press, 1999. [*IBD*]

"Naturalism and Genealogy." In *Morality, Reflection, and Ideology*, edited by E. Harcourt. Oxford: Oxford University Press, 2000.

"Philosophy as a Humanistic Discipline." Third Annual Royal Institute of Philosophy Lecture, 2000. *Philosophy* 75 (October 2000). [*PHD*]

"Die Zukunft der Philosophie." *Deutsche Zeitschrift für Philosophie* 48 (2000). English text: "What Might Philosophy Become?" [*PHD*]

"Understanding Homer: Literature, History and Ideal Anthropology." In *Being Human: Anthropological Universality in Transdisciplinary Perspectives*, edited by Neil Roughley. Berlin: Walter de Gruyter, 2000. [*SP*]

"Liberalism and Loss." In *The Legacy of Isaiah Berlin*, edited by Mark Lilla, Ronald Dworkin, and Robert Silvers. New York: New York Review of Books, 2001.

"Some Further Notes on Internal and External Reasons." In *Varieties of Practical Reasoning*, edited by Elijah Millgram. Cambridge: MIT Press, 2001.

"Foreword: Some Philosophical Recollections." In *Wittgensteinian Themes: Essays in Honour of David Pears*, edited by David Charles and William Child. Oxford: Oxford University Press, 2001.

"From Freedom to Liberty: The Construction of a Political Value." *Philosophy and Public Affairs* 30 (2001). [*IBD*]

Introduction to Friedrich Nietzsche, *The Gay Science*, edited by Bernard Williams, translated by Josefine Nauckhoff. Cambridge: Cambridge University Press, 2001. [*SP*]

"Why Philosophy Needs History." *London Review of Books*, October 17, 2002.

"Plato's Construction of Intrinsic Goodness." In *Perspectives on Greek Philosophy: S. V. Keeling Memorial Lectures in Ancient Philosophy 1991–2002*, edited by R. W. Sharples. London: Ashgate, 2003. [*SP*]

"Relativism, History, and the Existence of Values." In Joseph Raz et al., *The Practice of Value*, edited by R. Jay Wallace. Oxford: Oxford University Press, 2003.

"Unerträgliches Leiden." In *Zum Glück*, edited by Susan Neiman and Matthias Kroß. Berlin: Akademie Verlag, 2004. English text: "Unbearable Suffering." [*SP*]

"Realism and Moralism in Political Theory." [IBD]
"The Liberalism of Fear." [IBD]
"Human Rights and Relativism." [IBD]
"Conflicts of Liberty and Equality." [IBD]
"Censorship." [IBD]
"Humanitarianism and the Right to Intervene." [IBD]
"Three Reasons for Talking about Collingwood." [SP]
"The Human Prejudice." [PHD]

SELECTED REVIEWS

Moral Judgement, by D. Daiches Raphael. *Mind* (1957).
The Contemplative Activity, by Pepita Haezrahi. *Mind* (1957).
Language and the Pursuit of Truth, by John Wilson. *Times Literary Supplement*, January 11, 1957 (published anonymously).
The Revolution in Philosophy, by A. J. Ayer et al., edited by G. Ryle. *Philosophy* (1958).
Aesthetics and Criticism, by H. Osborne. *Mind* (1958).
Plato Today, by R.H.S. Crossman. *Spectator*, July 11, 1959.
English Philosophy since 1900, by G. J. Warnock. *Philosophy* (1959).
The Four Loves, by C. S. Lewis. *Spectator*, April 1, 1960.
The Forms of Things Unknown, by Herbert Read. *Spectator*, July 29, 1960.
Descartes, *Discourse on Method*, translated by A. Wollaston. *Spectator*, August 26, 1960.
The Liberal Hour, by J. K. Galbraith; *Kennedy or Nixon?*, by Arthur Schlesinger, Jr. *Spectator*, November 4, 1960.
Thought and Action, by Stuart Hampshire. *Encounter* (1960).
Ethics since 1900, by Mary Warnock. *Philosophical Books* (1960).
Sketch for a Theory of the Emotions. by J.-P. Sartre. *Spectator*, August 3, 1962.
Sense and Sensibilia: Philosophical Essays, by J. L. Austin. *Oxford Magazine*, December 6, 1962.
The Concept of a Person, by A. J. Ayer. *New Statesman*, September 27, 1963.
Morals and Markets, by H. B. Acton. *Guardian*, April 1, 1971.
Responsibility, by Jonathan Glover. *Mental Health* (1971).
Education and the Development of Reason, edited by R. F. Deardon, P. H. Hirst, and R. S. Peters. *Times Literary Supplement*, April 1972.
A Theory of Justice, by John Rawls. *Spectator*, June 22, 1972.
Beyond Freedom and Justice, by B. F. Skinner. *Observer*, March 1972.
Essays on Austin, edited by G. J. Warnock and J. O. Urmson. *New Statesman*, August 31, 1973.
What Computers Cannot Do, by Hubert Dreyfus. *New York Review*, October 1973.
Essays on Wisdom, edited by Renford Bambrough. *Times Literary Supplement*, August 31, 1974.
The Socialist Idea, edited by Stuart Hampshire and L. Kolakowski. *Observer*, January 5, 1975.

Anarchy, State, and Utopia, by R. Nozick. *Times Literary Supplement*, January 17, 1975.

The Life of Bertrand Russell, by R. W. Clark; *The Tamarisk Tree: My Quest for Liberty and Love*, by Dora Russell; *My Father Bertrand Russell*, by Katharine Tait; and *Bertrand Russell*, by A. J. Ayer. *New York Review*, March 4, 1976.

"Where Chomsky Stands." *New York Review*, November 11, 1976.

Ethics of Fetal Research, by Paul Ramsey. *Times Literary Supplement*, September 5, 1975.

The Selfish Gene, by R. Dawkins. *New Scientist*, November 4, 1976.

The Fire and the Sun, by Iris Murdoch. *New Statesman*, August 5, 1977.

Moore: G. E. Moore and the Cambridge Apostles, by Paul Levy. *Observer*, October 28, 1979.

Thinking, by G. Ryle, edited by K. Kolenda. *London Review of Books*, October 1979.

Life Chances, by R. Dahrendorf. *Observer*, January 27, 1980.

Rubbish Theory, by Michael Thompson. *London Review of Books*, February 1980.

Lying, by Sissela Bok. *Political Quarterly* (1980).

Logic and Society and *Ulysses and the Sirens*, by Jon Elster. *London Review of Books*, May 1, 1980.

The Culture of Narcissism, by Christopher Lasch; *Nihilism and Culture*, by Johan Goudsblom. *London Review of Books*, July 17, 1980.

Religion and Public Doctrine in England, by M. Cowling. *London Review of Books*, April 2, 1981.

Nietzsche on Tragedy, by M. S. Silk; *Nietzsche: A Critical Life*, by Ronald Hayman; *Nietzsche, Volume I: The Will to Power as Art*, by Martin Heidegger, translated by David Farrell. *London Review of Books*, May 1981.

After Virtue, by A. MacIntyre. *Sunday Times*, November 22, 1981.

Philosophical Explanations, by R. Nozick. *New York Review of Books*, February 18, 1982.

The Miracle of Theism, by John Mackie. *Times Literary Supplement*, March 11, 1983.

Offensive Literature, by John Sutherland. *London Review of Books*, March 17, 1983.

Consequences of Pragmatism, by R. Rorty. *New York Review of Books*, April 28, 1983. Reprinted in *Reading Rorty*, edited by Alan Malachowski. Oxford: Blackwell, 1990.

Collected Papers of Bertrand Russell, vol. 1. *Observer*, January 22, 1984.

Reasons and Persons, by D. Parfit. *London Review of Books*, June 7, 1984.

Critical Philosophy and *Journal of Applied Philosophy*. *Times Higher Education Supplement*, June 15, 1984.

Wickedness, by Mary Midgley. *Observer*, October 7, 1984.

Secrets, by Sissela Bok; *The Secrets File*, by D. Wilson. *London Review of Books*, October 18, 1984.

Choice and Consequence, by Thomas Schelling. *Economics and Philosophy* (1985).

Privacy: Studies in Social and Cultural History, by Barrington Moore, Jr. *New York Review of Books*, April 25, 1985.

Ordinary Vices, by Judith Shklar; *Immorality*, by Ronald Milo. *London Review of Books*, June 6, 1985.

The Right to Know, by Clive Ponting; *The Price of Freedom*, by Judith Cook. *Times Literary Supplement*, October 4, 1985.

Taking Sides, by Michael Harrington. *New York Times Book Review* [mid-1980s?].

A Matter of Principle, by Ronald Dworkin. *London Review of Books*, April 17, 1986.

The View from Nowhere, by Thomas Nagel. *London Review of Books*, August 7, 1986.

The Society of Mind, by Marvin Minsky. *New York Review of Books*, 1987.

Whose Justice? Which Rationality? by Alasdair MacIntyre. *Los Angeles Tribune*, 1988.

Reprint: *London Review of Books*, January 5, 1989.

Intellectuals, by Paul Johnson. *New York Review of Books*, July 20, 1989.

Contingency, Irony, and Solidarity, by Richard Rorty. *London Review of Books*, November 1989.

Sources of the Self, by Charles Taylor. *New York Review of Books*, October 1990.

Realism with a Human Face, by Hilary Putnam. *London Review of Books*, February 7, 1991.

The Saturated Self, by Kenneth J. Gergen. *New York Times*, June 23, 1991.

Political Liberalism, by John Rawls. *London Review of Books*, May 13, 1993.

Inequality Reexamined, by Amartya Sen. *London Review of Books*, November 1993.

The Therapy of Desire, by Martha Nussbaum. *London Review of Books*, October 1994.

Several books by Umberto Eco. *New York Review of Books*, February 2, 1995.

The Last Word, by Thomas Nagel. *New York Review of Books*, November 19, 1998.